Sams Teach Yourself HTML and XHTML in 24 Hours, Sixth Edition

Copyright © 2003 by Sams Publishing

International Standard Book Number: 0-672-32520-9

Library of Congress Catalog Card Number: 2002114452

Printed in the United States of America

First Printing: May 2003

06   05   04   03   4   3   2

Trademarks

All terms mentioned in this book that are known to be trademarks or service marks have been appropriately capitalized. Sams cannot attest to the accuracy of this information. Use of a term in this book should not be regarded as affect-ing the validity of any trademark or service mark.

Warning and Disclaimer

Every effort has been made to make this book as complete and as accurate as possible, but no warranty or fitness is implied. The information provided is on an "as is" basis. The author and the publisher shall have neither liability or responsibility to any person or entity with respect to any loss or damages aris-ing from the information contained in this book.

Bulk Sales

Sams offers excellent discounts on this book when ordered in quantity for bulk purchases or special sales. For more information, please contact:

> **U.S. Corporate and Government Sales**
> **1-800-382-3419**
> corpsales@pearsontechgroup.com

For sales outside of the U.S., please contact:

> **International Sales**
> **+1-317-581-3793**
> international@pearsontechgroup.com

ACQUISITIONS EDITOR
Betsy Brown

DEVELOPMENT EDITOR
Damon Jordan

MANAGING EDITOR
Charlotte Clapp

INDEXER
Mandie Frank

PROOFREADER
Mike Henry

TECHNICAL EDITOR
Robyn Ness

DESIGNER
Gary Adair

LAYOUT TECHNICIANS
Stacey Richwine-DeRome
Susan Geiselman
Michelle Mitchell

SAMS
Teach Yourself

HTML and XHTML

Dick Oliver
Michael Morrison

SIXTH EDITION

SAMS   *201 West 103rd St., Indianapolis, Indiana, 46290 USA*

Contents at a Glance

Table of Contents

About the Authors

DICK OLIVER (dicko@netletter.com) is the tall, dark, handsome author of lots of great books and software, including *Web Page Wizardry*, *Netscape Unleashed*, *Create Your Own Web Page Graphics*, and *Tricks of the Graphics Gurus*. He is also the president of Cedar Software and the warped mind behind the Nonlinear Nonsense Netletter at http://netletter.com (and many other Web sites). When he isn't banging on a keyboard, he's usually snowboarding, sledding, skiing, or warming up by the woodstove in his cozy Northern Vermont home (where they celebrate a day of summer each year, too). He likes writing HTML, eating killer-spicy Indian food, and waltzing wildly around the office with his daughters--not necessarily in that order. He also thinks it's pretty cool that authors get to write their own "About the Authors" sections.

MICHAEL MORRISON is a writer, developer, toy inventor, and author of a variety of nerdy books and interactive Web-based courses. In addition to his primary profession as a writer and geek for hire, Michael is the creative lead at Stalefish Labs (http://www.stalefishlabs.com), an entertainment company he co-founded with his wife, Masheed. The first commercial debut for Stalefish Labs is a "lounge game" titled *Tall Tales: The Game of Legends, Humdingers, and Creative One-Upmanship*. Michael encourages you to visit the Tall Tales game Web site at http://www.talltalesgame.com/ and buy dozens of games for your friends and family. When not glued to his computer, playing hockey, skateboarding, or watching movies with his wife, Michael enjoys hanging out by his koi pond. You can visit Michael on the Web at http://www.michaelmorrison.com/.

Dedication

This book is dedicated to my mother, Darlene Hewins, who had to teach herself HTML before the book was written, and told me in no uncertain terms that I'd better do a lot better job than those other books.

—Dick Oliver

To my wife, Masheed, who is always on board for my far-out schemes and pet projects, and highly supportive of my night job too.

—Michael Morrison

Acknowledgments

This book would certainly not exist today were it not for the author's loving family, who brought enough fresh carrot juice, tender popcorn, and buttery kisses to sustain him through the long hours of its creation.

Special thanks must also go to the folks at the Buffalo Mountain Food Cooperative in Hardwick, Vermont, for providing the carrots, popcorn, and butter.

—Dick Oliver

I'd like to thank Dick for allowing me to be a part of this project, and for all of my buddies at Sams who are always such a pleasure to work with.

—Michael Morrison

We Want to Hear from You!

As the reader of this book, you are our most important critic and commentator. We value your opinion and want to know what we're doing right, what we could do better, what areas you'd like to see us publish in, and any other words of wisdom you're willing to pass our way.

You can email or write me directly to let me know what you did or didn't like about this book—as well as what we can do to make our books stronger.

Please note that I cannot help you with technical problems related to the topic of this book, and that due to the high volume of mail I receive, I might not be able to reply to every message.

When you write, please be sure to include this book's title and author as well as your name and phone or email address. I will carefully review your comments and share them with the author and editors who worked on the book.

Email: webdev@samspublishing.com

Mail: Mark Taber
            Associate Publisher
            Sams Publishing
            201 West 103rd Street
            Indianapolis, IN 46290 USA

Reader Services

For more information about this book or others from Sams Publishing, visit our Web site at www.samspublishing.com. Type the ISBN (excluding hyphens) or the title of the book in the Search box to find the book you're looking for.

Put Your HTML Page Online Today

In the next 24 hours, more than 100,000 new Web pages will be posted in publicly accessible areas of the Internet. At least as many pages will be placed on private intranets where they will be viewed by businesspeople connected to local networks. Every one of those pages—like over 100 million pages already online—will use Hypertext Markup Language, or HTML.

If you read on, your Web pages will be among those that appear on the Internet in the next 24 hours. This will also be the day that you acquire one of the most valuable skills in the world today: mastery of HTML.

Can you really learn to create top-quality Web pages yourself, without any specialized software, in less time than it takes to schedule and wait for an appointment with a highly paid HTML wizard? Can this thin, easy-to-read book really enable you to teach yourself state-of-the-art Web page publishing?

Yes. In fact, within two hours of starting this book, someone with no previous HTML experience at all can have a Web page ready to place on the Internet's World Wide Web.

How can you learn the language of the Web so fast? By example. This book breaks HTML down into simple steps that anyone can learn quickly, and shows you exactly how to tackle each step. Every HTML example is pictured directly above the Web page it will produce. You see it done, you read a brief, plain-English explanation of how it works, and you immediately do the same thing with your own page. Ten minutes later, you're on to the next step.

The next day, you're marveling at your own impressive pages on the Internet.

Beyond HTML

This book isn't just about HTML because HTML isn't the only thing you need to know to create Web pages today. My goal is to give you all the skills you need to create a stunning, state-of-the-art Web site in just 24 short, easy lessons. I've received literally thousands of email messages from readers telling me that the earlier editions of this book achieved that goal better than any other book available.

Go ahead and scan the bookstore shelves. You'll discover that the book you're holding now is the only one on the market that covers all the following key skills and technologies in plain English that even beginners will understand.

- XHTML (Extended Hypertext Markup Language) and XML (eXtensible Markup Language) are the new standards for Web page creation. Every example in this book (and on the accompanying Web site) is fully XHTML and XML compatible, so you won't have to relearn anything as XHTML and XML replace old-fashioned HTML.

> Do you have existing Web pages that you need to bring up to date so they're compatible with the new standards? If so, Hour 24, "Planning for the Future of HTML," and Appendix D, "Migrating from HTML to XHTML," give you complete, easy-to-follow instructions for converting HTML pages into XHTML.

- At the same time, all the examples you learn here have been tested for compatibility with the latest version of every major Web browser. That includes Microsoft Internet Explorer, Netscape Navigator, and Opera. You'll learn from the start to be compatible with the past, yet ready for the future.

- Hours 8 through 11 teach you to design and create your own Web page graphics (including animations) using industry-standard software you can download and try for free. Creating graphics is the single most important part of producing a great-looking site—and one that most HTML books leave out.

- Along with HTML, you'll learn how to use Cascading Style Sheets (CSS), JavaScript, and Dynamic HTML (DHTML) in Hours 12 through 20. Your Web pages will be interactive and enchanting, not static and unresponsive.

- The technical stuff is not enough, so I also include the advice you need when setting up a Web site to achieve your real-world goals. Key details—designing an effective page layout, posting your page to the Internet with FTP software, organizing and managing multiple pages, and getting your pages to appear high on the query lists at all the major Internet search sites—are all covered in enough depth to get you beyond the snags that often trip people up.

- You may be aware that graphical Web site editors such as Microsoft FrontPage and Macromedia DreamWeaver make Web design accessible to people that don't know anything about HTML—but these tools also make it more necessary than ever to understand HTML yourself so you can create pages that do exactly what you want and are easy to read and maintain. Throughout the book, I include notes telling you when the What-You-See-Is-What-You-Get editors are helpful and when you're better off coding the HTML yourself.

All these essentials (which some authors treat like extras, or don't discuss at all) are what made the first five editions of this book non-stop bestsellers. For this edition, I've continued to incorporate the email feedback of thousands of readers to make every lesson easy, fast, and foolproof. I've also revised and updated the hands-on examples for you to experience online and modify to suit your own purposes—nearly 300 example pages in all. The color quick-reference sheets and updated reference appendixes are sure to keep this volume at your side long after you've become an experienced Webmaster.

How to Use This Book

There are several ways to go through this book, and the best way for you depends on your situation. Here are five recommended options. Pick the one that matches your needs.

1. *"I need to get some text on the Internet today. Then I can worry about making it look pretty later."*
   - Read Hour 1, "Understanding HTML and XHTML."
   - Read Hour 2, "Create a Web Page Right Now."
   - Read Hour 4, "Publishing Your HTML Pages."
   - Put your first page on the Internet!
     (Total work time: 2–4 hours)
   - Read the rest of the book and update your pages as you learn more HTML.

2. *"I need a basic Web page with text and graphics on the Internet as soon as possible. Then I can work on improving it and adding more pages."*
   - Read Hour 1, "Understanding HTML and XHTML."
   - Read Hour 2, "Create a Web Page Right Now."
   - Read Hour 8, "Creating Your Own Web Page Graphics."
   - Read Hour 9, "Putting Graphics on a Web Page."
   - Read Hour 4, "Publishing Your HTML Pages."
   - Put your first page on the Internet!
     (Total work time: 4–8 hours)
   - Read the rest of the book and update your pages as you learn more HTML.

3. *"I need a professional-looking business Web site with an order form right away. Then I can continue to improve and develop my site over time."*

- Read all four hours in Part I, "Your First Web Page."
- Read Hour 17, "Web Page Scripting for Non-Programmers."
- Read Hour 19, "Creating HTML Forms."
- Read Hour 8, "Creating Your Own Web Page Graphics."
- Read Hour 9, "Putting Graphics on a Web Page."
- Read Hour 10, "Custom Backgrounds and Colors."
- Put your pages and order form on the Internet!
    (Total work time: 8–12 hours)
- Read the rest of the book, and update your pages as you learn more HTML.

4. *"I need to develop a creative and attractive 'identity' Web site on a tight schedule. Then I need to develop many pages for our corporate intranet as well."*

- Read all four hours in Part I, "Your First Web Page."
- Read all four hours in Part II, "Web Page Text."
- Read all four hours in Part III, "Web Page Graphics."
- Read all four hours in Part IV, "Web Page Design."
- Put your pages on the Internet and your intranet!
    (Total work time: 10–16 hours)
- Read the rest of the book and update your pages as you learn more HTML.

5. *"I need to build a cutting-edge interactive Web site or HTML-based multimedia presentation—fast!"*

- Read this whole book.
- Put your pages on the Internet and/or CD-ROM!
    (Total work time: 16–24 hours)
- Review and use the techniques you've learned to continue improving and developing your site.

It may take a day or two for an Internet service provider to set up a host computer for your pages, as discussed in Hour 4. If you want to get your pages online immediately, read Hour 4 now so you can have a place on the Internet all ready for your first page.

No matter which of these approaches you take, you'll benefit from the unique presentation elements that make this book the fastest possible way to learn HTML.

Visual Examples

Every example in this book is illustrated in two parts. The text you type in to make an HTML page is shown first, with all HTML commands highlighted. The resulting Web page is shown as it will appear to people who view it with the world's most popular Web browser, Microsoft Internet Explorer. You'll often be able to adapt the example to your own pages without reading any of the accompanying text at all.

Though the figures use Microsoft Internet Explorer, I always tell you if the page will look different in other browsers or older versions. Everything in this book works with both Netscape Navigator and Microsoft Internet Explorer, as well as Opera.

Special Highlighted Elements

 As you go through each hour, sections marked To Do guide you in applying what you just learned to your own Web pages at once.

 Whenever a new term is used, it is highlighted with a special icon like this one. No flipping back and forth to the Glossary!

 Tips and tricks to save you precious time are set aside so you can spot them quickly.

 Crucial information you should be sure not to miss is also highlighted.

Coffee Break sections give you a chance to take a quick break and have some fun exploring online examples.

 When there's something you need to watch out for, you'll be warned about it in these sections.

Q&A, Quiz, and Exercises

Every hour ends with a short question-and-answer session that addresses the kind of "dumb questions" everyone wishes they dared to ask. A brief but complete quiz lets you test yourself to be sure you understand everything presented in the hour. Finally, one or two optional exercises give you a chance to practice your new skills before you move on.

The *24-Hour HTML Café*

Every sample page illustrated in this book, plus more than 150 more-complete Web pages designed to reinforce and expand your knowledge of HTML, can be found at an Internet site called the *24-Hour HTML Café* (`www.24hourHTMLcafe.com`). I built and opened the Café especially to provide readers of this book with oodles more examples and reusable HTML pages than I could ever picture in a short book.

You'll also get to have some fun with whimsical "edutainment" pages and break-time surprises, plus an extensive hotlist of links to a wide variety of Internet resources to help you produce your own Web pages even faster. See you there!

PART I
Your First Web Page

Hour

HOUR 1

Understanding HTML and XHTML

Before you begin creating your own Web pages with HTML, you need a little background knowledge about what Web pages are, how to view and edit them, and what you can expect to achieve with them. It might also help to have a basic understanding of how HTML differs from XHTML, and why there are two different languages designed to do the same thing—create Web pages. This hour provides a quick summary of HTML and XHTML basics, and some practical tips to make the most of your time as a Web page author and publisher.

To Do

Here's a review of what you need to do before you're ready to use the rest of this book.

1. Get a computer. I used a computer with Windows XP to create the figures in this book, but you can use any Windows, Macintosh, or UNIX machine to create your Web pages. The speed of the computer itself doesn't matter much for accessing Web pages, but the speed of the

▼ computer's modem or network interface card (NIC) should ideally be at least 56Kbps, and faster is better. If you happen to have broadband Internet access via a cable or DSL modem, that's even better!

2. Get a connection to the Internet. You can either dial up an Internet service provider (ISP) by using the modem in your computer or connect through the local network of your school or business. Most ISPs now offer dial-up Internet service for about $20 per month. If you don't mind spending a little more, a cable or DSL Internet service can dramatically improve the browsing experience thanks to the speed and "always on" connection. The ISP, school, or business that provides your Internet connection can help you with the details of setting it up properly.

Not sure how to find an ISP? The best way is to comparison-shop online (using a friend's computer that's already connected to the Internet). You'll find a comprehensive list of all the national and regional ISPs at `http://thelist.internet.com/`.

If you have two or more computers at your home that you'd like to connect to the Internet, you might consider using a wireless network router to share an Internet connection. This hardware allows you to place multiple computers anywhere you want in your house without any concern over snaking network wires through rooms. More importantly, you get the benefit of having all of the computers connected to the Internet and sharing a single Internet connection. To find out more about setting up a wireless home network, visit `http://www.homenethelp.com/`.

3. Get Web browser software. This is the software your computer needs to retrieve and display HTML Web pages. The most popular browser programs are currently Microsoft Internet Explorer and Netscape Navigator. One or the other of these two Web browser programs is used by more than 95 percent of the people who look at Web pages, so it's a good idea to get them both. You can buy them at a software retailer, or download them free over the Internet at `http://www.microsoft.com/` and `http://home.netscape.com/`.

4. Explore! Use Microsoft Internet Explorer or Netscape Navigator to look around the Internet for Web pages that are similar in content or appearance to those you'd like to create. Note what frustrates you about some pages, what attracts you and keeps you reading, and what makes you come back to some pages over and over again. If there is a particular topic that interests you, consider searching for it using a popular search engine such as Google (`http://www.google.com/`).

If you plan to put your HTML pages on the Internet (as opposed to publishing them on CD-ROM or a local intranet), you'll need to transfer them to a computer that is connected to the Internet 24 hours a day. The same company or school that provides you with Internet access may also let you put Web pages on their computer; if not, you may need to pay another company to host your pages.

You can start learning HTML with this book right away and wait to find an Internet host for your pages when they're done. However, if you want to have a place on the Internet ready for your very first page as soon as it is finished, you may want to read Hour 4, "Publishing Your HTML Pages," before you continue.

What Is a Web Page?

Once upon a time, back when there weren't any footprints on the moon, some far-sighted folks decided to see whether they could connect several major computer networks together. I'll spare you the names and stories (there are plenty of both), but the eventual result was the "mother of all networks," which we call the Internet.

Until 1990, accessing information through the Internet was a rather technical affair. It was so hard, in fact, that even Ph.D.-holding physicists were often frustrated when trying to swap data. One such physicist, the now famous Tim Berners-Lee, cooked up a way to easily cross-reference text on the Internet through "hypertext" links. This wasn't a new idea, but his simple Hypertext Markup Language (HTML) managed to thrive while more ambitious hypertext projects floundered.

NEW TERM *Hypertext* originally meant text stored in electronic form with cross-reference links between pages. It is now a broader term that refers to just about any object (text, images, files, and so on) that can be linked to other objects.

Hypertext Markup Language (HTML) is a language for describing how pages of text, graphics, and other information are organized, formatted, and linked together.

By 1993, almost 100 computers throughout the world were equipped to serve up HTML pages. Those interlinked pages were dubbed the *World Wide Web* (WWW), and several Web browser programs had been written to allow people to view Web pages. Because of the popularity of the Web, a few programmers soon wrote Web browsers that could view graphics images along with the text on a Web page. One of these programmers was Marc Andressen; he went on to become rich and famous, selling one of the world's most popular Web browsers, Netscape Navigator.

Today, HTML pages are the standard interface to the Internet. They can include animated graphics, sound and video, complete interactive programs, and good old-fashioned text. Millions of Web pages are retrieved and viewed each day from thousands of Web server computers around the world. Incidentally, the term "web" arose from the fact that Web pages are linked together in such a way that they form a massive web of information, roughly akin to a spider's web.

The Web is rapidly becoming a mass-market medium, as high-speed Internet connections through TV cables, modernized phone lines, and direct satellite feeds become increasingly commonplace. You can already browse the Web using a small box attached to your television instead of using your computer, with the cost of such devices likely to fall sharply over the next few years. In other words, it may not be necessary to rely on a computer for Web browsing in the near future.

Yet the Internet is no longer the only place you'll find HTML. Most private corporate networks (called *intranets*), now use HTML to provide business information to employees and clients. HTML is now the interface of choice for publishing presentations on CD-ROM and the very popular high-capacity digital versatile disk (DVD) format. Microsoft has even integrated HTML directly into the Windows operating system, allowing every storage folder in your computer to be associated with an HTML page and hypertext links to other folders and pages.

In short, HTML is everywhere. Fortunately, you're in the right place to find out how HTML Web pages work and how to create them.

There are actually two flavors of HTML. One is called HTML 4 and the other is called XHTML 1.1. The X stands for eXtensible, and you'll find out later in this lesson why it isn't called HTML 5. You'll also find out what all this has to do with another new language called XML.

The most important thing to know from the outset is that all the examples in this book are compatible with both HTML 4 and XHTML (as well as XML) and should be fully compatible with future versions of any software that interprets any Web page language.

If you have other books on creating Web pages, the example HTML in those books may look slightly different than what you see in this one. Even though the old-fashioned format shown in those books will work in the current crop of Web browsers, I strongly recommend that you use the more modern approach shown in this book; this will ensure that your pages remain usable as far into the future as possible.

How Web Pages Work

When you are viewing Web pages, they look a lot like paper pages. At first glance, the process of displaying a Web page is simple: You tell your computer which page you want to see, and the page appears on your screen. If the page is stored on a disk inside your computer, it appears almost instantly. If it is located on some other computer, you might have to wait for it to be retrieved.

Of course, Web pages can do some very convenient things that paper pages can't. For example, you can't point to the words "continued on page 57" in a paper magazine and expect page 57 to automatically appear before your eyes. Nor can you tap your finger on the bottom of a paper order form and expect it to reach the company's order fulfillment department five seconds later. You're not likely to see animated pictures or hear voices talk to you from most paper pages either (newfangled greeting cards aside). All these things are commonplace on Web pages.

But there are some deeper differences between Web pages and paper pages that you'll need to be aware of as a Web page author. For one thing, what appears as a single page on your screen may actually be an assembly of elements located in many different computer files. In fact, it's possible (though uncommon) to create a page that combines text from a computer in Australia with pictures from a computer in Russia and sounds from a computer in Canada.

Figure 1.1 shows a typical page as shown by Microsoft Internet Explorer, the world's most popular software for viewing Web pages. The page in Figure 1.1 would look roughly the same if viewed in Netscape Navigator, which runs a close second in popularity to Microsoft Internet Explorer. I say "roughly" because Web browsers don't always interpret Web pages exactly the same, even though in theory they should. For the sake of simplicity, let's for now assume that Internet Explorer and Navigator display pages without any major differences.

A Web browser such as Internet Explorer does much more than just retrieve a file and put it on the screen. It actually assembles the component parts of a page and arranges those parts according to commands hidden in the text by the author. Those commands are written in HTML.

NEW TERM   A *Web browser* is a computer program that interprets HTML commands to collect, arrange, and display the parts of a Web page.

Listing 1.1 shows the text, including the HTML commands, I typed to create the page in Figure 1.1. This text file can be read and edited with any word processor or text editor. It looks a bit strange with all those odd symbols and code words, but the text file itself doesn't include any embedded images, boldface text, or other special formatting. The words between < and > are HTML tags.

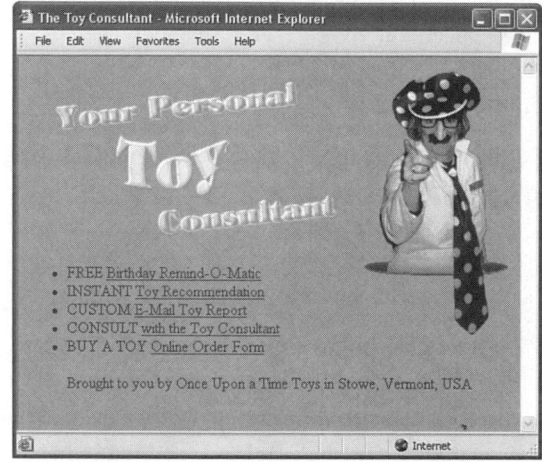

FIGURE 1.1

A Web browser assembles separate text and image files to display them as an integrated page.

LISTING 1.1   Text Used to Create the Page in Figure 1.1

```
<html><head><title>The Toy Consultant</title></head>
<body background="toyback3.gif" bgcolor="magenta" text="blue" link="purple"
vlink="white" alink="magenta">
<img src="ologist4b.gif" align="right" />
<img src="toycon.gif" align="top" />
<ul>
<li>FREE <a href="remind.htm">Birthday Remind-O-Matic</a></li>
<li>INSTANT <a href="commend.htm">Toy Recommendation</a></li>
<li>CUSTOM <a href="report.htm">E-Mail Toy Report</a></li>
<li>CONSULT <a href="consult.htm">with the Toy Consultant</a></li>
<li>BUY A TOY <a href="order.htm">Online Order Form</a></b></li>
</ul>
<div align="center">Brought to you by Once Upon a Time Toys in Stowe,
Vermont, USA</div>
</body></html>
```

Internet Explorer reads the commands in the HTML code shown in Listing 1.1 and then displays all the images and formatting you see in Figure 1.1. The coded HTML commands in the text instruct the browser to look for separate image files and display them along with the text. Other commands tell it which text to display in boldface and how to break up the lines of text on the page.

To see the HTML commands for any page on the Web, click with the right mouse button (or hold down the control key while clicking if you're using a Macintosh computer), and then select View Source from the pop-up menu. This is a great way to get an intuitive idea how HTML works and learn by others' examples.

Some Web pages use an advanced feature called frames to display more than one HTML page at the same time. In Netscape Navigator and Microsoft Internet Explorer, you can view the HTML commands for any frame by right-clicking it and selecting View Frame Source. Other Web browsers have slightly different menu commands for viewing the HTML source code.

Regardless of how you go about the viewing the source for existing Web pages, keep in mind that many commercial Web pages use complex HTML code that can be difficult to read and understand.

The Pieces and Parts of a Web Page

You'll learn how to understand and write HTML commands soon. The important point to note right now is that creating a Web page is just a matter of typing some text. You can type and save that text with any word processor or text editor you have on hand. You then open the text file with Microsoft Internet Explorer, Netscape Navigator, or any other HTML-compatible software to see it as a Web page.

When you want graphics, sound, animations, video, and interactive programming to appear on a Web page, you don't insert them into the text file directly, as you would if you were creating a document in most paper-oriented page layout programs such as Microsoft Word and Adobe Acrobat. Instead, you type HTML text commands telling the Web browser where to find the media files. The media files themselves remain separate, even though the Web browser will make them *look* as if they're part of the same document when it displays the page.

For example, the HTML document in Listing 1.1 refers to three separate graphics images. Figure 1.2 shows these three image files being edited in the graphics program Microsoft Photo Editor, which ships standard with Microsoft Office.

You could use any graphics program you like to modify or replace these images at any time, even the simple Paint program that comes standard with all versions of Windows. Changing the graphics can make a big difference in how the page looks, even if you don't make any changes to the HTML text file. You can also use the same image on any number of pages while storing only one copy of the graphics file. You'll learn much more about incorporating graphics files into Web pages in Part III, "Web Page Graphics."

FIGURE 1.2
Though text and graphics appear integrated in Figure 1.1, the graphics files are actually stored, and can be edited, separately.

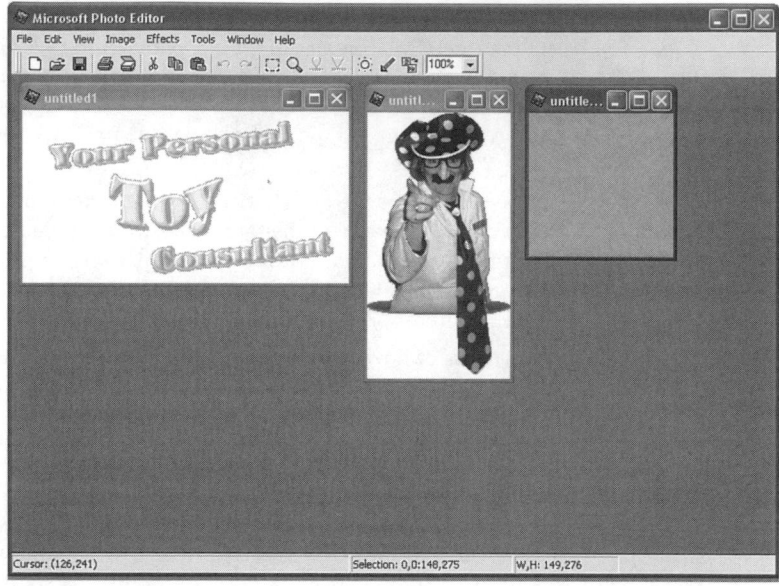

There are two basic approaches to making an HTML page: You can type out the text and HTML commands yourself with a text editor, or you can use graphical software that generates the HTML commands for you.

You will be able to follow along with this book and learn HTML much more easily if you work with an editor that shows the actual HTML text. Any word processor or text editor you already have—even the Windows Notepad or Macintosh TextEdit editor will do nicely.

For now, I strongly recommend that you do not use a graphical, What-You-See-Is-What-You-Get (WYSIWYG) Web page editor such as Microsoft FrontPage or Macromedia Dreamweaver. You'll likely find it easier and more educational to start out with a simple text editor while you're just learning HTML, and then progress on to visual tools once you have a better understanding of what's going on under the hood of your Web pages.

The Many Faces of HTML

It's important to understand that a single Web page can take on many different appearances, depending upon who views it and with what they view it. Figure 1.3 is the same Web page pictured earlier in Figure 1.1, as seen with the Pocket PC version of the Internet Explorer Web browser. The screen on Pocket PC handheld devices is only 240×320 in size, which is considerably smaller than the 640×480, 800×600, and higher resolution screens that most desktop PCs use these days.

FIGURE 1.3

The page from Figure 1.1 looks very different in the Pocket PC version of Internet Explorer.

As you can see, the Pocket PC view on the Web page is considerably different from its desktop counterpart. In fact, it doesn't look very good at all because the page isn't designed to scale down well to such a small screen. This distinction in Web page views is important to grasp early in your HTML education because it hammers home the point that you don't have a whole lot of control over how your pages are viewed. Or more accurately, you don't have much control over the size of the area in which your pages are viewed. Beyond that, browsers are reasonably consistent in rendering the actual content on your pages.

What this means is that most Web pages will look the same in Netscape Navigator as they do in Microsoft Internet Explorer, and they will also look the same on PCs, Macintoshes, and UNIX machines. The page in Figure 1.1, for example, would look the same on any of these machines as long as the size of the viewing window, fonts, and program settings were the same on each machine.

Now for the bad news. Even users of the same version of the same Web browser can alter how a page appears by choosing different display options and/or changing the size of the viewing window. Both Netscape Navigator and Microsoft Internet Explorer allow users to override the background and fonts specified by the Web page author with those of their own choosing. Screen resolution, window size, and optional toolbars can also change how much of a page someone sees when it first appears. The Pocket PC example in Figure 1.3 illustrates this point quite clearly.

To continue the study of how Web pages change at different screen resolutions and display settings, take a look at the page in Figure 1.4, which is viewed at 1024×768 resolution with a large size font. Compare this figure with Figure 1.1, which shows the same page at 800×600 with default font settings. Unfortunately, you as a Web page author have no direct control over the display settings on a particular computer; each individual who looks at your pages can always choose whatever settings he or she prefers by select-ing Edit, Preferences in Netscape Navigator or by selecting Tools, Internet Options in Microsoft Internet Explorer.

FIGURE 1.4

The page from Figure 1.1, displayed by Microsoft Internet Explorer at a higher resolution with larger fonts.

You can't even assume that people will be viewing your Web pages on a computer screen. The page in Figures 1.1, 1.3, and 1.4 might also be read on a low-resolution television screen or a high-resolution paper printout (see Figure 1.5).

FIGURE 1.5

Web browsers usually change the back-ground to white when sending pages to a printer.

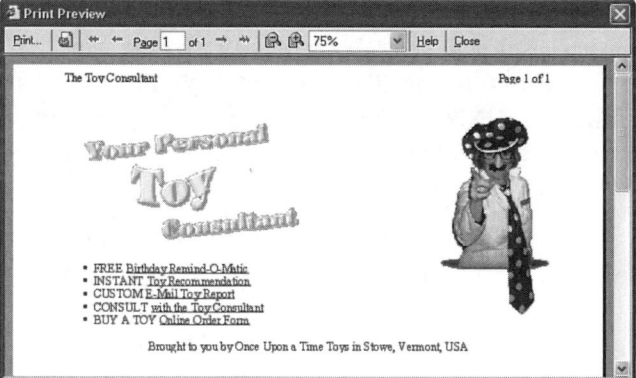

As you learn to make your own Web pages, remember how many different forms they can take when people view them. Some Web page authors fall into the trap of trying to make pages appear "perfect" on their computer and are sorely disappointed the first time they discover that it looks different on someone else's screen. (Even worse, some authors put silly messages on their pages demanding that everyone change the size of their view-ing window and font settings to match the author's computer, or proclaiming "This page

1

is best viewed by such-and-such." If you've ever encountered such messages, I'm sure you ignored them just like everyone else does.)

In Part IV, "Web Page Design," you'll find many tips and tricks for ensuring that your pages look great in the widest variety of situations.

> In this book you encounter many example Web pages. At the accompanying *24-Hour HTML Café* Web site (http://www.24hourHTMLcafe.com/), you'll find all those examples in living color, along with many more sample pages to explore.
>
> To get to the online examples for each hour in the book, click that hour number on the clock marked "Hour by Hour Examples from the Book" at http://www.24hourHTMLcafe.com/.
>
> You can go directly to a specific hour by entering an address like the following into your Web browser:
>
> http://www.24hourHTMLcafe.com/hour1/

The Scoop on HTML, XML, and XHTML

As you learned earlier in the lesson, HTML in its early days was great because it allowed scientists to share information over the Internet in an efficient and relatively structured manner. It wasn't until later that Web browsers caught on and HTML started being used to code more than scientific papers. HTML quickly went from a tidy little markup language for researchers to a full-blown online publishing language. And once it was established that HTML could be jazzed up for graphical browsing, the creators of Web browsers pretty much went crazy by adding lots of nifty features to the language. While these new features were neat at first, they compromised the simple design of HTML and introduced lots of inconsistencies when it came to how browsers displayed Web pages. The problem was that most new features only worked on one browser or another, and you were out of luck if you happened to be running the wrong browser. HTML had started to resemble a bad remodeling job on a house that really should've been left alone. As it turns out, some of the browser-specific features that turned up during this time have now been adopted as standards while others were dropped completely.

As with most revolutions, the birth of the Web was very chaotic, and the modifications to HTML reflected that chaos. In the past few years a significant effort has been made to reel in the inconsistencies of HTML and attempt to restore some order to the language. The problem with disorder in HTML is that it results in Web browsers having to guess at how a page is to be displayed, which is not a good thing. Ideally, a Web page designer should be able to define exactly how a page is to look and have it look the same regardless of what kind of browser or operating system someone is using. Better still, a designer should be able to define exactly what a page *means*, and have it look consistent across different browsers and platforms. This utopia is still off in the future somewhere, but a language called XML (Extensible Markup Language) is playing a significant role in leading us toward it.

NEW TERM   *XML* (Extensible Markup Language) is a language used to create other markup languages, such as HTML, that describe structured information.

XML is a general language used to create other languages such as HTML. I know this sounds a little strange, but it really just means that XML provides a basic structure and set of rules to which any markup language must adhere. Using XML, you can create a unique markup language to describe just about any kind of information, including Web pages. Knowing that XML is a language for creating other markup languages, you could create your own version of HTML using XML. You could even create a markup language called BCCML (Bottle Cap Collection Markup Language), for example, which you could use to create and manage your extensive collection of rare bottle caps. The point is that XML lays the ground rules for organizing information in a consistent manner, and that information can be anything from Web pages to bottle caps.

You might be thinking that bottle caps don't have anything to do with the Web, so why mention them? The reason is because XML is not entirely about Web pages. XML is actually broader than the Web in that it can be used to represent any kind of information on any kind of computer. If you can visualize all of the information whizzing around the globe between computers, mobile phones, handheld computers, televisions, and radios, you can start to understand why XML has much broader ramifications than just cleaning up Web pages. However, one of the first applications of XML is to restore some order to the Web, which is why XML is relevant to you learning HTML.

If XML describes data better than HTML, does it mean that XML is set to upstage HTML as the markup language of choice for the Web? No. XML is not a replacement for HTML, or even a competitor of HTML; XML's impact on HTML has to do with cleaning up HTML. HTML is a relatively unstructured language that could benefit from the rules of XML. The natural merger of the two technologies is to make HTML adhere to the rules and structure of XML. To accomplish this merger, a new version of HTML was formulated that adheres to the stricter rules of XML. The new XML-compliant version of HTML is known as XHTML. Fortunately for you, you'll actually be learning XHTML throughout this book since it is really just a cleaner version of HTML.

NEW TERM   *XHTML* (Extensible Hypertext Markup Language) is a version of HTML that is compliant with the stricter rules of XML.

Earlier in the lesson I referred to HTML as HTML 4, which is the latest version of HTML. XML and XHTML also have versions, with XML 1 being the latest version of XML, and XHTML 2 being the latest version of XHTML. XHTML 2 is very new and has yet to be supported in any major Web browsers, so this book sticks with teaching you XHTML 1.1. You'll learn more details about XHTML 1.1, HTML 4, and their relationship with each other as you progress through the book and create working Web pages.

1

Summary

This hour introduced the basics of what Web pages are and how they work. You learned that coded HTML commands are included in the text of a Web page, but images and other media are stored in separate files. You also learned why typing HTML text yourself is often better than using a graphical editor to create HTML commands for you, especially when you're starting out learning HTML. You saw that a single Web page can look very different, depending upon what software and hardware are used to display it. Finally, you learned about XML and XHTML, and how they relate to HTML.

Q&A

Q I'm stuck on my first page. It didn't work. What did I do wrong?

A That first page is always the hardest. For a step-by-step analysis of what might have gone wrong and how to fix it, refer to Appendix A, "Readers' Most Frequently Asked Questions." (You'll find that appendix handy anytime you have a question that doesn't seem to be answered elsewhere in the book.)

Q I'm still not quite sure what the difference between a "Web page" and an "HTML page" is. And how are these different from a "home page" or a "Web site"?

A If you want to get technical, I suppose a "Web page" would have to be a page located on the Internet instead of a disk on your own computer. But in practice, the terms "Web page" and "HTML page" are used interchangeably. A "Web site" is one or more pages that are created together and related in content, like the pages of a book. "Home page" usually means the first page people visit when they look at a Web site, though some people use home page to mean any Web page. Others use home page to mean a personal page, as opposed to a corporate Web site.

Q I've looked at the HTML "source" of some Web pages on the Internet, and it looks frighteningly difficult to learn. Do I have to think like a computer programmer to learn this stuff?

A Though complex HTML pages can indeed look daunting, learning HTML is several orders of magnitude easier than other computer languages like BASIC, C, and Java. You don't need any experience or skill as a computer programmer to be a very successful HTML author. The reason the HTML code for many commercial Web pages looks complicated is because it was likely created by a visual Web design tool, as opposed to being hand-coded; visual tools have a knack for making code difficult to read! Keep in mind that the apparent complexity in large pages could also be the natural result of changes and improvements over a long period of time; every Web page is built a piece at a time.

Q Do I need to be connected to the Internet constantly while I create HTML pages?

A No. In fact, you don't need any Internet connection at all if you only want to produce Web pages for publication on a CD-ROM, Zip or floppy disk, or local network. You also don't need a connection while you're developing pages that you aren't ready to publish online. In fact, I've spent months creating entire Web sites offline on my hard disk before placing them on the Internet. Hour 2, "Create a Web Page Right Now," gives more detailed instructions for working with Web pages offline.

Workshop

The workshop contains quiz questions and activities to help you solidify your understanding of the material covered. Try to answer all questions before looking at the "Answers" section that follows.

Quiz

1. Define the terms *Internet*, *Web page*, and *World Wide Web*.

2. How many files would you need to store on your computer to make a Web page with some text and two images on it?

3. Can you create Web pages with Microsoft Word or WordPerfect?

Answers

1. The Internet is the "network of networks" that connects millions of computers around the globe.

   A Web page is a text document that uses commands in a special language called HTML to add formatting, graphics and other media, and links to other pages.

   The World Wide Web is a collective name for all the Web pages on the Internet.

2. At least three files: one for the text (which includes the HTML commands), and one for each graphics image. In some cases, you might need more files to add a background pattern, sound, or interactive features to the page.

3. Yes, or with any other word processor on any computer (as long as the word processor will save plain text or ASCII files). Just keep in mind that word processors usually save files with extra formatting information by default, which is why you have to save the file as plain text for it to work as a Web page. It's a little simpler to just stick with a pure text editor such as Windows Notepad or TextEdit for the Macintosh.

Exercises

At the end of each hour in this book, you'll find some suggestions for optional exercises to reinforce and expand what you learned in the hour. However, because you're undoubtedly eager to get started learning HTML, let's skip the warm-up calisthenics for Hour 1 and dive right into Hour 2, "Create a Web Page Right Now."

HOUR 2

Create a Web Page Right Now

This hour guides you through the creation of your first Web page. The best way to follow along with this hour is to actually create a Web page as you read and model it after the sample pages developed here in the book. If you're a little nervous about jumping right in, you might want to read this hour once to get the general idea and then go through it again at your computer while you work on your own page. But I encourage you to throw caution aside and dive right in!

As mentioned in Hour 1, "Understanding HTML and XHTML," you can use any text editor or word processor to create HTML Web pages. Though you may eventually want to use an editor especially designed for HTML, for this hour I recommend you use Windows Notepad or the Macintosh TextEdit editor that came with your computer. That way you won't have to learn a new software program at the same time you're learning HTML.

> I encourage you not to try creating your first HTML page with Microsoft
> Word or any other HTML-compatible word processor; most of these pro-
> grams attempt to rewrite your HTML for you in strange ways, potentially
> leaving you totally confused.

To Do

Before you begin working with this hour, you should start with some text that you want
to put on a Web page.

1. Find (or write) a few paragraphs of text about yourself, your company, or the
   intended subject.

2. Be sure to save it as plain, standard ASCII text. Notepad and most simple text editors always save files as plain text, but you may need to choose it as an option
   (after selecting File, Save As) if you're using another program.

3. As you go through this hour, you will add HTML commands (called *tags*) to the
   text file, making it into a Web page. Use Notepad or some other simple text editor
   to do this; don't use Word or WordPad!

4. Always give files containing HTML tags a name ending in .html when you save
   them. This is important: If you forget to type the .html at the end of the filename
   when you save the file, most text editors will give it some other extension (such as
   .txt or .doc). If that happens, you won't be able to find it when you try to look at it
   with a Web browser. In other words, Web browsers expect Web pages to have a file
   extension of .html; you may also encounter Web pages with a file extension of
   .htm, which is also acceptable. There are also other file extensions used on the Web
   such as .asp (Microsoft Active Server Pages), but they are typically related to technologies beyond the scope of HTML.

> If you're using TextEdit on a Macintosh computer, the steps for creating a
> Web page are a little different. You must first select Make Plain Text from
> the Format menu and then change the preferences under the Saving header
> by unchecking the box for Append '.txt' Extension to Plain Text Files. Also,
> the default preferences are set to show .html documents as they would
> appear in a browser, which won't allow you to edit them. To fix this, check
> Ignore Rich Text Commands in HTML Files under the Rich Text Processing
> header.

Getting Started with a Simple Web Page

Listing 2.1 shows the text you would type and save to create a simple HTML page. If you opened this file with a Web browser such as Internet Explorer, you would see the page in Figure 2.1. Every Web page you create must include the `<html>`, `<head>`, `<title>`, and `<body>` tags.

LISTING 2.1 The `<html>`, `<head>`, `<title>`, and `<body>` Tags

```
<html>
<head><title>The First Web Page</title></head>
<body>
In the beginning, Tim created the HyperText Markup Language.
The Internet was without form and void, and text was upon
the face of the monitor and the Hands of Tim were moving over
the face of the keyboard. And Tim said, Let there be links;
and there were links. And Tim saw that the links were good;
and Tim separated the links from the text. Tim called the
links Anchors, and the text He called Other Stuff.
And the whole thing together was the first Web Page.
</body>
</html>
```

In Listing 2.1, as in every HTML page, the words starting with < and ending with > are actually coded commands. These coded commands are called HTML *tags* because they "tag" pieces of text and tell the Web browser what kind of text it is. This allows the Web browser to display the text appropriately.

 **NEW TERM** An HTML *tag* is a coded command used to indicate how part of a Web page should be displayed.

 In Listing 2.1, HTML tags are printed darker than the rest of the text so you can easily spot them. When you type your own HTML files, all the text will be the same color (unless you are using a special HTML editing program that uses color to highlight tags, such as Microsoft FrontPage or Macromedia Dreamweaver). Some fancier commercial HTML editors go a step further than highlighting code by also assisting you with the coding—they may complete tags for you and also validate your code as you enter it.

FIGURE 2.1

When you view the Web page in Listing 2.1 with a Web browser, only the actual title and body text are displayed.

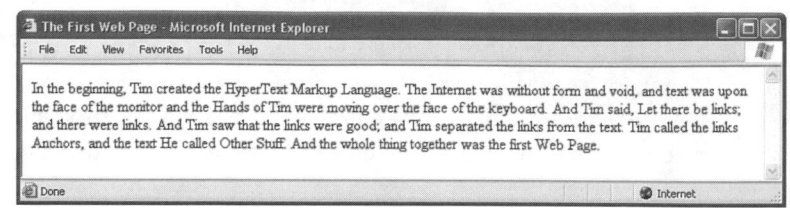

The First Web Page - Microsoft Internet Explorer

File   Edit   View   Favorites   Tools   Help

In the beginning, Tim created the HyperText Markup Language. The Internet was without form and void, and text was upon the face of the monitor and the Hands of Tim were moving over the face of the keyboard. And Tim said, Let there be links; and there were links. And Tim saw that the links were good; and Tim separated the links from the text. Tim called the links Anchors, and the text He called Other Stuff. And the whole thing together was the first Web Page.

Done   Internet

Figure 2.1 may look a little bit different than your Web browser does (even if you are using the same version of Internet Explorer) because I have hidden all the button bars. All the figures in this book have the button bars hidden to leave more room for the Web pages themselves.

Before you learn what the HTML tags in Listing 2.1 mean, you might want to see exactly how I went about creating and viewing the document itself:

1. Type all the text in Listing 2.1, including the HTML tags, in Windows Notepad (or Macintosh TextEdit).

2. Select File, Save As and be sure to select Text Documents as the file type.

3. Name the file `myfirst.html`.

4. Choose the folder on your hard drive where you would like to keep your Web pages—and remember which one you choose! Click the Save or OK button to save the file.

5. Now start up Netscape Navigator or Microsoft Internet Explorer. (Leave Notepad running, too. That way you can easily switch back and forth between viewing and editing your page.)

You don't need to be connected to the Internet to view a Web page stored on your own computer. If your Web browser program tries to connect to the Internet every time you start it, it is being a bad browser and you must discipline it severely. The appropriate disciplinary action will depend on your breed of browser:

- In Microsoft Internet Explorer for Windows, select Tools, Internet Options; click the General tab and click Use Blank under Home page. Under Macintosh OS X, look in the application preferences under the Browser Display set, and click the Use None button in the Home Page cluster.

> • In Netscape Navigator, select Edit, Preferences; choose the Navigator category and select Blank Page under Navigator Starts With.
>
> This teaches your browser not to run off and fetch a page from the Internet every time it starts.

6. In Microsoft Internet Explorer, select File, Open and click Browse. If you're using Netscape Navigator, select File, Open Page and click the Choose File button. Navigate to the appropriate folder and select the `myfirst.html` file. You can also drag and drop the `myfirst.html` file onto the browser window.

Voilà! You should see the page in Figure 2.1.

HTML Tags Every Web Page Must Have

The time has come for the secret language of HTML tags to be revealed to you. When you understand this language, you will have creative powers far beyond those of other humans. Don't tell the other humans, but it's really pretty easy.

Most HTML tags have two parts: an *opening tag*, which indicates where a piece of text begins, and a *closing tag*, which indicates where the piece of text ends. Closing tags start with a / (forward slash) just after the < symbol. Another type of tag is the *empty tag*, which is unique in that it doesn't involve a pair of matching opening and closing tags. Instead, an empty tag consists of a single tag that starts with a < and ends with a / just before the > symbol.

New Term An *opening tag* is an HTML tag that indicates the start of an HTML command; the text affected by the command appears after the opening tag. Opening tags always begin with < and end with >, as in `<html>`.

New Term A *closing tag* is an HTML tag that indicates the end of an HTML command; the text affected by the command appears before the closing tag. Closing tags always begin with `</` and end with >, as in `</html>`.

New Term An *empty tag* is an HTML tag that issues an HTML command without enclosing any text in the page. Empty tags always begin with < and end with `/>`, as in `<br />`.

For example, the `<body>` tag in Listing 2.1 tells the Web browser where the actual body text of the page begins, and `</body>` indicates where it ends. Everything between the `<body>` and `</body>` tags will appear in the main display area of the Web browser window, as you can see if you refer back to Figure 2.1.

Web browsers display any text between `<title>` and `</title>` at the very top of the browser window, as you can also see in Figure 2.1. The title text is also used to identify the page on the Netscape Navigator Bookmarks menu or in the Microsoft Internet Explorer Favorites list. It's important to provide a title for your pages so that visitors to the page can properly bookmark it for future reference.

You will use the `<body>` and `<title>` tags in every HTML page you create because every Web page needs a title and some body text. You will also use the other two tags shown in Listing 2.1, `<html>` and `<head>`. Putting `<html>` at the very beginning of a document simply indicates that this is a Web page. The `</html>` at the end indicates that the Web page is over.

Within a page, there is a head section and a body section, each of which is identified by `<head>` and `<body>` tags. The idea is that information in the head of the page somehow describes the page but isn't actually displayed by a Web browser. Information placed in the body, however, is displayed by a Web browser. The `<head>` tag always appears near the beginning of the HTML code for a page, just after the opening `<html>` tag.

The `<title>` tag used to identify the title of a page appears within the head of the page, which means it is placed after the opening `<head>` tag and before the closing `</head>` tag. (Hour 21, "Organizing and Managing a Web Site," reveals some other advanced header information that can go between `<head>` and `</head>`, but none of it is necessary for most Web pages.)

You may find it convenient to create and save a *bare-bones page* with just the opening and closing `<html>`, `<head>`, `<title>`, and `<body>` tags, similar to the document in Listing 2.1. You can then open that document as a starting point whenever you want to make a new Web page and save yourself from typing out all those obligatory tags every time.

(This won't be necessary if you use a dedicated HTML editing program, which usually puts these tags in automatically when you begin a new page.)

Organizing a Page with Paragraphs and Line Breaks

When a Web browser displays HTML pages, it pays no attention to line endings or the number of spaces between words. For example, the top poem in Listing 2.2 appears with a single space between all words in Figure 2.2. When the text reaches the edge of the browser window, it automatically wraps down to the next line, no matter where the line breaks were in the original HTML file.

LISTING 2.2 HTML for the Page Shown in Figure 2.2

```
<html>
<head>
<title>The Advertising Agency Song</title>
</head>
<body>
When your client's    hopping mad,
put his picture in the ad.

If he still should    prove refractory,
add a picture of his factory.

<hr />

<p>When your client's hopping mad,<br />
put his picture in the ad.</p>
<p>If he still should prove refractory,<br />
add a picture of his factory.</p>
</body>
</html>
```

FIGURE 2.2

When the HTML in Listing 2.2 is viewed as a Web page, line and paragraph breaks only appear where there are <br /> and <p> tags.

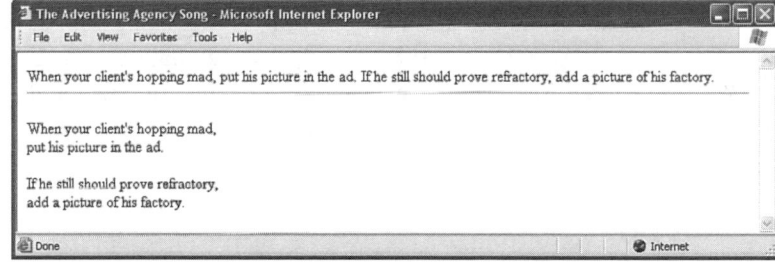

You must use HTML tags to control where line and paragraph breaks actually appear. To skip a line between paragraphs, put a `<p>` tag at the beginning of each paragraph and a `</p>` tag at the end. In other words, enclose the text of the paragraph within a pair of matching `<p>` and `</p>` tags.

The `<br />` tag forces a line break within a paragraph. Unlike the other tags you've seen so far, `<br />` doesn't require a closing `</br>` tag—this is one of those empty tags I was talking about earlier. This is also an example of where XHTML enters the Web page picture because normal HTML doesn't require the / in empty tags. However, the newer XHTML standard does, so it's important for you to stick to the latest standards and create Web pages that are coded properly—always code empty tags so that they end with />. If you're itching to find out more details about XHTML and how it compares to HTML, see Hour 24, "Planning for the Future of HTML."

> Note that most Web pages you see on the Internet today use `<br>` instead of `<br />`, and the current crop of Web browser software treats them both the same. However, you may save yourself a lot of work rewriting your pages in the future if you get in the habit of using the newer `<br />` form of the tag now.
>
> Likewise, the closing `</p>` tag is always optional in HTML 4 and is often left out by Web page authors today. Closing `</p>` tags are required by the new XHTML standard, so I recommend that you always include them. Developing clean HTML coding habits is a very important part of becoming a successful Web page designer.

The poem in Listing 2.2 and Figure 2.2 shows the `<br />` and `<p>` tags being used to separate the lines and verses of a nursery rhyme and to separate two paragraphs of text commenting on the rhyme.

You might have also noticed the `<hr />` tag in Listing 2.2, which causes a horizontal rule line to appear in Figure 2.2. Inserting a horizontal rule with the `<hr />` tag also causes a line break, even if you don't include a `<br />` tag along with it. For a little extra blank space above or below a horizontal rule, you can put a `<p>` tag before the `<hr />` tag and a `</p>` tag after it, effectively placing the horizontal rule within its own paragraph.

Like `<br />`, the `<hr />` horizontal rule tag is an empty tag and therefore never gets a closing `</hr>` tag.

To Do

Take a passage of text and try your hand at formatting it as proper HTML:

1. Add `<html><head><title>My Title</title></head><body>` to the beginning of the text (using your own title for your page instead of *My Title*).

2. Add `</body></html>` to the very end of the text.

3. Add a `<p>` tag at the beginning of each paragraph and a `</p>` tag at the end of each paragraph.

4. Use `<br />` tags anywhere you want single-spaced line breaks.

5. Use `<hr />` to draw horizontal rules separating major sections of text, or wherever you'd like to see a line across the page.

▼

▼   6. Save the file as *mypage*.html (using your own filename instead of *mypage*). If you are using a word processor, always be sure to save HTML files in plain text or ASCII format.

7. Open the file with Netscape Navigator or Microsoft Internet Explorer to see your Web page.

8. If something doesn't look right, go back to the text editor to make corrections and save the file again. You then need to click Reload (in Netscape Navigator) or Refresh (in Microsoft Internet Explorer) to see the changes you made to the Web
▲   page.

Calling Out Text with Headings

When you browse through Web pages on the Internet, you'll notice that many of them have a heading at the top that appears larger and bolder than the rest of the text. Listing 2.3 is a simple Web page containing examples of the three largest heading sizes you can make with HTML. Any text between <h1> and </h1> tags will appear as a large heading. <h2> and <h3> make smaller headings, and so on down the line of heading tags.

LISTING 2.3   Heading Tags

```
<html>
<head><title>Teach Yourself</title></head>
<body>
<h1>Teach Yourself Clock Programming in 13 Hours</h1>
<p>Tired of blinking VCRs and Microwaves? Embarrassed that
every fax from your office says it was sent from the year 1907?
Wondering whether you're ten, sixteen, or twenty-two minutes
late for work when all your LEDs and LCDs disagree?</p>
<h2>Take charge of your time.</h2>
<p>Pick up a copy of Teach Yourself Clock Programming in 13
Hours, and you'll never have to ignore another flashing
12:00AM again. In just 13 easy one-hour lessons, you'll learn
to set the time and date you want on any digital device, from
your bedside radio to the office copier.</p>
<h3>Complete, comprehensive, and FAST.</h3>
<p>Popular makes and models from every major appliance
manufacturer are covered, from convection ovens to car
stereos. PLUS special appendixes on VCR and fax programming
will take you beyond time, into the hallowed realms of
prescheduled recording and late-night "paper Spam".</p>
<p>Never ask your spouse how to reset the nuker again. Get
Teach Yourself Clock Programming in 13 Hours today.</p>
</body>
</html>
```

As you can see in Figure 2.3, the HTML that creates headings couldn't be simpler. For a big level 1 heading, put an <h1> tag at the beginning and an </h1> tag at the end. For a slightly smaller level 2 heading, use <h2> and </h2>, and for a little level 3 heading, use <h3> and </h3>.

FIGURE 2.3

The <h1>, <h2>, *and* <h3> *tags in Listing 2.3 make the three progressively smaller headings shown here.*

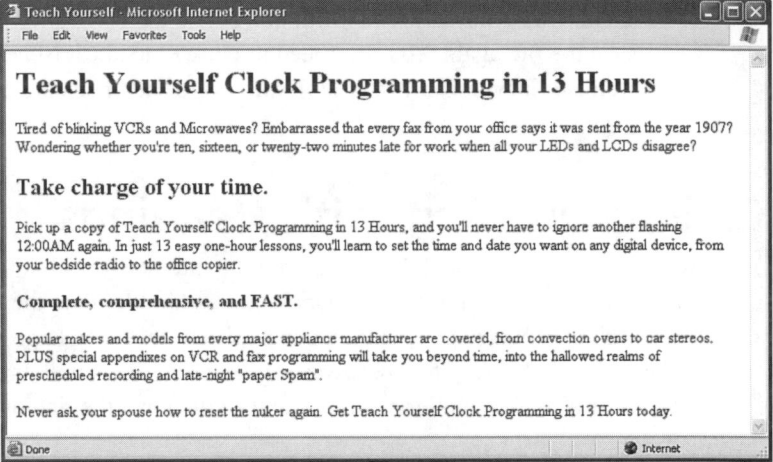

Theoretically, you can also use <h4>, <h5>, and <h6> to make progressively less important headings, but nobody uses these very much—after all, what's the point of a heading if it's not big and bold? Besides, most Web browsers don't show a noticeable difference between these and the small <h3> headings anyway.

On many Web pages nowadays, graphical images of ornately rendered letters and logos are often used in place of the ordinary text headings discussed in this hour. You'll discover how to create graphics and put them on your pages in Part III, "Web Page Graphics." However, old-fashioned text headings are still widely used and have the advantage of being transferred and displayed almost instantly, no matter how fast or slow the reader's connection to the Internet is.

It's important to remember the difference between a *title* and a *heading*. These two words are often interchangeable in day-to-day English, but when you're talking HTML, <title> gives the entire page an identifying name that isn't displayed on the page itself, but only on the browser window's title bar. The heading tags, on the other hand, cause some text on the page to be displayed with visual emphasis. There can only be one

<title> per page, but you can have as many <h1>, <h2>, and <h3> headings as you want, in any order that suits your fancy. In terms of HTML code, the title must be placed in the head of the page, while headings are placed in the body.

You'll learn to take complete control over the appearance of text on your Web pages in Part II, "Web Page Text." Even so, headings provide the easiest and most popular way to draw extra attention to important text.

Peeking at Other People's Pages

Given the visual and sometimes audio pizzazz present in many popular Web pages, you probably realize that the simple text pages described in this hour are only the tip of the HTML iceberg. Now that you know the basics, you may surprise yourself with how much of the rest you can pick up just by looking at other people's pages on the Internet. As mentioned in Hour 1, you can see the HTML for any page by right-clicking and selecting View Source in Netscape Navigator or Microsoft Internet Explorer.

Don't worry if you aren't yet able to decipher what some HTML tags do or exactly how to use them yourself. You'll find out about all that in the next few hours. However, sneaking a preview now will show you the tags that you do know in action and give you a taste of what you'll soon be able to do with your Web pages.

> The HTML goodies at my *24-Hour HTML Café* are especially designed to be intuitive and easy to understand.
>
> The HTML used in the main entrance page at http://www.24hourHTMLcafe.com/ may look a bit intimidating now, but you'll soon learn how to develop sophisticated sites like this yourself. For some less intimidating example pages, go to http://www.24hourHTMLcafe.com/hour2/.
>
> Click the link to each example page, and then use View, Page Source in Netscape Navigator (View, Source in Microsoft Internet Explorer) to look at the HTML code I wrote to create that page.

Summary

In this hour you've been introduced to the most basic and important HTML tags. By adding these coded commands to any plain text document, you can quickly transform it into a bona fide Web page.

The first step in creating a Web page is to put a few obligatory HTML tags at the beginning and end, including a title for the page. You then mark where paragraphs and lines end, and add horizontal rules and headings if you want them. Table 2.1 summarizes all the tags introduced in this hour.

TABLE 2.1   HTML Tags Covered in Hour 2

Tag	Function
`<html>...</html>`	Encloses the entire HTML document.
`<head>...</head>`	Encloses the head of the HTML document.
`<title>...</title>`	Indicates the title of the document. Used within `<head>`.
`<body>...</body>`	Encloses the body of the HTML document.
`<p>...</p>`	A paragraph; skips a line between paragraphs.
` `	A line break.
`<hr />`	A horizontal rule line.
`<h1>...</h1>`	A first-level heading.
`<h2>...</h2>`	A second-level heading.
`<h3>...</h3>`	A third-level heading.
`<h4>...</h4>`	A fourth-level heading (seldom used).
`<h5>...</h5>`	A fifth-level heading (seldom used).
`<h6>...</h6>`	A sixth-level heading (seldom used).

Q&A

Q I've created a Web page, but when I open the file in my Web browser I see all the text including the HTML tags. Sometimes I even see weird gobbledygook characters at the top of the page! What did I do wrong?

A You didn't save the file as plain text. Try saving the file again, being careful to save it as Text Only or ASCII Text. If you can't quite figure out how to get your word processor to do that, don't stress. Just type your HTML files in Notepad or TextEdit instead and everything should work just fine. (Also, always make sure the filename of your Web page ends in .html or .htm.)

Q I have this HTML Web page on my computer now. How do I get it on the Internet so everyone else can see it?

A Hour 4, "Publishing Your HTML Pages," explains how to put your pages on the Internet as well as how to get them ready for publishing on a local network or CD-ROM.

Q I want "Fred's Fresh Fish" to appear both at the top of my page and on people's bookmark (or favorites) lists when they bookmark my page. How can I get it to appear both places?

A Make a heading at the top of your page with the same text as the title, like this:

```
<html><head><title>Fred's Fresh Fish</title></head>
<body><h1>Fred's Fresh Fish</h1>
...the rest of the page goes here...
</body></html>
```

Q I've seen Web pages on the Internet that don't have `<html>` tags at the beginning. I've also seen pages with some other weird tags in front of the `<html>` tag. You said pages always have to start with `<html>`. What's the deal?

A Many Web browsers will forgive you if you forget to put in the `<html>` tag and will display the page correctly anyway. Yet it's a very good idea to include it because some software does need it to identify the page as valid HTML.

In fact, the official HTML standard goes one step further and recommends that you put a tag at the beginning that looks like this: `<!DOCTYPE HTML PUBLIC "-//IETF//DTD HTML//EN//4.0">`. Although it isn't very obvious, this tag indicates that your document conforms to the HTML 4 standard. No software that I'm aware of thus far, including Web browsers, pays attention to this tag, however. A similar tag also exists for identifying XHTML Web pages. For now you don't need to worry about including either tag in your Web pages.

Workshop

The workshop contains quiz questions and activities to help you solidify your understanding of the material covered. Try to answer all questions before looking at the "Answers" section that follows.

Quiz

1. What four tags are required in every HTML page?

2. Insert the appropriate line break and paragraph break tags to format the following poems with a blank line between them:

    Good night, God bless you,
    Go to bed and undress you.

    Good night, sweet repose,
    Half the bed and all the clothes.

3. Write the HTML for the following to appear one after the other:
    - A small heading with the words, "We are Proud to Present"
    - A horizontal rule across the page
    - A large heading with the one word, "Orbit"
    - A medium-sized heading with the words, "The Geometric Juggler"
    - Another horizontal rule

4. Write a complete HTML Web page with the title "Foo Bar" and a heading at the top which reads "Happy Hour at the Foo Bar", followed by the words "Come on down!" in regular type.

Answers

1. `<html>`, `<head>`, `<title>`, and `<body>` (along with their closing tags, `</html>`, `</head>`, `</title>`, and `</body>`).

2.
```
<p>Good night, God bless you,<br />
Go to bed and undress you.</p>
<p>Good night, sweet repose,<br />
Half the bed and all the clothes.</p>
```

3.
```
<h3>We are Proud to Present</h3>
<hr />
<h1>Orbit</h1>
<h2>The Geometric Juggler</h2>
<hr />
```

4.
```
<html>
<head><title>Foo Bar</title></head>
<body>
<h1>Happy Hour at the Foo Bar</h1>
Come on Down!
</body></html>
```

Exercises

- Even if your main goal in reading this book is to create Web pages for your business, you might want to make a personal Web page just for practice. Type a few paragraphs to introduce yourself to the world, and use the HTML tags you've learned in this hour to make them into a Web page.

- You'll be using the HTML tags covered in this hour so often that you'll want to commit them to memory. The best way to do that is to take some time now and create several Web pages before you go on. You can try creating some basic pages with serious information you want to post on the Internet, or just use your imagination and make some fun pages.

HOUR 3

Linking to Other Web Pages

In the previous two hours you learned how to use HTML tags to create a Web page with some text on it. However, at this point the Web page is an island unto itself, with no connection to anything else. To make it a "real" Web page you need to connect it to the rest of the World Wide Web—or at least to your own personal or corporate web of pages.

This hour shows you how to create *hypertext links*—those words that take you from one Web page to another when you click them with your mouse. You learn how to create links that go to another part of the same page in Hour 7, "Creating Text Links."

Although the same HTML tag you study in this hour is also used to make graphical images into clickable links, graphical links aren't explicitly discussed here. You'll find out about those in Hour 9, "Putting Graphics on a Web Page." For now you'll focus your energy on linking to other pages via words, not graphics.

Linking to Another Web Page

The tag to create a link is called <a>, which stands for anchor. While the word "anchor" might seem a little obscure when describing links, it has to do with the fact that you can use the <a> tag to identify a particular spot within a Web page—an anchor point. Granted, there are certainly better words out there that would make more sense, but we're stuck with anchor so just go with it! Within the <a> tag, you put the address of the page to link to in quotes after href=, like the following:

```
<a href="http://www.stalefishlabs.com/products.html">click here!</a>
```

This link displays the words click here! in blue with an underline. When a user clicks those, she would see the Web page named products.htm, which is located on the Web server computer whose address is www.stalefishlabs.com—just as if she had typed the address into the Web browser by hand. (By the way, Internet addresses are also called *Uniform Resource Locators*, or *URLs*, by techie types.)

Getting back to the <a> tag, href stands for hypertext reference and is an *attribute* of the <a> tag. An *attribute* is an additional piece of information associated with a tag that provides further details about the tag. You'll learn more about attributes in Hour 5, "Basic Text Alignment and Formatting."

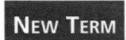 **NEW TERM** An *attribute* is an additional piece of information associated with a tag that provides further details about the tag. For example, the href attribute of the <a> tag identifies the address of the page to which you are linking.

 As you may know, you can leave out the http:// at the front of any address when typing it into most Web browsers. However, you cannot leave that part out when you type an Internet address into an <a href> link on a Web page.

 One thing you can often leave out of an address is the actual name of the HTML page. Most computers on the Internet automatically pull up the home page for a particular address or directory folder. For example, you can use http://www.stalefishlabs.com to refer to the page located at http://www.stalefishlabs.com/index.html because my server computer knows index.html is the page you should see first (see Hour 4, "Publishing Your HTML Pages").

Listing 3.1 includes a number of `<a>` tags, which show up as underlined links in Figure 3.1. The addresses for the links are given in the `href` attributes. For example, clicking the words `Eiffel Tower` in Figure 3.1 will take you to the page located at `http://www.abcparislive.com/eiffel_tower_webcams.htm` as shown in Figure 3.2.

LISTING 3.1   `<a>` Tags

```html
<html><head><title>You Aren't There</title></head><body><h1>Wonders of the
World</h1>Vacations aren't cheap. But who needs them anymore, with somany live
cameras connected to the World Wide Web? Pack apicnic, and you can visit just
about any international
attraction you want. Stop off at the <a
href="http://www.earthcam.com/usa/nevada/lasvegas/mgmgrand/">
MGM Grand in Las Vegas</a> on your way to
<a href="http://www.fallsview.com/Stream/PanLive.shtml">Niagra
Falls</a>. Then hop on a virtual Concorde jet and zip across
the ocean to Paris where you can take in the
<a href="http://www.abcparislive.com/eiffel_tower_webcams.htm">
Eiffel Tower</a>.</p>
</body>
</html>
```

FIGURE 3.1

The HTML in Listing 3.1 produces this page, with links appearing as blue or purple underlined text.

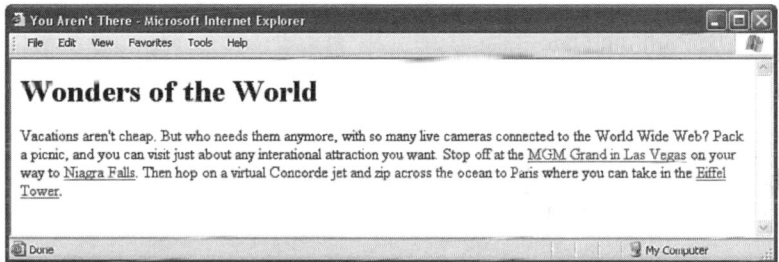

 You can easily transfer the address of a page from your Web browser to your own HTML page by using the Windows or Macintosh clipboard. Just highlight the address in the Location, Address, Bookmark Properties, or Edit Favorites box in your Web browser, and select Edit, Copy (or press Ctrl+C or Command+C on the Mac). Then type `<a href="` and select Edit, Paste (Ctrl+V or Command+V) in your HTML (text) editor.

FIGURE 3.2

Clicking the Eiffel Tower link in Figure 3.1 retrieves the Paris Live Eiffel Tower Cams page from the Internet.

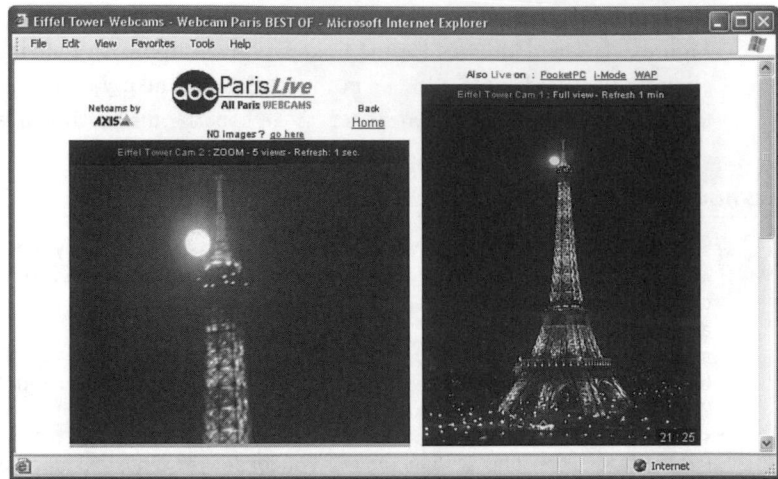

Linking Between Your Own Pages

One exception to the rule earlier about needing to include `http://` before each address specified in the `href` attribute is when you're dealing with links between files on the same computer or Web server. When you create a link from one page to another page on the same computer, it isn't necessary to specify a complete Internet address. In fact, if the two pages are stored in the same folder, you can simply use the name of the HTML file:

```
<a href="pagetwo.htm">click here to go to page 2.</a>
```

As an example, Listing 3.2 and Figure 3.3 show a quiz page with a link to the answers page in Listing 3.3 and Figure 3.4. The answers page contains a link back to the quiz page. Because the page in Listing 3.2 links to another page in the same directory, the filename can be used in place of a complete address.

LISTING 3.2   Linking to Another Page in the Same Directory

```
<html>
<head><title>History Quiz</title></head>
<body>
<h1>History Quiz</h1>
<p>Complete the following rhymes. (Example: William the Conqueror played cruel
tricks
on the Saxons in... ten sixty-six.)</p>
<p>1. Columbus sailed the ocean blue in...<br />
2. The Spanish Armada met its fate in...<br />
3. London burnt like rotten sticks in...<br />
4. Tricky Dickie served his time in...<br />
```

```
5. Billy C. went on a spree in...</p>
<p><a href="answers.htm">Click here for answers.</a></p>
</body>
</html>
```

LISTING 3.3 This Is the `answers.htm` file; Listing 3.2 Is `quizzer.htm`, to Which This Page Links Back

```
<html
<head><title>History Quiz</title></head>
<body><h1>History Quiz Answers</h1>
<p>1. ...fourteen hundred and ninety-two.<br />
2. ...fifteen hundred and eighty eight.<br />
3. ...sixteen hundred and sixty-six.<br />
4. ...nineteen hundred and sixty-nine.<br />
5. ...nineteen hundred and ninety-three.</p>
<p><a href="quizzer.htm">Click here for the questions.</a></p>
</body>
</html>
```

FIGURE 3.3

This is the quizzer.htm *file listed in Listing 3.2 and referred to by the link in Listing 3.3.*

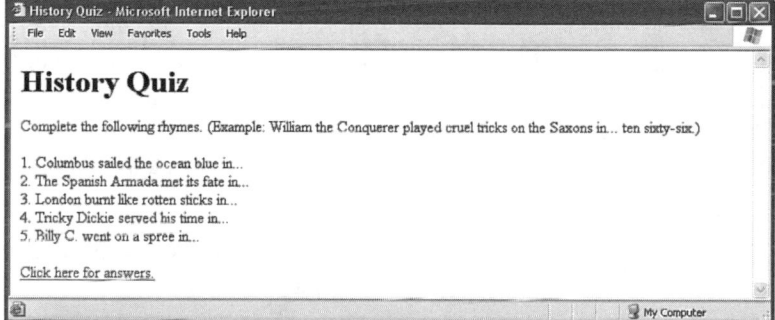

FIGURE 3.4

Click here for answers *in Figure 3.3 takes you here.* Click here for the questions *takes you back to Figure 3.3.*

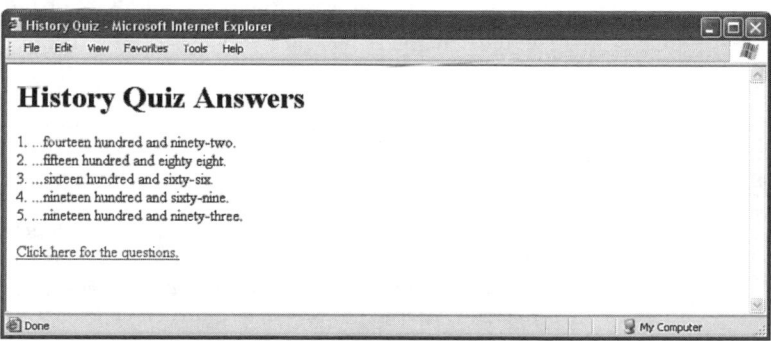

Using filenames instead of complete Internet addresses saves you a lot of typing. More importantly, the links between your pages will work properly no matter where the group of pages is stored. You can test the links while the files are still on your computer's hard drive. You can then move them to a computer on the Internet, or to a CD-ROM or DVD disk, and all the links will still work correctly. There is nothing magic about this simplified approach to identifying Web pages—it all has to do with Web page addressing, which you learn about next.

At the *24-Hour HTML Café*, you'll find some fun sample pages demonstrating hypertext links, including a tour of Indigestible Ingestibles Research sites on the Internet and a light-hearted literary history quiz. These intriguing pages can be found, along with the other examples from this hour, at `http://www.24hourhtmlcafe.com/hour3/`.

Addressing Web Pages

The simplest way to organize Web pages for an individual Web site is to place them all in the same folder together. When files are stored together like this, you can link to them by simply providing the name of the file in the `href` attribute of the `<a>` tag. If you have many pages, you may want to put them in more than one folder for better organization. In that case, you still shouldn't use the full Internet address to link between them. You can use *relative addresses*, which include only enough information to find one page from another.

 **NEW TERM**   A *relative address* describes the path from one Web page to another, instead of a full (or *absolute*) Internet address.

For instance, suppose you are creating a page named `zoo.htm` in a directory folder named `webpages` on your hard drive. You want to include a link to a page named `african.htm`, which is in a subfolder named `elephants` within `webpages`. The link would look like the following:

```
<a href="elephants/african.htm">learn about african elephants.</a>
```

The / forward slash is always used to separate directory folders in HTML. Don't use the \ backslash normally used in Windows and DOS! I apologize if the reference to DOS was shocking, but believe it or not there are still a few remnants of it in the Windows operating system, such as backslashes.

The african.htm page might contain a link back to the main zoo.htm page:

```
<a href="../zoo.htm">return to the zoo.</a>
```

The double dot (..) is a special code that indicates the folder containing the current folder—in other words, the parent folder. (The .. means the same thing in Windows, Macintosh, and UNIX.) In truth, specifying a filename by itself is also a form of relative addressing because you're saying that the file resides in the current folder.

If you use relative addressing consistently throughout your Web pages, you can move the pages to another folder, disk drive, or Web server without changing the links. Or using the example, everything will work as long as you always put african.htm inside a subfolder named elephants.

> The general rule surrounding relative addressing (cow.html) versus absolute addressing (http://www.accsyst.com/cow.html) is that you should use relative addressing when linking to files that are stored together, such as files that are all part of the same Web site. Absolute addressing should be used when you're linking to files somewhere else—another computer, another disk drive, or more commonly, another Web site on the Internet.

Relative addresses can span quite complex directory structures if necessary; Hour 21, "Organizing and Managing a Web Site," offers more detailed advice for organizing and linking among large numbers of Web pages.

To Do

You probably created a page or two of your own while working through Hour 2, "Create a Web Page Right Now." Now is a great time to add a few more pages and link them together:

- Use a home page as a main entrance and central hub to which all of your other pages are connected. If you created a page about yourself or your business in Hour 2, use that as your home page. You also might like to make a new page now for this purpose.

- On the home page, put a list of <a href> links to the other HTML files you've created (or plan to create soon). Be sure that the exact spelling of the filename, including any capitalization, is correct in every link.

- On every other page, include a link at the bottom (or top) leading back to your home page. That makes it simple and easy to navigate around your site.

- You may also want to include a list of links to sites on the Internet, either on your home page or a separate hotlist page. People often include a list of their friends'

▼ personal pages on their own home page. (Businesses, however, should be careful
not to lead potential customers away to other sites too quickly—there's no guaran-
▲ tee they'll come back!)

> There is one good reason to sometimes use the complete address of your
> own pages in links. If someone saves one of your pages on his own hard
> drive, none of the links to your other pages from that page will work unless
> he downloads all of the pages or you've included full addresses.
>
> A good middle-of-the-road solution to this addressing problem involves
> including a link with the full address of your main home page at the bottom
> of every page, and use simple filenames or relative addresses in all the rest
> of the links.

Remember to only use filenames (or *relative addressing*) for links between your own
pages, but full Internet addresses for links to other sites.

Opening a Link in a New Browser Window

Now that you have a handle on how to create addresses for links, I want to share one
additional little linking trick. I'm referring to opening a linked page in a new browser
window, which leaves the original page still open in its original window. To accomplish
this feat, you simply include an additional attribute in the `<a>` tag called `target`. You must
set the `target` attribute to `_blank` for this nifty little trick to work, as the following example shows:

```
<a href="../zoo.htm" target="_blank">return to the zoo.</a>
```

When someone clicks the linked text in this example, the `zoo.htm` Web page is opened in
a completely new browser window. I don't encourage you to use this technique too much
because most people don't enjoy new browser windows popping up everywhere. One
scenario where I've found it useful is when you link to a page that isn't located on your
site. This can be a helpful way to keep your site active in the background so you aren't
forgotten when the link is followed!

Summary

The `<a>` tag is what makes hypertext "hyper." With it, you can create clickable links
between pages, as well as links to specific anchor points on any page. This hour focused
on creating simple links to other pages using either relative or absolute addressing to
identify the pages.

When creating links to other people's pages, you learned that it's important to include the full Internet address of each page in an `<a href>` tag. For links between your own pages, include just the filenames and enough directory information to get from one page to another.

Table 3.1 summarizes the `<a>` tag discussed in this hour.

TABLE 3.1 HTML Tags and Attributes Covered in Hour 3

Tag/Attribute	Function
`<a>...</a>`	With the `href` attribute, creates a link to another document or anchor.
Attributes	
`href="..."`	The address of the document or anchor point to link to.
`target="_blank"`	Opens the linked page in a new browser window.

Q&A

Q When I make links, some of them are blue and some of them are purple. Why? How come most of the links I see on the Internet aren't blue and purple?

A A link appears blue to anyone who hasn't recently visited the page to which it points. Once you visit a page, any links to it turn purple. These colors can be (and often are) changed to match any color scheme a Web page author wants, so many links you see on the Web won't be blue and purple. (Hour 10, "Custom Backgrounds and Colors," tells how to change the colors of text and links on your Web pages.)

Q What happens if I link to a page on the Internet and then the person who owns that page deletes or moves it?

A That depends on how that person has set up his server computer. Usually, people see a message saying `page not found` or something to that effect when they click the link. They can still click the Back button to return to your page.

Q One of my links works fine on my computer, but when I put the pages on the Internet it doesn't work anymore. What's up?

A The most likely culprits are

- Capitalization problems. On Windows computers, linking to a file named `Freddy.htm` with `<a href="freddy.htm">` will work. On most Web servers (which are often UNIX machines), the link must be `<a href="freddy.htm">`

(or you must change the name of the file to `freddy.htm`). To make matters worse, some text editors and file transfer programs actually change the capitalization without telling you! The best solution is to stick with all lowercase filenames for Web pages.

- **Spaces in filenames.** Most Web servers don't allow filenames with spaces. For example, you should never name a Web page, `my page.htm`. Instead, call it `mypage.htm` or `MyPage.htm`.

- **Local absolute addresses.** If for some reason you link to a file using a local absolute address, such as `C:\mywebsite\news.html`, the link won't work when you place the file on the Internet. You should never use local absolute addresses; when this occurs it is usually an accident caused from a temporary link created just to test part of a page. So, be careful to remove any test links like this before publishing a page on the Web.

The next hour explains how to upload files to a Web site and how to rename files once they're online so that you can make sure the spelling and capitalization are perfect.

Workshop

The workshop contains quiz questions and activities to help you solidify your understanding of the material covered. Try to answer all questions before looking at the "Answers" section that follows.

Quiz

1. Your best friend from elementary school finds you on the Internet and says he wants to trade home page links. How do you put a link to his page at `www.cheapsuits.com/~billybob/` on your page?

2. Your home page will be at `http://www.mysite.com/home.htm` when you put it on the Internet. Write the HTML code to go on that page so that when someone clicks the words `all about me`, they see the page located at `http://www.mysite.com/mylife.htm`.

3. You plan to publish a CD-ROM disk containing HTML pages. How do you create a link from a page in the `\guide` directory folder to the `\guide\maine\katahdin.htm` page?

4. How about a link from `\guide\maine\katahdin.htm` to the `\guide\arizona\superstitions.htm` page?

Answers

1. Put the following on your page:

```
<a href="http://www.cheapsuits.com/~billybob/">
my buddy billy bob's page of inexpensive businesswear</a>
```

2. `<a href="mylife.htm">all about me</a>`

   The following would work equally well, though it would be harder to test on your hard drive:

   ```
   <a href="http://www.mysite.com/mylife.htm">all about me</a>
   ```

3. `<a href="maine/katahdin.htm">mount katahdin</a>`

4. `<a href="../arizona/superstitions.htm">`

   `the superstition range</a>`

Exercises

To make a formatted list of your favorite sites, click the Bookmarks button on the toolbar in Netscape Navigator, click Edit Bookmarks, and then select File, Save As. You can then open that bookmark page in any text editor and add other text and HTML formatting as you prefer. (Alas, there's no easy way to export your Microsoft Internet Explorer favorites list as a single Web page, but I'm working on it!)

Hour **4**

Publishing Your HTML Pages

Here it is, the hour you've been waiting for! Your Web pages are ready for the world to see, and this hour explains how to get them to appear before the eyes of your intended audience, whether it's your circle of friends or co-workers, or the entire online world.

The most obvious avenue for publishing Web pages is, of course, the Internet, but you may want to limit the distribution of your pages to a local intranet within your organization, instead of making them available to the general public. You may also choose to distribute your Web pages on CD-ROMs, floppy disks, Zip disks, DVD-ROMs, or even USB memory cards.

This hour covers all of these options and offers advice for designing your pages to work best with whichever distribution method you choose.

NEW TERM   An *intranet* is a private network with access restricted to one organization, but which uses the same technical standards and protocols as the global public Internet.

To Do

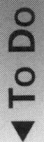

Before you read about publishing your pages, you should give some thought to which methods of distribution you will be using.

- If you want your pages to be visible to as many people as possible all over the world, Internet publishing is a must. However, don't rule out other distribution methods; you can easily adapt Internet-based pages for distribution on disks or local networks.

- If you want to reach only employees of your organization, publish on your local intranet only.

- If you want to provide very large graphics, multimedia, or other content that would be too slow to transfer over even a cable or DSL modem connection, consider publishing on a CD-ROM. You can easily link the CD-ROM to an Internet Web site and offer the CD-ROM to people who find you through the Internet, but want the full experience.

- If you plan to make a presentation at a meeting and would also like to publish related material on the Internet or an intranet, why not use HTML instead of old-fashioned PowerPoint slides as a visual aid? You can even place the files on a floppy disk, a Zip disk, or burn one-off CD-ROMs if necessary for people to take home.

Setting Up Web Space on the Internet

NEW TERM To make an HTML page part of the publicly accessible World Wide Web, you need to put it on a *Web server* (a computer permanently connected to the Internet and equipped to send out Web pages on request). If you run your own Web server, this procedure is simply a matter of copying the file to the right directory folder. However, you may not have access to a Web server that you can use to host your own Web site, in which case you'll need to use a Web server run by an Internet service provider (ISP) to host your pages.

NEW TERM A *Web server* is a computer permanently connected to the Internet that uses special software to deliver Web pages upon request by Web browsers.

Almost all ISPs that offer Internet access also now offer space in which to place your own personal Web pages for little or no additional cost, though you may have to pay extra if your site attracts a huge number of visitors or includes very large multimedia files. Make sure to check with the company you're getting Internet access from to see if any Web space is built into your standard account. This is often a great way to get started with creating a Web site because the space is usually free and readily available.

Even if it's free initially, you don't have to use the same company that provides you with Internet access to host your pages, especially if they don't
offer advanced features such as shopping cart and online merchant services.
If you run a high-traffic business Web site, you may get more features and
more reliable service from a company that specializes solely in Web hosting.
To comparison shop the hosting services offered by various Internet service
providers, go to the list of ISPs at `http://thelist.internet.com/`.

Web hosting prices for a business site start well under $50 per month, but you usually
pay more when lots of people start viewing your pages. For a site with about a hundred
different Web pages, I have paid as little as $9 per month when a few thousand people
looked at my pages, and as much as $2,000 per month when hundreds of thousands of
people looked at my pages. The pricing ultimately comes down to how much traffic your
site gets from Web users, although early on you can probably expect traffic to be fairly
light. Keep in mind also that Web hosting prices are getting more and more affordable,
so you're likely to find a suitable hosting service on the lower end of the range I've mentioned.

Free Web hosting services such as Geocities (`http://geocities.yahoo.com/`), Tripod
(`http://www.tripod.lycos.com/`), and Angelfire (`http://www.angelfire.lycos.com/`) are very
popular with Web page authors—and yes, they really are free—although most such services require that you include advertisements of their choosing on your pages. The other
issue with these free services is that they often display pop-up ads to people viewing
your pages, which can be annoying.

One of the most important choices you'll need to make when you set up a
Web site is the name you want to use as the site's address. If you don't pay
to register a unique domain name of your own, which runs around $30 per
year, your site's address will include the name of your Internet service
provider (`http://www.shore.net/~smith/` for example). If you're willing to
pay for it and register a name, you can choose any name that isn't already
used by another company (`http://www.mister-smith.com/` for example).

If your Web hosting service doesn't offer domain name registration, you can
use a domain service such as `http://www.easydns.com/`, `http://www.regis-
ter.com/`, or `http://www.networksolutions.com/`. Prior to registering a new
name, you must first perform a search to see if the name is available; each
domain name service offers such a search service at no charge. Keep in mind
that you can register a domain name even if you aren't ready to publish
your Web site; this is a good idea if you want to make sure you don't lose
the name while you build your site.

Transferring Pages to a Web Server

When a Web server computer sends Web pages to people through the Internet, it uses an information exchange standard called *Hypertext Transfer Protocol* (*HTTP*). To upload a page to your Web site, however, you usually need software that uses a different communications standard called *File Transfer Protocol* (*FTP*).

New Term   *FTP* is the standard that your file transfer software must adhere to when sending files to a Web server. After you've published files to a Web server using FTP, the server then sends those files out to anyone who asks for them using HTTP. Here's an easy way to remember the protocols: FTP is used to upload your HTML files to the Web server, while HTTP is used by Web browsers to download and view your Web pages.

You'll most likely need to get four important pieces of information from your Web hosting service before you can put pages up on your Web site:

1. Your *account name* (sometimes called a *username* or *user ID*). If the same company provides you with both Internet access and Web hosting, the account name for your Web site will probably be the same as your email account name.
2. Your *password*. This may also be the same as your email password.
3. The *FTP address* for your site. Note that this address may or may not be the same as the address people go to when they view your Web pages in a Web browser.
4. The *folder* where your Web page files should be placed. You can sometimes place them in the root folder of the Web server, which is the topmost folder on the server, but often you need to go into a subdirectory named www or public, or the same as your domain name.

Next, you need to decide which software you'll use to send your pages to the Web server and maintain your site. This hour covers five options:

- Microsoft Internet Explorer
- Netscape Composer (comes with Navigator)
- Microsoft FrontPage (or similar Web development software)
- FTP software (such as CuteFTP or WS_FTP)
- Windows Web Publishing Wizard

Which of these do I recommend? It depends on your situation. If you plan on developing a complex Web site, you will find that a program such as Microsoft FrontPage saves you a lot of time by helping manage changing links between pages and automatically keeping track of which pages have changed and need updating. However, for the beginning Web page author and anyone who only plans to have a modest site with a few personal or business pages, it's easier to learn and use a simple FTP program such as CuteFTP. If you just want to get your pages online without bothering to set up any new software at all, you can get the job done with the Web browser you already have or with the standard Windows Web Publishing Wizard.

The next few sections cover the details of publishing Web pages using each of the previously mentioned approaches. You may end up trying several of the approaches before deciding which technique is best for your needs.

Using Microsoft Internet Explorer

As you might guess from the name, Microsoft Internet Explorer for Windows was designed to work much like the Windows Explorer file manager that comes with Windows. When you enter an FTP address in the Address bar of Internet Explorer, you can cut, paste, delete, and rename any file or directory folder on the Web server just as if it were on your computer's own hard drive.

If you're using the Windows version of Internet Explorer, follow these steps to upload a page you've created on your hard drive so that it will appear on your Web site online:

1. Start Microsoft Internet Explorer. Click the Address bar, type My Computer, press the Enter key, and you will see all of the drives and folders available on your computer. Navigate to where the page you created is currently located. Note that going to the folder by selecting File, Open won't work—you have to navigate to the page within Explorer.

2. Click once on the file you want to upload to your Web site to highlight it. As in any Windows program, you can select multiple files by holding down the Shift or Ctrl key as you click on the files. Be sure to include any graphics files (see Hour 9) that need to go with the HTML file.

3. Select Edit, Copy (see Figure 4.1).

4

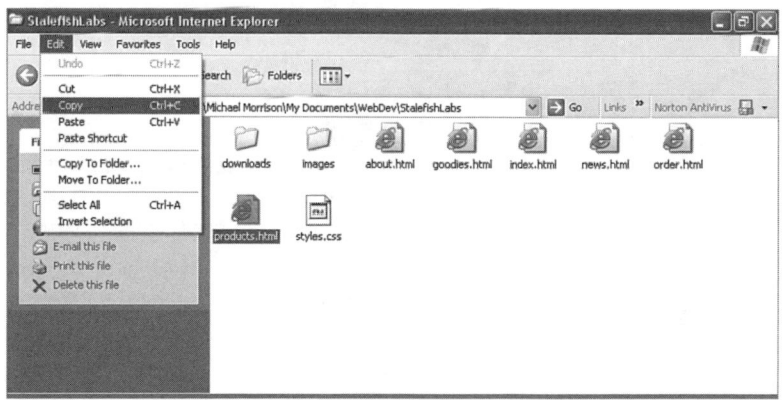

4. Now click the Address bar again in Internet Explorer and enter your Web account name, password, and site address in the following format:

   ftp://*myname*:*mypassword*@*siteaddress.net*/*home*/*web*/*wherever*/

   Put your account name and password for accessing the site instead of *myname* and *mypassword*, the FTP address for your site instead of *siteaddress.net*, and the top-level directory where your Web pages go on the server instead of */home/web/wherever/*.

5. Wait until the Web server folder is opened in Internet Explorer, and then select Edit, Paste. The file(s) will be transferred from your hard drive to the Web server (see Figure 4.2).

6. Test your page by returning to Navigator and entering the URL of the Web page. You're on the Web!

To delete or rename a file or folder on the Web server, right-click it and select Delete or Rename, just as you would with local files in an Windows application.

FIGURE 4.2

Microsoft Internet Explorer uses the familiar Windows Explorer interface to paste files into folders on a distant Web server computer.

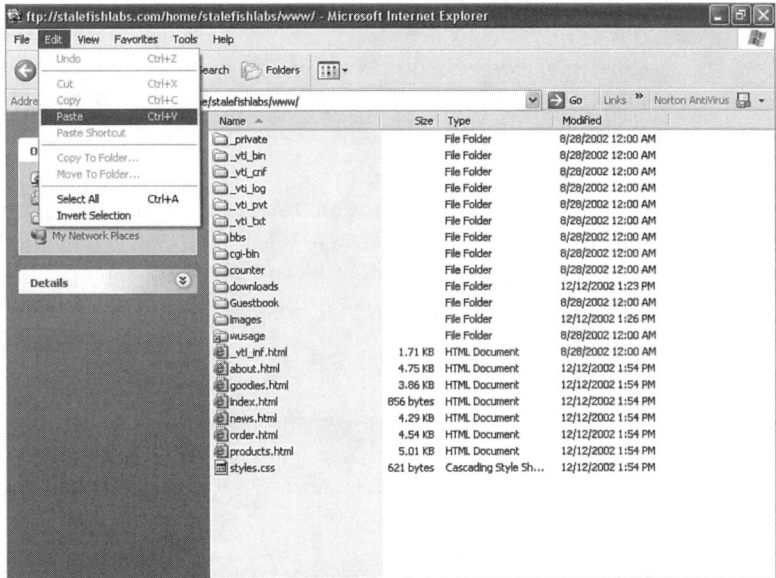

You can take follow the first three steps with Windows Explorer instead of Internet Explorer. Another good technique for transferring files in Windows is to drag and drop them from Windows Explorer into Internet Explorer, as opposed to using the copy-and-paste approach.

Once you've successfully published the file onto the Web server, it's very important that you test it by entering the name of the Web page in the Address bar of Internet Explorer, and pressing the Enter key. If you've registered a domain name for the site, you'll probably enter the domain name followed by a forward slash (/) followed by the Web page file name. Otherwise, you'll need to enter the exact name of your Web server as provided by your Web hosting service provider, followed by a slash and the file name.

> You cannot directly transfer a file from one folder on an FTP site to another folder on an FTP site. If you want to do that, you need to transfer the file to your hard drive first and then transfer it back to the new location on the FTP site.

Using Netscape Composer

Many people don't realize that the Netscape Navigator Web browser can also upload pages to a Web server. Unlike Internet Explorer, however, Navigator allows you to use a different application called Netscape Composer, which is included in the Navigator installation. In actuality, Composer is a complete Web page development tool that you can use as an HTML editor if you choose. For now I want to focus on using it to publish Web pages, but you are free to tinker with it as a Web page creation tool. Following are the steps required to publish HTML files using Netscape Composer:

1. Run Composer from your Netscape Navigator installation folder, or just select Composer from the Window menu to run it.

2. Click File, Open and select the file you'd like to publish.

3. Click the Publish button on the Composer toolbar, and then enter the Web server information required to access your Web storage space. This information includes the FTP (publishing) address for your site, the HTTP address for viewing the site, and your account name and password for accessing the site (Figure 4.3). Check the Save Password check box if you want Composer to remember your user name and password for publishing future pages. Wait while the files are transferred.

4. Test your page by returning to Navigator and entering the URL of the Web page.

Even though Netscape Composer can send files to any Web server on the Internet, specialized FTP programs such as CuteFTP and WS_FTP offer much more control for managing your Web pages. For example, Composer doesn't give you any way to delete an old Web page or change the name of a Web page on the Web server computer. For these reasons, at some point you'll probably want something more than a Web browser to maintain your Web site.

FIGURE 4.3

You can connect to your Web hosting service and publish your HTML pages using Netscape Composer's Publish feature.

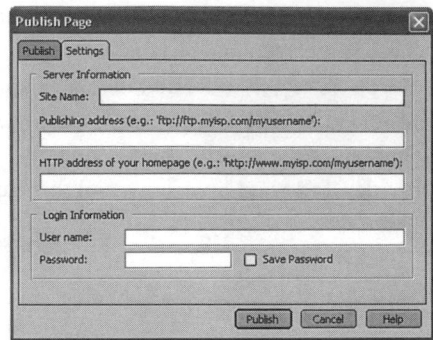

Using Microsoft FrontPage

While using Internet Explorer or Netscape to publish a few pages is certainly a reasonable approach to consider, there are more advanced options out there if you're looking for a complete Web development software package. One such package is Microsoft FrontPage for Windows, which is also a useful tool for creating Web pages once you get a solid handle on HTML. FrontPage turns publishing your entire Web site into a one-step, automated process. Whether you've created one or one hundred pages, you can put them all online by selecting File, Publish Web (see Figure 4.4). There are also Macintosh-compatible tools for publishing Web pages, which you learn about in a moment.

FIGURE 4.4

Microsoft FrontPage makes it easy to upload many pages at once—or to upload just those pages you made changes to.

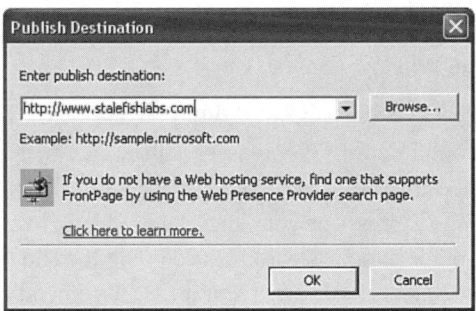

The first time you publish pages to a particular site, you are asked to specify the location of the Web server, which simply means to enter the FTP address your Web hosting service gave you (or the HTTP address, if the Web server has FrontPage extensions installed).

You are then asked to enter your account name and password. FrontPage automatically uploads all pages that you've changed since your last update; it keeps track of which pages you've modified since the last publish. Other Web development software, including Macromedia Dreamweaver and Adobe GoLive, also offers similar automated uploading and site management features.

Be very careful to include the correct subdirectory when you tell FrontPage where to publish the Web. For example, my Web host (sover.net) requires my pages to go in a directory folder named www, so I must publish to

ftp.sover.net/www/

I once forgot to include the www/ at the end, and before I knew it FrontPage had placed a large number of pages in the wrong directory. FrontPage doesn't offer any easy way to delete those pages without deleting them from my hard drive, so I ended up using another FTP program to get rid of them.

Using FTP Software

If you don't like any of the preceding options for publishing Web pages, or if you just want a little more control over how HTML files and related resources are organized on a Web server, you need to consider using FTP software. FTP software allows you to transfer, delete, and rename files on a Web server, as well as create, rename, and delete folders. This gives you a great deal of control over how your Web sites are organized. There are many FTP programs out there, most of which are free or require a relatively minimal registration fee. CuteFTP is a popular FTP program for Windows that I've used with success. An evaluation version of CuteFTP is available for free download from the CuteFTP Web site at http://www.cuteftp.com/. Figure 4.5 shows CuteFTP in action as it displays files on a Web server.

The makers of CuteFTP, GlobalSCAPE, also offer affordable Web hosting that includes a free copy of CuteFTP.

If you aren't using a Windows computer, don't worry, because there are plenty of FTP software packages similar to CuteFTP that you can use on other operating systems such as Macintosh and UNIX systems. Fetch is a popular Macintosh FTP program (http://www.fetchsoftworks.com/), while gFTP is a good option if you're using a computer that runs UNIX (`http://gftp.seul.org/`). You can also use your favorite search engine to perform a search on "ftp client" or "ftp software" and see what else you find.

FIGURE 4.5
CuteFTP is a powerful and user-friendly FTP program that individuals can use for free.

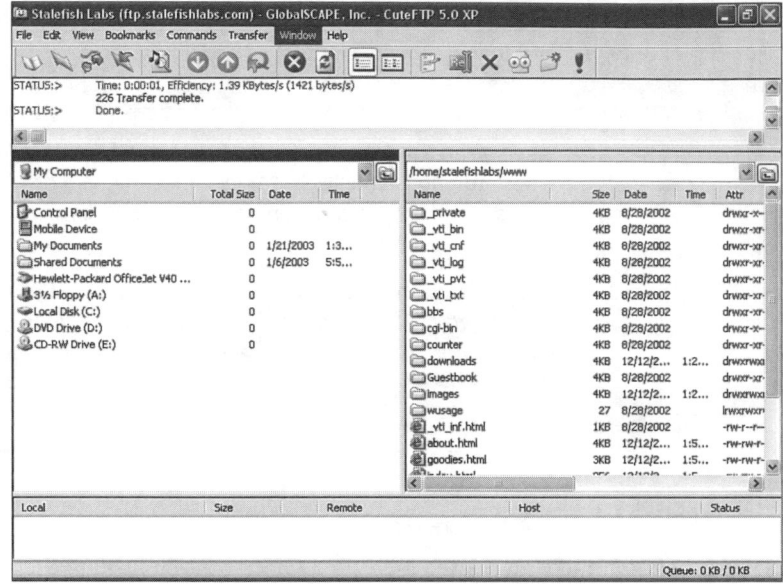

Another popular Windows FTP program is WS_FTP, which is available online at `http://www.ipswitch.com/`. From that site you can download an evaluation version of WS_FTP for free, or purchase the full version online.

Regardless of what kind of computer you're using and what FTP software you select, the process of publishing Web pages is very straightforward. I'll show you steps using CuteFTP as an example, but you should be able to follow along in virtually any FTP program. Just follow these steps:

1. Before you can access the Web server, you must tell your FTP program its address, as well as your account name and password (Figure 4.6). Clicking the Edit button allows you to specify additional information about the FTP site (Figure 4.7). 2. Here's how to fill in each of the items in Figures 4.6 and 4.7:

   - The site label is the name you'll use to refer to your own site. Nobody else will see this name, so enter whatever you want.

   - The host address is the FTP address of the Web server to which you need to send your Web pages. This usually (but not always) starts with ftp. Notice that it may or may not resemble the address that other people will use to view your Web pages. The ISP that runs your Web server will be able to tell you the correct address to enter here.

FIGURE 4.6

CuteFTP includes an intuitive FTP site manager, although most Web page authors need only a single FTP site entry.

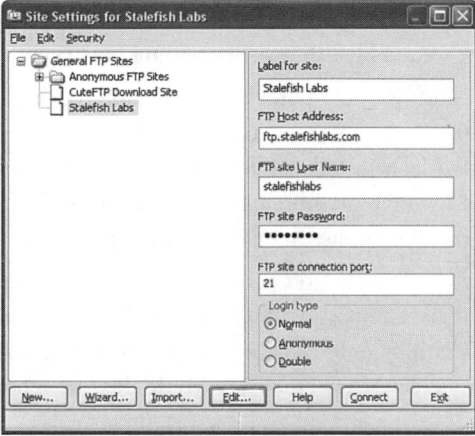

FIGURE 4.7

Clicking the Site Settings Edit button brings up this dialog box.

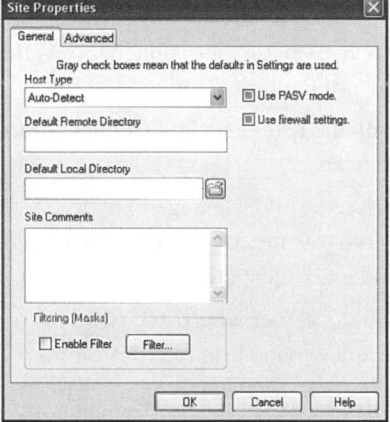

- The company that runs the Web server also issues your user ID and password. Be aware that CuteFTP (and most other FTP programs) remember your password automatically, which means that anyone who has physical access to your computer can modify your Web site.

- You should set the Login Type to Normal unless somebody important tells you otherwise. (The Anonymous setting is for downloading files from public FTP services that don't require user IDs or passwords.)

- Set the Transfer Type to Auto-Detect. (This automatically sends HTML and other text files using a slightly different protocol than images and other non-text files to ensure complete compatibility with all types of computers.)

- The Host Type should also be set to Auto-Detect, unless you have trouble connecting. In that case, you need to find out what type of computer you're connecting to and pick the corresponding host type.

- For the Default Remote Directory, fill in the name of the main directory folder on the Web server where your Web pages will be located. Your Web service provider will tell you the name of this directory. (In some cases, you don't need to enter anything here because the Web server computer will automatically put you in the directory when you connect to it.)

- You can leave both Remote Directory Filter and Local Directory Filter both blank. (This is where you would enter wildcards such as `*.htm*` if you want to see files ending only in `.htm` or `.html` when you connect to this site. All other files, such as `.gif` and `.jpg`, would then be ignored.)

- For the Default Local Directory, enter the drive and directory folder on your computer's hard drive where you keep your Web pages.

- Normally, you won't need to change any settings on the Advanced tab unless you experience problems with your connection. If that happens, have your ISP help you figure out the best settings.

3. When you're finished with the settings, click Connect to establish a connection with the Web server computer.

   Most server computers issue a short message to everyone who connects to them. Many FTP programs ignore this message, but CuteFTP presents it to you. It seldom says anything important, so just click OK.

4. Once you're connected to the server, you'll see two lists of files, as shown earlier in Figure 4.5. The left window pane lists the files on your computer, while the right pane lists the files on the server computer.

   To transfer a Web page to the server, select the HTML file and any accompanying image files in the left window. (Remember that you can hold down the Ctrl key and click with the mouse to select multiple files in any Windows program.) Then select Transfer, Upload, or click the Upload button on the toolbar.

   CuteFTP also contains commands that delete or rename files (either on your computer or on the server), as well as commands to make and change directory folders.

Most Web servers have a special name for the file that should be sent if a user doesn't include a specific filename when he requests a page. For example, if you go to `http://netletter.com/`, my Web server will automatically give you the `welcome.htm` file. Other Web servers use different names for the default file, such as `index.html`.

Be sure to ask your ISP for the default filename so you can give your home page that name.

5. You can immediately view the page you just put on the Web server by entering the URL of the page in a Web browser.

6. When you're finished sending and modifying files on the Web server, select FTP, Disconnect to close the connection.

Most FTP programs remember the settings for each FTP connection you make, so the next time you need to upload Web pages, you won't need to fill in all the information in step 2. You can just click Connect, select the pages you want to send, and click the Upload button.

4

Most Web servers are set up so that any documents placed onto them are immediately made available to the entire World Wide Web. However, a few require that users manually change file permission settings, which control who is allowed to access individual files. Your ISP can tell you exactly how to change permission settings on their server and whether it's necessary to do so.

Using the Windows Web Publishing Wizard

Thus far we've kind of moved up the scale of Web publishing options from the most simple to the most powerful. Now I'd like to take a step back and show you one last option that is extremely simple, yet admittedly somewhat limited. I'm referring to the Web Publishing Wizard that ships standard with Windows XP (both Home and Professional). The Web Publishing Wizard is extremely easy to use, but it is limited in terms of what kinds of Web hosting services it supports. So, if you're using a service that isn't supported, you'll have to go with a different approach to publish your pages.

One of the default Web service providers supported by the Web Publishing Wizard is MSN Groups, which is an online community that is part of MSN (Microsoft Network). You can learn more about MSN Groups at `http://groups.msn.com/`.

As its name implies, the Web Publishing Wizard uses a familiar wizard interface, which means you publish Web pages by answering a series of questions presented in a succession of windows. To publish pages with the Web Publishing Wizard, you must start out in Windows Explorer. Here are the steps to follow:

1. Start Windows Explorer and navigate to the folder containing the HTML file(s) you want to publish. Click Publish this folder to the Web in the left side of the Explorer window.

2. The Web Publishing Wizard will appear. Click the Next button to get started uploading the pages.

3. Select your Web hosting service provider from the list shown in the Web Publishing Wizard (see Figure 4.8). If your provider isn't shown, you may want to skip ahead to the next section and try a different approach to uploading your files.

FIGURE 4.8

The Windows Web Publishing Wizard provides a simple approach to publishing Web pages as long as you're using a supported Web hosting provider to host your pages.

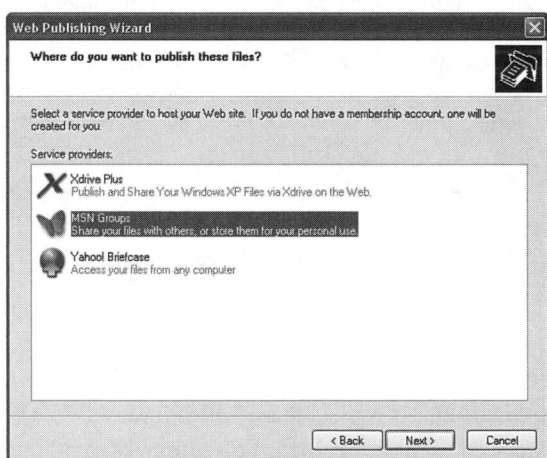

4. Enter the information required of the Web hosting service provider that you selected. This information varies depending upon the specific service provider, so you may want to check with your provider if you aren't sure what the wizard is asking you to enter.

5. Proceed through the final step of the wizard, and your pages will be uploaded to the Web server. This may take a few minutes if you're uploading a bunch of files or if your Internet connection isn't too speedy.

6. Test your Web page by launching your Web browser and entering the URL of the page.

Making a File Available for Downloading

Now that you know the scoop about getting your Web pages online, it's worth addressing another issue closely related to publishing HTML files. I'm referring to files other than Web pages that you want to make available online. Whether it's a Zip file containing your art portfolio, or an Excel spreadsheet with sales numbers, it's often useful to publish files on the Internet that aren't Web pages.

To make a file available on the Web that isn't a Web page, just upload the file to your Web site as if it were an HTML file, following the instructions earlier in this hour for uploading. Once the file is uploaded to the Web server, you need to create a link to the file on one of your Web pages, as explained in Hour 3. For example, if the file were called artfolio.zip, the link would look like this:

```
<a href="artfolio.zip">Click here to download my art portfolio.</a>
```

Remember that some Web host services charge by the number of bytes sent out, so you need to be careful about posting huge multi-megabyte files if a lot of people will be downloading them. For example, if 10,000 people a day download a 2MB file from your site, it might start costing you some serious money and overburden your Web server. Of course, short of you creating the next Yahoo! or eBay, that's a lot of traffic for a Web site by most normal standards.

4

Other HTML Publishing Options

Publishing HTML pages online is obviously the number one reason to learn HTML and create Web pages. However, this doesn't mean there aren't situations where other forms of publishing aren't viable. For example, you might want to distribute CD-ROMS at a trade show with marketing materials designed as HTML pages. You may also want to include HTML-based instructional manuals on floppy disks, Zip disks, or CD-ROMs for students at a training seminar. These are just two examples of how HTML pages can be used in publishing scenarios that don't involve the Internet. The next couple of sections provide additional information about these publishing options.

Putting Web Pages on an Intranet

Although the approach you learned for publishing pages to the global Internet will often work with private corporate intranets, the internal workings of intranets vary considerably from company to company. In some cases, you may need to use an FTP program to send files to an intranet server. In others, you may be able to transfer files by using the same file management program you use on your own computer. You may also need to adjust permission settings or make special allowances for the firewall that insulates a private intranet from the public Internet.

The best advice I can give regarding publishing to an intranet is to consult with your systems administrator. He or she can help you put your Web pages on the company server in a way that best ensures their accessibility and security.

Putting Web Pages on Disk

Unless you were hired to create documents for a company intranet, you have probably assumed that the Internet is the best way to get your pages in front of the eyes of the world, and for the most part this is true. There are, however, three major incentives for considering distribution on some form of disk instead:

- Currently, more people have disk drives than Internet connections.
- Disks can deliver information to the computer screen much faster than people can download it from the Internet.
- You can distribute disks to a select audience, regardless of whether they are connected to the Internet or any particular intranet.

In the very near future, as Web-enabled televisions and high-speed networks become more commonplace, these advantages may disappear. For now, publishing on disk can be an excellent way to provide a bigger, faster, more tightly targeted HTML presentation than you can on today's Internet. And perhaps more importantly, you can deliver it to people when Internet access isn't readily available.

Publishing on 1.44MB floppy disks or 100MB Zip disks is simply a matter of copying files from your hard disk with any file management program. You just need to keep in mind that any links starting with http:// will work only if and when someone reading your pages is also connected to the Internet. The cost associated with disks is reasonable, although Zip disks are considerably more expensive than floppy disks.

Never use a drive letter (such as C:) in <a href> link tags on your Web pages; otherwise, they won't work when you copy the files to a different disk. Refer to Hour 3 for more details on how to make links that will work both on disk and on the Internet.

Publishing on CD-ROM or DVD-ROM disks isn't much more complicated than the floppy or Zip disk approach; you either need a drive (and accompanying software) capable of creating the disks, or you can send the files to a disk mastering and duplication company. Costs for CD-ROM duplication is surprisingly low, often cheaper than the floppy/Zip disk approach, especially when you consider how much information you can store on a CD-ROM (650 MB). DVD-ROM pricing is a little more volatile, and expensive, but it will eventually be similar to CD-ROM.

Web browser software is always necessary for reading HTML pages. However, these days almost everyone has a Web browser, so you may not need to supply one with your Web pages. If you do want to include a browser, you might consider Opera, which includes most of the basic features of Netscape Navigator and Microsoft Internet Explorer but is small enough to fit on a single 1.44MB floppy disk and can be freely distributed in the form of a 30-day evaluation version. (You can download Opera at http://www.operasoftware.com/.)

Microsoft and Netscape are also often willing to allow their browsers to be included on CD-ROMs if you ask nicely in writing or pay them a licensing fee. Never give out copies of Microsoft or Netscape software without written permission, since these companies aren't afraid to flex their enormous legal muscles to ensure that you obtain proper licensing.

Testing Your Web Pages

Whenever you transfer Web pages to an Internet site, intranet server, or disk, you should immediately test every page thoroughly.

The following checklist will help make sure everything on your pages behaves the way you expected.

1. Before you transfer the pages, follow all of these steps to test the pages while they're on your hard drive. After you transfer the pages to the master disk or Web server, test them again—if your pages are on the Internet, preferably through a 56Kbps modem connection to try them out under a minimal connection speed.

2. Do each of the following steps with the latest version of Netscape Navigator, the latest Microsoft Internet Explorer, and at least one other browser such as Opera. Testing with an older version of Navigator or Internet Explorer isn't a bad idea either since many people still use outdated versions and some pages will appear differently.

3. If possible, use a computer with 800×600 resolution for testing purposes. If pages look good at this resolution, they'll probably look fine at larger resolutions, too. (Additional testing at 1,024×768 or 1,600×1,200 resolution can't hurt.) You might also consider testing at 640×480, since there are bound to be a few people out there still using smaller low-res monitors.

4. Turn off auto image loading in Netscape Navigator before you start testing, so you can see what each page looks like without the graphics. Check your `alt` tag messages and then click the Load Images button on the toolbar to load the graphics and review the page carefully again. Hour 9, "Putting Graphics on a Web Page," explains how to place images on a page, along with how the `alt` tag works.

5. Use your browser's font size settings to look at each page in a variety of font sizes, to ensure that your careful layout doesn't fall to pieces.

6. Start at the home page and systematically follow every link. (Use the Back button to return after each link, and then click the next link on the page.)

7. Wait for each page to completely finish loading, and scroll all the way down to make sure all images appear where they should.

8. If you have a complex site, it may help to make a checklist of all the pages on your site to ensure they all get tested.

9. Time how long it takes each page to load through a 56Kbps modem, preferably when connected through a different ISP than the one that runs the Web server. Multiply that time by 2 to find out how long 28.8Kbps modem users will have to wait to see the page. Is the information on that page valuable enough to keep them from going elsewhere before the page finishes loading? Granted, not to many people will be using such a slow connection, but it's worth at least considering.

If your pages pass all those tests, you can be pretty certain that they'll look great to every Internet surfer in the world.

Summary

This hour gave you the basic knowledge you need to choose among the most common distribution methods for Web pages. It also stepped you through the process of placing

Web pages on a Web server computer by using commonly available file transfer software. Finally, it offered a checklist to help you thoroughly test your Web pages once they are in place.

Q&A

Q **When I try to send pages to my Web site from home, it works fine. When I try it from the computer at work, I get error messages. Any idea what the problem might be?**

A The company where you work probably has a *firewall*, which is a layer of security protecting their local network from tampering via the Internet. You need to set some special configuration options in your FTP program to help it get through the firewall when you send files. Your company's network administrator can help you with the details.

Q **I don't know which ISP to choose—there are so many!**

A Obviously, you should compare prices of the companies listed at `http://thelist.internet.com`. You should also ask for the names of some customers with sites about the same size you're planning on having; ask those customers (via email) how happy they are with the company's service and support. Also, make sure that your ISP has at least two major (T3 or bigger) connections to the Internet, preferably provided to them by two different network companies.

Q **All the tests you recommend would take longer than creating my pages! Can't I get away with less testing?**

A If your pages aren't intended to make money or provide an important service, it's probably not a big deal if they look funny to some people or produce errors once in a while. In that case, just test each page with a couple of different window and font sizes and call it good. However, if you need to project a professional image, there is no substitute for rigorous testing.

Q **I wanted to name my site** `lizardlover.com` **but someone beat me to it. Is there anything I can do?**

A Well, if you operated a reptilian pet store and your company was named Lizard Lover, Inc., before the other person registered the domain name, you could always try suing them, but even if you don't have the budget to take on their legal army, you may still be able to register `lizardlover.org`, `lizardlover.net`, or possibly even `lizardlover.biz` (if you aren't scooped again).

4

Workshop

The workshop contains quiz questions and activities to help you solidify your understanding of the material covered. Try to answer all questions before looking at the "Answers" section that follows.

Quiz

1. How do you put a few Web pages on a floppy disk?

2. Suppose your ISP tells you to put your pages in the default main directory at ftp.bigisp.net, that your username is rastro, and that your password is rorry_rel-roy. You have the Web pages all ready to go in the \webpages folder on your C drive. Where do you put all that information in CuteFTP so you can get the files on the Internet?

3. What address would you enter in Netscape Navigator to view the Web pages you uploaded in question 2?

4. If the following Web page is named mypage.htm, which files would you need to transfer to the Web server to put it on the Internet?

```
<html><head><title>My Page</title></head>
<body background="joy.gif">
<img src="me.jpg" align="right" />
<h1>My Web Page</h1>
<p>Oh happy joy I have a page on the Web!</p>
<a href="otherpage.htm">Click here for my other page.</a>
</body></html>
```

Answers

1. Just copy the HTML files and image files from your hard drive to the disk. Anyone can then insert the disk in his or her computer, start the Web browser, and open the pages right from the floppy.

2. Click the New button in the FTP Site Manager window, and then enter the following information:

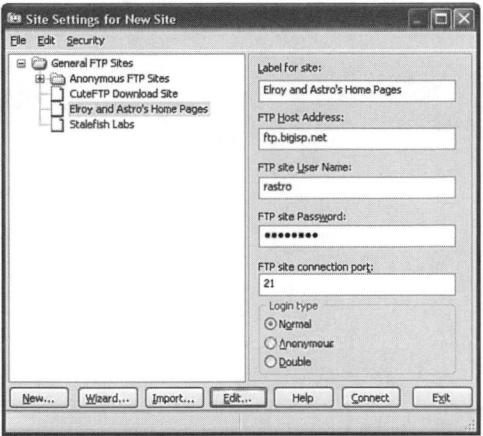

3. You can't tell from the information given in question 2. A good guess would be `http://www.bigisp.net/~elroy/`, but you might choose a completely different domain name, such as `http://elroy-and-astro.com/`.

4. You need to transfer all three of the following files into the same directory on the Web server:

```
mypage.htm
joy.jpg
me.gif
```

If you want the link on that page to work, you must also transfer this one, as well as any image files that are referred to in that HTML file:

```
otherpage.htm
```

Exercises

Put your pages on the Internet already!

PART II
Web Page Text

Hour

HOUR 5

Basic Text Alignment and Formatting

In the early days of the Web, text was displayed in only one font and in one size. If you've been around computers long enough to remember what it was like before mice and graphical operating systems entered the picture, you know what I'm talking about because text formatting in those days involved making sure you pressed Enter to start a new paragraph! HTML makes it possible to control the appearance of text and how it is aligned and displayed on a Web page. This hour tackles the basics of text alignment and formatting, while the next hour digs deeper into the nuts and bolts of text formatting to share with you some advanced tips and tricks.

Another important topic covered in this hour is lists, which provide a means of listing multiple items in HTML. Since lists are so common in Web pages, HTML provides tags that automatically indent text and add numbers or bullets in front of each listed item. You find out in this hour how to format numbered and bulleted lists, not to mention definition lists, which can be used as a simple way to indent content on a page.

To Do

You can make the most of this hour if you have some text that needs to be indented or centered to be presentable.

- Any type of outline, bullet points from a presentation, numbered steps, glossary, or list of textual information from a database will serve as good material with which to work.

- If the text you'll be using is from a word processor or database program, be sure to save it to a new file in plain text or ASCII format. You can then add the appropriate HTML tags to format it as you go through this lesson.

Aligning Text on a Page

It's easy to take for granted the fact that most paragraphs are automatically aligned to the left when you're reading information on the Web. However, there are certainly situations where you may choose to align content to the right or even the center of a page. HTML gives you the option to align a single HTML element, such as a paragraph of text, or entire sections of a page. Before we get into the details of these two alignment approaches, however, let's briefly recap how attributes work.

In Hour 3, "Linking to Other Web Pages," you briefly learned how attributes are used to provide additional information related to an HTML tag. Attributes are very important in even the simplest of Web pages, so it's important that you get comfortable using them. As an example, attributes are used to determine the alignment of paragraphs. When you begin a paragraph with the `<p>` tag, you can specify whether the text in that paragraph should be aligned to the left margin, right margin, or center of the page by setting the `align` attribute.

 *Attributes* are special code words used inside an HTML tag to control exactly what the tag does.

Aligning a Paragraph

To align a paragraph to the right margin, you place `align="right"` inside the `<p>` tag at the beginning of the paragraph. To center a paragraph, use `<p align="center">`. Similarly, the tag to align a paragraph to the left is `<p align="left">`. (For the record, this last alignment setting is seldom used because paragraphs are always aligned to the left by default when you use plain old `<p>`.)

Every attribute in HTML has a default value that is assumed if you don't set the attribute yourself. In the case of the `align` attribute of the `<p>` tag, the default value is `left`, so using the bare bones `<p>` tag has the same effect as `<p align="left">`. Learning the default values for common attributes is an important part of becoming a good Web page developer.

The `align` attribute is not just reserved for the `<p>` tag. In fact, you can use the `align` attribute with just about any HTML tag that contains text, including `<h1>`, `<h2>`, the other heading tags, and some tags you will meet later. There are many other attributes besides `align`. You will find out how to use them as you learn more HTML tags.

According to the official HTML 4 standard, it doesn't matter whether tags and attributes are in uppercase or lowercase letters. However, the newer XHTML standard requires tags and attributes to be lowercase, so it's a very good idea to make all of your HTML code lowercase now for future compatibility. The newer standard also requires quotation marks around attribute values.

For example, the following code is technically acceptable in popular Web browsers:

```
<P ALIGN=CENTER>
```

However, this code does not conform to the latest standards for how Web pages should be designed going into the future because it is in uppercase and the attribute `center` isn't in quotes. If you want to stay compatible with upcoming standards and software, you should always use the following instead:

```
<p align="center">
```

Keep in mind that sometimes the same attribute name can have different meanings when used with different tags. For instance, you will discover in Hour 9, "Putting Graphics on a Web Page," that `align="left"` does something quite different when used with the `<img>` image tag than it does with the text tags discussed in this hour.

Aligning an Entire Section of a Page

When you want to set the alignment of more than one paragraph or heading at a time, you can use the `align` attribute with the `<div>`, or *division*, tag. By itself, `<div>` and its corresponding closing `</div>` tag actually don't do anything at all—which would seem to make it a peculiarly useless tag!

5

Yet if you include an `align` attribute, `<div>` becomes quite useful indeed. Everything you put between `<div align="center">` and `</div>`, for example, is centered. This may include lines of text, paragraphs, headings, images, and all the other things you'll learn how to put on Web pages in upcoming lessons. Likewise, `<div align="right">` will right-align everything down to the next `</div>` tag.

> Later in the book you find out that the `<div>` tag is also useful as a means of organizing text for applying special formatting styles.

Listing 5.1 demonstrates the `align` attribute with both the `<p>` and `<div>` tags. The results are shown in Figure 5.1. You'll learn many more advanced uses of the `<div>` tag in Hour 14, "Formatting Pages with Style Sheets," and Hour 15, "Making the Most of Style Sheets."

LISTING 5.1   The align Attribute

```
<html>
<head><title>Bohemia</title></head>
<body>
<div align="center">
  <h2>Bohemia</h2>
  <b>by Dorothy Parker</b>
</div>
<p align="left">
Authors and actors and artists and such<br />
Never know nothing, and never know much.<br />
Sculptors and singers and those of their kidney<br />
Tell their affairs from Seattle to Sydney.</p>
<p align="center">
Playwrights and poets and such horses' necks<br />
Start off from anywhere, end up at sex.<br />
Diarists, critics, and similar roe<br />
Never say nothing, and never say no.</p>
<p align="right">
People Who Do Things exceed my endurance;<br />
God, for a man that solicits insurance!</p>
</body></html>
```

FIGURE **5.1**

The alignment settings in Listing 5.1, as they appear in a Web browser.

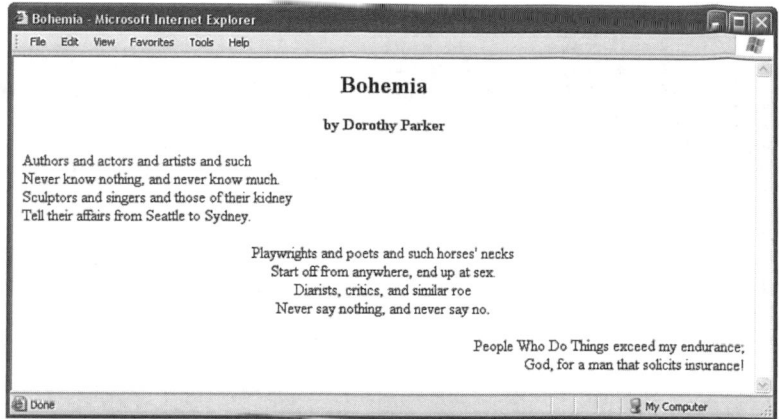

The Three Types of HTML Lists

It's often useful to present information on a Web page as a list of items. There are three basic types of HTML lists. All three are shown in Figure 5.2, and Listing 5.2 reveals the HTML to construct them:

- The bulleted list is called an *unordered list*. It opens with the `<ul>` tag and closes with `</ul>`. It looks just like an ordered list, except that bullets appear at each `<li>` tag instead of numbers.

- The numbered list is called an *ordered list*. It begins with the `<ol>` tag and ends with a closing `</ol>` tag. Numbers and line breaks appear automatically at each `<li>` tag, and the entire list is indented.

- The list of terms and their meanings is called a *definition list*. It starts with the `<dl>` and ends with `</dl>`. The `<dt>` tag goes in front of each term to be defined, with a `<dd>` tag in front of each definition. Line breaks and indentations appear automatically.

NEW TERM *Ordered lists* are indented lists that have numbers or letters in front of each item. *Unordered lists* are indented lists with a special bullet symbol in front of each item. *Definition lists* are indented lists without any number or symbol in front of each item.

LISTING 5.2 Unordered Lists, Ordered Lists, and Definition Lists

```
<html><head><title>How to be Proper</title></head>
<body>
Basic Etiquette for a Gentlemen Greeting a Lady Aquaintance
```

LISTING 5.2   continued

```html
<ul>
<li>Wait for her acknowledging bow before tipping your
hat.</li>
<li>Use the hand farthest from her to raise the hat.</li>
<li>Walk with her if she expresses a wish to converse; Never
make a lady stand talking in the street.</li>
<li>When walking, the lady must always have the wall.</li>
</ul>
Recourse for a Lady Toward Unpleasant Men Who Persist in Bowing
<ol>
<li>A simple stare of iciness should suffice in most
instances.</li>
<li>A cold bow discourages familiarity without offering
insult.</li>
<li>As a last resort: "Sir, I have not the honour of your
aquaintance."</li>
</ol>
Proper Address of Royalty
<dl>
<dt>Your Majesty</dt>
<dd>To the king or queen.</dd>
<dt>Your Royal Highness</dt>
<dd>To the monarch's spouse, children, and siblings.</dd>
<dt>Your Highness</dt>
<dd>To nephews, nieces, and cousins of the sovereign.</dd>
</dl>
</body></html>
```

FIGURE 5.2

The three types of HTML lists, as they appear in Internet Explorer.

Remember that different Web browsers can display Web pages quite differently. The HTML standard doesn't specify exactly how Web browsers should format lists, so people using older Web browsers may not see the same indentation that you see.

Software of the future may also format HTML lists differently, though all current Web browsers now display lists in almost exactly the same way.

Placing Lists Within Lists

Although definition lists are officially supposed to be used for defining terms, many Web page authors use them anywhere they'd like to see some indentation. In practice, you can indent any text simply by putting `<dl><dd>` at the beginning of it and `</dd></dl>` at the end. However, a better approach to indenting text is to use the `<blockquote>` tag, which indents content without the presumption of a definition.

You can indent items further by *nesting* one list inside another, like the following:

```
<dl><dd>this item will be indented</dd>
<dl><dd>this will be indented further</dd>
<dl><dl><dd>and this will be indented very far indeed</dd>
</dl></dl></dl></dl>
```

Just make sure you always have the same number of closing `</dl>` tags as opening `<dl>` tags.

Ordered and unordered lists can also be nested inside one another, down to as many levels as you want. In Listing 5.3, a complex indented outline is constructed from several unordered lists. You'll notice in Figure 5.3 that Internet Explorer automatically uses a different type of bullet for each of the first three levels of indentation, making the list very easy to read.

LISTING 5.3 Using Lists to Build Outlines

```
<html><head><title>Gloves</title></head>
<body>
<h2>Gloves</h2>
<ul><li><b>Power</b>
    <ul><li>Sega VR</li>
        <li>Surgical</li>
        <li>Elbow length, white</li>
    </ul></li>
    <li><b>Rec</b>
```

5

LISTING 5.3   continued

```
<ul><li><b>Sporting</b>
    <ul><li>Boxing</li>
        <li>Driving</li>
        <li>Biking</li>
    </ul></li>
    <li><b>Evening</b>
    <ul><li>Elbow length, black</li>
        <li>Latex</li>
    </ul></li>
</ul></li>
<li><b>Cute</b>
<ul><li>Swedish, fake fur</li>
    <li>Kid</li>
    <li>Golf</li>
</ul></li>
</ul>
</body></html>
```

FIGURE 5.3
Multilevel unordered lists are neatly indented and bulleted for readability.

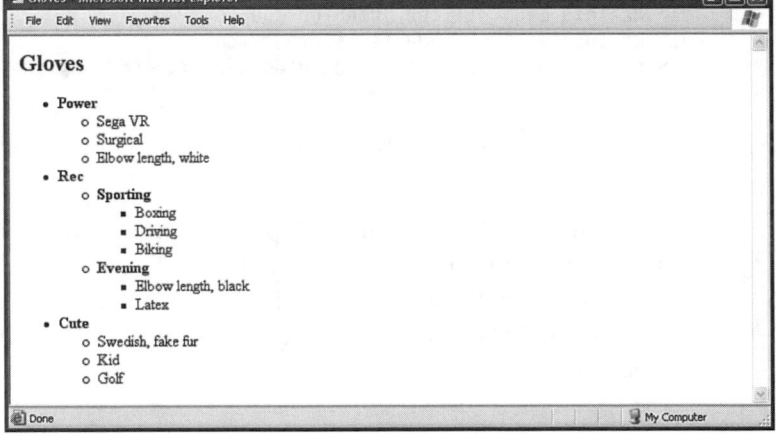

Some of the text in the unordered list in Figure 5.3 has been bolded for effect. You learn how to apply such formatting effects to text in Hour 6, "Advanced Text Formatting."

As shown in Figure 5.3, Internet Explorer (and Netscape Navigator) will normally use a solid disc for the first-level bullet, a hollow circle for the second-level bullet, and a solid square for all deeper levels. However, you can explicitly choose which type of bullet to use for any level by using `<ul type="disc">`, `<ul type="circle">`, or `<ul type="square">` instead of `<ul>`.

You can even change the bullet for any single point within an unordered list by using the `type` attribute in the `<li>` tag. For example, the following would display a hollow circle in front of the words `extra` and `super`, but a solid square in front of the word `special`:

```
<ul type="circle">
<li>extra</li>
<li>super</li>
<li type="square">special</li>
</ul>
```

The `type` attribute also works with ordered lists, but instead of choosing a type of bullet, you choose the type of numbers or letters to place in front of each item. Listing 5.4 shows how to use roman numerals (`type="I"`), capital letters (`type="A"`), and lowercase letters (`type="a"`) along with ordinary numbers in a multilevel list. In Figure 5.4, you can see the resulting nicely formatted outline.

Although Listing 5.4 only uses the `type` attribute with the `<ol>` tag, you can also use it for specific `<li>` tags within a list (though it's hard to imagine a situation where you would want to). You can also explicitly specify ordinary numbering with `type="1"`, and you can make lowercase roman numerals with `type="i"`.

Here's one more seldom-used but handy-when-you-need-it trick: You can start an ordered list with any number (or letter) with the `start` attribute. `<ol start="3">`, for example, starts a numbered list at 3 instead of 1. Individual points can be renumbered with the `value` attribute (`<li value="12">` for example).

 Note that you must always use numbers with the `start` and `value` attributes. To make a list that starts with the capital letter C, for example, you need to type `<ol type="A" start="3">`.

LISTING 5.4   Using the type Attribute in Multitiered Lists

```
<html><head><title>Advice from the Golf Guru</title></head>
<body>
<h2>How to Win at Golf</h2>
<ol type="I"><li>Training
  <ol><li>Mental prep
    <ol type="A"><li>Watch PGA on TV religiously</li>
      <li>Get that computer game with Jack whatsisname</li>
      <li>Rent "personal victory" subliminal tapes</li>
```

5

LISTING 5.4   continued

```
      </ol></li>
      <li>Equipage
      <ol type="A"><li>Make sure your putter has a pro autograph
                      on it</li>
        <li>Pick up a bargain bag of tees-n-balls at Costco</li>
      </ol></li>
      <li>Diet
      <ol type="A"><li>Avoid baseball or football food
        <ol type="a"><li>No hotdogs</li>
          <li>No pretzels</li>
          <li>No peanuts and Crackerjacks</li>
        </ol></li>
        <li>Drink cheap white wine only, no beer</li>
      </ol></li>
    </ol></li>
    <li>Pre-game
    <ol><li>Dress
      <ol type="A">
        <li>Put on shorts, even if it's freezing</li>
        <li>Buy a new hat if you lost last time</li>
      </ol></li>
      <li>Location and Scheduling
      <ol type="A">
        <li>Select a course where your spouse won't find you</li>
        <li>To save on fees, play where your buddy works</li>
      </ol></li>
      <li>Opponent
      <ol type="A">
        <li>Look for: overconfidence, inexperience</li>
        <li>Shun: suntan, stethescope, strident walk,
                          florida accent</li>
        <li>Buy opponent as many pre-game drinks as possible</li>
      </ol></li>
    </ol></li>
    <li>On the Course
    <ol><li>Tee first, then develop severe hayfever</li>
        <li>Drive cart over opponent's ball to degrade
                          aerodynamics</li>
        <li>Say "fore" just before ball makes contact with
            opponent</li>
        <li>Always replace divots when putting</li>
        <li>Water cooler holes are a good time to correct any
                          errors in ball placement</li>
        <li>Never record strokes taken when opponent is
            urinating</li>
      </ol></li>
    </ol>
  </body></html>
```

FIGURE 5.4

*A well-formatted out-
line can make almost
any plan look more
plausible.*

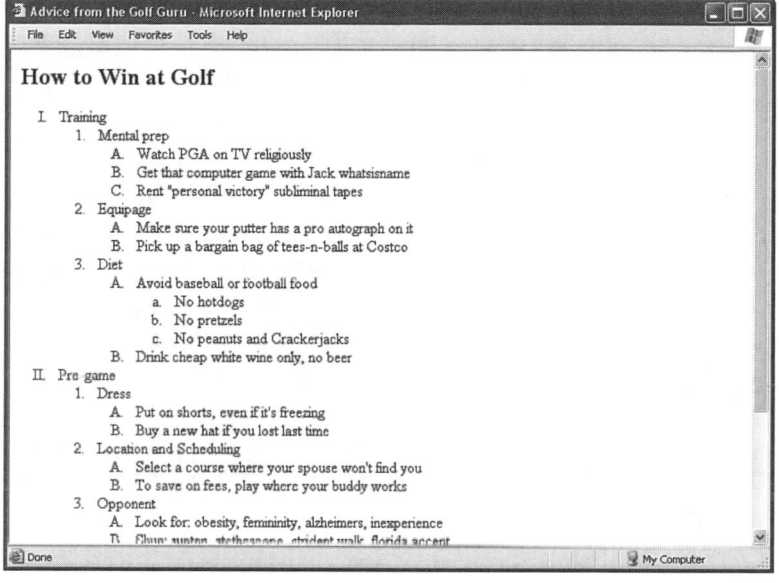

FIGURE 5.4

*A well-formatted out-
line can make almost
any plan look more
plausible.*

By combining ordered, unordered, and definition lists within one another,
you can organize the most complex information in a readable and attractive
way. To get your creative juices flowing, I've created a list of lists for you to
browse through before you begin organizing your own HTML lists.

To check it out, go to the 24-Hour HTML Café at
`http://www.24hourhtmlcafe.com/hour5/`.

Click the list-o-mania link and have some fun trying to figure out what the
real titles of the example lists might be, based upon the information they
contain. Answers are given—as a nested HTML list, of course—at the end of
the page.

To Do

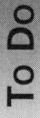

Take a list or two of your own and try to find the best way to present the information so
it can be easily understood.

1. Which type of list or combination of list types best suits your list? Use ordered
   lists only for lists that actually have a natural order to them. Try to avoid more than
   seven bullet points in a row in any unordered list; otherwise, the list will be hard to
   read. Use definition lists whenever indenting is sufficient to convey the structure of
   your information.

▼   2. Start each list (or new level within a multitiered list) with an `<ol>`, `<ul>`, or `<dl>`. Start each point within the list with `<li>`. Use the `type` attribute if you want non-standard bullets or letters instead of numbers.

        3. If you want a blank line between list items, use `<li><p>` and `</p></li>` instead of just `<li>` and `</li>`.

        4. Be very careful to close every `<li>` list item with a `</li>` tag. End every `<ol>` list with `</ol>`, and make sure that each `<ul>` or `<dl>` has a corresponding `</ul>` or
▲   `</dl>`. Unclosed lists can make pages look very strange, and can even cause some Web browsers not to display the list at all.

Summary

In this hour you learned that attributes are used to specify options and special behavior of many HTML tags, and you also learned to use the `align` attribute to center or right-justify text.

You also found out how to create and combine three basic types of HTML list: ordered lists, unordered lists, and definition lists. Lists can be placed within other lists to create outlines and other complex arrangements of text.

Table 5.1 lists all the tags and attributes covered in this hour.

TABLE 5.1   HTML Tags and Attributes Covered in Hour 5

Tag/Attribute	Function
`<div>...</div>`	A region of text to be formatted.
`align="..."`	Align text to `center`, `left`, or `right`. (Can also be used with `<p>`, `<h1>`, `<h2>`, `<h3>`, and so on.)
`<ol>...</ol>`	An ordered (numbered) list.
Attributes	
`type="..."`	The type of numerals used to label the list. Possible values are `A`, `a`, `I`, `i`, `1`.
`start="..."`	The value with which to start this list.
`<ul>...</ul>`	An unordered (bulleted) list.
Attributes	
`type="..."`	The bullet dingbat used to mark list items. Possible values are `disc`, `circle`, and `square`.
`<li>...</li>`	A list item for use with `<ol>` or `<ul>`.

TABLE 5.1 continued

Tag/Attribute	Function
Attributes	
type="..."	The type of bullet or number used to label this item. Possible values are disc, circle, square, a, A, i, I, 1.
value="..."	The numeric value this list item should have (affects this item and all below it in <ol> lists).
<dl>...</dl>	A definition list.
<dt>...</dt>	A definition term, as part of a definition list.
<dd>...</dd>	The corresponding definition to a definition term, as part of a definition list.

Q&A

Q **Most Web pages I've seen on the Internet use `<center>` instead of `<div align="center">`. Should I be using `<center>` to make sure my pages are compatible with older Web browsers?**

A For maximum compatibility, you might prefer to use both the obsolete `<center>` tag and the new `<div align="center">` tag, like this: `<div align="center"><center>`. This text will be centered in both old and new browsers. Don't forget to end the centered section with `</center></div>`. On the other hand, current Web browsers display content fine when it's centered with `<div align="center">`, so the `<center>` tag is only important if you're concerned about the minority of users still using old browsers. Even this minority will go away over time as older computers are retired.

Q **I've seen pages on the Internet that use three-dimensional little balls or other special graphics for bullets. How do they do that?**

A That trick is a little bit beyond what this hour covers. You'll find out how to do it yourself at the end of Hour 9, "Putting Graphics on a Web Page."

Q **How do I "full justify" text, so that both the left and right margins are flush?**

A You don't, at least not with HTML alone. HTML 4 does not support full-justified text by itself. You can full-justify text using style sheets, which you learn about in Hours 14 and 15.

Workshop

The workshop contains quiz questions and activities to help you solidify your understanding of the material covered. Try to answer all questions before looking at the "Answers" section that follows.

Quiz

1. How would you center everything on an entire page?

2. Write HTML to create the following ordered list:

   X. Xylophone

   Y. Yak

   Z. Zebra

3. How would you indent a single word and put a square bullet in front of it?

4. Use a definition list to show that the word "glunch" means "a look of disdain, anger, or displeasure" and that the word "glumpy" means "sullen, morose, or sulky."

5. Write the HTML to create the following indentation effect:

   Apple pie,

      pudding,

        and pancake,

   All begin with an A.

Answers

1. Put `<div align="center">` immediately after the `<body>` tag at the top of the page, and `</div>` just before the `</body>` tag at the end of the page.

2. `<ol type="a" start="24"><li>xylophone</li><li>yak</li><li>zebra</li></ol>`

   The following alternative will also do the same thing:

   `<ol type="a"><li value="24">xylophone</li><li>yak</li><li>zebra</li></ol>`

3. `<ul type="square"><li>supercalifragilisticexpealidocious</li></ul>`

   (Putting the `type="square"` in the `<li>` tag would give the same result because there's only one item in this list.)

4. ```
<dl>
<dt>glunch</dt><dd>a look of disdain, anger, or displeasure</dd>
<dt>glumpy</dt><dd>sullen, morose, or sulky</dd>
</dl>
```

5. ```
<dl><dt>apple pie,</dt>
   <dd>pudding,</dd>
   <dl><dd>and pancake</dd></dl>
   all begin with an a.</dl>
```

Exercises

Try producing an ordered list outlining the information you'd like to put on your Web pages. This will give you practice formatting HTML lists and also give you a head start on thinking about the issues covered in Part VI, "Building a Web Site."

5

HOUR 6

Advanced Text Formatting

The previous hour established some ground rules in regard to how text is formatted and arranged in HTML. This hour continues the discussion by looking more closely at how to format text and control the appearance of text on your pages. You'll learn to incorporate boldface, italics, superscripts, subscripts, underlining, and strikethrough text into your pages, as well as how to choose typefaces and font sizes.

This chapter also shows you how to create special symbols, such as the copyright mark, and European language characters such as the é in Café.

There are two completely different approaches to controlling text formatting and alignment in HTML 4. The tags you study in this lesson (and the align attribute from Hour 5, "Basic Text Alignment and Formatting") are the "old way," which is actually officially discouraged. The "new way" is introduced in Hour 14, "Formatting Pages with Style Sheets."

You're no doubt wondering why learn something that's already out of date? Because style sheets only became supported by Web browsers fairly recently, a significant number of people still use older browsers that don't support style sheets very well. If you want your pages to look right to everyone—not just those who use the latest software technology—you'll need to know everything in this lesson. In other words, it's a good idea to know how to use both approaches to text formatting and alignment.

All the tricks introduced in this lesson (and the previous one) will work with nearly any Web browser, old or new.

To Do

Before you proceed, you should get some text to work with so you can practice formatting it as you read this hour's lesson.

- Any text will do, but try to find (or type) some text that you want to put onto a Web page. The text from a company brochure or from your personal résumé might be a good choice.
- If the text is from a word processor file, be sure to save it as plain text or ASCII text before adding any HTML tags.
- Add the `<html>`, `<head>`, `<title>`, and `<body>` tags (discussed in Hour 2, "Create a Web Page Right Now") before you use the tags introduced in this chapter to format the body text.

Boldface, Italics, and Special Formatting

Way back in the age of the typewriter, we were content with plain text and an occasional underline for emphasis. Today, **boldface** and *italicized* text have become de rigueur in all paper communication. Naturally, you can add bold and italic text to your Web pages too.

For boldface text, put the `<b>` tag at the beginning of the text and `</b>` at the end. Similarly, you can make any text italic by enclosing it between `<i>` and `</i>`.

You can *nest* one type of formatting inside another. For instance, if you want some text to be both bold and italic, put `<b><i>` in front of it and `</i></b>` after it. To avoid confusing some Web browsers, be careful to close the tags in the opposite order you opened them in. For example, don't do this:

```
<b>Bold, <i>bold and elegant,</b> or just plain elegant.</i>
```

Instead, do it this way:

```
<b>Bold, <i>bold and elegant,</i></b><i>or just plain elegant.</i>
```

Similarly, you should always close any `<b>`, `<i>`, or other formatting tags that occur within an `<li>` list item or heading before you end the `</li>`. Most of the `<i>` and `</i>` tags in the following list may seem redundant, but adhering to this good form ensures that your pages fully meet the new XHTML standards, which may save you having to rewrite them in the future.

```
<ul>
<li><i>Important Stuff</i></li>
<li><i>Critical Information</i></li>
<li><i>Highly Sensitive Material</i></li>
<li>Nothing All That Useful</li>
</ul>
```

You can also use the `<b>` tag within headings, but boldface usually won't show in headings because they are already bold.

There are actually two ways to make text display as boldface; the `<b>` tag and the `<strong>` tag do the same thing in most Web browsers. Likewise, all popular browsers today interpret both `<i>` and `<em>` as italics.

Many purists prefer the `<strong>` and `<em>` tags because they imply only that the text should receive special emphasis, rather than dictating exactly how that effect should be achieved. Meanwhile, the vast majority of Web authors use the shorter and easier-to-remember `<b>` and `<i>` tags. I'll use `<b>` and `<i>` throughout this book, but if you like to be philosophically pure, by all means use `<strong>` and `<em>` instead.

From an XML perspective, `<strong>` and `<em>` are better tags to use because they add meaning to text, along with affecting how the text should be displayed. An even better approach for altering the appearance of text is to use style sheets, which are covered in Hours 14 and 15.

In addition to `<b>`, `<i>`, `<em>`, and `<strong>`, there are several other HTML tags for adding special formatting to text. Table 6.1 summarizes all of them (including the boldface and italic tags), and Listing 6.1 and Figure 6.1 demonstrate each of them in action.

6

TABLE 6.1 HTML Tags That Add Special Formatting to Text

Tag	Function
`<small>`	Small text
`<big>`	Big text
`<sup>`	Superscript text
`<sub>`	Subscript text

continued

TABLE 6.1   continued

Tag	Function
`<strike>`	Strikethrough text (draws a line through text)
`<u>`	Underline text
`<em>` or `<i>`	Emphasized (italic) text
`<strong>` or `<b>`	Strong (boldface) text
`<tt>`	Monospaced text (typewriter font)
`<pre>`	Monospaced text, preserving spaces and line breaks

Use the <u> tag sparingly, if at all. People expect underlined text to be a link, and may get confused if you underline text that isn't a link. If you're wondering how to get rid of the underlining for links, you find out later in Hours 14 and 15 when you learn how to use style sheets. While we're at it, it's also important to mention that the <u> and <strike> tag are *deprecated*, which means they have been phased out of the HTML language. They are still supported in Web browsers, and likely will be for quite a while, but the preferred approach to creating underlined and strikethrough text is style sheets, which are tackled in Hours 14 and 15.

LISTING 6.1   Special Formatting Tags

```
<html><head><title>The Micracle Product</title></head>
<body>
<u>New</u> <sup>Super</sup><strong>Strength</strong>
H<sub>2</sub>O <em>plus</em> will <strike>strike out</strike>
any stain, <big>big</big> or <small>small</small>.<br />
Look for new <sup>Super</sup><b>Strength</b> H<sub>2</sub>O
<i>plus</i> in a stream near you.
<p><tt>NUTRITION INFORMATION</tt> (void where prohibited)</p>
<pre>
                Calories  Grams   USRDA
                /Serving  of Fat  Moisture
Regular            3        4      100%
Unleaded           3        2      100%
Organic            2        3       99%
Sugar Free         0        1      110%
</pre>
</body></html>
```

The <tt> tag usually changes the typeface to Courier New, a monospaced font. (*Monospaced* means that all the letters and spaces are the same width.) However, Web browsers let users change the monospaced `<tt>` font to the typeface of their choice (under Tools, Internet Options, Fonts in Microsoft Internet Explorer and Edit, Preferences, Appearance, Fonts in Netscape Navigator). The monospaced font may not even be monospaced for some users, though the vast majority of people stick with the standard fonts that their browsers come set up with.

FIGURE 6.1

Here's what all character formatting from Listing 6.1 looks like.

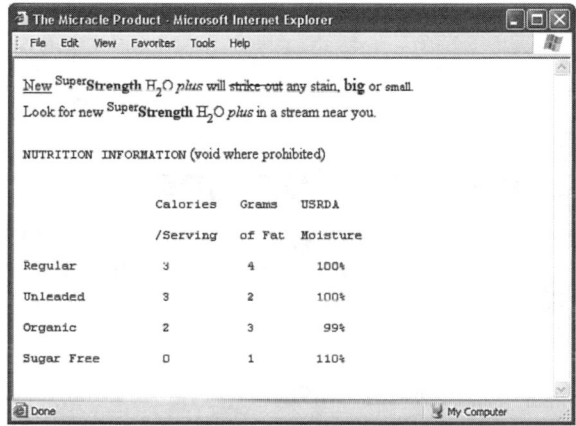

 In Internet Explorer for Macintosh, you can change browser fonts in the Language/Fonts section of the application preferences.

The `<pre>` tag causes text to appear in the monospaced font, but it also does something else unique and useful. As you learned in Hour 2, multiple spaces and line breaks are normally ignored in HTML files, but `<pre>` causes exact spacing and line breaks to be preserved. For example, without `<pre>`, the text at the end of Figure 6.1 would look like the following:

```
calories grams usrda /serving of fat moisture regular
3 4 100% unleaded 3 2 100% organic 2 3 99% sugar free 0 1 110%
```

Even if you added `<br />` tags at the end of every line, the columns wouldn't line up properly. However, when you put `<pre>` at the beginning and `</pre>` at the end, the columns line up properly because the exact spaces are kept—no `<br />` tags are needed.

There are fancier ways to make columns of text line up, and you learn all about them in Hour 13, "Advanced Layout with Tables." The `<pre>` tag gives you a quick and easy way to preserve the alignment of any monospaced text files you might want to transfer to a Web page with a minimum of effort.

6

> You can use the `<pre>` tag as a quick way to insert extra vertical space between paragraphs. For example, to put several blank lines between the words up and down, you could type this:
>
> up`<pre>`
>
>
>
> `</pre>`down

Tweaking the Font Size and Color

The `<big>`, `<small>`, and `<tt>` tags give you some rudimentary control over the size and appearance of the text on your pages. Generally, you should try sticking to those tags until you are ready for the advanced font formatting controls discussed in Hours 14 and 15.

However, there may be times when you'd just like a bit more control over the size and appearance of your text while maintaining as much compatibility with older Web browsers as possible. For those times, you can use the officially discouraged but widely used `<font>` tag.

For example, the following HTML will change the size and color of some text on a page:

`<font size="5" color="purple">this text will be big and purple.</font>`

The `size` attribute can take any value from 1 (tiny) to 7 (fairly big), with 3 being the default size. (If you need VERY big fonts, you'll need to use style sheets as explained in Hours 14 and 15.)

The `color` attribute can take any of the following standard color names: black, white, red, green, blue, yellow, aqua, fuchsia, gray, lime, maroon, purple, navy, olive, silver, or teal.

The actual size and exact color of the font depends upon each user's screen resolution and preference settings, but you can be assured that `size=6` is a lot bigger than `size=2` and that `color="red"` certainly shows its fire.

You learn more about controlling the color of the text on your pages in Hour 10, "Custom Backgrounds and Colors." That lesson also shows you how to create your own custom colors and control the color of text links.

Selecting a Font Typeface

If you've ever used fonts in a word processor or desktop publishing program, you understand how important they are in establishing a certain look for text. The `face` attribute of the `<font>` tag allows you to specify the typeface that should be used to display text—and was been the source of much rejoicing among Webmasters who were awfully sick of Times and Courier in the early days of the Web!

The page in Listing 6.2 and Figure 6.2 uses these font controls to present a quick but colorful history lesson. Notice how `<font>` tags can be nested inside one another, changing some aspects of the font's appearance while leaving others the same. For example, even when `<font>` tags change the size and color of the letters in A HISTORY OF EVERYTHING, the typeface specified in the first `<font>` tag still applies. Likewise, the `<font>` tags that make small capital letters do not change the color, so the entire line ends up maroon.

LISTING 6.2 The `<font>` Tags

```
<html><head><title>A History</title></head>
<body>
<font face="Lucida Sans Unicode, Arial, Helvetica">
  <font size="5" color="green">
    A H<font size="4"><b>ISTORY OF</b></font>
    E<font size="4"><b>VERYTHING</b></font>
  </font><br />
  <font face="Lucida Handwriting">
        It starts with a <b>bang</b>.
  </font>
Then everything <b>inflates</b> like a super-balloon tied up
with <b>super-strings</b>, until the whole mess curdles into
millions of <b>milky ways</b>. <b>Starlight</b> hits the <b>
volcanic rocks</b>, and cooks up some tasty <b>double-helix</b>
treats. They get eaten by each other, the <b>fittest</b> (and
least tasty) <b>survive</b>, a <b>meteor</b> kills the <b>
big</b> ones, and when it all <b>freezes over</b> the <b>
smart</b> ones move into <b>caves</b> and start a <b>fire</b>.
Growing <b>grass</b> turns out to be more fun than chasing <b>
woolly mammoths</b>, so the <b>agriculturalists</b> start a <b>
revolution</b>. The <b>pharoahs, ceasars, kings,</b> and <b>
fuhrers</b> mostly win but eventually lose, so the <b>
scientists</b> and <b>industrialists</b> revolt this time.
Japan gets <b>nuked</b> and takes over the <b>world
economy</b>, the <b>Berlin wall</b> and <b>Soviets</b> fall,
and the <b>United States</b> all sue <b>Microsoft</b> over
the <b>Internet</b>.
</font>
<font face="Lucida Handwriting"><i>The end.</i></font>
</body></html>
```

6

FIGURE 6.2

If you have the Lucida Sans Unicode and Lucida Sans fonts installed on your computer, they will be used to display the page in Listing 6.2.

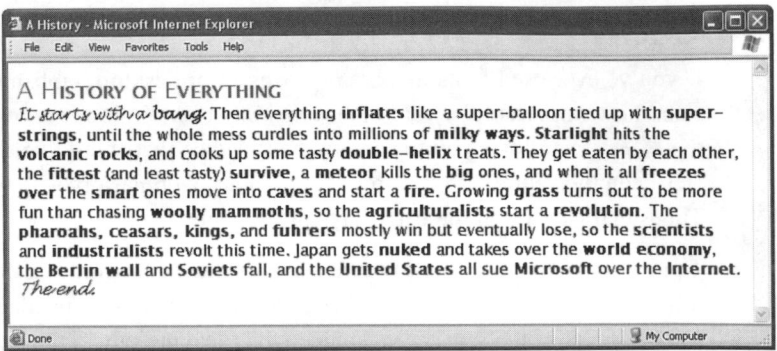

The following is the code to set the typeface used for most of the text in Listing 6.2:

```
<font face="lucida sans unicode, arial, helvetica">
```

If your Web browser can find a font named Lucida Sans Unicode on a user's system, that font is used. Otherwise, the browser will look for Arial or Helvetica. Figure 6.3 shows how the page would look on a computer that didn't have Lucida Sans Unicode or Lucida Sans installed, but did have the Arial font. If none of those fonts could be found, the browser will display the text using the default font (usually Times New Roman) .

FIGURE 6.3

If you don't have Lucida Sans Unicode and Lucida Sans fonts installed, the text from Listing 6.2 would appear in Arial or Times New Roman.

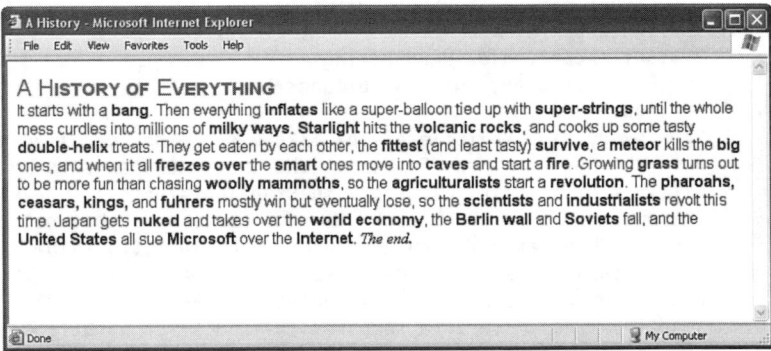

Since only fonts that each user has on his system show up, you have no real control over which fonts appear on your pages. Furthermore, the exact spelling of the font names is important, and many common fonts go by several slightly different names. This means that the only absolutely reliable choices beyond Times New Roman are Arial (on Windows machines) and Helvetica (on Macintosh machines). Don't be afraid to specify other fonts, but make sure your pages look acceptable in Times New Roman as well.

> To see a list of the most common fonts used on the Web, and to find out which of them are installed on your computer, visit the *24-Hour HTML Café* at http://24hourhtmlcafe.com/hour6/.
>
> You'll also find some whimsical examples of how text formatting can liven up a page.

Working with Special Characters

Most fonts now include special characters for European languages, such as the accented é in Café. There are also a few mathematical symbols and special punctuation marks such as the circular • bullet.

You can insert these special characters at any point in an HTML document by looking up the appropriate codes in Table 6.2. You'll find an even more extensive list of codes for multiple character sets online at http://hotwired.lycos.com/webmonkey/reference/special_characters/.

For example, the word Café would look like this:

```
caf&#233;
```

NEW TERM HTML uses a special code known as a *character entity* to represent special characters such as © and ®. Character entities are always specified starting with a & and ending with a ;. Table 6.2 lists the most commonly used character entities, although HTML supports many more.

> Looking for the copyright © and registered trademark ® symbols? The codes you need are © and ® respectively.
>
> To create an unregistered trademark ™ symbol, use ^{tm} or <small>^{tm}</small> for a smaller version.

Although you can specify character entities by number, each symbol also has a mnemonic name that is often easier to remember. Here is another way to write Café:

```
caf&eacute;
```

Notice that there are also codes for the angle brackets, quotation, and ampersand in Table 6.2. You need to use the codes if you want these symbols to appear on your pages; otherwise, the Web browser interprets them as HTML commands.

In Listing 6.3 and Figure 6.4, several of the symbols from Table 6.2 are shown in use.

6

LISTING 6.3   Special Character Codes

```html
<html><head><title>Punctuation Lines</title></head>
<body>
Q: What should you do when a British banker picks a fight with
you?<br />
A: &pound; some &cent;&cent; into him.
<hr />
Q: What do you call it when a judge takes part of a law off the
books?<br />
A: &sect; violence.
<hr />
Q: What did the football coach get from the locker room vending
machine in the middle of the game?<br />
A: A &frac14; back at &frac12; time.
<hr />
Q: How hot did it get when the police detective interrogated
the mathematician?<br />
A: x&sup3;&deg;
<hr />
Q: What does a punctilious plagarist do?<br />
A: &copy;
<hr />
</body></html>
```

FIGURE 6.4

This is how the HTML page in Listing 6.3 will look in most Web browsers.

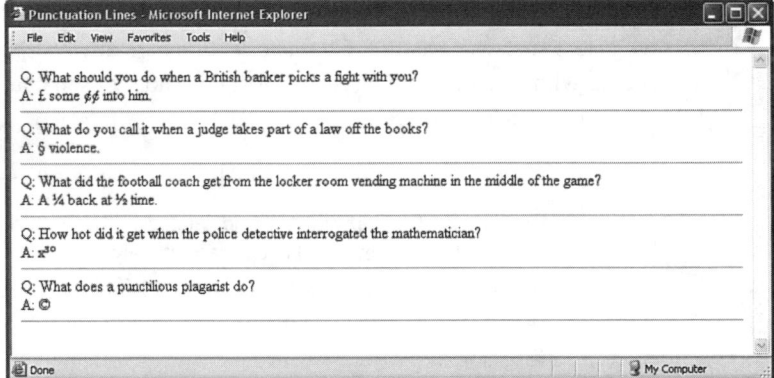

TABLE 6.2   Commonly Used English Language Special Characters

Character	Numeric Code	Code Name	Description
"	"	"	Quotation mark
&	&	&	Ampersand
<	<	<	Less than
>	>	>	Greater than

TABLE 6.2 continued

Character	Numeric Code	Code Name	Description
¢	&#162;	&cent;	Cent sign
£	&#163;	&pound;	Pound sterling
¦	&#166;	¦ or &brkbar;	Broken vertical bar
§	&#167;	&sect;	Section sign
©	&#169;	&copy;	Copyright
®	&#174;	&reg;	Registered trademark
°	&#176;	&deg;	Degree sign
±	&#177;	&plusmn;	Plus or minus
^{2}	&#178;	&sup2;	Superscript two
^{3}	&#179;	&sup3;	Superscript three
·	&#183;	&middot;	Middle dot
^{1}	&#185;	&sup1;	Superscript one
¼	&#188;	&frac14;	Fraction one-fourth
½	&#189;	&frac12;	Fraction one-half
¾	&#190;	&frac34;	Fraction three-fourths
Æ	&#198;	&AElig;	Capital AE ligature
æ	&#230;	&aelig;	Small ae ligature
É	&#201;	&Eacute;	Accented capital E
é	&#233;	&eacute;	Accented small e
×	&#215;	&times;	Multiply sign
÷	&#247;	&divide;	Division sign

Summary

6

This hour showed you how to make text appear as boldface or italic, or with superscripts, subscripts, underlines, crossed-out text, special symbols, and accented letters. You saw how to make everything line up properly in preformatted passages of monospaced text and how to control the size, color, and typeface of any section of text on a Web page.

Table 6.3 summarizes the tags and attributes discussed in this hour. Don't feel like you have to memorize all these tags, by the way! That's why you have this book: You can look them up when you need them. Remember that all the HTML tags are listed in Appendix C, "Complete HTML 4 Quick Reference."

TABLE 6.3   HTML Tags and Attributes Covered in Hour 6

Tag/Attribute	Function
`<em>...</em>`	Emphasis (usually italic).
`<strong>...</strong>`	Stronger emphasis (usually bold).
`<b>...</b>`	Boldface text.
`<i>...</i>`	Italic text.
`<tt>...</tt>`	Typewriter (monospaced) font.
`<pre>...</pre>`	Preformatted text (exact line endings and spacing will be preserved—usually rendered in a monospaced font).
`<big>...</big>`	Text is slightly larger than normal.
`<small>...</small>`	Text is slightly smaller than normal.
`<sub>...</sub>`	Subscript.
`<sup>...</sup>`	Superscript.
`<strike>...</strike>`	Puts a strikethrough in text.
`<font>...</font>`	Controls the appearance of the enclosed text.
Attributes	
`size="..."`	The size of the font, from 1 to 7. Default is 3. Can also be specified as a value relative to the current size; for example, +2 or -1.
`color="..."`	Changes the color of the text.
`face="..."`	Name of font to use if it can be found on the user's system. Commas can separate multiple font names, and the first font on the list that can be found will be used.

Q&A

Q Other books talk about some text formatting tags that you didn't cover in this hour, such as `<code>` and `<address>`. Shouldn't I know about them?

A There are a number of tags in HTML that indicate what kind of information is contained in some text. The `<address>` tag, for example, was supposed to be put around addresses. The only visible effect of `<address>` in most browsers, however, is making the text italic. Web page authors today most often simply use the `<i>` or `<em>` tag instead. Similarly, `<code>` and `<kbd>` do essentially the same thing as `<tt>`. You may also read about `<var>`, `<samp>`, or `<dfn>` in some older HTML references, but nobody uses them in ordinary Web pages.

One tag that you might occasionally find handy is `<blockquote>`, which indents all the text until the closing `</blockquote>`. Some Web page authors use `<blockquote>` on all or part of a page as a quick and easy way to widen the left and right margins. However, later in the book you'll find that style sheets provide a much better way of controlling margins.

Q How do I find out the exact name for a font I have on my computer?

A On a Windows or Macintosh computer, open the Control Panel and click the Fonts folder—the fonts on your system are listed. Use the exact spelling of font names when specifying them in the `<font face>` tag.

Q How do I put Kanji, Arabic, Chinese, and other non-European characters on my pages?

A First of all, everyone you want to be able to read these characters on your pages must have the appropriate language fonts installed. They must also have selected that language character set and font in their Web browser. You can use the Character Map program in Windows (or a similar program in other operating systems) to get the numerical codes for each character in any language font; click Start, All Programs, Accessories, and then System Tools to find Character Map. If the character you want has a code of 214, use `&#214;` to place it on a Web page.

The best way to include a short message in an Asian language (such as `we speak tamil—call us!`) is to include it as a graphics image. That way everyone will see it, even if they use English as their primary language for Web browsing.

Workshop

The workshop contains quiz questions and activities to help you solidify your understanding of the material covered. Try to answer all questions before looking at the "Answers" section that follows.

Quiz

1. Write the HTML to produce the following:

   Come for ~~cheap~~ free H$_2$O on May 7th at 9:00PM

2. What's the difference between the following two lines of HTML?

   ```
   deep <tt>s p   a   a   c e</tt> quest
   deep <pre>s p   a   a   c e</pre> quest
   ```

6

3. How would you say, "We're having our annual Impeachment Day SALE today," in normal-sized blue text, but with the word "SALE" in the largest possible size in bright red?

4. How do you say "© 2004, Webwonks Inc." on a Web page?

Answers

1. ```
   come for <strike>cheap</strike> free h<sub>2</sub>o on may
   7<sup><u>th</u></sup> at 9:00<small>PM</small>
   ```

2. The line using `<tt>` will look like this:

   Deep s p a a c e Quest

   The line using `<pre>` will produce the following three lines of text on the Web page.

   ```
   deep
   s p   a   a c e
   quest
   ```

3. ```
   <font color="blue">We're having our annual Impeachment Day
   <font color="red" size=7>SALE</font> today!</font>
   ```

4. ```
   &copy; 2004, webwonks inc.
   ```

   The following produces the same result:

   ```
   &#169; 2004, webwonks inc.
   ```

Exercises

Professional typesetters use small capitals for the AM and PM in clock times. They also use superscripts for dates like the 7th or 1st. Use the `<small>` and `<sup>` tags to typeset important dates and times correctly on your Web pages.
   ```

HOUR 7

Creating Text Links

In Hour 3, "Linking to Other Web Pages," you learned to use the `<a>` tag to create links between HTML pages. This hour takes linking a step or two forward by showing you how to use the same tag to allow viewers to jump between different parts of the same Web page. This allows you to break a document into sections, and opens up opportunities for creating a table of contents with links or to put a link at the bottom of a page that returns you to the top. You'll find out how to link to a specific point within a separate page, too.

Links aren't just for connecting Web pages with each other; this lesson also tells you how to embed a live link to your email address in a Web page, so readers can instantly compose and send messages to you.

Linking Within a Page Using Anchors

If you recall from Hour 3, the `<a>` tag got its name from the word "anchor," which means a link serves as a designation for a spot in a Web page. So far you've only seen how to use the `<a>` tag to link to somewhere else, but that's only half of its usefulness.

Identifying Locations in a Page with Anchors

The `<a>` tag is also used to mark a spot on a page as an anchor. This allows you to create a link that points to that exact spot. Listing 7.1 demonstrates a link to an anchor within a page. To see how such links are made, take a look ahead at the first `<a>` tag in the listing:

```
<a id="top"></a>
```

 An *anchor* is a named point on a Web page. The same tag is used to create hypertext links and anchors (which explains why the tag is named `<a>`).

This use of the `<a>` anchor tag gives a name to the specific point on the page where the tag occurs. The `</a>` tag must be included, and a unique name assigned to the `id` or `name` attribute, but no text between `<a>` and `</a>` is necessary. The `id` attribute is recommended for compatibility with XHTML, but both attributes are acceptable from a purely HTML perspective. In the past the problem has been that the `id` attribute wasn't supported in browsers, but recent versions of browsers support the attribute. I recommend either using the `id` attribute alone or using both attributes if you're very concerned about users on older browsers. Getting back to the `<a>` tag, it creates an anchor that can then be linked to from this page or any other Web page.

Linking to Anchor Locations

To link to an anchor on a page, you use the `href` attribute of the `<a>` tag. Take a look at the last `<a>` tag in Listing 7.1 to see what I mean:

```
<a href="#top">Return to Index.</a>
```

The `#` symbol means that the word `top` refers to a named anchor point within the current document, rather than to a separate page. When a reader clicks `Return to Index.`, the Web browser displays the part of the page starting with the `<a id="top">` tag.

LISTING 7.1   An `<a>` Tag with an `id` Attribute

```
<html><head><title>Alphabetical Shakespeare</title></head>
<body>
<a id="top"></a>
<h2>First Lines of Every Shakespearean Sonnet</h2>
Don't ya just hate when you go a-courting, and there you are
down on one knee about to rattle off a totally romantic
Shakespearean sonnet, and zap! You space it. <i>"Um... It was,
uh... I think it started with a B..."</i>
```

LISTING 7.1   continued

```
<p>Well, appearest thou no longer the dork. Simply pull this
page up on your laptop computer, click on the first letter of
the sonnet you want, and get an instant reminder of the first
line to get you started. <i>"Beshrew that heart that makes my
heart to groan..."</i> She's putty in your hands.</p>
<h3 align="center">Alphabetical Index<br />
(click on a letter)<br />
<a href="#A">A</a> <a href="#B">B</a> <a href="#C">C</a>
<a href="#D">D</a> <a href="#E">E</a> <a href="#F">F</a>
<a href="#G">G</a> <a href="#H">H</a> <a href="#I">I</a>
<a href="#J">J</a> <a href="#K">K</a> <a href="#L">L</a>
<a href="#M">M</a> <a href="#N">N</a> <a href="#O">O</a>
<a href="#P">P</a> <a href="#Q">Q</a> <a href="#R">R</a>
<a href="#S">S</a> <a href="#T">T</a> <a href="#U">U</a>
<a href="#V">V</a> <a href="#W">W</a> <a href="#X">X</a>
<a href="#Y">Y</a> <a href="#Z">Z</a></h3>
<p><hr /></p><a id="A"></a>
<h2>A</h2>
A woman's face with nature's own hand painted,<br />
Accuse me thus, that I have scanted all,<br />
Against my love shall be as I am now<br />
Against that time (if ever that time come)<br />
Ah wherefore with infection should he live,<br />
Alack what poverty my muse brings forth,<br />
Alas 'tis true, I have gone here and there,<br />
As a decrepit father takes delight,<br />
As an unperfect actor on the stage,<br />
As fast as thou shalt wane so fast thou grow'st,<br />
<p><a href="#top"><i>Return to Index.</i></a></p><hr />
...
<a id="Y"></a><h2>Y</h2>
Your love and pity doth th' impression fill,<br />
<p><a href="#top"><i>Return to Index.</i></a></p><hr />
<a id="Z"></a><h2>Z</h2>
(No sonnets start with Z.)<br />
<p><a href="#top">Return to Index.</a></p>
<hr />
</body></html>
```

Here's an easy way to remember the difference between these two types of <a> tags: <a href> is what you click, and <a id> is where you go when you click there. Similarly, each of the <a href> links in Listing 7.1 makes an underlined link leading to a corresponding <a id> anchor. Clicking the letter B under alphabetical index in Figure 7.1, for instance, takes you to the part of the page shown in Figure 7.2.

7

FIGURE 7.1
The <a id> tags in Listing 7.1 don't appear at all on the Web page. The <a href> tags appear as underlined links.

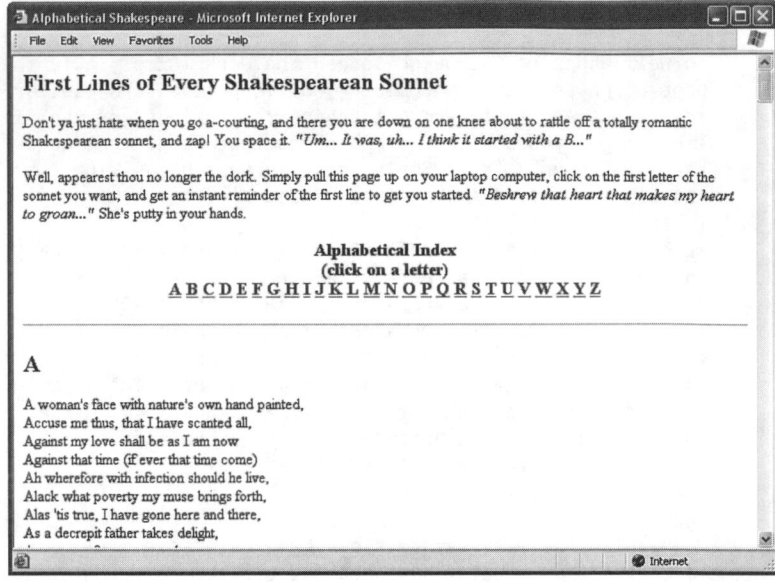

FIGURE 7.2
Clicking the letter B in Figure 7.1 takes you to the appropriate section of the same page.

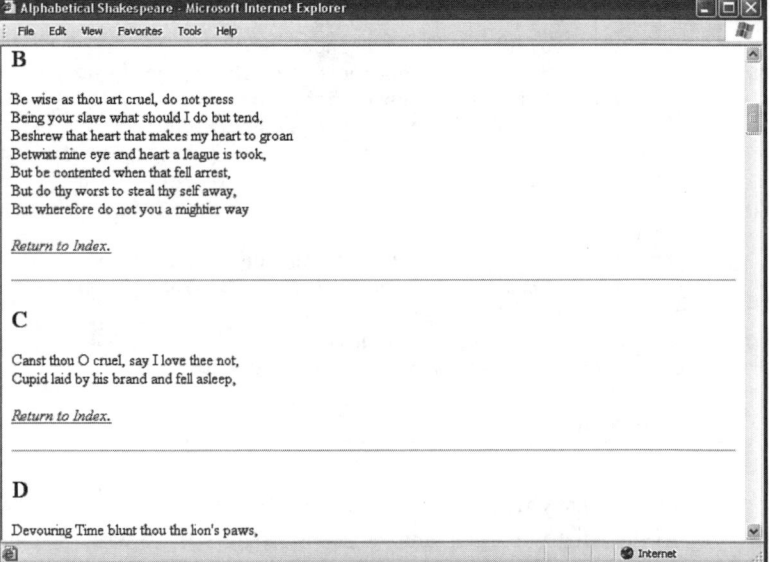

To Do

Now that you have several pages of your own linked together, you might want to add an index at the top of your home page so people can easily get an overview of what your pages have to offer:

▼   • Place `<a id>` tags in front of each major topic on your home page or any longish
       page you make.

     • Copy each of the major topic headings to a list at the top of the page, and enclose
▲   each heading in an `<a href>` linking to the corresponding `<a id>` tag.

> One of the most common uses for the `<a id>` tag is creating an alphabetical
> index. The bad news for anyone with an alphabetical list that he wants to
> index is that typing out 26 links to 26 anchors is a rather tedious endeavor.
> The good news is that I've already done it for you and dropped off the
> indexed page at the *24-Hour HTML Café*:
> `http://www.24hourhtmlcafe.com/hour7/`.
>
> Click the Instant Alphabetical Index link and select File, Save As to save the
> document to your hard drive. You can then cut and paste your own alpha-
> betical information after each letter.

Linking to a Specific Part of Another Page

You can even link to a named anchor on another page by including the address or name
of that page followed by # and the anchor name. Listing 7.2 shows several examples,
such as the following:

```
<a href="sonnets.htm#131">
You're bossy, ugly and smelly, but I still love you.</a>
```

Clicking `You're bossy, ugly and smelly, but I still love you.`, which is shown in
Figure 7.3, brings up the page named `sonnets.htm` and goes directly to the point where `<a
id="131"></a>` occurs on that page (see Figure 7.4). (The HTML for `sonnets.htm` is not
listed here because it is quite long. It's just a bunch of sappy old sonnets with `<a id>` tags
in front of each one.) Note that anchor names can be numbers, words, or any combination of letters and numbers. In this case, I used the sonnet number.

LISTING 7.2   Using the Page Address and Anchor Name in the `<a href>` Tag

```
<html><head><title>Topical Shakespeare</title></head>
<body>
<h2>Shakespearean Sonnets for Every Occasion</h2>
<p>Choose your message for a genuine Shakespearean sonnet which
expresses your feelings with tact and grace.</p>
<i><a href="sonnets.htm#131">
You're bossy, ugly and smelly, but I still love you.</a><br />
<a href="sonnets.htm#2">
```

7

LISTING 7.2 continued

```
Life is short. Let's make babies.</a><br />
<a href="sonnets.htm#140">
Say you love me or I'll tell lies about you.</a><br />
<a href="sonnets.htm#31">
You remind me of all my old girlfriends.</a><br />
<a href="sonnets.htm#57">
You abuse me, but you know I love it.</a><br />
<a href="sonnets.htm#141">
I think you're hideous, but I'm desperate.</a><br />
<a href="sonnets.htm#150">
You don't deserve me, but take me anyway.</a><br />
<a href="sonnets.htm#36">
I feel bad about leaving, but see ya later.</a></i>
</body></html>
```

FIGURE 7.3

This page is listed in Listing 7.2. All the links on this page go to different parts of a separate page named sonnets.htm.

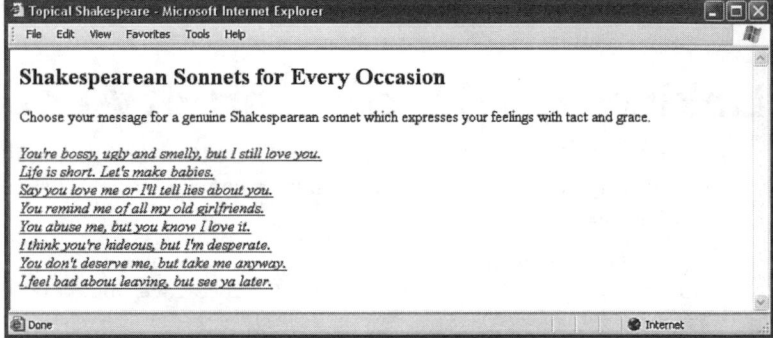

FIGURE 7.4

Clicking the bossy link in Figure 7.3 brings you directly to this part of the sonnets.htm *page. HTML for this page isn't shown.*

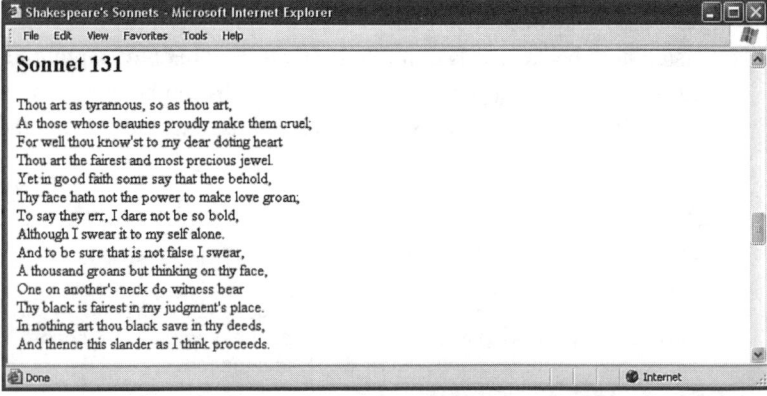

Be sure to only include the # symbol in `<a href>` link tags. Don't put a # symbol in the `<a id>` or `<a name>` tag; links to that name won't work in that case.

Linking Your Email Address into a Page

In addition to linking between pages and between parts of a single page, the `<a>` tag allows you to link to your email address. This is the simplest way to enable readers of your Web pages to "talk back" to you. Of course, you could just tell them your email address and trust them to type it into whatever email program they use if they want to say something to you, but that would be much more error prone. You can make it almost completely effortless for them to send you messages by providing a clickable link to your email address.

An HTML link to an email address looks like the following:

```
<a href="mailto:dicko@netletter.com">Send me an email message.</a>
```

The words `Send me an email message.` will appear just like any other `<a>` link (as underlined text in the color you set for links in the `link` or `vlink` attributes of the `<body>` tag). When someone clicks the link in most Web browsers, she gets a window in which to type a message that is immediately sent to you—whatever email program the person uses to send and receive email will automatically be used.

If you want people to see your actual email address (so they can make note of it or send a message using a different email program), include it both in the `href` attribute and as part of the message between the `<a>` and `</a>` tags.

For example, the HTML in Listing 7.3 is an email directory page for a club of aging German philosophers. (I know that Wittgenstein's English, but he was born in Austria, so they let him in the club anyway.) The resulting page in Figure 7.5 lists the club officers with a clickable email link for each.

LISTING 7.3 Using the `<a>` Tag to Link to Email Addresses

```
<html><head><title>GPhC E-Mail Directory</title></head>
<body>
<h2>German Philosopher's Club<br />E-Mail Directory</h2>
<ul>
<li><p><a href="mailto:manny@24hourhtmlcafe.com">
    <i>Emmanuel Kant, President</i><br />
       manny@24hourhtmlcafe.com</a></p></li>
```

7

LISTING 7.3   continued

```
<li><p><a href="mailto:marty@24hourhtmlcafe.com">
   <i>Martin Heidegger, Secretary</i><br />
      marty@24hourhtmlcafe.com</a></p></li>
<li><p><a href="mailto:will-fred@24hourhtmlcafe.com">
   <i>Georg Wilhelm Friedrick Hegel, Senior Officer</i><br />
      will-fred@24hourhtmlcafe.com</a></p></li>
<li><p><a href="mailto:fred-will@24hourhtmlcafe.com">
   <i>Friedrick Wilhelm Nietzche, Junior Officer</i><br />
      fred-will@24hourhtmlcafe.com</a></p></li>
<li><p><a href="mailto:jj@24hourhtmlcafe.com">
   <i>Ludwig J.J. Wittgenstein,
      Administrative Assistant</i><br />
      jj@24hourhtmlcafe.com</a></p></li>
</ul>
</body>
</html>
```

FIGURE 7.5

The `mailto:` *links in Listing 7.3 look just like* `http://` *links on the page.*

When someone clicks the top link in Figure 7.5, a separate window (see Figure 7.6) opens; the window has spaces for a subject line and email message. The email address from the link is automatically entered, and the user can simply click the mail button to send the message.

It is customary to put an email link to the Web page author at the bottom of every Web page. Not only does this make it easy for others to contact you, it also gives them a way to tell you about any problems with the page that your testing may have missed.

FIGURE 7.6

FIGURE 7.6

Clicking the top link in Figure 7.5 brings up this email window (or the email software set up on your computer).

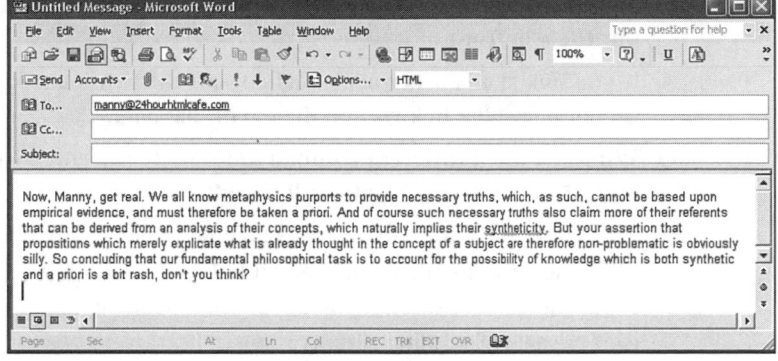

Summary

This hour has shown you two uses for the `<a>` tag not covered in Hour 3. You learned how to create named anchor points within a page and how to create links to a specific anchor. You also saw how to link to your email address so readers can easily send you messages. Table 7.1 summarizes the two attributes of the `<a>` tag discussed in this hour.

TABLE 7.1 HTML Tags and Attributes Covered in Hour 7

Tag/Attribute	Function
`<a>...</a>`	With the `href` attribute, creates a link to another document or anchor; with the `name` attribute, creates an anchor that can be linked to.
Attributes	
`href="..."`	The address of the document or anchor point to which to link.
`id="..."`	The name for this anchor point in the document.
`name="..."`	The name for this anchor point in the document; not compliant with XHTML, but otherwise equivalent to `id`.

Q&A

Q Can I put both `href` and `id` in the same `<a>` tag? Would I want to for any reason?

A You can, and it might save you some typing if you have a named anchor point and a link right next to each other. It's generally better, however, to use `<a href>` and `<a id>` separately to avoid confusion because they play very different roles in an HTML document.

7

Q What happens if I accidentally spell the name of an anchor wrong or forget to put the # in front of it?

A If you link to an anchor name that doesn't exist within a page or misspell the anchor name, the link goes to the top of that page.

Q What if I use a different company to handle my email than handles my Web pages? Will my email links still work?

A Yes. You can put any email address on the Internet into a link, and it will work fine. The only situation where email links won't work is when the person who clicks the link doesn't have an email program set up on his computer, and therefore isn't capable of sending email.

Workshop

The workshop contains quiz questions and activities to help you solidify your understanding of the material covered. Try to answer all questions before looking at the "Answers" section that follows.

Quiz

1. Write the HTML to make it possible for someone clicking the words "About the authors" at the top of the page to skip down to a list of credits at the bottom of the page.

2. Suppose your company has three employees and you want to create a company directory page listing some information about each of them. Write the HTML for that page and the HTML to link to one of the employees from another page.

3. If your email address is bon@soir.com, how would you make the text "goodnight greeting" into a link that people can click to compose and send you an email message?

Answers

1. Type this at the top of the page:

   ```
   <a href="#credits">about the authors</a>
   ```

   Type this at the beginning of the credits section:

   ```
   <a id="credits"></a>
   ```

2. The company directory page would look like the following:

   ```
   <html><head><title>company directory</title></head>
   <body><h1>company directory</h1>
   <a id="jones"><h2>jane jones</h2>
   ```

```
ms. jones is our accountant... etc.
<a id="smith"><h2>sam smith</h2>
mr. smith is our salesman.. etc.
<a id="bharwaniji"><h2>r.k. satjiv bharwahniji</h2>
mr. bharwahniji is our president... etc.
</body></html>
```

If the file were named `directory.htm`, a link to one employee's information from another page would look like the following:

```
<a href="directory.htm#bharwaniji">about our president</a>
```

3. Type the following on your Web page:

```
send me a <a href="mailto:bon@soir.com">goodnight greeting</a>!
```

Exercises

- When you link back to your home page from other pages, you might want to skip some of the introductory information at the top of the home page. Using a link to a named anchor just below that introductory information will avoid presenting it to people who have already read it, making your pages seem less repetitive. Also, if any pages on your site are longer than two screens of information when displayed in a Web browser, consider putting a link at the bottom of the page back up to the top.

- Look through your Web pages and consider whether there are any places in the text where you'd like to make it easy for people to respond to what you're saying. Include a link right there to your email address. You can never provide too many opportunities for people to contact you and tell you what they need or think about your products, especially if you're running a business.

7

PART III
Web Page Graphics

Hour

Hour **8**

Creating Your Own Web Page Graphics

You don't have to be an artist to put high-impact graphics and creative type on your Web pages. You don't need to spend hundreds or thousands of dollars on software, either. This hour tells you how to create the images you need to make visually exciting Web pages. Though the example figures in this chapter use a popular Windows graphics program (Paint Shop Pro from Jasc Software), you can easily follow along with any major Windows or Macintosh graphics application.

This hour is only concerned with creating the actual graphics files for Web images, so it doesn't actually discuss any HTML tags at all. In Hour 9, "Putting Graphics on a Web Page," you'll see how to integrate your graphics with your HTML pages.

One of the best ways to save time creating the graphics and media files for Web pages is, of course, to avoid creating them altogether. Grabbing a graphic from any Web page is as simple as right-clicking it (or holding down the button, on a Macintosh mouse) and selecting Save Image As in Netscape Navigator or Save Picture As in Microsoft Explorer. Extracting a background image from a page is just as easy: Right-click it and select Save Background As.

You may also want to consider royalty-free clip art, which doesn't require you to get copyright permission. A good source of clip art online is Microsoft's Design Gallery Live, which is located at `http://dgl.microsoft.com/`.

Any image or media clip you see on any Web site is instantly reusable provided the copyright holder grants (or sells) you the right to copy it. Make sure to ask before using any copyrighted media on your own pages. To learn more about Web piracy, visit `http://www.pirated-sites.com/`. Along with potentially getting you in a lot of legal trouble, taking images without permission is considered highly unprofessional, not to mention unethical.

Choosing Graphics Software

You can use almost any computer graphics program to create graphics images for your Web pages, from the simple paint program that comes free with your computer's operating system to an expensive professional program such as Adobe Photoshop. If you have a digital camera or scanner attached to your computer, it probably came with some graphics software capable of creating Web page graphics.

Adobe Photoshop is without a doubt the cream of the crop when it comes to image editing programs. However, it is expensive and quite complex if you don't have experience working with computer graphics. Adobe now offers a more affordable, easier to use version of Photoshop called Photoshop Elements, which you might want to take a look at. For more information on Adobe's products, visit the Adobe Web site at `http://www.adobe.com/`.

If you already have software you think might be good for creating Web graphics, try using it to do everything described in this hour. If it can't do some of the tasks covered here, it probably won't be a good tool for Web graphics. In that case, you might want to consider downloading the evaluation version of Paint Shop Pro or Adobe Photoshop

Elements if you're using a Windows computer, or Adobe Photoshop Elements if you're using a Macintosh.

To Do

An excellent and inexpensive program that provides everything you're likely to need for Web images is Paint Shop Pro from Jasc, Inc. If you are using a Windows computer, you can download a fully functional evaluation copy of Paint Shop Pro before reading the rest of this lesson. (Macintosh users should download Adobe Photoshop Elements from `http://www.adobe.com/` instead, because Paint Shop Pro is currently available for Windows only. There is also a version of Photoshop Elements for Windows if you're partial to Adobe products.)

1. Start your Web browser and go to `http://www.Jasc.com/`.

2. Click the "free downloads" link, followed by "Trial Software," and choose Paint Shop Pro.

3. Make sure you download the evaluation version, and then click the download site nearest you; the file will transfer to your hard drive. You are asked to confirm where you want to put the file on your hard drive—be sure to remember which folder it goes into!

4. Once the download transfer is complete, use Windows Explorer to find the file you downloaded and double-click it to install Paint Shop Pro.

> The Paint Shop Pro software you can get online is a fully functional shareware evaluation copy. If you find it useful for working with Web page images, you'll want to register the program with Jasc Software for a fee. The evaluation copy of Paint Shop Pro is only good for 30 days, so you'll have to make up your mind at some point about registering the software or finding an alternative.

Almost all the graphics you see in this book were created with Paint Shop Pro, and this chapter uses Paint Shop Pro to illustrate several key Web graphics techniques you'll need to know. Of course, there are so many ways to produce images with Paint Shop Pro I can't even begin to explain them all. If you'd like a quick but complete tutorial on using Paint Shop Pro to make high-impact Web page graphics, I recommend *Sams Teach Yourself Paint Shop Pro in 24 Hours*.

The Least You Need to Know About Graphics

Two forces are always at odds when you post graphics and multimedia on the Internet. Your eyes and ears want everything to be as detailed and accurate as possible, but your clock and wallet want files to be as small as possible. Intricate, colorful graphics mean big file sizes, which can take a long time to transfer even over a fast connection.

How do you maximize the quality of your presentation while minimizing file size? To make these choices, you need to understand how color and resolution work together to create a subjective sense of quality.

NEW TERM The *resolution* of an image is the number of individual dots, or *pixels* (the individual dots that make up a digital image), that make up an image. Large, high-resolution images generally take longer to transfer and display than small, low-resolution images. Resolution is usually specified as the width times the height of the image, in pixels; a 300×200 image, for example, is 300 pixels wide and 200 pixels high.

NEW TERM You might be surprised to find that resolution isn't the most significant factor determining an image file's storage size (and transfer time). This is because images used on Web pages are always stored and transferred in *compressed* form. *Image compression* is the mathematical manipulation that images are put through to squeeze out repetitive patterns. The mathematics of image compression is complex, but the basic idea is that repeating patterns or large areas of the same color can be squeezed out when the image is stored on a disk. This makes the image file much smaller and allows it to be transferred faster over the Internet. The Web browser program can then restore the original appearance of the image when the image is displayed.

In the rest of this hour, you'll learn exactly how to create graphics with big visual impact and small file sizes. The techniques you'll use to accomplish this depend on the contents and purpose of each image. There are as many uses for Web page graphics as there are Web pages, but four types of graphics are by far the most common:

- Photos of people, products, or places
- Graphical banners and logos
- Snazzy-looking buttons or icons to link between pages
- Background textures or wallpaper to go behind pages

The last of these is covered in Hour 10, "Custom Backgrounds and Colors," but you can learn to create the other three kinds of graphics right now.

Preparing Photographic Images

To put photos on your Web pages, you need some kind of scanner or digital camera. You'll often need to use the custom software that comes with your scanner or camera to save pictures on your hard drive. Note, however, that you can control just about any scanner directly from Paint Shop Pro and most other graphics programs—see the software documentation for details.

> If you don't have a scanner or digital camera, any Kodak film-developing store can transfer photos from 35mm film to a CD-ROM for a modest fee. You can then use Paint Shop Pro to open and modify the Kodak Photo-CD files. Some large photo developers other than Kodak also offer similar digitizing services.

Once you have the pictures, you can use Paint Shop Pro (or another similar graphics program) to get them ready for the Web.

Cropping an Image

You want Web page graphics to be as compact as possible, so you'll usually need to crop or reduce the size of your digital photos. Follow these steps to crop a picture in Paint Shop Pro:

1. Click the rectangular selection tool on the tools palette. (The tools palette is shown in the left in Figure 8.1. You can drag it wherever you want it, so it may be in a different place on your screen.)

2. Click the top-left corner of the portion of the image you want to keep, and hold down the left mouse button while you drag down to the lower-right corner.

3. Select Image, Crop to Selection to crop the image.

FIGURE 8.1

Use the rectangular selection tool to crop images as tightly as possible.

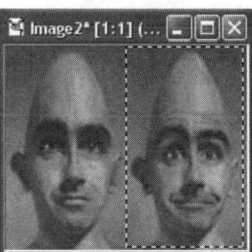

Even after cropping, your image may be larger than it needs to be for a Web page. Generally, a complex photograph should be no more than 300×300 pixels, and a simpler photo can look fine at 100×50 or so.

Notice that in Paint Shop Pro the resolution of the current image is shown at the bottom-right corner of the window. The image may look larger or smaller than it really is because Paint Shop Pro automatically adjusts the image to fit in the window while you're working on it. (The current magnification ratio is shown just above each image, in the title bar.) To see the image at the size it will appear on a Web page, select View, Normal Viewing (1:1) .

Resizing an Image

To change an image's resolution, and therefore its apparent size, use the Image, Resize command. (Notice that in some software, including earlier versions of Paint Shop Pro, this option is called Resample.) You'll get the Resize dialog box shown in Figure 8.2.

FIGURE 8.2

To change the size of an image, select Image, Resize to get this dialog box.

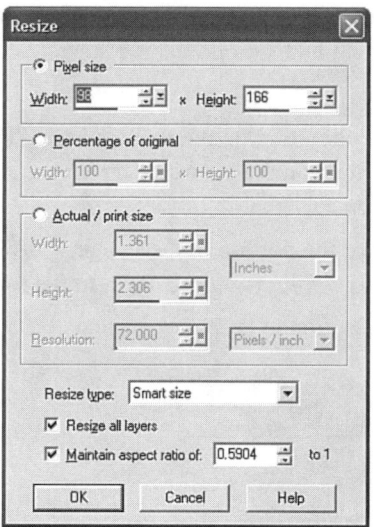

You'll almost always want Smart Size, Resize All Layers, and Maintain Aspect Ratio Of selected (near the bottom of the dialog box). If you opt to maintain the aspect ratio, when you enter the width you'd like the image to be, the height will be calculated automatically to keep the image from squishing out of shape. It also works the same way if you specify the height and allow Paint Shop Pro to alter the width automatically.

Tweaking Image Colors

Many photographs will require some color correction to look their best on a computer screen. Like most photo-editing programs, Paint Shop Pro offers many options for adjusting an image's brightness, contrast, and color balance.

Most of these options are pretty intuitive, but the most important and powerful one may be unfamiliar if you're not an old graphics pro. Whenever an image appears too dark or too light, select Colors, Adjust, Gamma Correction. For most images, this works better than Colors, Adjust, Brightness/Contrast, because it doesn't wash out bright or dark areas.

As shown in Figure 8.3, you can move the sliders in the Gamma Correction dialog box to adjust the correction factor until the image looks about right. (Numbers above 1 make the image lighter, and numbers between 1 and 0 make the image darker.) If the color in the image seems a little off, try deselecting the Link check box, which allows you to move the Red, Green, and Blue sliders separately and to adjust the color balance.

FIGURE 8.3

Gamma correction is the best way to fix images that are too dark or too light.

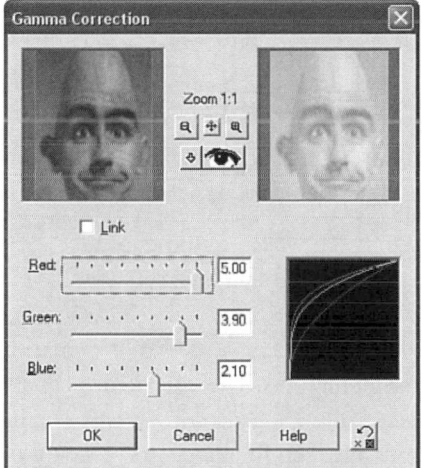

Most of the other image editing tools in Paint Shop Pro offer small preview windows like the one in Figure 8.3, so a little playful experimentation is the best way to find out what each of them does.

Controlling JPEG Compression

Photographic images look best when saved in the JPEG file format. When you're finished adjusting the size and appearance of your photo, select File, Save As and choose the JPEG-JFIF Compliant file type with Standard Encoding, as shown in Figure 8.4.

Figure 8.4 shows the Save Options dialog box you'll see when you click the Options button. You can control the compression ratio for saving JPEG files by adjusting the Compression Factor setting between 1 percent (high quality, large file size) and 99 percent (low quality, small file size).

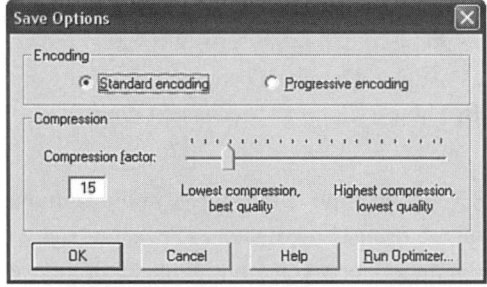

FIGURE 8.4

Paint Shop Pro allows you to trade reduced file size for image quality when saving JPEG images.

You may want to experiment a bit to see how various JPEG compression levels affect the quality of your images, but 25 percent compression is generally a good compromise between speed and quality for most photographic images.

Creating Banners and Buttons

Graphics that you create from scratch, such as banners and buttons, require you to make considerations uniquely different than photographs.

The first decision you need to make when you produce a banner or button is how big it should be. The majority of people accessing the Web now have a computer with one of the following two screen sizes: 800×600 pixels or 1,024×768 pixels. You should generally plan your graphics so that they will always fit in the smaller of these screens, with room to spare for scrollbars and margins. The crucial size constraint is the horizontal width of your pages because scrolling a page horizontally is a huge hassle and source of confusion for Web users. Vertically scrolling a page is much more acceptable, so it's okay if your pages are taller than the minimum screen sizes.

If you really want to ensure maximum compatibility with every user, you should design your pages for 640×480 pixel screens, but the drawback here is that your pages will look small on higher resolution screens. Generally speaking, it's safe to assume an 800×600 resolution for the vast majority of Web users.

8

Assuming you target a minimum resolution of 800×600 pixels, this means that full-sized banners and title graphics should be no more than 770 pixels wide by 430 pixels tall, which is the maximum viewable area of the page once you've accounted for scrollbars, toolbars, and other parts of the browser window. Photos and large artwork should be from 100 to 300 pixels in each dimension, and smaller buttons and icons should be 20 to 100 pixels tall and wide.

Figure 8.5 shows the dialog box you get when you select File, New to start a new image. You should always begin with 16.7 million colors (24 bit) as the image type. You can always change its size later with Image, Crop or Image, Canvas Size; don't worry if you aren't sure exactly how big it needs to be.

For the background color, you should usually choose white to match the background that most Web browsers use for Web pages. (You'll see how to change a page's background color in Hour 10.) When you know you'll be making a page with a background other than white, you can choose a different background color.

FIGURE 8.5

You need to decide on the approximate size of an image before you start working on it.

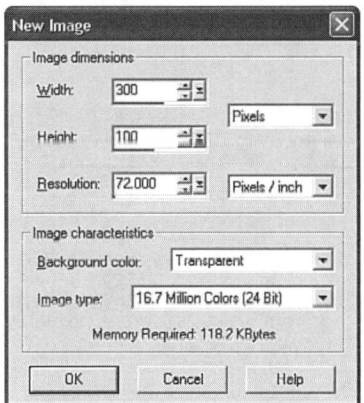

When you enter the width and height of the image in pixels and click OK, you are faced with a blank canvas—an intimidating sight if you're as art-phobic as most of us! Fortunately, computer graphics programs such as Paint Shop Pro make it amazingly easy to produce professional-looking graphics for most Web page applications.

Often, you will want to incorporate some fancy lettering into your Web page graphics. For example, you might want to put a title banner at the top of your page that uses a decorative font with a drop-shadow or other special effects. To accomplish this in Paint Shop Pro, perform the following steps:

1. Choose the color you want the lettering to be from the color palette on the right edge of the Paint Shop Pro window. (Press the letter C to make the color palette appear if you don't see it.)

2. Click the A tool on the toolbar, and then click anywhere on the image. The Text Entry dialog box shown in Figure 8.6 appears.

3. Choose a font and point size for the lettering, and make sure Floating and Antialias are selected under Create As. (This smoothes the edges of the text.) Click OK.

4. Click anywhere in the image, and then grab and drag the text with the mouse to position it where you want it (usually in the center of the image) .

FIGURE 8.6

Use Paint Shop Pro's text tool to create elegant lettering in a graphics image.

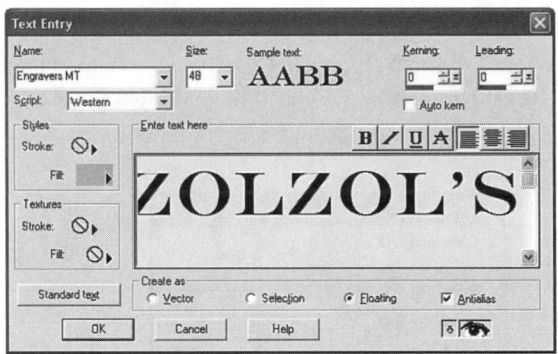

The list of fonts you see when you use the text tool will almost certainly be different than those shown in Figure 8.6. You will see only the fonts previously installed on your computer, which are probably somewhat different than those installed on my computer.

When you first put the text onto the image, it shimmers with a moving dotted outline. This means that it is selected and that any special effects you choose from the menu will apply to the shape of the letters you just made. For example, you might select Effects, 3D Effects, Chisel to add a chiseled outline around the text. Figure 8.7 shows the dialog box that would appear.

Notice that you can adjust the chisel effect and see the results in a small preview window before you actually apply them to the image. This makes it very easy to learn what various effects do simply by experimenting with them. Using only the text tool and the four choices on the Image, Effects submenu (Buttonize, Chisel, Cutout, and Drop Shadow), you can create quite a variety of useful and attractive Web graphics.

FIGURE 8.7

Like most menu choices in Paint Shop Pro, the Image, Effects, Chisel command gives you an easy-to-use preview.

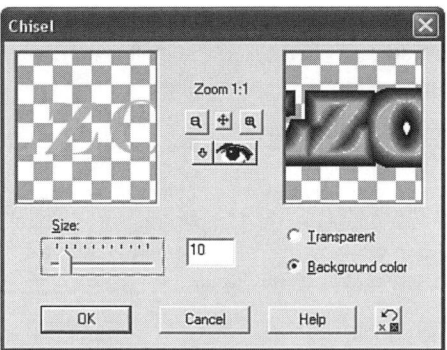

You may also want to deform, blur, sharpen, or otherwise play around with your text after you've applied an effect to it. To do so, simply select Effects, Effect Browser and select an effect to use. You get a dialog box like the one shown in Figure 8.8, which lets you pick from a list of effects and preview each one.

FIGURE 8.8

Select Effects, Effect Browser to play with all the image-altering special effects available, and then choose the one you want.

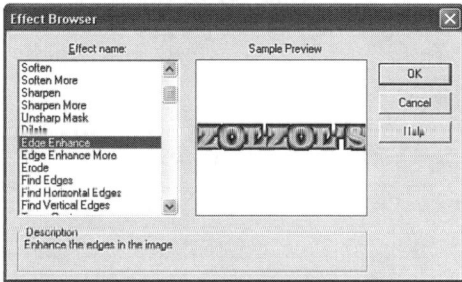

In the figure, the Edge Enhance filter from the Effect Browser is being used, which adds a sparkly effect to the chiseled lettering. You can have a lot of fun playing around with all the different options in the effect browser!

Reducing the Number of Colors in an Image

One of the most effective ways to reduce the size, and therefore the download time for an image, is to reduce the number of colors used in the image. This can drastically reduce the visual quality of some photographic images, but works great for most banners, buttons, and other icons.

In Paint Shop Pro, you can do this by selecting Colors, Decrease Color Depth. (Most other graphics programs have a similar option.) Choose 16 Colors (4 bit) when your image has very few colors in it. If the image has lots of colors (or the image doesn't look good when you try 16 Colors), select Colors, Decrease Color Depth, 256 Colors (8 bit) instead. The software will automatically find the best palette of 16 or 256 colors for approximating the full range of colors in the image.

 Even if you only use two or three colors in an image, you should still select Colors, Reduce Color Depth, 16 Colors before you save it. If you don't, the image file will waste some space "leaving room for" lots of colors—even though very few are actually in use.

When you reduce the number of colors in an image, you will see a dialog box with several choices (see Figure 8.9). For Web page images, you will almost always want to choose Optimized Octree and Nearest Color. Leave all the options on the right side of the dialog box unchecked; they will seldom improve the quality of an image noticeably.

FIGURE 8.9

Reducing the number of colors in an image can dramatically decrease file size without dramatically changing the appearance of the image.

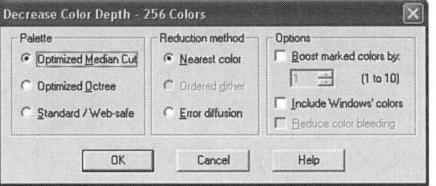

 Dithering (also called *error diffusion* in Paint Shop Pro) is a technique used by image-editing programs to simulate a color that isn't in the color palette with alternating pixels of two similar colors. For example, a dithered pink color would consist of alternating pixels of red and white pixels, which give the general impression of pink. Dithering can make images look better in some cases, but should usually be avoided for Web page graphics. Why? It substantially increases the information complexity of an image, and that almost always results in much larger file sizes and slower downloads.

You'll be glad to know that there is a special file format for images with a limited number of colors; it's called the Graphics Interchange Format (GIF). To save a GIF image in Paint Shop Pro, select File, Save As and choose CompuServe Graphics Interchange (*.gif) as the image type. The GIF image format is designed for images that contain areas of solid colors, such as Web page titles and other illustrated graphics; the GIF format is not ideal for photographs.

The GIF image format is important because it allows you to specify a transparent color, which means the background of the Web page will show through those areas of an image. Another newer image format called PNG (pronounced "ping") is similar to GIF, but not as widely supported.

8

Interlaced GIFs and Progressive JPEGs

Both the GIF and JPEG image file formats offer a nifty feature that makes images appear faster than they otherwise could. An image can be stored in such a way that a "rough draft" of the image appears quickly, and the details are filled in as the download finishes. This has a profound psychological effect, because it gives people something to look at instead of drumming their fingers, waiting for a large image to pour slowly onto the screen.

A file stored with this feature is called an *interlaced GIF* or *progressive JPEG*. Despite the different names, the visual results are similar with either format.

NEW TERM   An *interlaced GIF* file is an image that appears blocky at first, and then more and more detailed as it finishes downloading. Similarly, a *progressive JPEG* file appears blurry at first and then gradually comes into focus.

Most graphics programs that can handle GIF files enable you to choose whether to save them interlaced or noninterlaced. In Paint Shop Pro, for example, you can choose Version 89a and Interlaced by clicking the Options button in the Save As dialog box just before you save a GIF file (see Figure 8.10).

FIGURE 8.10

Paint Shop Pro lets you save interlaced GIF images, which appear to display faster when loading.

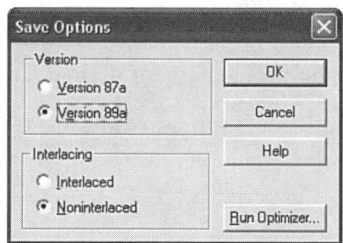

To save a progressive JPEG file, select Save As (or Save Copy As), choose the JPEG-JFIF Compliant image type, click the Options button, and select Progressive Encoding. Virtually all GIF and JPEG images used on the Web these days take advantage of interlacing and progression to provide a better browsing experience for Web surfers.

 Image files smaller than about 3KB will usually load so fast that nobody will ever see the interlacing or progressive display anyway. In fact, very small images may actually load more slowly when interlaced. Save these tricks for larger images.

Creating Animated Web Graphics

The GIF image format allows you to create animated images that can be used to add some motion and spice up any Web page. They also transfer much faster than most video or multimedia files. The latest version of Paint Shop Pro includes a module called Animation Shop, which is designed especially for creating Web page GIF animations. There are a few other GIF animation programs available, including both freeware and advanced commercial software packages. Animation Shop offers the best mix of great features, ease of use, and low price.

The first step in creating a GIF animation is to create a series of images to be displayed one after the other. Each of these images is called a *frame*. (By the way, this use of the word *frame* has nothing whatsoever to do with the *frames* you learn about in Hour 16, "Multi-Page Layout with Frames.") You can use any graphics software you like to make the images, though Paint Shop Pro is an obvious choice if you plan on using Animation Shop to put the animation together.

If you know how to use Paint Shop Pro's (or any other advanced graphics software) Layers feature, you'll find that creating animation frames is easier because you can easily turn parts of a picture on and off to make variations or move layers to simulate motion. Don't fret, however; layer manipulation is a bit beyond you at the moment. You can easily make very effective animations by copying an ordinary one-layer image and painting on some variations, or moving some parts of it around to make the next frame.

When you have your animation's individual frames ready, use Colors, Decrease Color Depth to limit them to 256 or 16 colors, and then save each of them as a separate GIF file.

To Do

If you would like to work with the same three animation frames I use for the first example in this hour, you'll find them at the sites:

http://www.24hourHTMLcafe.com/hour8/noburn1.gif

http://www.24hourHTMLcafe.com/hour8/noburn2.gif

http://www.24hourHTMLcafe.com/hour8/noburn3.gif

Assembling Images into an Animation

8

Once you have the individual GIF files saved, select File, Jasc Software Products, Launch Animation Shop from within Paint Shop Pro to start putting them together into a single animation file.

> The fastest way to create a simple GIF animation with Animation Shop is to select File, Animation Wizard. This starts an "interview" that leads you through all the steps discussed next.
>
> In this hour, however, I show you how to create animations by hand, without using the Animation Wizard. This will give you a head start when you want to use the advanced animation tricks discussed toward the end of the chapter.

The basic idea here couldn't be simpler: You just need to tell Animation Shop which pictures to show and in what order. There are also a couple of other picky details you need to specify: how long to show each picture before moving on to the next one and how many times to repeat the whole sequence. Follow this step-by-step procedure to assemble an animation:

1. Select File, Open (in Animation Shop, not in Paint Shop Pro). Select the image file that you want to be the first frame of the animation. It will appear as shown in Figure 8.11. Notice that the transparency is preserved, as indicated by the gray checkerboard pattern showing through.

FIGURE 8.11

This is a single-frame GIF image as it first appears when opened in Animation Shop.

2. Select Animation, Insert Frames, From File to get the dialog box shown in Figure 8.12. Click the Add File button and choose the image you want to appear second

in the animation. Click Add File again to add the third frame, and so forth, until the list contains all the images you made for this animation. Click OK.

FIGURE 8.12
Selecting Edit, Insert Frames, From File gives you this dialog box. The Add File button lets you choose an image to add to the animation.

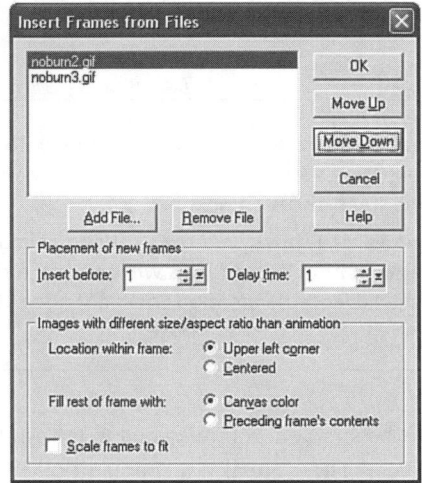

3. You should now see all the frames laid out next to each other like a filmstrip (see Figure 8.13). You can use the scrollbar to move forward and back through the film-strip if all the frames aren't visible at once. If you'd like to see a preview of the animation, select View, Animation. If any frames are in the wrong order, simply grab and drag them into the proper positions with the mouse.

FIGURE 8.13
Animation Shop displays all of an animation's frames side-by-side, like a filmstrip.

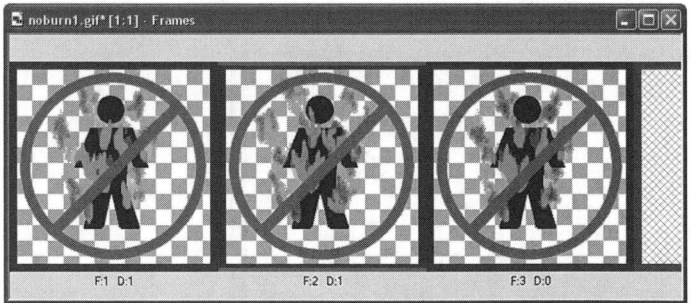

If you don't tell it any different, Animation Shop normally puts a tenth of a second between each frame of the animation. That was actually about right for my little burning-man icon. However, you will often want to control the length of time each individual frame is displayed before the next one replaces it.

4. To set the timing for a frame, click it; the border around it will turn blue and red. Select Edit, Frame Properties; alternatively, you can right-click the frame and pick

8

Properties from the pop-up menu. You'll get a dialog box that allows you to specify the display time in hundredths of a second.

5. One final detail, and your animation will be done! Select Edit, Animation Properties (alternatively, right-click the gray area below the filmstrip and pick Properties from the pop-up menu) to get the Animation Properties dialog box. I want my flames to flicker as long as someone is viewing my animation, so I chose Repeat the Animation Indefinitely. In some cases, however, you may want your animation sequence to play only once (or some other number of times) before stopping to display the last frame as a still image. In that case, you'd select the second choice and enter the number of repetitions.

6. Your animation is complete. Select File, Save As to save it. You are presented with a slider control that allows you to choose a balance between good image quality and small file size. Animation Shop usually does an excellent job of choosing the most appropriate optimizations for you based on the slider setting. Move the slider up for better image quality, down for smaller file size.

How do you decide where it goes? Animation Shop helps there, too. Pick a setting and click Next. After some chugging and crunching, you'll see a report like the one shown in Figure 8.14. This makes it much easier for you to decide how big too big is and return to adjust the slider by clicking Back. When the file size seems acceptable, click Finish.

FIGURE 8.14

This report helps you decide whether you found the right balance of image quality versus file size.

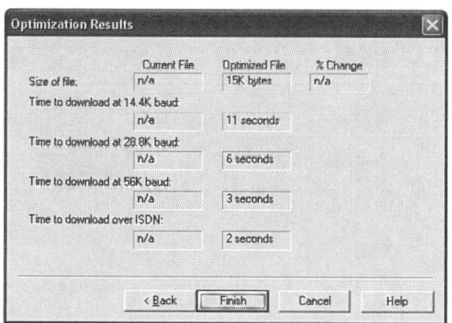

Generating Transitions and Text Effects

Animation Shop (like some other GIF animation programs) can do much more than just collect multiple GIF images into a single animation file. It can also generate some impressive special effects and even create scrolling text banners all by itself. There's not room in this book to explain in detail how to use these features, but they're easy enough that you can probably pick it up on your own with a little help from the Animation Shop online help system.

Just to get you started, Figures 8.15 and 8.16 show a transition and text effect being con-structed. One uses the image transition feature (Effects, Insert Image Transition) to dis-solve between a picture of the word ATTENTION and a picture of the word WARNING. (I made these two pictures in Paint Shop Pro ahead of time.) The other uses text transitions (Effects, Insert Text Effect) to scroll the words NO SPONTANEOUS COMBUSTION smoothly across a white background. This didn't require any images at all, since the text transition effects generate their own pictures of the text as they do their magic.

FIGURE 8.15

Use Effects, Insert Image Transition to generate fades, wipes, dissolves, and other automatic transitions between images.

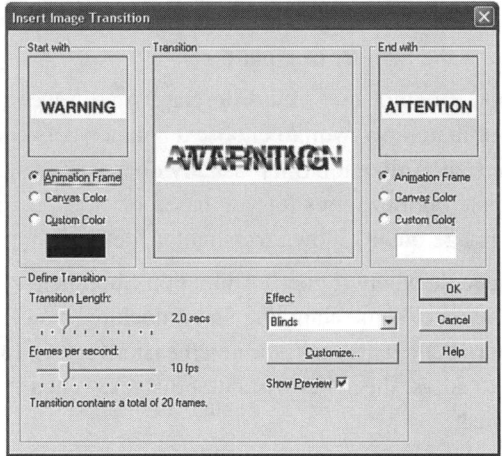

FIGURE 8.16

Use Effects, Insert Text Effect to generate mov-ing text and special-effect text over a frame or a set of frames.

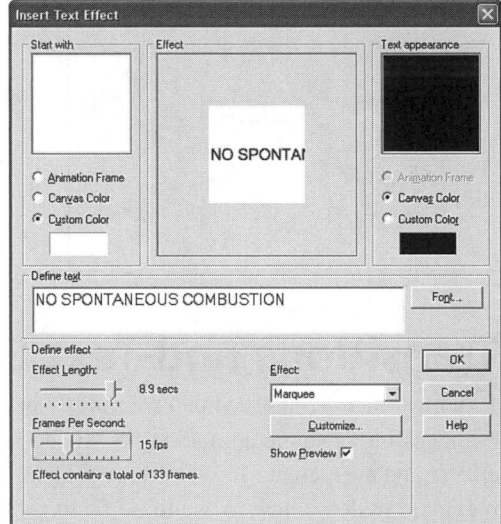

Once you get started with Web page animation, it's hard not to get carried away. I couldn't resist adding a flashing neon sign to the *24-Hour HTML Café*. In the examples page for this hour (http://www.24hourHTMLcafe.com/hour8/), you'll also find links to several other animations that you are welcome to reuse for your own pages. (The book that turns its own pages is especially popular.)

Summary

In this hour you learned the basics of preparing graphics for use on Web pages. You saw how to download and use the popular graphics program Paint Shop Pro when working with photos, banners, buttons, and other Web page images (though the techniques you learned will work with many other graphics programs as well). You also found out how to decide among the various graphics file formats used for Web page graphics, and how to make images that appear in stages, for the illusion of speed.

Q&A

Q Shouldn't I just hire a graphics artist to design my pages instead of learning all this stuff?

A If you have plenty of money and need a visually impressive site—or if you think that ugly building with chartreuse trim that people are always complaining about actually looks pretty nice—hiring some professional help might not be a bad idea. Remember, however, that you probably know what you want better than anyone else does, which often counts more than artistic skills in producing a good Web page.

Q I've produced graphics for printing on paper. Is making Web page graphics much different?

A Yes. In fact, many of the rules for print graphics are reversed on the Web. Web page graphics have to be low-resolution, while print graphics should be as high-resolution as possible. White washes out black on computer screens, while black bleeds into white on paper. Also, someone may stop a Web page when only half the graphics are done. Try to avoid falling into old habits if you've done a lot of print graphics design.

Q I have a Windows AVI video clip. Can I turn it into a GIF animation?

A Yes. Simply open the AVI file with Animation Shop to convert it to a GIF animation. (You are given the option to reduce the number of frames; it's usually a good idea to sample every third frame or so to keep the file size down to reasonable pro-portions.) You can also embed AVI files directly into Web pages, as discussed in Hour 20, "Embedding Multimedia in Web Pages."

Workshop

The workshop contains quiz questions and activities to help you solidify your under-standing of the material covered. Try to answer all questions before looking at the "Answers" section that follows.

Quiz

1. Suppose you have a scanned picture of a horse that you need to put on a Web page. How big should you make it, and in what file format should you save it?

2. Your company logo is a black letter Z with a red circle behind it. What size should you draw or scan it, and in what file format should you save it for use on your Web page?

3. Should you save a 100×50 pixel button graphic as an interlaced GIF file?

4. How would you modify a GIF animation that repeats infinitely to instead play only three times before stopping?

Answers

1. Depending on how important the image is to your page, as small as 100×40 pixels or as large as 300×120 pixels. The JPEG format, with about 50 percent compres-sion, would be best.

2. About 100×100 pixels is generally good for a logo, but a simple graphic like that will compress very well; you could make it up to 300×300 pixels if you want. Save it as a 16-color GIF file.

3. No. A small file like that will load just as fast or faster without interlacing.

4. Using Paint Shop Pro, for example, you first open the animation in Animation Shop; select Edit, Animation Properties; choose Play It and enter the number 3.

Exercises

- If you have an archive of company (or personal) photos, look through it to find a few that might enhance your Web site. Scan them (or send them out to be scanned) so that you'll have a library of graphics all ready to draw from as you produce more pages in the future. If you have photos taken on a digital camera, you can obviously skip the scan step and jump straight into prepping the images for your Web pages.

- Before you start designing graphics for an important business site, try spicing up your own personal home page. This will give you a chance to learn Paint Shop Pro (or your other graphics software) so you'll look like you know what you're doing when you tackle it at work.

8

HOUR 9

Putting Graphics on a Web Page

In Hour 8, "Creating Your Own Web Page Graphics," you learned how to make digital images for your Web pages, both still and animated. This hour shows you how easy it is to put those graphics on your pages with HTML. Fortunately, there is nothing special you have to do to place an animated image on a Web page, as compared to a still image.

To Do

You should get two or three images ready now so you can try putting them on your own pages as you follow along with this hour.

If you have some image files already saved in the GIF or JPEG format (the filenames will end in `.gif` or `.jpg`), use those. Otherwise, you can just grab some graphics I've put on the Internet for you to practice with. Here's how:

1. Enter the following address into your Web browser:

   `http://www.24hourHTMLcafe.com/hour9/images.htm`

   You should see a page with four images of hats and stars at the bottom.

▼   2. Save each of the graphics to your computer's hard drive by right-clicking each image (or holding down the mouse button if you use a Macintosh computer), and then selecting Save Image As from the pop-up menu. Put the graphics on your hard drive in whichever folder you use for creating Web pages.

3. As you read this lesson, use these image files to practice putting images on your pages. (It's also fine to use any graphics you created while reading the previous

▲   lesson.)

At the *24-Hour HTML Café*, you'll find live links to many graphics and multi-media hot lists and sites, where you can find ready-to-use graphics. To access these links, go to http://www.24hourHTMLcafe.com/hotsites.htm.

The familiar Web search engines and directories such as yahoo.com, hotbot.com, and infoseek.go.com can become a gold mine of graphics images just by leading you to sites related to your own theme. They can also help you discover the oodles of sites specifically dedicated to providing free and cheap access to reusable media collections. Also, don't forget Microsoft's massive clip art library, Design Gallery Live, which is located at http://dgl.microsoft.com/.

Placing an Image on a Web Page

To put an image on a Web page, first move the image file into the same folder as the HTML text file. Insert the following HTML tag at the point in the text where you want the image to appear. Use the name of your image file instead of *myimage.gif*:

```
<img src="myimage.gif" />
```

Listing 9.1, for example, inserts several images at the top and bottom of the page. Whenever a Web browser displays the HTML file in Listing 9.1, it will automatically retrieve and display the image files as shown in Figure 9.1.

LISTING 9.1   Use the `<img />` Tag

```
<html>
<head><title>ZOLZOL's New &amp; Used Planets</title></head>
<body>
<img src="zolzol2.jpg" alt="Friendly Fen" />
<img src="zolsign2.gif" alt="ZOLZOL New and Used Planets" />
<img src="zolzol1.jpg" alt="Honest Han" />
<h1><img src="zolmodel.gif" alt="HomeStar 12" />
The HomeStar Model 12</h1>
```

LISTING 9.1 continued

```
<h3><i>Manufactured Home Planets for Today's Lifeforms</i></h3>
<p>Tired of sinking endless time and resources into the same
old run-down ecosystem? Maybe it's time to think about the
<b>modern solution</b> to all your environmental problems!
Why spend a fortune on another filthy, volcano-stained planet
riddled with unsightly hurricanes and lightning storms, when
you can own a <b>factory new</b> manufactured planet for a
fraction of the price? We custom-build each HomeStar Model 12
to your race's specifications, with your choice of sky and
ground colors, synthetic Sim Veg landscaping, and odor-free
Quick-Gro hydroponic agricultural systems. Call ZOLZOL's for
a <b>free quotation</b> today!</p>
<p><small>(Orbital installation may incur additional fees, and
may require local zoning permits.)</small></p>
<div align="center">
<a href="zolzol.htm"><img src="zolhome.gif" border="0"
alt="ZOLZOL Home Page" /><br />
Click here for more bargains!</a></div>
</body></html>
```

FIGURE 9.1

When a Web browser displays the HTML page in Listing 9.1, it adds the images named zolzol2.jpg, zol-sign2.gif, zolzol1.jpg, zolmodel.gif, *and* zolhome.gif.

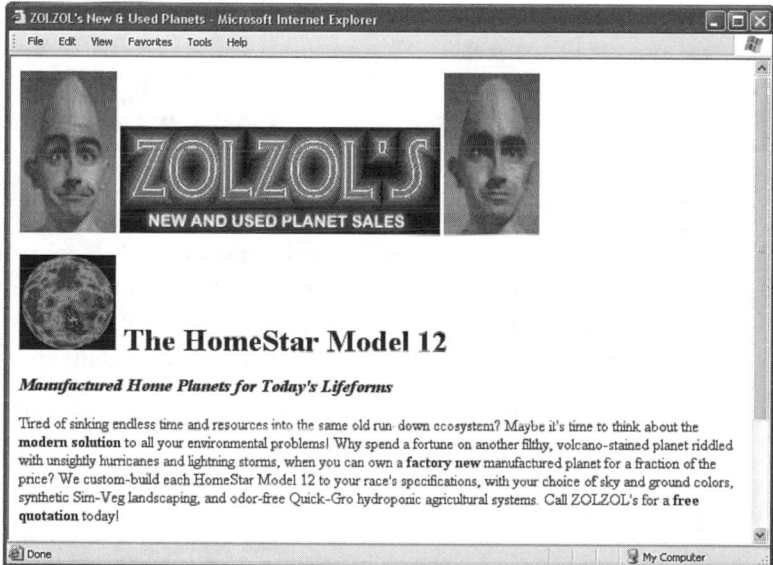

If you guessed that img stands for *image*, you're right; src stands for *source*, which is a reference to the location of the image file. (As discussed in Hour 1, "Understanding HTML and XHTML," a Web page image is always stored in a separate file from the text, even though it appears to be part of the same page when viewed in a browser.)

Just as with the `<a href>` tag (covered in Hour 3, "Linking to Other Web Pages"), you can specify any complete Internet address as the `<img src>`. Alternatively, you can specify just the filename if an image will be located in the same directory folder as the HTML file. You may also use relative addresses such as `photos/birdy.jpg` or `../smiley.gif`.

Theoretically, you can include an image from any Internet Web page within your own pages. For example, you could include a picture of my family by putting the following on your Web page:

`<img src="http://www.netletter.com/dicko/olivers.gif" />`

The image would be retrieved from my server computer whenever your page was displayed. You could do this, but you shouldn't! Not only is it bad manners (it often costs people money whenever you pull something from their server computer), it can also make your pages display more slowly. You also have no way of controlling whether the image has been changed or deleted.

If someone gives you permission to republish an image from one of his pages, always transfer a copy of that image to your computer and use a local file reference such as `<img src="olivers.gif" />`. In other words, you should host all images used on your pages.

Describing an Image with Text

Each `<img />` tag in Listing 9.1 includes a short text message, such as `alt="friendly fen"`. The `alt` stands for *alternate text* because this message will appear in place of the image if a user turns off automatic image downloading in her Web browser preferences. Everyone else will see the message you put in the `alt` attribute too—because graphics files sometimes take a while to transfer over the Internet, most Web browsers show the text on a page first with the `alt` messages in place of the graphics (as shown in Figure 9.2).

Even after the graphics replace the `alt` messages, the `alt` message typically appears in a little box whenever the mouse pointer passes over an image. The `alt` message also helps anyone who is visually impaired (or is using a voice-based telephone interface to read the Web page).

You should include a suitable `alt` attribute in every `<img />` tag on your Web pages, keeping in mind the variety of situations where people might see that message. A very brief description of the image is usually best, but Web page authors sometimes put short advertising messages or subtle humor in their `alt` messages. For small or unimportant images, it's tempting to omit the `alt` message altogether, but I should point out that it is technically a required attribute of the `<img />` tag. This doesn't mean your page won't display properly, but it does mean you'll be in violation of the latest XHTML standards. I recommend assigning an empty text message to `alt` if you absolutely don't need it (`alt=""`).

FIGURE 9.2

People will see the `alt` *messages while they wait for the graphics to appear.*

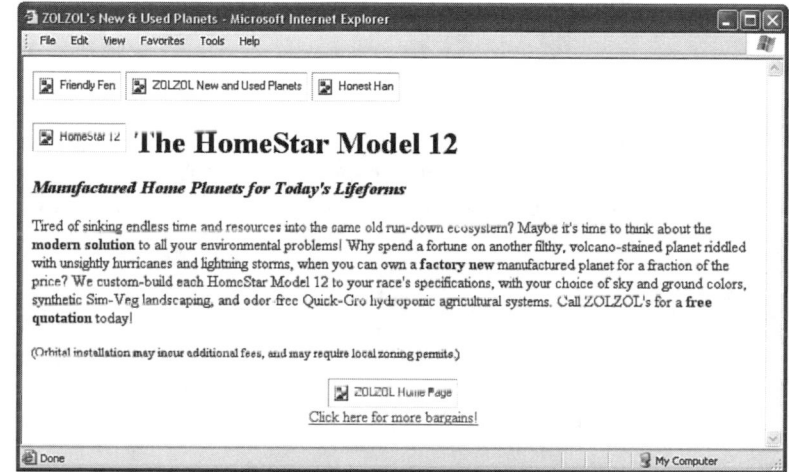

Not every `<img />` tag in this book adheres to the rule about the `alt` attribute being a requirement. It's not that I've been lazy; it's just sometimes easier to explain a point without adding in extra code. In real Web pages, you should try hard to always provide an `alt` attribute for every `<img />` tag. This also applies to the `src` attribute of the `<img />` tag, which is required as well. Of course, the `<img />` tag wouldn't be very useful without the `src` attribute, so this one is a little more obvious.

Turning Images into Links

You can make any image into a clickable link to another page with the same `<a href>` tag used to make text links. Figure 9.2 shows an example; clicking the big button at the bottom of the page (or the words `Click here for more bargains!`) retrieves the page named `zolzol.htm`.

Normally, Web browsers draw a colored rectangle around the edge of each image link. Like text links, the rectangle usually appears blue to people who haven't visited the link recently, and purple to people who have. Since you seldom, if ever, want this unsightly line around your beautiful buttons, you should usually include `border="0"` in any `<img />` tag within a link. (You learn more about the `border` attribute in Hour 12, "Page Design and Layout.")

All the same linking rules and possibilities discussed in Hours 3 and 7 apply to image links exactly as they do for text links. (You can link to another part of the same page with `<a href="#name">` and `<a id="name">`, for example.)

Aligning Images

Similarly to text, images can be aligned on the page using special attributes. Not only can you align images horizontally, but you can also align them vertically with respect to text and other images that surround them.

Horizontal Image Alignment

As discussed in Hour 5, "Basic Text Alignment and Formatting," you can use `<div align="center">`, `<div align="right">`, and `<div align="left">` to align part of page to the center, right margin, or left margin. These tags affect both text and images.

For example, the last `<img />` tag in Listing 9.1 occurs between the `<div align="center">` tag and the closing `</div>` tag. This causes the image (as well as the text below it) to be centered on the page. Like text, images are normally lined up with the left margin unless a `<div align="center">` or `<div align="right">` tag indicates that they should be centered or right-justified. In other words, `left` is the default value of the `align` attribute.

As the first three images in Listing 9.2 and Figure 9.3 demonstrate, you can also use `<div align="center">` to center more than one image at a time. Since there are no `<br />` or `<p>` tags between them, the three images all appear on one line and the entire line is centered horizontally in the browser window.

You can also make text wrap around images, as the paragraph around the pictures of Mars and Venus in the lower-middle part of Figure 9.3 does. You do this by including an `align` attribute within the `<img />` tag itself, as shown in the fifth and sixth `<img />` tags in Listing 9.2, which I've repeated here for clarity:

```
<img src="zolmoon.gif" align="absmiddle" />
<img src="zolsol4.gif" align="right" />
```

`<img align="left" />` aligns the image to the left and causes text to wrap around the right side of it. As you'd expect, `<img align="right" />` aligns the image to the right and causes text to wrap around the left side of it.

You can't use <img align="center" /> because text won't wrap around a centered image. You must use <div align="center"> if you want an image to be centered on the page, as I did with the top image in Figure 9.3.

> Notice that align means something different in an <img /> tag than it does in a <div> tag. <img align="right" /> will align an image to the right and cause any text that follows to wrap around the image. <div align="right" />, on the other hand, just controls the alignment and never causes text to wrap around images.

Vertical Image Alignment

Sometimes, you may want to insert a small image right in the middle of a line of text; or you might like to put a single line of text next to an image as a caption. In either case, it would be handy to have some control over how the text and images line up vertically. Should the bottom of the image line up with the bottom of the letters, or should the text and images all be arranged so their middles line up? You can choose between these and several other options:

- To line up the top of an image with the top of the tallest image or letter on the same line, use <img align="top" />.

- To line up the bottom of an image with the bottom of the text, use <img align="bottom" />.

- To line up the bottom of an image with the bottom of the lowest image or letter on the same line, use <img align="absbottom" />. (If there are some larger images on the same line, align="absbottom" might place an image lower than align="bottom".)

- To line up the middle of an image with the baseline of the text, use <img align="middle" />.

- To line up the middle of an image with the overall vertical center of everything on the line, use <img align="absmiddle" />. This might be higher or lower than align="middle", depending upon the size and alignment of other images on the same line.

Three of these options are illustrated in Listing 9.2 and Figure 9.3. The ZOLZOL's logo is aligned with the top of the photos on either side of it by using align="top"; the picture of the water planet uses align="middle" to line up the baseline of the words Sol III with the center of the Earth; and the little image of the moon is lined up in the exact center of the text around it using align="absmiddle".

If you don't include any align attribute in an `<img />` tag, the image will line up with the bottom of any text next to it. That means you never actually have to type in `align="bottom"` because it is assumed by default.

In fact, you probably won't use any of the vertical alignment settings much; the vast majority of Web page images use either `align="left"`, `align="right"`, or no align attribute at all. Don't worry about memorizing all these options—you can always refer to this book if you ever do need them.

LISTING 9.2   Horizontal Alignment, Vertical Alignment, and Text Wrapping

```html
<html>
<head><title>ZOLZOL's New &amp; Used Planets</title></head>
<body>
<div align="center">
<img src="zolzol2.jpg" />
<img src="zolsign2.gif" align="top" />
<img src="zolzol1.jpg" /></div>
<h1><img src="zolsol3.gif" align="middle" /> Sol III</h1>
<h3><i>A real water planet at a desert planet price!</i></h3>
<p>This baby has its <b>original ecosystem</b> still installed,
and comes pre-populated by a technologically-savvy <b>ideal
slave species</b>! <i>PLUS:</i> <b>atmospheric oxygen</b>,
plenty of hydrocarbons, <b>H<sub>2</sub>O by the gigaton</b>,
and a wide range of metals, all pre-mined and ready for
off-planet shipment asan <b>immediate source of income</b>
for you and your families! So pack up the kids, hop in the
battlecruiser, and move onto this barely-used world today!
Did we mention the huge, close moon?
<img src="zolmoon.gif" align="absmiddle" />
<b>What a space base!</b> Don't let this once-in-a-millenium
opportunity pass you buy: <b> call ZOLZOL's</b> to place your
bid for Sol III* <b>right now!</b></p>
<p><img src="zolsol2.gif" align="left" />
<img src="zolsol4.gif" align="right" />
(And don't forget to bid on Sol III's sister planets, Sol II and
Sol IV! With a little investment in these great fixer-uppers, you
could have the <b>three-planet home of your
dreams</b> for one low price. <b>Call NOW!</b>)</p>
<br clear="all" /><hr />
<p><small><b>*Disclaimer:</b> One or more races on this planet
may possess chemical and/or nuclear weapons. All sales are final.
Invasion and enslavement of native species is the sole
responsibility of the customer and ZolZol's makes no warrantees,
expressed or implied. ZolZol believes this planet to be in
inhabititable condition, but some environmental degradation is
normal for speciated worlds.</small></p>
```

LISTING 9.2 continued

```
<div align="center">
<a href="zolzol.htm"><img src="zolhome.gif" border="0" /></a>
<a href="zolnew.htm"><img src="zolnew.gif" border="0" /></a>
<a href="zoljunk.htm"><img src="zoljunk.gif" border="0" /></a>
</div>
</body></html>
```

9

FIGURE 9.3

The HTML page listed in Listing 9.2, as it appears in a Web browser.

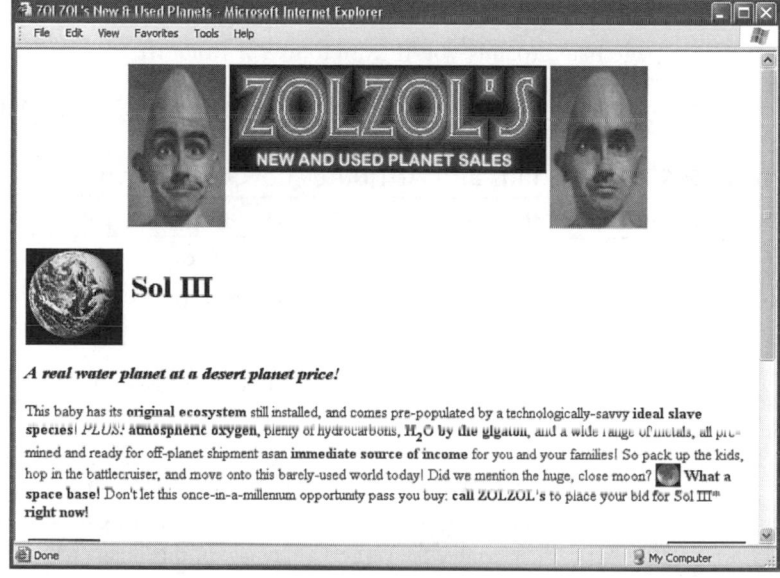

To Do

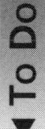

Try adding some images to your Web pages now, and experiment with all the different values of align. To get you started, here's a quick review of how to add the magic hat image to any Web page. (See the "To Do" section at the beginning of this hour for help downloading the magic hat image.)

- Copy the magic.gif image file to the same directory folder as the HTML file.

- With a text editor, add <img src="magic.gif" alt="Magic Hat"/> where you want the image to appear in the text.

- If you want the image to be centered, put <div align="center"> before the <img /> tag and </div> after it. To wrap text around the image instead, add align="right" or align="left" to the <img /> tag.

- If you have time for a little more experimentation, try combining multiple images of various sizes (such as the stars and the magic hats) with various vertical alignment settings.

Summary

This hour has shown you how to use the `<img />` tag to place graphics images on your Web pages. You learned to include a short text message to appear in place of the image as it loads and to appear whenever someone moves their mouse pointer over the image. You also learned to control the horizontal and vertical alignment of each image and how to make text wrap around the left or right of an image.

Finally, you learned how to make images into "buttons" that link to other pages by using the same `<a>` tag introduced in Hour 3. You also got a sneak preview of the kind of custom page backgrounds you'll learn to use in Hour 10.

Table 9.1 summarizes the attributes of the `<img />` tag covered in this hour.

TABLE 9.1   HTML Tags and Attributes Covered in Hour 9

Tag/Attribute	Function
`<img />`	Places an image file within the page.
	Attributes
`src="..."`	The address or filename of the image.
`alt="..."`	A text message that is displayed in place of the image, or in a small box over the image.
`align="..."`	Determines the alignment of the given image. If `left` or `right`, the image is aligned to the left or right column, and all following text flows beside that image. All other values, such as `top`, `middle`, `bottom`, `absmiddle`, or `absbottom`, determine the vertical alignment of this image with other items in the same line.

Q&A

Q I found a nice image on a Web page on the Internet. Can I just use Save Image As to save a copy and then put the image on my Web pages?

A It's easy to do that, but unfortunately it's also illegal in most countries if you don't have permission to reuse the image; of course, this excludes images found on royalty-free clip art Web sites. You should first get written permission from the original creator of the image. Most Web pages include the author's email address, which makes it a simple matter to ask for permission—a lot simpler than going to court!

Q **How long a message can I put after `alt=` in an `<img />` tag?**

A Theoretically, as long as you want. For practicality, you should keep the message short enough so that it will fit in less space than the image itself. For big images, 10 words may be fine. For small images, a single word is better.

Q **I used the `<img />` tag just like you said, but all I get is a little box with an X or some shapes in it when I view the page. What's wrong?**

A The broken image icon you're seeing can mean one of two things: Either the Web browser couldn't find the image file, or the image isn't saved in a format the browser can understand. To solve either one of these problems, open the image file by using Paint Shop Pro (or your favorite graphics software), select Save As, and be sure to save the file in either the GIF or JPEG format. Also make sure you save it in the same folder as the Web page that contains the `<img />` tag referring to it and that the filename on the disk precisely matches the filename you put in the `<img />` tag (including capitalization).

Q **How do I control both the horizontal and vertical alignment of an image at once?**

A The short answer is that you can't. For example, if you type `<img align="right" align="middle" src="myimage.gif">`, the `align="middle"` will be ignored.

There are ways around this limitation, however. In Part IV, "Web Page Design," you will discover several techniques for positioning text and images exactly where you want them in both horizontal and vertical directions. You can think of the align attribute as a quick and simple, yet limited method of aligning images and text.

Q **Why do the examples in this book put a slash at the end of every `<img />` tag? None of the Web pages I see on the Internet do that.**

A As discussed in Hour 2 (yes, I know that was a long time ago), the new XML and XTHML standards require any tag that doesn't have a closing tag to include a slash at the end. Though it may be unlikely that anyone will ever write software that fails to accept the traditional `<img>` tag without the slash, I use `<img />` just to be on the safe side. (Remember, people once thought it was unlikely that four-digit year codes for dates would ever be necessary in the software they were writing...)

Workshop

The workshop contains quiz questions and activities to help you solidify your understanding of the material covered. Try to answer all questions before looking at the "Answers" section that follows.

Quiz

1. How would you insert an image file named `elephant.jpg` at the very top of a Web page?

2. How would you make the word `Elephant` appear whenever the actual `elephant.jpg` image couldn't be displayed by a Web browser?

3. Write the HTML to make the `elephant.jpg` image appear on the right side of the page, with a big headline reading `"Elephants of the World Unite!"` on the left side of the page next to it.

4. Write the HTML to make a tiny image of a mouse (named `mouse.jpg`) appear between the words `"Wee sleekit, cow'rin,"` and the words `"tim'rous beastie"`.

5. Suppose you have a large picture of a standing elephant named `elephant.jpg`. Now make a small image named `fly.jpg` appear to the left of the elephant's head and `mouse.jpg` appear next to the elephant's right foot.

Answers

1. Copy the image file into the same directory folder as the HTML text file, and type `<img src="elephant.jpg" alt="" />` immediately after the `<body>` tag in the HTML text file.

2. Use the following HTML:

   ```
   <img src="elephant.jpg" alt="elephant" />
   ```

3. ```
   <img src="elephant.jpg" align="right" />
   <h1>Elephants of the World Unite!</h1>
   ```

4. ```
   Wee sleekit, cow'rin,<img src="mouse.jpg" alt="" />tim'rous beastie
   ```

5. ```
   <img src="fly.jpg" alt="" align="top" />
   <img src="elephant.jpg" alt="" />
   <img src="mouse.jpg" alt="" />
   ```

Exercises

Try using any small image as a "bullet" to make lists with more flair. If you also want the list to be indented, use the `<dl>` definition list and `<dd>` for each item (instead of `<ul>` and `<li>`, which would give the standard boring bullets). Here's a quick example, using the `star.gif` file from my sample images page:

```
<dl><dd><img src="star.gif" />A murder of crows</dd>
<dd><img src="star.gif" />A rafter of turkeys</dd>
<dd><img src="star.gif" />A muster of peacocks</dd></dl>
```
```

Hour **10**

Custom Backgrounds and Colors

Nearly every sample Web page in Hours 1 through 9 has a white background and black text. In this hour, you'll find out how to make pages with background and text colors of your choosing. You'll also discover how to make your own custom background graphics and how to let the background show through parts of any image you put on your Web pages.

The World Wide Web Consortium (W3C)—the group that created the HTML 4 standard—recommends that you control the colors on your Web pages using style sheets instead of the regular HTML tags discussed in this hour.

In Hours 14 and 15 you'll learn all about using style sheets and why they are officially recommended. However, style sheets are a little more complex than the techniques you learn in this lesson, and they are fairly new in the grand scheme of the Web. So, it's helpful to know how to dress up pages the old way before you move on to learning the new way. Web browsers will likely support both approaches for the foreseeable future.

This hour also explains how to make transparent images and background tiles—techniques that will come in handy whether or not you are using style sheets.

To Do

The black-and-white figures printed in this book obviously don't convey colors very accurately, so you may want to view the sample pages online. You can also try the colors on your own Web pages as you read about how to make them.

To find all the examples from this hour online, go to
http://www.24hourHTMLcafe.com/hour10/.

Exploring Background and Text Colors

Specifying a background color other than white for a Web page is easier than you probably realize. For example, to specify blue as the background color for a page, put bgcolor="blue" inside the <body> tag. Of course, you can use many colors other than blue. You can choose from the 16 standard Windows colors: black, white, red, green, blue, yellow, magenta, cyan, purple, gray, lime, maroon, navy, olive, silver, and teal. (You can call magenta by the name *fuchsia* and cyan by the name *aqua* if you want to feel more artsy and less geeky.)

You can also specify colors for text and links in the <body> tag. For example, in Figure 10.1 you'll notice the following <body> tag:

```
<body bgcolor="teal" text="fuchsia" link="yellow" vlink="lime" alink="red">
```

As you probably guessed, text="fuchsia" makes the text fuchsia (which is the same as magenta). There are three separate attributes for link colors:

- link="yellow" makes links that haven't been visited recently yellow.
- vlink="lime" makes recently visited links lime green.
- alink="red" makes links briefly blink red when someone clicks them.

Here's a neat trick: If you make the vlink color the same as the bgcolor color, links to pages that a visitor has already seen will become invisible. This can make your page seem "smart"—offering people only links to places they haven't been. (Note, however, that it may also annoy anybody who wants to return to a page they've already seen! In other words, use this trick with caution.)

Listing 10.1 and Figure 10.1 illustrate how color can be used in combination with links. Because I used pure, beautiful teal as the background color in the graphics images, they blend right into the background of the Web page. (I didn't need to use transparent images, which you'll learn about later in this hour.)

LISTING 10.1   Specifying Color in the <body> Tag

```
<html><head><title>The Teal and the Fuchsia</title></head>
<body bgcolor="teal" text="fuchsia"
 link="yellow" vlink="lime" alink="red">
<img src="c.gif" align="right" />
<h1><a href="index.htm">CREDLEY HIGH SCHOOL</a></h1>
<h2>"The Old Teal and Fuchsia"</h2>
<div align="center">
<i><b>Oh, hail! Hail! Sing Credley!<br />
Our colors jump and shout!<br />
Deep teal like ocean's highest waves,<br />
Fuchsia like blossoms bursting out!</b></i>
<p><i><b><img src="cheer.gif" align="left" />
As Credley conquers every team<br />
So do our brilliant colors peal<br />
From mountain tops &amp; florist shops<br />
Sweet sacred fuchsia, holy teal!</b></i></p>
<p><i><b>Our men are tough as vinyl siding<br />
Our women, strong as plastic socks<br />
Our colors tell our story truly<br />
We may be ugly, but we rock!</b></i></p>
</div></body></html>
```

FIGURE 10.1

On a color screen, this ever-so-attractive page has a teal background, fuchsia body text, and yellow link text, as specified in Listing 10.1.

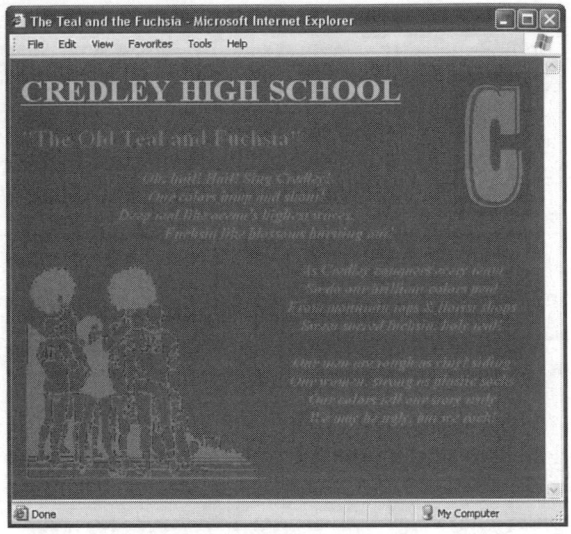

Specifying Custom Colors

If the 16 named colors don't include the exact hue you're after, you can mix your own custom colors by specifying how much red, green, and blue light should be mixed into each color. It works a little bit like Play-Doh—just mix in the amounts of red, blue, and green you want to get the appropriate color.

The format is `#rrggbb` where `rr`, `gg`, and `bb` are two-digit hexadecimal values for the red, green, and blue components of the color. If you're not familiar with hexadecimal numbers, don't sweat it. Just remember that `ff` is the maximum and `00` is the minimum, and use one of the following codes for each component:

- `ff` means full brightness
- `cc` means 80 percent brightness
- `99` means 60 percent brightness
- `66` means 40 percent brightness
- `33` means 20 percent brightness
- `00` means none of this color component

For example, bright red is `#ff0000`, dark green is `#003300`, bluish-purple is `#660099`, and medium-gray is `#999999`. To make a page with a red background, dark green text, and bluish-purple links that turn white when you click them and gray when you've visited them, the HTML would look like the following:

```
<body bgcolor="#ff0000" text="#003300" link="#660099" alink="#ffffff"
vlink="#999999">
```

Though the colors you specify in the `<body>` tag apply to all text on the page, you can also use either color names or hexadecimal color codes to change the color of a particular word or section of text by using the `<font>` tag. This is discussed in Hour 6, "Advanced Text Formatting."

For a very handy chart showing the 216 most commonly used hexadecimal color codes, along with the colors they create, go to `http://www.24hourHTMLcafe.com/colors/`.

You can then choose any of the standard 16 text colors to see how each of them looks as compared to every color in the table.

You should be aware that different computer monitors may display colors in very different hues. I recently designed a page with a beautiful blue background for a company I work for, only to find out later that the president of the company saw it on his computer as a lovely purple background! Neutral, earth-tone colors such as medium gray, tan, and ivory can lead to even more unpredictable results on many computer monitors, and may even seem to change color on one monitor depending on lighting conditions in the room and the time of day.

The moral of the story: Try to stick to the named colors and don't waste time mucking with hexadecimal color codes, unless you have precise control over your intended audience's computer displays or your willing to test your page on a variety of different monitors. Of course, testing your pages on different computers is very important, and should be done anyway.

You can set the color of an individual link to a different color than the rest by putting a `<font>` tag with a `color` attribute *after* the `<a href>`. (Also include a `</font>` tag before the `</a>` tag.) For example, the following would make a green link:

```
Visit the <a href="thumb.htm"><font color="green">Green
Thumb page</font></a> to become a better gardener.
```

Using Background Image Tiles

Background tiles let you specify an image to be used as a wallpaper pattern behind all text and graphics in a document. You put the image filename after `background=` in the `<body>` tag at the beginning of your page:

```
<body background="image.jpg">
```

Like other Web graphics, background tiles must be in either the GIF or JPEG file format, and you can create them by using Paint Shop Pro or any other graphics software. For example, the tile.gif file referred to by the <body> tag in Listing 10.2 is an image of one small tile. As you can see in Figure 10.2, most Web browsers will repeat the image behind any text and images on the page, like floor tile.

LISTING 10.2 Tiling Background Images with the background Attribute of the <body> Tag

```
<html><head><title>Motawi Tileworks</title></head>
<body background="tile.gif">
<img src="mtworks.gif" />
<p><img src="motawis.gif" align="left" />
Karim and Nawal Motawi (brother and sister) welcome you to
<a href="http://www.motawi.com">Motawi Tileworks</a>, an art tile
studio specializing in the Arts &amp; Crafts style. We create
low-relief and polychrome tiles as accents and as art pieces, as
well as many varieties of flat tiles, architectural borders, trims,
and custom pieces.</p>
<div align="center">
<h2><a href="http://www.motawi.com">www.motawi.com</a></h2>
33 North Staebler, Suite 2, Ann Arbor, MI 48103<br />
tel: (734) 213-0017 fax: (734) 213-2569
</div></body></html>
```

FIGURE 10.2

The tile.gif file (specified in Listing 10.2 and shown in Figure 10.3) is automatically repeated to cover the entire page.

Tiled background images should be implemented with great care to avoid distracting from the main content of the page itself. Many pages on the Web are almost impossible to read due to overdone backgrounds.

Before you include your company logo or baby pictures as wallpaper behind your Web pages, stop and think. If you had an important message to send someone on a piece of paper, would you write it over the top of the letterhead logo or on the blank part of the page? Backgrounds should be like fine papers: attractive, yet unobtrusive.

Working with Transparent Images

You will see how to make your own background tiles later in this hour, but first a word about how to let the background show through parts of your foreground graphics.

Web page images are always rectangular. However, the astute observer of Figure 10.2 (that's you) will notice that the background tiles show through portions of the images, and therefore the title and picture don't look rectangular at all. This works because portions of the image are transparent, which allows the background to show through. You'll often want to use partially transparent images to make graphics look good over any background color or background image tile.

Figure 10.3 shows the images from Figure 10.2, as they looked in Paint Shop Pro when I created them. (Figure 10.3 also shows the single tile used for the background in Figure 10.2.)

FIGURE 10.3

When I saved two of these images in Paint Shop Pro, I made the background color transparent. (The third image, at the lower right, is the background tile.)

To make part of an image transparent, the image must have 256 or fewer colors, and you must save it in the GIF file format. (JPEG images can't be made transparent.) Most graphics programs that support the GIF format allow you to specify one color to be transparent.

It's worth mentioning that there is another image format newer than GIF that is rapidly gaining acceptance on the Web. I'm referring to the PNG format (pronounced "ping"), which is also ideally suited for illustrative images and images with transparency. In fact, the PNG format is superior to GIF in many ways, especially in regard to transparency. As the PNG format becomes more widely accepted, expect to see more and more Web pages designed to use PNG images instead of GIF images. All of the latest Web browsers already support PNG images. For more information on the PNG image format, visit `http://www.libpng.org/pub/png/pngintro.html`.

To Do

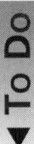

Follow these steps to save a transparent GIF in Paint Shop Pro:

1. Select Colors, Decrease Color Depth, 256 Colors (8-bit) or Colors, Decrease Color Depth, 16 Colors (4-bit), and check the Optimized Octree and Nearest Color boxes. (This is recommended in Hour 8, "Creating Your Own Web Page Graphics.")

2. Choose the eyedropper tool and right-click the color you want to make transparent.

3. Select Colors, View Palette Transparency. If any part of the image is already set to be transparent, you will see a gray checkered pattern in that part now.

4. Select Colors, Set Palette Transparency.

5. You should see the dialog box shown in Figure 10.4. Choose Set the Transparency Value to the Current Background Color, and then click OK.

6. The transparent parts of the image turn to a gray checkerboard pattern. (If you hadn't already selected View Palette Transparency in step 3, you would need to click the Proof button shown in Figure 10.4 to see the transparency effect.)

7. You can use any of the painting tools to touch up parts of the image where there is too little or too much of the transparent background color.

8. When everything looks right, select File, Save As (or File, Save Copy As) and choose CompuServe Graphics Interchange (*.gif) as the file type.

If you select Colors, View Palette Transparency (or when you click the Proof button as shown in Figure 10.4), Paint Shop Pro shows transparent regions of an image with a gray checkerboard pattern. You can change the grid size and colors used under File, Preferences, General Program Preferences, Transparency.

FIGURE 10.4

This dialog box appears when you select Colors, Set Palette Transparency. You will usually want the middle option.

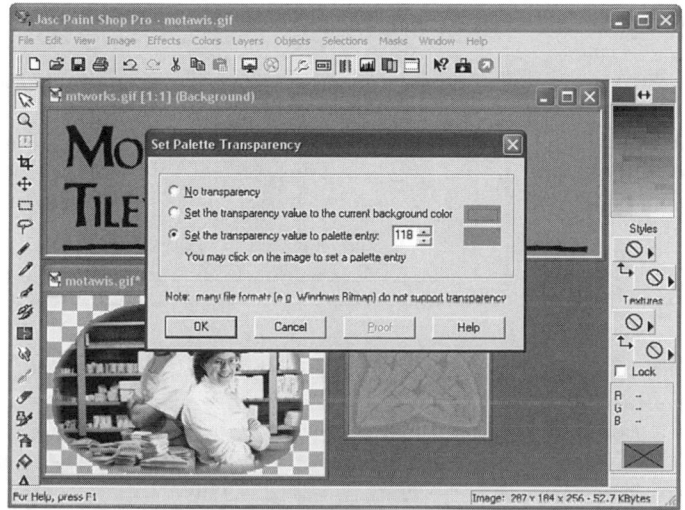

10

Creating Your Own Backgrounds

Any GIF or JPEG image can be used as a background tile. Pages look best, however, when the top edge of a background tile matches seamlessly with the bottom edge, and the left edge matches with the right.

If you're clever and have some time to spend on it, you can turn any image into a seamless tile by meticulously cutting and pasting, while touching up the edges. Paint Shop Pro provides a much easier way to automatically make any texture into a seamless tile: Simply use the rectangular selection tool to choose the area you want to make into a tile, and then choose Selections, Convert to Seamless Pattern. Paint Shop Pro crops the image and uses a sophisticated automatic procedure to overlay and blur together opposite sides of the image.

Figure 10.5 shows a section I cropped out of an image of the planet Jupiter, taken from a NASA image archive. The resulting tile—shown as the background of a Web page in Figure 10.6—tiles seamlessly, but has the tone and texture of the eye of Jove himself.

You'll find similar features in other graphics programs, including Photoshop (use Filter, Other, Offset with Wrap Turned On), Kai's Power Tools, and the Macintosh programs Mordant and Tilery.

FIGURE **10.5**

Paint Shop Pro can automatically take any region of an image and turn it into a background pattern that can be easily made into tiles.

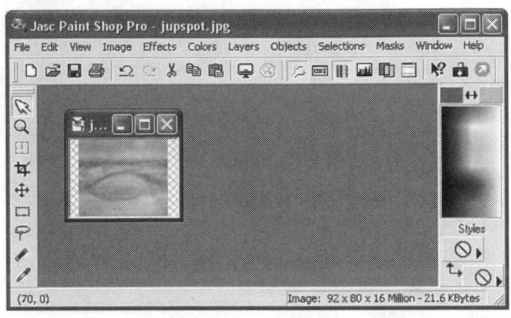

FIGURE **10.6**

These are the results of Figure 10.5 used as a background image for a Web page.

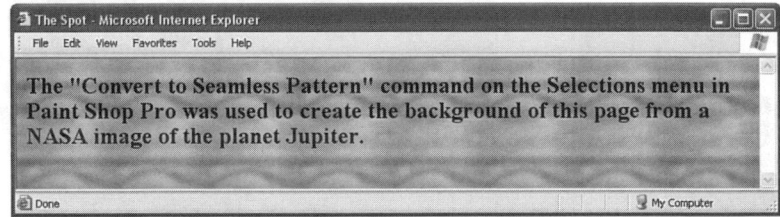

To Do

Here are some tips for making your own background tiles with Paint Shop Pro:

- If you have a scanner or digital camera, try using some textures from around the house or office, such as the top of a wooden desk, leaves of houseplants, or clothing.

- Using the Image, Blur, Blur More filter on an image (as I did with the Jupiter picture in Figures 10.5 and 10.6) before you turn it into a seamless tile will help it look better as a background. Using Colors, Adjust, Brightness and Contrast is usually also necessary to keep the background subtle in color variation.

- When you select an area to be turned into a tile, try to choose part of the image that is fairly uniform in brightness from side to side. Otherwise, the tile may not look seamless even after you use Convert to Seamless Pattern.

- You must also use an image big enough so that you can leave at least the width and height of the tile on either side of your selection. If you don't, when you select Convert to Seamless Pattern you'll get a message saying `Your selection is too close to the edge to complete this operation`.

- You can also make some almost-automatic textures with the paper texture feature in the paintbrush style palette in Paint Shop Pro. You can make great paper textures, too, by selecting Image, Noise, Add followed by Image, Blur, Blur and Colors, Colorize.

> If you just cannot seem to get the pattern you want, there are hundreds of sites on the Internet that offer public domain background images that are free or inexpensive and professionally designed.

Summary

In this hour you learned how to set the background and text colors for a Web page. You also found out how to make a tiled background image appear behind a Web page, how to make foreground images partially transparent so the background shows through, and how to create seamless image tiles for use as backgrounds.

Table 10.1 summarizes the attributes of the <body> tag discussed in this hour.

TABLE 10.1 Attributes of the *<body>* Tag Covered in Hour 10

Attributes	Function
`<body>...</body>`	Encloses the body (text and tags) of the HTML document
`background="..."`	The name or address of the image to tile on the page background
`bgcolor="..."`	The color of the page background
`text="..."`	The color of the page's text
`link="..."`	The color of unfollowed links
`alink="..."`	The color of activated links
`vlink="..."`	The color of followed links

Q&A

Q Don't Web browsers let people choose their own background and text color preferences?

A Yes, Web browsers allow users to override the colors you, as a Web page author, specify. Some may see your white-on-blue page as green-on-white or their own favorite colors instead, but very few people use this option. The colors specified in the <body> tag will usually be seen.

Q I've heard that there are 231 "browser-safe colors" that I should use on Web pages, and that I shouldn't use any other colors. Is that true?

A Here's the real story: There are 231 colors that will appear less "fuzzy" to people who operate their computers in a 256-color video mode. (The other 25 colors are used for menus and stuff like that.) Some Web page authors try to stick to those colors. However, true-color or high-color computer displays are all but standard these days, and they show all colors with equal clarity. So, if your graphics program can display color values in hexadecimal format, feel free to plug those codes straight into your pages for custom colors.

Q My background image looks okay in my graphics editing program, but has weird white or colored gaps or dots in it when it comes up behind a Web page. Why?

A There are two possibilities: If the background image you're using is a GIF file, it probably has transparency turned on, which makes one of the colors in the image turn white (or whatever color you specified in the `body bgcolor` attribute). The solution is to open the file with your graphics program and turn off the transparency. (In Paint Shop Pro, select Colors, Set Palette Transparency, and pick No transparency.) Resave the file.

If a JPEG or non-transparent GIF image looks spotty when you put it on a Web page, it may just be the Web browser's dithering. That's the method the software uses to try to show more colors than your system is set up to display at once by mixing colored dots together side-by-side. There's not much you can do about it, though you'll find hints for minimizing the problem in Hour 8, "Creating Your Own Web Page Graphics."

Workshop

The workshop contains quiz questions and activities to help you solidify your understanding of the material covered. Try to answer all questions before looking at the "Answers" section that follows.

Quiz

1. How would you give a Web page a black background and make all text, including links, bright green?

2. How would you make an image file named `texture.jpg` appear as a repeating tile behind the text and images on a Web page with white text and red links that turn blue after being followed?

3. If `elephant.jpg` is a JPEG image of an elephant standing in front of a solid white backdrop, how do you make the backdrop transparent so only the elephant shows on a Web page?

Answers

1. Put the following at the beginning of the Web page:

```
<body bgcolor="black"
text="lime" link="lime" vlink="lime" alink="black">
```

The following would do exactly the same thing:

```
<body bgcolor="#000000"
text="#00ff00" link="#00ff00" vlink="#00ff00" alink="#000000">
```

2.
```
<body background="texture.jpg"
text="white" link="red" vlink="blue" alink="black">
```

3. Open the image in Paint Shop Pro and then use Colors, Decrease Color Depth, 256 Colors to pick the best 256 colors for the image. Right-click the white area, select Colors, Set Palette Transparency; elect to make the background color transparent. Touch up any off-white spots that didn't become transparent and then use File, Save As to save it in the GIF 89a format.

Exercises

- Try getting creative with some background tiles that don't use Convert to Seamless Pattern. You'll discover some sneaky tricks for making background tiles that don't look like background tiles in Hour 12, "Page Design and Layout," but I bet you can figure out some interesting ones on your own right now. (Hint: What if you made a background tile 2,000 pixels wide and 10 pixels tall?)

- If you have some photos of objects for a Web-based catalog, consider taking the time to paint a transparent color carefully around the edges of them. (Sometimes the magic wand tool in your image editor can help automate this process.) You can also use Paint Shop Pro's Image, Effects, Drop Shadow feature to add a slight shadow behind or beneath each object, so it appears to stand out from the background.

10

Hour **11**

Graphical Links and Imagemaps

If you haven't been skipping around too much and you've read Hour 9, "Putting Graphics on a Web Page," you know how to make an image link to another document. (If you don't quite recall how to do it right now, it looks like this: `<a href="gohere.htm"><img src="image.gif" /></a>`.)

You can also divide an image into regions that link to different documents, depending upon where someone clicks. This is called an *imagemap*, and any image can be made into an imagemap. A Web site with medical information might show an image of the human body and bring up different pages of advice for each body part. A map of the world could allow people to click any country for regional information. Many people use imagemaps to create a "navigation bar" that integrates icons for each page on their Web site into one cohesive imagemap.

NEW TERM	An *imagemap* is an image on a Web page that leads to two or more different links, depending on which part of the image is clicked. Modern Web browsers use *client-side imagemaps*, but you can also create *server-side imagemaps* for compatibility with old browsers.

Netscape Navigator and Microsoft Internet Explorer allow you to choose between two different methods for implementing imagemaps. Nowadays, all your imagemaps should be done using the latest method, which is called a client-side imagemap. There really is no longer any reason to make them work the old-fashioned server-side way since Web browsers have been supporting client-side imagemaps for years.

Why Imagemaps Aren't Always Necessary

The first thing I must say about imagemaps is that you probably won't need to use them except in very special cases! It's almost always easier and more efficient to use several ordinary images, placed right next to one another, with a separate link for each image.

For example, imagine that you wanted to make a Web page that looks like Figure 11.1, with each of the glowing words leading to a different link. The obvious approach is to use a single imagemap for the entire central graphic. You'll see how to do that later this hour.

However, the better solution is to cut the graphic into pieces by using Paint Shop Pro (or any other graphics program) and make each piece a separate image on the Web page. This way, the page is compatible with all versions of all Web browsers without requiring any server scripting or advanced HTML. Figure 11.2 shows how to cut the picture so that each link area is a separate image. Listing 11.1 shows the HTML that creates the page in Figure 11.1, using the images in Figure 11.2.

FIGURE 11.1

You can create this page using ordinary <img /> *tags and* <a href> *links; imagemaps aren't always necessary.*

FIGURE 11.2

To avoid using imagemaps, you need to cut the image on the top left into the seven images on the right. (Cut and paste using the rectangular selection tool.)

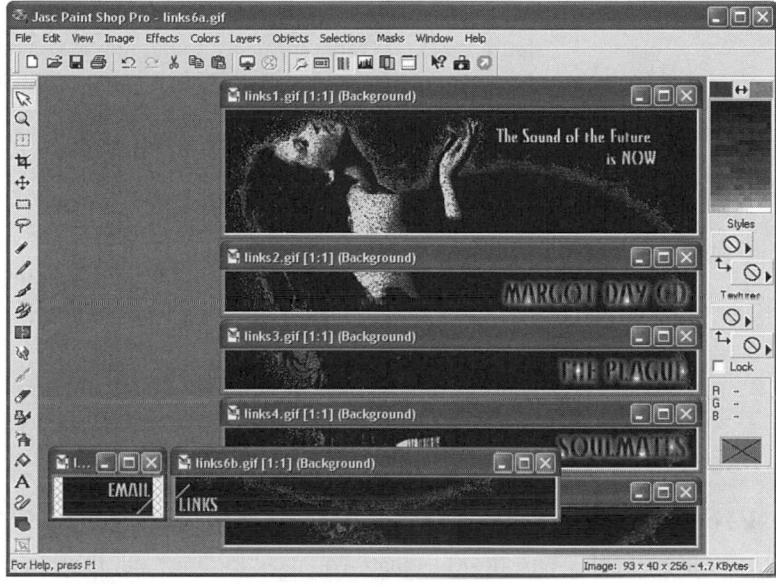

LISTING 11.1 Using the Images in Figure 11.2 to Implement the Page in Figure 11.1

```html
<html><head><title>FUTURE RECORDS</title></head>
<body bgcolor="#000008" background="fade2.gif" text="F0F0F0"
link="F000FF" vlink="8000F0" alink="8080FF">
<img src="future2.gif" width="320" height="108" alt="FUTURE RECORDS" />
<div align="center">
<img src="links1.gif" width="490" height="127"
   alt="The Sound of the Future is NOW" /><br />
<a href="http://www.margotday.com/margotcd.htm"><img
   src="links2.gif" width="490" height="40" border="0"
   alt="MARGOT DAY CD" /></a><br />
<a href="http://www.margotday.com/plague.htm"><img
   src="links3.gif" width="490" height="40" border="0"
   alt="THE PLAGUE" /></a><br />
<a href="http://www.margotday.com/soulmate.htm"><img
   src="links4.gif" width="490" height="40" border="0"
   alt="SOULMATES" /></a><br />
<img src="links5.gif" width="490" height="40" /><br />
<a href="mailto:margot@together.net"><img
   src="links6a.gif" width="93" height="40" border="0"
   alt="EMAIL" /></a><a
   href="http://www.margotday.com/links.htm"><img
   src="links6b.gif" width="397" height="40" border="0"
   alt="LINKS" /></a></div>
</body></html>
```

Notice that I was very careful not to put any spaces or line breaks in the bottom two `<img />` tags in Listing 11.1. A space or line break between `<img />` tags creates a small space between the images on the page, and the illusion of everything fitting together into one big image would be totally destroyed.

When *would* you want to use an imagemap, then? Only when the parts of an image you want to link are so numerous or oddly arranged that it would be a big hassle to chop the image into smaller images.

That does happen from time to time, so it's a good idea to know how to create imagemaps when you truly need to. The rest of this hour shows you how.

Mapping Regions Within an Image

To make any type of imagemap, you need to figure out the numerical pixel coordinates of each region within the image that you want to turn into a clickable link. An easy way to do this is to open the image with Paint Shop Pro and watch the coordinates at the bottom of the screen as you use the rectangle selection tool to select a rectangular region of the image (see Figure 11.3). When the mouse button is down, the coordinates at the bottom of the screen show both the top-left and bottom-right corners of the rectangle. When the mouse button isn't down, only the x,y position of the mouse is shown.

You could use the whole image in Figure 11.3 as an imagemap, linking to seven Web pages about the various literary genres. To do so, you would first need to decide which region of the image should be linked to each Web page. You can use rectangles, circles, and irregular polygons as regions. Figure 11.4 shows an example of how you might divide the image into these shapes.

Graphical Web page editors such as Microsoft FrontPage, Macromedia Dreamweaver, and Adobe GoLive allow you to paint *hotspots* onto an imagemap (see Figure 11.4) interactively and then generate the necessary HTML for you. This is one situation where a graphical editor is very handy to have around.

There are also programs available that let you highlight a rectangle with your mouse and automatically spew out imagemap coordinates into a file for you to cut-and-paste into your HTML, but they are rather cumbersome to use. If you don't have access to FrontPage or another good graphical Web page editor, you can easily locate the pixel coordinates in Paint Shop Pro or your favorite general-purpose graphics program.

FIGURE 11.3

An image editor can easily give the coordinates for imagemap regions without mucking about with special image-mapping utilities.

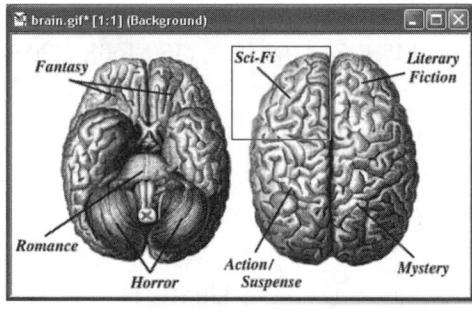

FIGURE 11.4

Microsoft FrontPage lets you draw clickable hotspot links onto your imagemaps with your mouse.

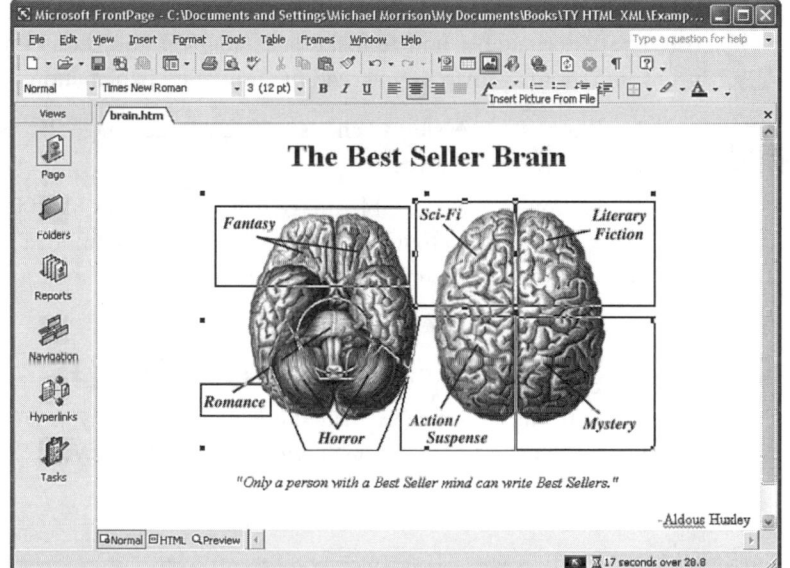

To create the imagemap, first jot down the pixel coordinates of the top-left and bottom-right corners of each rectangular region shown in Figure 11.4. You also need to locate and record the center point and radius of the circle, as well as the coordinates of each corner of the irregularly shaped regions. (If you want to follow along with this by using an image of your own, just write the coordinates on a piece of paper for now. You'll see exactly how to put them into an HTML file momentarily.)

These coordinates are as follows:

- Fantasy (region 1): A rectangle from 15,15 to 220,100.
- Romance (region 2): A rectangle from 0,200 to 75,235 and a circle centered at 140,150 with radius 40.

- Horror (region 3): An irregular polygon with corners at the following eight points: (70,175), (90,155), (125,195), (160,195), (190,160), (220,185), (185,270), and (110,270).

- Sci-Fi (region 4): A rectangle from 225,10 to 330,120.

- Literary Fiction (region 5): A rectangle from 330,10 to 475,120.

- Action/Suspense (region 6): An irregular polygon with corners at the following five points: (230,130), (330,130), (330,270), (210,270), and (210,230).

- Mystery (region 7): A rectangle from 330,130 to 475,270.

To Do

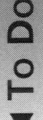

You'll better remember how to make imagemaps if you get an image of your own and turn it into an imagemap as you read the following explanation.

- For starters, it's easiest to choose a fairly large image that is visually divided into roughly rectangular regions.

- If you don't have a suitable image handy, use Paint Shop Pro (or your favorite graphics program) to make one. One easy and useful idea is to put a word or an icon for each of your important pages together into a button bar or signpost.

▲

Creating Client-Side Imagemaps

Once you have the coordinates written down, you're ready to create an HTML imagemap. Type the following just after the `<body>` tag in your Web page:

```
<map id="brainmap">
```

The `id` and `name` attributes play the same role in the `<map>` tag, so you could have also entered the previous code as this:

```
<map name="brainmap">
```

However, XML standards require the use of `id` instead of `name`, which is why I've stuck with it throughout this lesson (and the rest of the book for that matter).

You can use whatever name you want if `brainmap` doesn't describe the image you're using very well.

Now you need to type an `<area />` tag for each region of the image. Listing 11.2 shows how you would define the eight regions of the brain image with HTML code.

LISTING 11.2   The <map> and <area /> Tags Define the Regions of an Imagemap

```
<html><head><title>Best Seller Brain</title></head>
<body>
<map id="brainmap">
<area shape="rect" coords="15,15,220,100" href="fantasy.htm" alt="Fantasy"/>
<area shape="rect" coords="0,200,75,235" href="romance.htm" alt="Romance"/>
<area shape="circle" coords="140,150,40" href="romance.htm" alt="Romance"/>
<area shape="poly" coords="70,175, 90,135, 125,195, 160,195,
    190,160, 220,185, 185,270, 110,270" href="horror.htm" alt="Horror"/>
<area shape="rect" coords="225,10,330,120" href="scifi.htm" alt="Sci-Fi"/>
<area shape="rect" coords="330,10,475,120" href="litfi.htm" alt="Lit-Fi"/>
<area shape="poly" coords="230,130, 330,130, 330,270, 210,270,
    210,230" href="action.htm" alt="Action"/>
<area shape="rect" coords="330,130,475,270" href="mystery.htm" alt="Mystery"/>
</map>
<div align="center">
<h1>The Best Seller Brain</h1>
<img src="brain.gif" usemap="#brainmap" border="0" />
<p><i>"Only a person with a Best Seller mind can write Best
Sellers."</i></p></div>
<div align="right">-Aldous Huxley</div>
</body></html>
```

11

Each <area /> tag in Listing 11.2 has three attributes:

- shape indicates whether the region is a rectangle (shape="rect"), a circle (shape="circle"), or an irregular polygon (shape="poly").

- coords gives the exact pixel coordinates for the region. For rectangles, give the x,y coordinates of the top-left corner followed by the x,y coordinates of the bottom-right corner. For circles, give the x,y center point followed by the radius in pixels. For polygons, list the x,y coordinates of all the corners, in connect-the-dots order.

- href specifies the page to which the region links. You can use any address or file-name that you would use in an ordinary <a href> link tag.

- alt allows you to provide a piece of text that is associated with the shape. Most browsers display this text in a small box when the user pauses with the mouse over the shape.

After the <area /> tags, you are done defining the imagemap; insert a closing </map> tag.

To place the actual imagemap on the page, you use an ordinary <img /> tag and add a usemap attribute:

```
<img src="brain.gif" usemap="#brainmap">
```

Use the name you put in the <map> tag (and don't forget the # symbol). In the listing I also included width and height attributes, which isn't a bad idea for any image on a Web page because it can help Web browsers lay out objects on a page a little faster.

It is also possible to put the map definition in a separate file by including that file's name in the usemap attribute, like the following:

```
<img src="thisthat.gif" usemap="maps.htm#thisthat">
```

For instance, if you used an imagemap on every page in your Web site, you could just put the `<map>` and `<area>` tags for it on one page instead of repeating it on every page it appears.

Figure 11.5 shows the imagemap in action. Notice that Microsoft Internet Explorer displays the link address for whatever region the mouse is moving over at the bottom of the window, just as it does for "normal" links. If someone clicked where the mouse cursor (the little hand) is shown in Figure 11.5, the page named fantasy.htm would come up.

FIGURE 11.5

The imagemap defined in Listing 11.2 as it appears on the Web page.

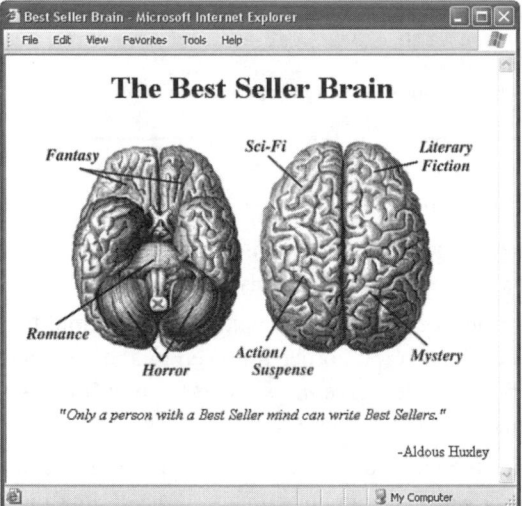

You may want to include text links at the bottom of your imagemap that lead to the same pages the map itself links to. This allows people who have older Web browsers—or who don't want to wait for the image to finish loading—to access those pages.

For an example—and a little tongue-in-cheek history lesson thrown into the bargain—click "The Immortal Presidents" at http://www.24hourHTMLcafe.com/hour11/.

Summary

This hour explained how to create imagemaps—links that lead to more than one place, depending on where you click an image—as well as why and how to avoid using them. You saw how to define rectangular and circular link regions within an image, as well as irregularly shaped polygonal regions. You saw how imagemaps, although highly specialized in function, can nonetheless be very useful in some situations. When used with discretion, imagemaps can be an important part of a Web page's user interface.

Table 11.1 is a summary of the tags and attributes covered in this hour.

TABLE 11.1   HTML Tags and Attributes Covered in Hour 11

Tag/Attribute	Function
`<img />`	Inserts an image into the document.
	Attributes
`src="..."`	The image's URL.
`usemap="..."`	The name of an imagemap specification for client-side image mapping. Used with `<map>` and `<area />`.
`<map>...</map>`	A client-side imagemap, referenced by `<img usemap="..." />`. Includes one or more `<area />` tags.
`<area />`	Defines a clickable link within a client-side imagemap.
	Attributes
`shape="..."`	The shape of the clickable area. Currently, `rect`, `poly`, and `circle` (or `round`) are the valid options.
`coords="..."`	The left, top, right, and bottom coordinates of the clickable region within an image.
`href="..."`	The URL that should be loaded when the area is clicked.

11

Q&A

Q I don't have Paint Shop Pro and my graphics software doesn't tell me x,y coordinates. How do I figure out the coordinates for my imagemaps?

A Here's a sneaky way to do it using Netscape Navigator. Put the image on a page with the `ismap` attribute and an `<a>` tag around it, like the following:

```
<a href="nowhere"><img src="myimage.gif" ismap="ismap" /></a>
```

When you view that page with Navigator, move the mouse over the image. You will see the coordinates in the status bar along the bottom of the window.

Q What happens if I overlap areas on an imagemap?

A You are allowed to overlap areas on an imagemap, just keep in mind that one area will have precedence over the other one when it comes to determining which link to follow. Precedence is assigned according to which areas are listed first in the imagemap. For example, the first area in the map has precedence over the second area if they overlap, which means a click in the overlapping portion of the areas will link to the first area. If you have an area within an imagemap that you don't want to link to anything, you can use this overlap trick to deliberately keep it from linking to anything—just place the "dead" area before other areas so that it will overlap them, and then leave off its href attribute.

Workshop

The workshop contains quiz questions and activities to help you solidify your understanding of the material covered. Try to answer all questions before looking at the "Answers" section that follows.

Quiz

1. You have a 200×200-pixel image named quarters.gif for your Web page. When viewers click the top-left quarter of the image, you want them to get a page named toplft.htm. When they click the top-right quarter, they should get toprgt.htm. Clicking the bottom left should bring up btmlft.htm, and the bottom right should lead to btmrgt.htm. Write the HTML to implement this as an imagemap.

2. How could you implement the effect described in question 1 without using imagemaps at all?

Answers

1.
```
<map id="quartersmap">
<area shape="rect" coords="0,0,99,99" href="toplft.htm" />
<area shape="rect" coords="100,0,199,99" href="toprgt.htm" />
<area shape="rect" coords="0,100,99,199" href="btmlft.htm" />
<area shape="rect" coords="100,100,199,199" href="btmrgt.htm" />
</map>
<img src="quarters.gif" width="200" height="200"
usemap="#quartersmap" />
```

2. Use a graphics program such as Paint Shop Pro to chop the image into four quarters and save them as separate images named toplft.gif, toprgt.gif, btmlft.gif, and btmrgt.gif. Then write this:

```
<a href="toplft.htm"><img src="toplft.gif"
width="100" height="100" border="0" /></a>
<a href="toprgt.htm"><img src="toprgt.gif"
width="100" height="100" border="0" /></a> <br />
<a href="btmlft.htm"><img src="btmlft.gif"
width="100" height="100" border="0" /></a>
<a href="btmrgt.htm"><img src="btmrgt.gif"
width="100" height="100" border="0" /></a>
```

Be careful to break the lines of the HTML *inside* the tags as shown in this code, to avoid introducing any spaces between the images.

Exercises

- If you have some pages containing short lists of links, see if you can cook up an interesting imagemap to use instead.

- Imagemaps are usually more engaging and attractive than a row of repetitive-looking icons or buttons. Can you come up with a visual metaphor related to your site that would make it easier—and maybe more fun—for people to navigate through your pages? (Thinking along these lines is a good preparation for the issues you'll be tackling in Part VI, "Building a Web Site," by the way.)

11

PART IV
Web Page Design

Hour

HOUR **12**

Page Design and Layout

You've learned in earlier hours how to create Web pages with text and images on them. This hour goes a step further by showing you some HTML tricks to control the spaces *between* your text and images. These tricks are essential for making your pages attractive and easy to read. This hour provides practical advice that helps you design attractive and highly readable pages, even if you're not a professional graphics designer.

This hour also teaches you how to ensure that your Web pages will appear as quickly as possible when people try to read them. This is essential for making a good impression with your pages, especially for people who will be accessing them through dial-up modem connections or wireless devices with slower access speeds.

When it comes to designing and laying out your pages, you might think that a graphical Web page layout tool such as Microsoft FrontPage or Macromedia Dreamweaver would be more intuitive and powerful than editing the HTML by hand, as you'll be doing in this hour.

It's true that designing your pages with an interactive graphical tool can be more intuitive, and I recommend that you have a good graphical tool like FrontPage available for that purpose.

However, you'll still be very glad to know the HTML you learn in this hour when it comes time to fine-tune all those little spacing problems that graphical tools tend to leave you with. This hour covers page design techniques that are essential to both writing HTML by hand and using a graphical tool.

To Do

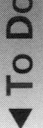

The techniques covered in this hour are intended to help you make the pages you've already created better and more efficient. Select some of the most important and impressive pages that you've made to date, and see if you can make them look even better.

- Choose pages with some graphics on them. Almost all tricks in this hour involve images.

- If you have a page you think might especially benefit from a creative layout or unique background, start with that one.

- You may have some text and images that you haven't gotten around to putting on a Web page yet. If so, this hour can help make those new pages your best yet.

- Copy the pages you select into their own folder, and play with new design possibilities for them as you read through this hour.

The Essentials of Web Page Design

So far, this book has focused on the exact mechanics of Web page creation using HTML. Before getting into the nitty-gritty of spacing and layout tricks, you should take a moment now to step back and think about the overall visual design of your Web pages. Now that you know basic HTML, you need to learn how to apply it wisely.

Every aspect of a Web page should reflect the goals that led you to create the page in the first place. Not only should the text and graphics themselves communicate your message, but the way you fit those elements together can make an enormous impact on the reader's perceptions of you and your company.

Table 12.1 is a checklist to help you think about the key design elements of a Web page. You should aim for most of your pages to meet the recommendations in this table, though some individual pages will undoubtedly need to break the rules.

TABLE 12.1   Key Elements of Web Page Design

Things to Consider	Suggested Guidelines
Text content	Between 100 and 500 words per page
Text breaks	A headline, rule, or image every 40 to 100 words (except in long articles or stories)
Page length	One to four screens (at 800×600 resolution)
File size	No more than 100KB per page, including images; animated GIFs can be up to 150KB per page
Speed	First screen of text and key images appear in under 3 seconds over a 56Kbps modem
Colors	Two to four thematic colors dominant
Fonts	No more than three fonts (in graphics and text)
Blank space	Background should show on at least 50% of page
Contrast	No color in background should be close to text color
Tone and style	All text and graphics consistent in mood and theme
Overall impact	Page as a whole should appear balanced and attractive

Most of the tips in Table 12.1 are common to any page design, on paper or electronic. Some, however, are particularly tricky to control on Web pages.

The next section of this hour presents some HTML commands for handling the blank space and overall visual impact of your pages. This lesson then wraps up with some techniques for meeting the speed requirements of today's Web, even when you use relatively large images.

Fine-Tuning Image Spacing and Borders

Listing 12.1 contains the code for a well-designed Web page that meets all the criteria outlined in Table 12.1. Too see what I'm talking about, take a look at Figures 12.1 and 12.2, which show the images used in the page, as well as the resulting page as viewed in a Web browser.

LISTING 12.1   Adding Blank Space Between Images and Text

```
<html><head><title>The Varieties of Proboscis</title></head>
<body background="wainscot.gif"
  text="green" link="maroon" vlink="green" alink="white">
<div align="center">
```

12

LISTING 12.1   continued

```
    <img src="vofp.gif" align="top" alt="" width="400" height="100" />
    <img src="bosc.gif" align="top" alt="" width="125" height="135" />
    <br /><img src="spacer.gif" alt="" width="20" height="20" /><br />
</div>
<h2><a href="point.htm">
<img src="point.gif" align="left" alt="" width="120" height="120"
border="3" hspace="20" vspace="5" />The Needle</a></h2>
Being perhaps the most refined and coveted variety, this
proboscis is favoured by accountants, lawyers, librarians,
and all persons of great intellect and bile.<br clear="left" />
<img src="spacer.gif" alt="" width="20" height="20" /><br />
<h2 align="right"><a href="arch.htm">
<img src="arch.gif" align="right" alt="" width="140" height="100"
border="3" hspace="20" vspace="5" />The Arch</a></h2>
An original inspiration for both Roman and Gothic architectural
motifs, this well-loved proboscis boasts an extensive history
in the fine arts.<br clear="right" />
<img src="spacer.gif" alt="" width="20" height="20" /><br />
<h2><a href="bulb.htm">
<img src="bulb.gif" align="left" alt="" width="140" height="100"
border="3" hspace="20" vspace="5" />The Bulb</a></h2>
A long-standing favorite of politicians and food service
professionals, this is the traditional proboscis of good
cheer and prolific oration.<br clear="left" />
<img src="spacer.gif" alt="" width="20" height="20" /><br />
<h2 align="right"><a href="hook.htm">
<img src="hook.gif" align="right" alt="" width="120" height="120"
border="3" hspace="20" vspace="5" />The Hook</a></h2>
This most visible and respected proboscis type commands prompt
attention and high regard in both religious and secular
circles.<br clear="right" />
<img src="spacer.gif" alt="" width="20" height="20" />
<div align="center">
  <img src="flourish.gif" alt="" width="136" height="30" />
  <p><a href="index.htm"><i>Return to the
  European Anatomy HomePage.</i></a></p>
</div></body></html>
```

 When you look at Figure 12.1, remember that Paint Shop Pro uses cross-hatching to indicate that a window is bigger than the image it contains, and a checkerboard pattern to indicate which regions of an image are transparent. For example, spacer.gif is actually a very small, entirely transparent square.

FIGURE 12.1

Here are five of the nine image files referred to in the Web page in Listing 12.1.

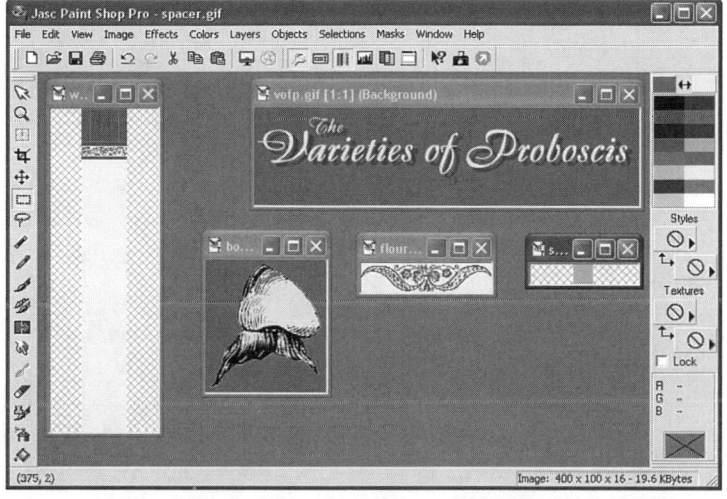

FIGURE 12.2

Thanks to generous spacing and a carefully premeditated layout, the HTML in Listing 12.1 looks great as a Web page.

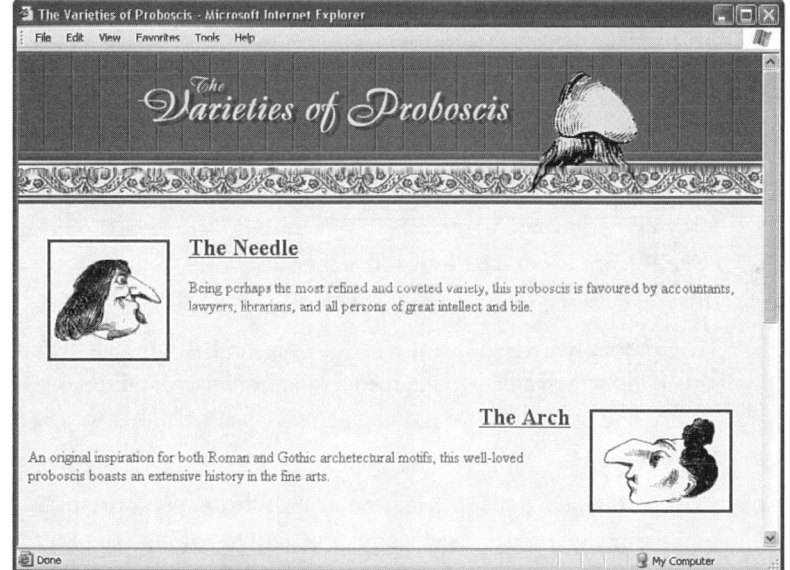

12

Notice the generous amount of space between images and paragraphs in Figure 12.2. Web browsers tend to crowd everything together, but you can easily add space using three different techniques:

- Use small, totally transparent images to leave room between other things. The spacer.gif file (shown in Figure 12.1 and referred to in Listing 12.1) creates 20 pixels of blank space between each of the main parts of this page.

- When you wrap text around an image by using `<img align="right" />` or `<img align="left" />`, you can skip past the bottom of that image at any time with `<br clear="right" />` or `<br clear="left" />`. If you have images on both the right and left, you can type `<br clear="all" />` to go past both of them. Keep in mind that this technique is not officially encouraged in HTML 4 even though it is convenient. The recommended approach involves the use of style sheets, which you learn about in Hours 14 and 15. I also recommend using style sheets, but the `clear` attribute is a quick-and-dirty option you can consider for short-term Web pages.

- You can add extra space on the left and right sides of any image with `hspace`. To add space on the top and bottom sides, use `vspace`. For example, each image in Figure 12.2 has 20 pixels of blank space to the left and right of it, and 5 pixels above and below it. This is because each `<img />` tag in Listing 12.1 includes the attributes `hspace="20" vspace="5"`. Similar to the `clear` attribute, `hspace` and `vspace` have been deprecated in HTML 4, so you are encouraged to use style sheets instead. I provide them here for completeness, however, because they are still widely used across the Web.

When using images as spacers, make sure you specify their `alt` tags as empty strings (`alt=""`). This keeps Web browsers from displaying any pop-up text when the user hovers over them with the mouse.

You'll learn about the `width` and `height` attributes of the `<img />` tag later in this lesson, in the "Specifying Image Width and Height" section.

You probably noticed that the `<img />` tags in Listing 12.1 also include a `border="3"` attribute, which enlarges the rectangular border around the images. The border is normally one pixel thick for any image inside an `<a>` link, but `border="3"` makes it three pixels thick.

As you learned in the previous hour, the most popular use of the `border` attribute is making the image border disappear completely by typing `border="0"`. This is especially handy with transparent images, which often look funny with a rectangle around them.

The color of the border will be the same as the color of any text links. In this page, images that link to pages someone hasn't visited yet will have maroon borders. Images that link to a recently visited page will have green borders.

I'm probably starting to sound like a broken record, but `border` is another one of those pesky deprecated attributes that is frowned upon in HTML 4. My suggestion is to use deprecated attributes with caution while you develop a mastery of style sheets. Style sheets represent the future of HTML formatting, so you might as well start thinking in terms of abandoning the old comfortable HTML formatting tags and attributes. However, as I said earlier, many of the deprecated attributes are still widely used (old habits die hard), so you need to understand how they work. You start learning about style sheets in Hour 14.

The Old Background Banner Trick

One of the most prominent tricks employed in the Web page in Figure 12.2 is the use of a 1,000-pixel-high background image (named `wainscot.gif`). Because the entire page is unlikely to be more than 1,000 pixels high, the background appears to repeat in the horizontal direction. Since the bottom part of the image is all the same color, it looks like the background is only a banner at the top of the page.

Unlike a foreground image used as a banner, however, this wainscoting will automatically size itself to go from "wall to wall" of any sized window. It takes up less space on a disk and transfers over the Internet faster because only one repetition of the pattern needs to be stored.

If you use this trick to make background banners on your own Web pages, you should make them at least 2,000 pixels high. The page shown in Figure 12.3 can actually become longer than 1,000 pixels when someone uses a very large font size, in which case the wainscoting visibly repeats at the very bottom or middle of the page.

"Hang on," you say, "143×1,000 is 143,000 pixels! Won't that make an enormous image file and take forever to download?" The answer is no; large areas of uniform color take up virtually no space at all when compressed in the GIF file format. (`wainscot.gif` is only a 3KB file.)

12

By using a very wide background that repeats vertically, you can easily make a repeating banner that runs down the left side of a page, too. If you don't want text to obscure the banner, put a very large, totally transparent image at the beginning of the HTML page with `<img align="left" />`.

Listing 12.2 shows the code for a page that uses a left-side banner created as a repeating background image. Figures 12.3 and 12.4 show the images used in the page, along with the page itself as viewed in a Web browser.

LISTING 12.2   Moving the Top Banner from Figure 12.2 to the Left Side

```
<html><head><title>The Varieties of Proboscis</title></head>
<body background="wainsco2.gif"
  text="green" link="maroon" vlink="green" alink="white">
<img src="vofp2.gif" align="left" alt="" width="170" height="1200"/>
<img src="spacer.gif" alt="" width="20" height="20" /><br />
<h2><a href="point.htm">
<img src="point.gif" align="right" alt="" width="120" height="120"
border="3" hspace="20" vspace="5" />The Needle</a></h2>
Being perhaps the most refined and coveted variety, this
proboscisis favoured by accountants, lawyers, librarians,
and all persons of great intellect and bile.<br clear="right" />
<img src="spacer.gif" alt="" width="20" height="20" /><br />
<h2 align="right"><a href="arch.htm">
<img src="arch.gif" align="right" alt="" width="140" height="100"
border="3" hspace="20" vspace="5" />The Arch</a></h2>
An original inspiration for both Roman and Gothic archetectural
motifs, this well-loved proboscis boasts an extensive history
in the fine arts.<br clear="right" />
<img src="spacer.gif" alt="" width="20" height="20" /><br />
<h2><a href="bulb.htm">
<img src="bulb.gif" align="right" alt="" width="140" height="100"
border="3" hspace="20" vspace="5" />The Bulb</a></h2>
A long-standing favourite of politicians and food service
professionals, this is the traditional proboscis of good cheer
and prolific oration.<br clear="right" />
<img src="spacer.gif" alt="" width="20" height="20" /><br />
<h2 align="right"><a href="hook.htm">
<img src="hook.gif" align="right" alt="" width="120" height="120"
border="3" hspace="20" vspace="5" />The Hook</a></h2>
This most visible and respected proboscis type commands prompt
attention and high regard in both religous and secular
circles.<br clear="right" />
<img src="spacer.gif" alt="" width="20" height="20" />
<div align="center">
  <img src="flourish.gif" alt="" width="136" height="30" />
  <p><a href="index.htm"><i>Return to the
  European Anatomy Home Page.</i></a></p>
</div></body></html>
```

If you use a left-aligned transparent banner, be sure to add enough blank space around the actual foreground image to fill the area on the page you want to cover. The Varieties of Proboscis title graphic in Figures 12.3 and 12.4, for example, is 170×1,200 pixels.

Because few people view Web pages in a window larger than 1600×1,200 pixels, vertically tiled background banners can safely be 2,000 pixels wide in most circumstances. However, keep in mind that there are now some extremely large monitors in use that push the screen size even larger than 1,600×1,200 pixels, so you might want to consider your target audience when deciding on the width of a background image to keep it from repeating.

FIGURE 12.3

The rotated graphics for a left-side banner. (Notice how I changed the direction of the light source and shadowing, too.)

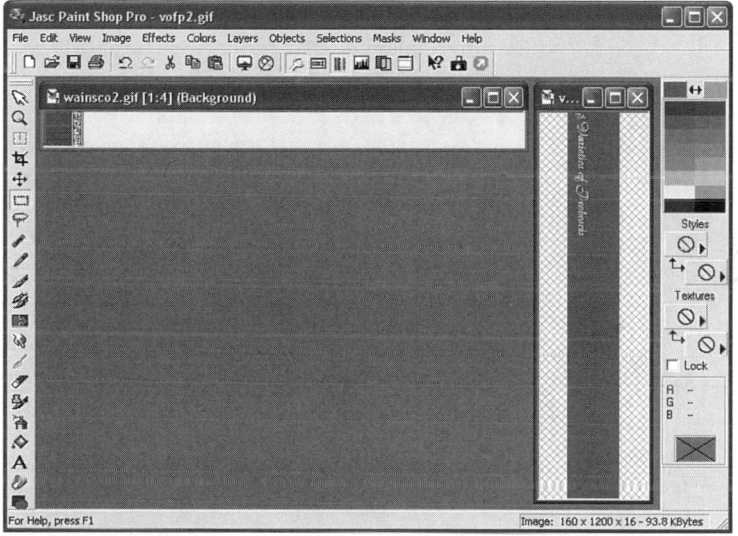

FIGURE 12.4

The HTML from Listing 12.2 and the banner from Figure 12.3, as they appear in Internet Explorer.

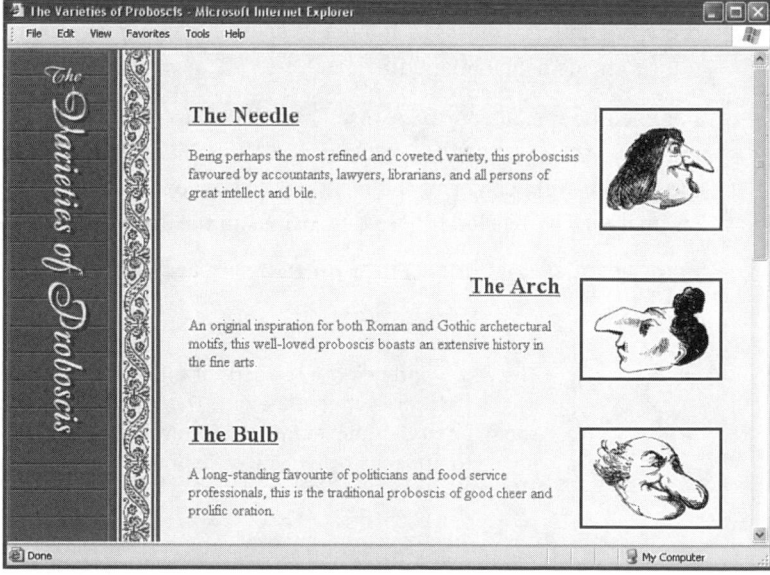

12

Note that I right-justified the other graphics in this sample page for aesthetic reasons and so that I could avoid using `<br clear="left" />`, which would skip all the way to the bottom of the left-justified banner graphic.

You'll sometimes choose to push the limits of HTML layout, and I encourage you to do so. The home page of the *24-Hour HTML Café* (`http://www.24hourHTMLcafe.com`) does exactly that—combining several tricks from this and other hours into a flexible layout that adjusts itself to the size of the browser window gracefully.

If you view the page in a small enough window (fewer than about 600 pixels wide), you'll notice that the images start crawling all over each other in ways God obviously never intended them to try. I could have solved this problem with tables (see Hour 13) or other advanced tricks, but I went for simplicity at the risk of annoying the relatively few people who look at the Web through extremely small windows.

Specifying Image Width and Height

Because text moves over the Internet much faster than do graphics, most Web browsers will display the text on a page before the images. This gives people something to read while they're waiting to see the pictures, which makes the whole page seem faster.

You can make sure that everything on your page appears as quickly as possible and in the right places by explicitly stating each image's width and height. That way, a Web browser can leave the right amount of space for that image as it lays out the page and return for the actual image file later.

For each image on your page, use Paint Shop Pro or another graphics program to find out the exact width and height in pixels. (In Paint Shop Pro, this information appears at the bottom-right corner of the main window when you move the mouse over any part of an image.) Then include those dimensions in the `<img />` tag, like this:

```
<img src="myimage.gif" alt="" width="200" height="100" />
```

The width and height specified for an image don't have to match the image's actual width and height. The Web browser program will try to squish or stretch the image to whatever size you specify. If you want an image to appear smaller, you're definitely better off resizing it in an image editor.

> Allowing a Web browser to resize an image usually makes it look very ugly due to the squishing or stretching, but there is one excellent use for it: You can save a very small, totally transparent image and use it as any size spacer by specifying the `width` and `height` of the blank region you want to create on your page.

Summary

This hour provided some guidelines for designing attractive, highly readable Web pages. It also explained how to create and control blank space on your pages, as well as how to put borders around images. You saw how to use backgrounds to create banners across the top or left edge of a page and how to make sure people always have text to look at while waiting for the images on your page.

Table 12.2 summarizes the tags and attributes discussed in this chapter.

TABLE 12.2   HTML Tags and Attributes Covered in Hour 12

Tag/Attribute	Function
`<img />`	Inserts an inline image into the document.
	Attributes
`src="..."`	The address of the image.
`alt="..."`	A text message that is displayed in place of the image, or in a small box over the image.
`align="..."`	Determines the alignment of the given image (see Hour 9, "Putting Graphics on a Web Page").
`vspace="..."`	The space between the image and the text above or below it.
`hspace="..."`	The space between the image and the text to its left or right.
`width="..."`	The width, in pixels, of the image. If `width` is not the actual width, the image is scaled to fit.
`height="..."`	The height, in pixels, of the image. If `height` is not the actual height, the image is scaled to fit.
`border="..."`	Draws a border of the specified value in pixels to be drawn around the image. In case the images are also links, `border` changes the size of the default link border.
` `	A line break.
	Attributes
`clear="..."`	Causes the text to stop flowing around any images. Possible values are `right`, `left`, `all`.

12

Q&A

Q **I'd like to know exactly how wide the margins of a page are so I can line up my background and foreground images the way I want.**

A Unfortunately, different browsers (and even the same browser on different types of computers) leave different amounts of space along the top and left side of a page, so you can't precisely line up foreground graphics with background images. Generally, you can expect the top and left margins to be 8 to 12 pixels.

The good news is that you'll learn an elegant and precise way to control margin width in Hour 14, "Formatting Pages with Style Sheets."

Q **I used a graphical layout program to design my pages, and when I put the pages online my images look blotchy and seem to take forever to show up. What can I do?**

A Here's what might be going on: When you place and resize an image in some graphical Web page layout programs (such as Adobe PageMill), the program simply changes the `width` and `height` attributes without actually resizing the image file itself. This usually makes the images look kind of crinkly, and can mean that what looks like a little 100×100-pixel image on the page may actually be a huge 2,000×2,000-pixel monster that takes half an hour to download.

Here's how you can fix it: Open the image in your favorite image editing software and resize it there so that the `width` and `height` attributes of the `<img />` tag match the actual image size.

Q **I've seen pages on the Web with multiple columns of text, wide margins, and other types of nice layouts you didn't discuss. How were those pages made?**

A Probably with the HTML table tags, which are discussed in Hour 13, "Advanced Layout with Tables," or with style sheets, discussed in Hours 14 and 15.

Workshop

The workshop contains quiz questions and activities to help you solidify your understanding of the material covered. Try to answer all questions before looking at the "Answers" section that follows.

Quiz

1. How would you wrap text around the right side of an image, leaving 40 pixels of space between the image and the text?

2. How could you insert exactly 80 pixels of blank space between two paragraphs of text?

3. If you have a circular button that links to another page, how do you prevent a rectangle from appearing around it?

4. What four attributes should you always include in every `<img />` tag as a matter of habit?

Answers

1. `<img src="myimage.gif" hspace="40" vspace="40" align="left" />`
   `Text goes here.`

2. Create a small image that is all one color and save it as `nothing.gif` with that color transparent. Then put the following tag between the two paragraphs of text:

   `<img src="nothing.gif" width="1" height="80" />`

3. Use the `border="0"` attribute, like the following:

   `<a href="another_page.htm"><img src="circle.gif" border="0" /></a>`

4. `src`, `alt`, `width`, and `height`. An example:

   `<img src="fred.jpg" alt="fat fred" width="300" height="100">`

Exercises

- Try creating a page with the wildest layout you can manage with the HTML tags you've learned so far. If you're resourceful, you should be able to create a staggered diagonal line of images or place short sentences of text almost anywhere on the page.

- Make a very large background—so big that people will see only one "tile" and you don't have to worry about it being seamless. Most Web browsers will display all foreground content (in front of the `bgcolor` you specify in the `<body>` tag) while the background image loads. Go ahead and play around with the creative possibilities that large backdrops open up.

12

Hour 13

Advanced Layout with Tables

One of the most powerful tools for creative Web page design is the *table*, which allows you to arrange text and graphics into multiple columns and rows. This hour shows you how to build HTML tables and how to control the spacing, layout, and appearance of the tables you create. You'll find that tables are not only useful for arranging information into rows and columns, but are also useful for laying out images and text on your pages.

 A *table* is an orderly arrangement of text and/or graphics into vertical *columns* and horizontal *rows*.

To Do

 As you read this hour, think about how arranging text into tables could benefit your Web pages. The following are some specific ideas to keep in mind:

- Of course, the most obvious application of tables is to organize tabular information, such as a multi-column list of names and numbers.

▼
- If you want more complex relationships between text and graphics than the `<img align="left" />` or `<img align="right" />` can provide, tables can do it.

- Tables can be used to draw borders around text or around several graphics images.

- Whenever you need multiple columns of text, tables are the answer.

For each of your pages that meets one of these criteria, try adding a table modeled after the examples in this hour. The "Exercises" section at the end of this hour offers a couple
▲ of detailed suggestions along these lines as well.

Creating a Simple Table

A table consists of rows of information with individual cells inside. To make tables, you have to start with a `<table>` tag. Of course, you end your tables with the `</table>` tag. If you want the table to have a border, use a `border` attribute to specify the width of the border in pixels. A border size of 0 (or leaving the `border` attribute out entirely) will make the border invisible, which is often handy when you are using a table as a page layout tool.

With the `<table>` tag in place, the next thing you need is the `<tr>` tag. The `<tr>` tag creates a table row, which contains one or more cells of information before the closing `</tr>`. To create these individual cells, you use the `<td>` tag. `<td>` stands for table data; you place the table information between the `<td>` and `</td>` tags.

NEW TERM A *cell* is a rectangular region that can contain any text, images, and HTML tags. Each row in a table is made up of at least one cell. Multiple cells within a row form columns in a table.

There is one more basic tag involved in building tables: The `<th>` tag works exactly like a `<td>` tag, except `<th>` indicates that the cell is part of the heading of the table. Most Web browsers render the text in `<th>` cells as centered and boldface.

You can create as many cells as you want, but each row in a table should have the same number of columns as the other rows. The HTML code in Listing 13.1 creates a simple table using only the four table tags I've mentioned thus far. Figure 13.1 shows the resulting page as viewed in a Web browser.

LISTING 13.1   Creating Tables with the `<table>`, `<tr>`, `<td>`, and `<th>` Tags

```
<html><head><title>Things to Fear</title></head>
<body>
<table>
<tr>
```

LISTING 13.1 continued

```
    <th>Description</th>
    <th>Size</th>
    <th>Weight</th>
  </tr>
  <tr>
    <td>.38 Special</td>
    <td>Five-inch barrel</td>
    <td>Twenty ounces</td>
  </tr>
  <tr>
    <td>Rhinoceros</td>
    <td>Twelve feet</td>
    <td>Up to two tons</td>
  </tr>
  <tr>
    <td>Broad Axe</td>
    <td>Thirty-inch blade</td>
    <td>Twelve pounds</td>
  </tr>
  </table>
  </body></html>
```

As you know, HTML ignores extra spaces between words and tags. However, you might find your HTML tables easier to read (and less prone to time-wasting errors) if you use spaces to indent <td> tags, as I did in Listing 13.1.

FIGURE 13.1

The HTML code in Listing 13.1 creates a table with four rows and three columns.

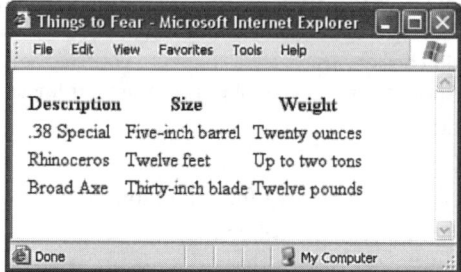

13

You can place virtually any HTML element into a table cell. However, tags used in one cell don't carry over to other cells, and tags from outside the table don't apply within the table. For example, if you wrote the following, the word there would be neither boldface nor italic because neither the `<b>` tag outside the table nor the `<i>` tag from the previous cell affects it (the `<i>` tag is also a problem because it needs to be closed with a `</i>` tag):

```
<b>
<table><tr>
  <td><i>hello</td>
  <td>there</td>
</tr></table>
</b>
```

To make both the words `hello` and `there` boldface, you would need to type this:

```
<table><tr>
  <td><b>hello</b></td>
  <td><b>there</b></td>
</tr></table>
```

Controlling the Size of Tables

Ordinarily, the size of a table and its individual cells automatically expand to fit the data you place into it. However, you can choose to control the exact size of the entire table by putting `width` and/or `height` attributes in the `<table>` tag. You can also control the size of each cell by putting `width` and `height` attributes in the individual `<td>` tags. The `width` and `height` attributes can be specified as either pixels or percentages. For example, the following code creates a table 500 pixels wide and 400 pixels high:

```
<table width="500" height="400">
```

> Just like many of the other attributes relating to layout and formatting, the `width` and `height` attributes are deprecated in HTML 4. They still work, but you should consider using style sheets to control the size of your tables. You get the whole scoop on style sheets in the next lesson.

To make the first cell of the table 20% of the total table width and the second cell 80% of the table width, you would type the following:

```
<table><tr>
  <td width="20%">skinny cell</td>
  <td width="80%">fat cell</td>
</tr></table>
```

When you use percentages instead of fixed pixel sizes, the table will resize automatically to fit any size browser window, while maintaining the aesthetic balance you're after.

Alignment and Spanning Within Tables

By default, anything you place inside a table cell is aligned to the left and vertically centered. You can align the contents of table cells both horizontally and vertically with the align and valign attributes.

You can apply these attributes to any <tr>, <td>, or <th> tag. Alignment attributes assigned to a <tr> tag apply to all cells in that row. Depending upon the size of your table, you can save yourself a considerable amount of time and effort by applying these attributes at the <tr> level and not in each individual <td> or <th> tag. The HTML code in Listing 13.2 uses valign="top" to bring the text to the top of each cell. Figure 13.2 shows the result.

LISTING 13.2 Alignment, Cell Spacing, Borders, and Background Colors in Tables

```
<html><head><title>Things to Fear</title></head>
<body>
<table border="2" cellpadding="8" cellspacing="3">
<tr bgcolor="silver">
  <th colspan="2">Description</th>
  <th>Size</th>
  <th>Weight</th>
  <th>Speed</th>
</tr>
<tr valign="top">
  <td><img src="handgun.gif" /></td>
  <td><h2>.38 Special</h2></td>
  <td>Five-inch barrel.</td>
  <td>Twenty ounces.</td>
  <td>Six rounds in four seconds.</td>
</tr>
<tr valign="top">
  <td><img src="rhino.gif" /></td>
  <td><h2>Rhinoceros</h2></td>
  <td>Twelve feet, horn to tail.</td>
  <td>Up to two tons.</td>
  <td>Thirty-five miles per hour in bursts.</td>
</tr>
<tr valign="top">
  <td><img src="axeman.gif" /></td>
  <td><h2>Broad Axe</h2></td>
  <td>Thirty-inch blade.</td>
  <td>Twelve pounds.</td>
  <td>Sixty miles per hour on impact.</td>
</tr>
</table>
</body></html>
```

13

FIGURE 13.2

The colspan *attribute
in Listing 13.2 allows
the top-left cell to span
multiple columns.*

At the top of Figure 13.2, a single cell spans two columns. This is accomplished with the colspan="2" attribute in the <th> tag for that cell. As you might guess, you can also use the rowspan attribute to create a cell that spans more than one row.

NEW TERM *Spanning* is the process of forcing a cell to stretch across more than one row or column of a table. The colspan attribute causes a cell to span across multiple columns, while the rowspan has the same effect on rows.

> Keeping the structure of rows and columns organized in your mind can be the most difficult part of creating tables with cells that span multiple columns or rows. The tiniest error can often throw the whole thing into disarray. You'll save yourself time and frustration by sketching your tables out on graph paper before you start writing the HTML to implement them.
>
> You can also use visual Web design software to arrange the rows and columns in your table. This can make table design much easier, as long as you choose a program (such as Microsoft FrontPage or Macromedia Dreamweaver) that creates well-formatted HTML that you can edit by hand when you choose.

Table Backgrounds and Spacing

There are a few tricks in Listing 13.2 that I haven't mentioned yet. You can give an entire table—and each individual row or cell in a table—its own background, distinct from any background you might use on the Web page itself. You do this by placing a bgcolor or background attribute in the <table>, <tr>, <td>, or <th> tag exactly as you would in the <body> tag (see Hour 10, "Custom Backgrounds and Colors"). To give an entire table a yellow background, for example, you would use <table bgcolor="yellow"> or the equivalent <table bgcolor="#ffff00">.

You can also control the space around the borders of a table with the cellpadding and cellspacing attributes. The cellspacing attribute sets the amount of space (in pixels) between table borders and between table cells themselves. The cellpadding attribute sets the amount of space around the edges of information in the cells. Setting the cellpadding value to 0 causes all the information in the table to align as closely as possible to the table borders, possibly even touching the borders. cellpadding and cellspacing give you good overall control of the table's appearance.

You saw the effect of background color and spacing attributes in Figure 13.2.

NEW TERM You can place an entire table within a cell of a different table, and the inner table will possess the qualities of the "parent" table. In other words, you can *nest* tables inside one another.

Nested tables open a vast universe of possibilities for creative Web page layout. For example, if you want a column of text to appear to the left of a table, you could create a two-column table with the text in one column and the subtable in the other column, like the following:

```
<table>
<tr><td>To the right, you see all our telephone numbers.</td>
<td>
  <table border="1">
  <tr><td>voice<td>802-888-2828</td></tr>
  <tr><td>fax  <td>802-888-6634</td></tr>
  <tr><td>data <td>802-888-3009</td></tr>
  </table>
</table>
```

Notice that the inner table has borders, but the outer table does not.

A drawback to nested tables is that if you get carried away and nest them too deeply it can slow down the rendering of the page in a browser. You definitely shouldn't go deeper than three levels without a very good reason, and two levels is really a more realistic limit if you can handle it.

13

Creative Page Layout with Tables

The boring, conventional way to use tables is for tabular arrangements of text and numbers. The real fun begins when you make the borders of your tables invisible and use them as guides for arranging graphics and columns of text any way you please. For an example, take a look at Listing 13.3, which contains the code for a page that relies on tables for its layout. The resulting page is displayed in Figure 13.3.

Although laying out pages with invisible tables is a highly popular and useful technique, it is technically discouraged by the World Wide Web Consortium (W3C), the standards body that oversees the future of the Web. The W3C promotes style sheets as the proper way to layout pages, as opposed to using tables. Although I agree with the W3C in principle, tables are simply too useful for page layout to completely ignore them. Don't worry, I teach you the style sheet approach to page layout in Hour 14, "Formatting Pages with Style Sheets." Style sheets are ultimately much more powerful than tables, so you definitely should consider using them for pages with more complex designs. Just keep in mind that some older browsers don't support style sheets, although they are well supported in more recent browsers.

While I worked on building this table, I left the borders visible so I could make sure everything was placed the way I wanted. Then, before incorporating this table into the final Web page, I removed the border="1" attribute from the <table> tag to make the lines invisible.

LISTING 13.3   Using Tables for Multiple Columns of Text or Wide Margins

```
<html><head><title>Mathew Eber, D.D.E.</title></head>
<body><div align="center">
<table cellspacing="10">
<tr valign="top">
<td><img src="handgun.gif" /><br />Five-inch barrel. Twenty
ounces. Six rounds in four seconds.</td>
<td><img src="rhino.gif" /><br />Twelve feet, horn to tail.
Up to two tons. Thirty-five miles per hour.</td>
<td><img src="axeman.gif" /><br />Thirty-inch blade. Twelve
pounds. Sixty miles per hour on impact.</td>
<td><img src="dentist.gif" /><br /><b>Two-millimeter bit.
Under an ounce. Fifty revolutions per second.</b></td>
</tr></table>
<table width="400"><tr><td align="center">
<h1>Visit the Dentist.</h1>
```

LISTING 13.3 continued

```
<h2>It's Really Not So Bad.</h2>
<p>Getting yourself to go to the dentist shouldn't be like
pulling teeth. Modern oral care is relatively painless and
inexpensive, compared to some of the alternatives. So make
an appointment today.</p>
<p><b>1-800-PAINLESS</b><br />
<i>Dr. Mathew Eber, D.D.E.</i></p>
</td></tr></table>
</div></body></html>
```

FIGURE 13.3

HTML tables give you greater flexibility and control when laying out your Web pages.

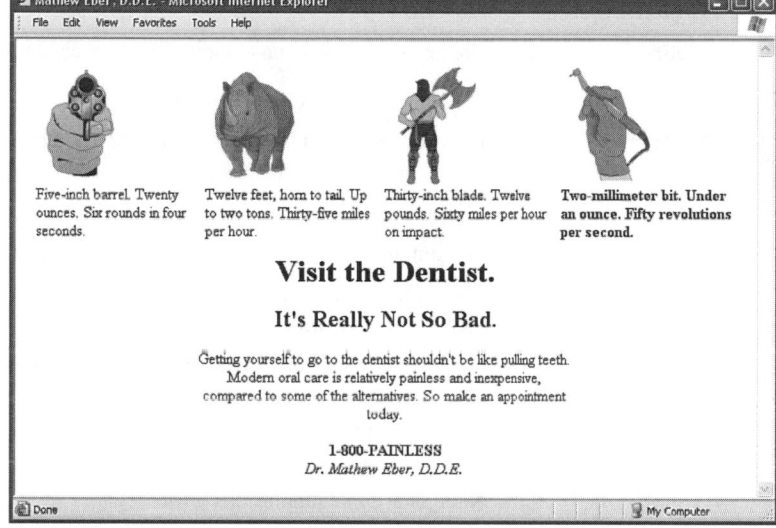

I used two different tables in Listing 13.3 and Figure 13.3. The first table allowed me to arrange the images and text into four columns. The second table let me confine the text to the middle 400 pixels of the screen, essentially giving me extra-wide margins. Remember both of these applications of tables—you'll probably find uses for them often!

13

For an example of how you can use tables for creative layout, click "LOOK: The Site of the '90s" at http://www.24hourHTMLcafe.com/hour13/.

Your real-world site will probably be a bit tamer than the LOOK site—but some of you will start getting even crazier ideas....

Summary

In this hour you learned to arrange text and images into organized arrangements or rows and columns, called tables. You learned the three basic tags for creating tables and many optional attributes for controlling the alignment, spacing, and appearance of tables. You also saw that tables can be used together and nested within one another for an even wider variety of layout options.

Table 13.1 summarizes the tags and attributes covered in this hour.

TABLE 13.1   HTML Tags and Attributes Covered in Hour 13

Tag/Attribute	Function
`<table>...</table>`	Creates a table that can contain any number of rows (`<tr>` tags).
Attributes	
`border="..."`	Indicates the width in pixels of the table borders. `border="0"` or omitting the `border` attribute, makes borders invisible.
`cellspacing="..."`	The amount of space between the cells in the table.
`cellpadding="..."`	The amount of space between the edges of the cell and its contents.
`width="..."`	The width of the table on the page, in either exact pixel values or as a percentage of page width.
`bgcolor="..."`	Background color of all cells in the table that do not contain their own `background` or `bgcolor` attribute.
`background="..."`	Background image to tile within all cells in the table that do not contain their own `background` or `bgcolor` attribute (some versions of Netscape Navigator don't support this attribute).
`<tr>...</tr>`	Defines a table row, containing one or more cells (`<td>` tags).
Attributes	
`align="..."`	The horizontal alignment of the contents of the cells within this row. Possible values are `left`, `right`, and `center`.
`valign="..."`	The vertical alignment of the contents of the cells within this row. Possible values are `top`, `middle`, and `bottom`.
`bgcolor="..."`	Background color of all cells in the row that do not contain their own `background` or `bgcolor` attributes.
`background="..."`	Background image to tile within all cells in the row that do not contain their own `background` or `bgcolor` attributes.
`<td>...</td>`	Defines a table data cell.

TABLE 13.1 continued

Tag/Attribute	Function
	Attributes
align="..."	The horizontal alignment of the contents of the cell. Possible values are left, right, and center.
valign="..."	The vertical alignment of the contents of the cell. Possible values are top, middle, and bottom.
rowspan="..."	The number of rows this cell will span.
colspan="..."	The number of columns this cell will span.
width="..."	The width of this column of cells, in exact pixel values or as a percentage of the table width.
bgcolor="..."	Background color of the cell.
background="..."	Background image to tile within the cell.
<th>...</th>	Defines a table heading cell. (Accepts all the same attributes as <td>.)

Q&A

Q I made a big table and when I load the page, nothing appears for a long time. Why the wait?

A Because the Web browser has to figure out the size of everything in the table before it can display any part of it, complex tables can take a while to appear on the screen. You can speed things up a bit by always including width and height tags for every graphics image within a table. Using width attributes in the <table> and <td> tags also helps.

Q I've noticed that a lot of pages on the Web have tables in which one cell changes while others stay the same. How do they do that?

A Those sites are using *frames*, not tables. Frames are similar to tables except that each frame contains a separate HTML page and can be updated independently of the others. The new *floating frames*, or *iframes*, can actually be put inside a table, so they can look just like a regular table even though the HTML that creates them is quite different. You'll find out how to make frames in Hour 16, "Multi-Page Layout with Frames."

13

Q I read in another book that there is a table `<caption>` tag, but you didn't mention it in this book. Why not?

A The `<caption>` tag isn't widely used, and considering how much you're learning at once here, I didn't think you needed an extra tag to memorize! Since you asked, however, all the `<caption>` tag does visually is center some text over the top of the table. You can easily do the same thing with the `<div align="center">` tag you're already familiar with, but the idea behind `<caption>` is that some highly intelligent future software might associate it with the table in some profound and meaningful way, thus facilitating communication with higher lifeforms and saving humanity from cosmic obscurity and almost-certain destruction. Or to put it a little more literally, the `<caption>` tag is used to identify the title of a table, which could have some usefulness if the page is processed by a non-visual browser.

Another HTML feature that is related to the `<caption>` tag is the `summary` attribute, which acts somewhat like a table equivalent of the `alt` attribute that is used with images. Whereas the `<caption>` tag is used to specify the title of a table, the `summary` attribute provides a brief description of a table. Both the `<caption>` tag and the `summary` attribute are considered accessibility features of HTML, which help aid users who don't use a traditional Web browser. To learn more about accessibility and how to design Web pages that are more accessible, visit this Web page at `http://aware.hwg.org/why/`.

Q Aren't there some new table tags in HTML 4? And isn't this a book about HTML 4?

A The HTML 4 standard introduces several new table tags not discussed in this book. The primary practical uses of these extensions are to prepare for some advanced features that Web browsers aren't fully supporting just yet, such as tables with their own scrollbars and more reliable reading of tables for visually impaired users. If either of these things is of direct concern to you, you can find out about the new tags at the W3C Web site (`http://www.w3c.org/`). The new tags do not directly affect how tables are displayed in any existing Web browser.

Don't worry—the new tags do not and will not make any of the table tags covered in this hour obsolete. They will all continue to work just as they do now.

Workshop

The workshop contains quiz questions and activities to help you solidify your understanding of the material covered. Try to answer all questions before looking at the "Answers" section that follows.

Quiz

1. You want a Web page with two columns of text side by side. How do you create it?

2. You think the columns you created for question 1 look too close together. How do you add 30 pixels of space between them?

3. Write the HTML to create the table shown in the following figure:

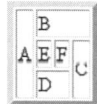

Answers

1. With the following table:
   ```
   <table>
   <tr>
     <td align="top">
   ...First column of text goes here...
     </td>
     <td align="top">
   ...Second column of text goes here...
     </td>
   </tr>
   </table>
   ```

2. Add `cellspacing="30"` to the `<table>` tag. (Alternatively, you could use `cellpadding="15"` to add 15 pixels of space inside the edge of each column.)

3.
   ```
   <table border="5">
   <tr>
     <td rowspan="3">A</td>
     <td colspan="3">B</td>
   </tr>
   <tr>
     <td>E</td>
     <td>F</td>
     <td rowspan="2">C</td>
   </tr>
   <tr>
     <td colspan="2">D</td>
   </tr>
   </table>
   ```

13

Exercises

- You can use a simple one-celled table with a border to draw a rectangle around any section of text on a Web page. By nesting that single-cell table in another two-column table, you can put a sidebar of text to the left or right side of your Web page. Outlined sections of text and sidebars are very common on printed paper pages, so you'll probably find uses for them on your Web pages, too.

- Do you have any pages where different visitors might be interested in different information? Use a table to present two or three columns of text, each with its own heading (and perhaps its own graphic). That way, something of interest to everyone will be visible at the top of the page when it first appears.

HOUR **14**

Formatting Pages with Style Sheets

In the previous hour I showed you how to use tables to layout pages in rows and columns. Tables have been used heavily across the Web as a page layout tool, but they're now being phased out for that particular purpose thanks to style sheets. Style sheets go much further than simply providing a better way to layout pages, however. Style sheets are now the preferred way to apply fonts, control margins, and tweak just about every other visible aspect of Web pages.

The concept behind style sheets is simple: You create a single style sheet document that specifies the fonts, colors, backgrounds, and other characteristics that establish a unique look for a Web site. You then link every page that should have that look to the style sheet, instead of specifying all those styles repeatedly in each separate document. When you decide to change your official corporate typeface or color scheme, you can modify all your Web pages at once just by changing one or two style sheets.

 A *style sheet* is a grouping of formatting instructions that can control the appearance of many HTML pages at once.

If style sheets accomplished this and nothing else, they'd save millions of dollars worth of Webmasters' time and become an integral part of most Web publishing projects. But they aim to do this and much more as well. The HTML style sheet standard enables you to set a great number of formatting characteristics that were never possible before with any amount of effort. These include exacting typeface controls, letter and line spacing, margins and page borders, and expanded support for non-European languages and characters. They also enable sizes and other measurements to be specified in familiar units such as inches, millimeters, points, and picas. You can also use style sheets to precisely position graphics and text anywhere on a Web page.

In short, style sheets bring the sophistication level of paper-oriented publishing to the Web. And they do so—you'll pardon the expression—with style.

 If you have three or more Web pages that share (or should share) similar formatting and fonts, you may want to create a style sheet for them as you read this hour. Even if you choose not to create a complete style sheet, you'll find it helpful to apply styles to individual HTML elements directly within a Web page.

A Basic Style Sheet

Despite their intimidating power, style sheets can be very simple to create. Consider the document in Figures 14.1 and 14.2. These documents share several properties that could be put into a common style sheet.

- They use the Book Antiqua font for body text and Prose Antique for headings.
- They use an image named `parchmnt.jpg` as a background tile.
- All text is maroon colored (on a color screen, not in this book!).
- They have wide margins and indented body text.
- There is lots of vertical space between lines of text.
- The footnotes are centered and in small print.

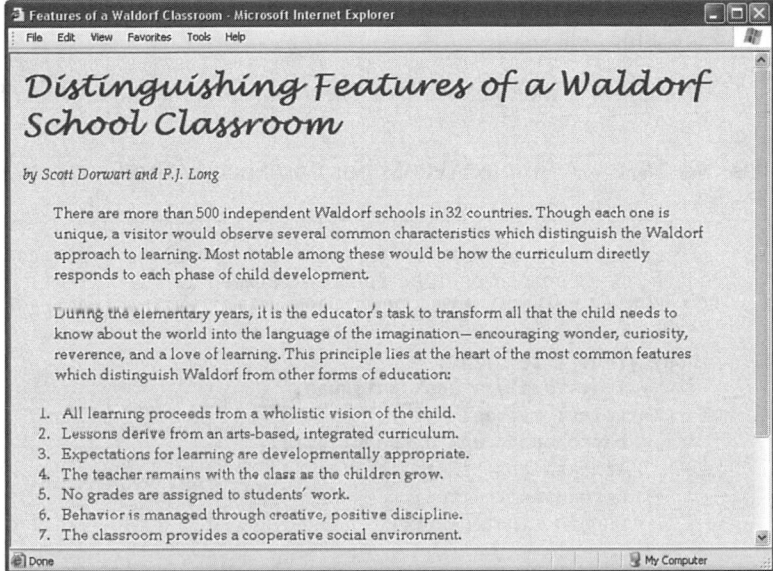

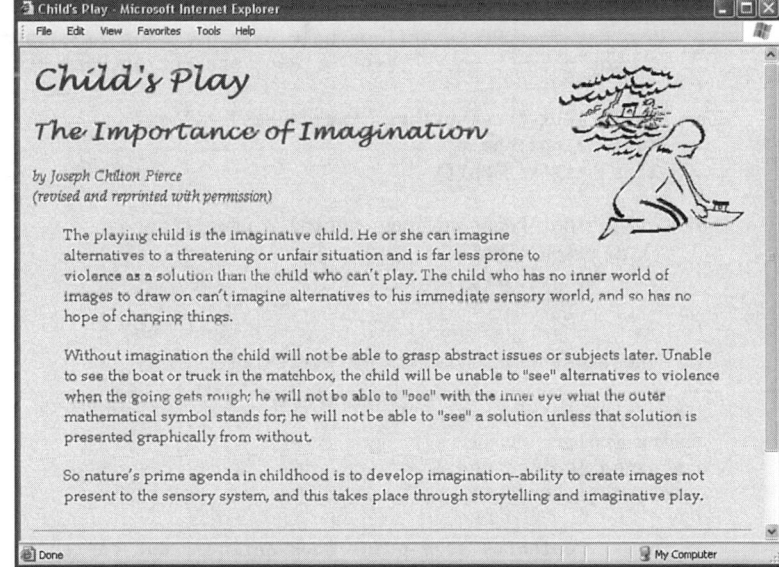

Some of these properties, such as text color, background tile, and centered small print, are easy to achieve with ordinary HTML tags. Others, such as line spacing and wide margins, are beyond the scope of standard HTML. All of them can now be achieved easily with style sheets.

Listing 14.1 shows how a style sheet that specified these properties would look.

LISTING 14.1   A Single Style Sheet Can Specify the Properties of Any Number of Pages

```
/* Make all body text maroon-colored 12-point Book Antiqua
   with 16-point vertical spacing between lines of text
   and 10-point margins. Use parchmnt.gif as the background.
*/
body {font-size: 12pt;
      font-family: "Book Antiqua";
      color: maroon;
      background: url(parchmnt.gif);
      line-height: 16pt;
      margin-left: 10pt;
      margin-right: 10pt;}

/* Indent paragraphs */
p {margin-left: 24pt;
   margin-right: 24pt;}

/* Make headings Prose Antique bold with generous line spacing.
   If user doesn't have Prose Antique, use Lucida Handwriting.
*/
h1 {font: 24pt ProseAntique, Lucida Handwriting;
    font-weight: bold;
    line-height: 30pt;}

h2 {font: 18pt ProseAntique, Lucida Handwriting;
    font-weight: bold;
    line-height: 22pt;}

/* Don't underline links, and make all links red.
   Make links flash black when activated.
*/
a {text-decoration: none;}
a:link {color: red;}
a:visited {color: red;}
a:active {color: black;}

/* Format footnotes as 9-point Book Antiqua, and center them. */
div.footnote {font-size: 9pt;
              line-height: 12pt;
              text-align: center;}
```

The first thing you'll undoubtedly notice about this style sheet is that it doesn't look anything like normal HTML. Style sheet specifications are really a separate language.

Of course, there are some familiar HTML tags in there. As you might guess, body, p, h1, h2, a, and div in the style sheet refer to the corresponding tags in the HTML documents to which the style sheet will be applied. In curly braces after each tag name are the specifications for how all text within that tag should appear.

In this case, all body text that isn't within some other tag should be rendered at a size of 12 points, in the Book Antiqua font if possible, and with the color maroon and 14 points between lines. The page should have 10-point margins, and the background should be the image found at the relative URL parchmnt.jpg.

Any paragraph starting with a <p> tag will be indented an additional 24 points. Any text within <h1> or <h2> tags should be rendered in boldface ProseAntique at a size of 24 points and 18 points, respectively. If a user doesn't have a font named ProseAntique installed, the Lucida Handwriting font will be used instead.

NEW TERM The pt after each measurement in Listing 14.1 means *points* (there are 72 points in an inch). If you prefer, you can specify any style sheet measurement in inches (in), centimeters (cm), pixels (px), or widths-of-a-letter-m, which are called ems (em) .

> The "point sizes" used in the HTML <font> tag are not the same as the point sizes specified in style sheets. <font size="3"> corresponds to approximately 12-point text, <font size="1"> is about 6-point text, and <font size="7"> (the maximum size for the font tag) is about 24-point text. You can specify font sizes as large as you like with style sheets, although some display devices and printers will not correctly handle fonts over 200 points.

To link this style sheet to the HTML documents, you include a <link /> tag in the <head> section of each document. Listing 14.2 is the HTML for the page in Figure 14.1. It contains the following <link /> tag:

```
<link rel="stylesheet" type="text/css" href="hhh.css" />
```

This assumes the style sheet was saved under the name hhh.css in the same directory folder as the HTML document. As long as the Web browser supports style sheets, and most modern browsers do, the properties specified in the style sheet will apply to the content in the page without the need for any <font> tags or other special HTML formatting.

14

LISTING 14.2   This Page Shown in Figure 14.1

```
<html><head><title>Features of a Waldorf Classroom</title>
<link rel="STYLESHEET" type="text/css" href="hhh.css" /></head>
<body>
<h1>Distinguishing Features of a Waldorf School Classroom</h1>
<i>by Scott Dorwart and P.J. Long</i>
<p>There are more than 500 independent Waldorf schools in 32
countries. Though each one is unique, a visitor would observe
several common characteristics which distinguish the Waldorf
approach to learning. Most notable among these would be how the
curriculum directly responds to each phase of child
development.</p>
<p>During the elementary years, it is the educator&rsquo;s task
to transform all that the child needs to know about the world
into the language of the imagination&mdash;encouraging wonder,
curiosity, reverence, and a love of learning. This principle
lies at the heart of the most common features which distinguish
Waldorf from other forms of education:</p>
<ol>
<li>All learning proceeds from a wholistic vision of the
child.</li>
<li>Lessons derive from an arts-based, integrated curriculum.</li>
<li>Expectations for learning are developmentally appropriate.</li>
<li>The teacher remains with the class as the children grow.</li>
<li>No grades are assigned to students&rsquo; work.</li>
<li>Behavior is managed through creative, positive discipline.</li>
<li>The classroom provides a cooperative social environment.</li>
</ol>
<div class="footnote"><hr />
<i>Scott Dorwart is a carpenter and father of two children who
attend the Green Mountain Waldorf School. P.J. Long is a
psychotherapist and mother of two.</i><hr />
<a href="http://netletter.com/GMWS/HHH.htm">Head, Heart,
Hands: A Waldorf Family Newsletter</a><br />
Published by <a href="http://netletter.com/GMWS/GMWS.htm">The Green
Mountain Waldorf School</a><hr />
</div>
</body></html>
```

In most Web browsers, you can see the commands in a style sheet by opening the .css file and using Notepad or another text editor as the helper
application to view the file. (To determine the name of the .css file, look at
the HTML source of any document that links to it.) To edit your own style
sheets, just use a text editor.

 Although CSS is widely supported in all modern Web browsers, it hasn't always enjoyed such wide support. Additionally, not every browser's support of CSS is flawless. To find out about how major browsers compare to each other in terms of CSS support, take a look at this Web site: `http://www.westciv.com/style_master/academy/browser_support/`.

Understanding CSS

The technology behind style sheets is called CSS, which stands for Cascading Style Sheets. CSS is a language that defines style constructs such as fonts, colors, and positioning, which are used to describe how information is displayed. As you've already seen, CSS styles are stored in style sheets, which contain *style rules* that apply styles to elements of a given type. Style sheet rules are usually placed in external style sheet documents with the file extension `.css`. This explains the naming of the `hhh.css` file you saw a moment ago.

NEW TERM   A *style rule* is a formatting instruction that can be applied to an element on a Web page, such as a paragraph of text or a link.

The "cascading" part of the name CSS refers to the manner in which style sheet rules are applied to elements in an HTML document. More specifically, styles in a CSS style sheet form a hierarchy where more specific styles override more general styles. It is the responsibility of CSS to determine the precedence of style rules according to this hierarchy, which gives the rules a cascading effect. If that sounds a bit confusing, just think of the cascading mechanism in CSS as being similar to genetic inheritance where general traits are passed on from a parent to a child, but more specific traits are entirely unique to the child; base style rules are applied throughout a style sheet but can be overridden by more specific style rules.

NEW TERM   You may notice that I use the term element a fair amount in this hour and the next. An element is simply a piece of information (content) in a Web page, such as an image, a paragraph, or a link.

There are actually two different languages to choose from when you create a style sheet. The first version of CSS is known as *Cascading Style Sheets Level 1*, or *CSS1*, and was created back in 1996. The newer CSS2 standard was created in 1998, and while that still seems like a long time ago, only recently has CSS2 fully caught on with Web browsers. With all the power and promise of CSS, browser support has always been an enormous problem. Fortunately, browsers have finally caught up for the most part, and you can now

14

safely use CSS2 style sheets without too much concern. Granted, you may still have a few users who haven't upgraded, but generally speaking it's safe to move forward with CSS2.

> If you know for a fact that the target audience for your Web pages is using very outdated computers and Web browsers, you should stick to CSS1, and possibly even no style sheets at all. This would be a rare group of people, however.

You'll find a complete reference guide to both the CSS1 and CSS2 style sheet languages at www.w3c.org, which is also where you can go to find out which styles are part of which CSS version. The rest of this hour explains how to put the information from those reference documents to use in a way that is compatible with the current generation of Web browsers.

A CSS Style Primer

You now have a basic knowledge of CSS style sheets and how they are based upon style rules that describe the appearance of information in Web pages. The next few sections of this lesson provide a quick overview of some of the most important styles, and allow you to get started using CSS in your own style sheets.

CSS includes a variety of style properties that are used to control fonts, colors, alignment, and margins, to name just a few facets of Web page styling. The style properties in CSS can be broadly grouped into two major categories:

- Layout properties
- Formatting properties

Layout properties consist of properties that impact the positioning of elements on a Web page. For example, layout properties allow you to control the width, height, margin, padding, and alignment of content, and even go so far as to allow you to place content at exact positions on a page. This is something impossible to carry out in HTML alone!

Layout Properties

CSS layout properties are used to determine how content is placed on a Web page. One of the most important layout properties is the display property, which describes how an element is displayed with respect to other elements. There are four possible values for the display property:

- block—The element is displayed on a new line, as in a new paragraph
- list-item—The element is displayed on a new line with a list-item mark (bullet) next to it
- inline—The element is displayed inline with the current paragraph
- none—The element is not displayed

It's easier to understand the display property if you visualize each element on a Web page occupying a rectangular area when displayed—the display property controls the manner in which this rectangular area is displayed. For example, the block value results in the element being placed on a new line by itself, while the inline value places the element next to the content just before it. The display property is one of the few style properties that you will define for most style rules. Following is an example of how to set the display property:

```
display:block;
```

> The display property relies on a concept known as *relative positioning*, which means that elements are positioned relative to the location of other elements on a page. CSS also supports *absolute positioning*, which allows you to place an element at an exact location on a page independent of other elements. You learn more about both of these types of positioning in the next hour, "Making the Most of Style Sheets."

You control the size of the rectangular area for an element with the width and height properties. Like many size-related CSS properties, width and height property values can be specified in several different units of measurement:

- in—Inches
- cm—Centimeters
- mm—Millimeters
- px—Pixels
- pt—Points

You can mix and match units however you choose within a style sheet, but it's generally a good idea to be consistent across a set of similar style properties. For example, you might want to stick with points for font properties or pixels for dimensions. Following is an example of setting the width of an element using pixel units:

```
width:200px;
```

14

Formatting Properties

CSS formatting properties are used to control the appearance of content on a Web page, as opposed to controlling the physical position of the content. One of the most popular formatting properties is the `border` property, which is used to establish a visible boundary around an element with a box or partial box. The following `border` properties provide a means of describing the borders of an element:

- `border-width`—The width of the border edge
- `border-color`—The color of the border edge
- `border-style`—The style of the border edge
- `border-left`—The left side of the border
- `border-right`—The right side of the border
- `border-top`—The top of the border
- `border-bottom`—The bottom of the border
- `border`—All of the border sides

The `border-width` property is used to establish the width of the border edge, and is often expressed in pixels, as the following code demonstrates:

```
border-width:5px;
```

Not surprisingly, the `border-color` and `border-style` properties are used to set the border color and style. Following is an example of how these two properties are set:

```
border-color:blue;
border-style:dotted;
```

The `border-style` property can be set to any of the following values:

- `solid`—A single-line border
- `double`—A double-line border
- `dashed`—A dashed border
- `dotted`—A dotted border
- `groove`—A border with a groove appearance
- `ridge`—A border with a ridge appearance
- `inset`—A border with an inset appearance
- `outset`—A border with an outset appearance
- `none`—No border

The default value of the `border-style` property is `none`, which is why elements don't have a border unless you set the border property to a different style. The most common border styles are the `solid` and `double` styles.

The `border-left`, `border-right`, `border-top`, and `border-bottom` properties allow you to set the border for each side of an element individually. If you want a border to appear the same on all four sides, you can use the single `border` property by itself. Following is an example of using the `border` property to set a border that consists of two red lines that are a total of ten pixels in width:

```
border:10px double red;
```

While the color of an element's border is set with the `border-color` property, the color of the inner region of an element is set using the `color` and `background-color` properties. The `color` property sets the color of text in an element (foreground), while the `background-color` property sets the color of the background behind the text. Following is an example of setting both color properties to predefined colors:

```
color:black;
background-color:orange;
```

You can also assign custom colors to these properties by specifying the colors in hexadecimal or as RGB (Red Green Blue) decimal values, just as you do in HTML:

```
background-color:#999999;
color:rgb(0,0,255);
```

You can also control the alignment and indentation of Web page content without too much trouble. This is accomplished with the `text-align` and `text-indent` properties, as the following code demonstrates:

```
text-align:center;
text-indent:12px;
```

Once you have an element properly aligned and indented, you might be interested in setting its font. The following font properties are used to set the various parameters associated with fonts:

- `font-family`—The family of the font
- `font-size`—The size of the font
- `font-style`—The style of the font (normal or italic)
- `font-weight`—The weight of the font (light, medium, bold, and so on)

The `font-family` property specifies a prioritized list of font family names. A prioritized list is used instead of a single value to provide alternatives in case a font isn't available on a given system. The `font-size` property specifies the size of the font using a unit of

14

measurement, usually points. Finally, the `font-style` property sets the style of the font, while the `font-weight` property sets the weight of the font. Following is an example of setting these font properties:

```
font-family: Arial, sans-serif;
font-size: 36pt;
font-style: italic;
font-weight: medium;
```

Now that you know a whole lot more about style properties and how they work, take a look back at Listing 14.1 and see if it makes a bit more sense. Here's a recap of the style properties used in that style sheet, which you can use as a guide for understanding how it works:

- `font`—Lets you set many font properties at once. You can specify a list of font names separated by commas; if the first is not available, the next is tried, and so on. You can also include the words bold and/or italic and a font size. Each of these font properties can be specified separately with `font-family:`, `font-size:`, `font-weight: bold`, and `font-style: italic` if you prefer.

- `line-height`—Also known in the publishing world as *leading*. This sets the height of each line of text, usually in points.

- `color`—Sets the text color, using the standard color names or hexadecimal color codes (see Hour 10, "Custom Backgrounds and Colors").

- `text-decoration`—Useful for turning link underlining off—simply set it to `none`. The values of `underline`, `italic`, and `line-through` are also supported.

- `text-align`—Aligns text to the `left`, `right`, or `center` (just like the `<div align>` HTML attribute), along with justifying the text with a value of `justify`.

- `text-indent`—Indents beyond the left margin by a specified amount. You can say how far to indent in units (`px`, `in`, `cm`, `mm`, `pt`, `pc`), or you can specify a percentage of the page width (such as 20%).

- `margin`—Sets the left and right margins to the same value, which can be in measurement units or a percentage of the page width. Use `margin-left` and `margin-right` if you want to set the left and right margins independently, and `margin-top` to set the top margin. You learn more about these style properties in the next hour.

- `background`—Places a solid color or image behind text, either with a color or `url(address)`, where address points to a background image tile. Note that this can be assigned not only to the `<body>` tag, but to any tag or span of text to highlight an area on a page.

Using Style Classes

This is a "teach yourself" book, so you don't have to go to a single class to learn how to give your pages great style, although you do need to learn what a style class is. Whenever you want some of the text on your pages to look different than the other text, you can create what amounts to a custom-built HTML tag. Each type of specially formatted text you define is called a *style class*.

NEW TERM A *style class* is a custom set of formatting specifications that can be applied to any passage of text in a Web page.

For example, suppose you wanted two different kinds of `<h1>` headings in your documents. You would create a style class for each one by putting the following text in the style sheet.

```
h1.silly {font: 36pt Comic Sans;}
h1.serious {font: 36pt Arial;}
```

To choose between the two style classes in an HTML page, you would use the `class` attribute, as follows:

```
<h1 class="silly">Marvin's Munchies Inc.</h1>
Text about Marvin's Muchies goes here.
<h1 class="serious">MMI Investor Information</h1>
Text for business investors goes here.
```

The words `Marvin's Munchies Inc.` would appear in 36-point Comic Sans to people whose browsers support style sheets (assuming you included a `<link />` to the style sheet at the top of the Web page and assuming the user has the Comic Sans font installed). The words `MMI Investor Information` would appear in the 36-point Arial font instead.

What if you want to create a style class that could be applied to any text, rather than just headings or some other particular tag? You can associate a style class with the `<div>` tag (which, as you may recall from Hour 5, "Basic Text Alignment and Formatting," can enclose any text but doesn't do anything except what its `align` or other attributes indicate).

You can essentially create your own custom HTML tag by using `div` followed by a period (.) followed by any style class name you make up and any style specifications you choose. That tag can control any number of font, spacing, and margin settings all at once. Wherever you want to apply your custom tag in a page, use a `<div>` tag with the `class=` attribute followed by the class name you created.

For example, the style sheet in Listing 14.1 includes the following style class specification:

14

```
div.footnote {font-size: 9pt;
              line-height: 12pt;
              text-align: center;}
```

This style class is applied in Figure Listing 14.2 with the following tag:

```
<div class="footnote">
```

Everything between that tag and the accompanying `</div>` tag in Listing 14.1 appears in 9-point centered text with 12-point vertical line spacing.

Specifying Inline Styles

In some situations, you might want to specify styles that will be used in only one Web page, in which case you can enclose a style sheet between `<style>` and `</style>` tags and include it directly in an HTML document. Style used in this manner must appear in the `head` of an HTML document. No `<link />` tag is needed, and you cannot refer to that style sheet from any other page (unless you copy it into the beginning of that document, too).

If you want to specify a style for only a small part of a page, such as an individual element, you can go one step further and put a `style` attribute within a `<p>`, `<div>`, or `<span>` tag. This type of style is known as an *inline style* because it is specified right there in the middle of the HTML code.

> `<span>` and `</span>` are *dummy* tags that do nothing in and of themselves except specify a range of text to apply any `style` attributes that you add. The only difference between `<div>` and `<span>` is that `<div>` forces a line break, while `<span>` doesn't. Therefore, you should use `<span>` to modify the style of any portion of text shorter than a paragraph.

Here's how a sample `style` attribute might look:

```
<p style="color: green">This text is green, but
<span style="color: red"> this text is red.</span>
Back to green again, but...</p>
<p>...now the green is over, and we're back to the default color for
this page.</p>
```

Although the effect of this example could be achieved as easily with the `<font color>` tag (see Hour 6, "Advanced Text Formatting"), many style specifications have no corresponding HTML tag. Beyond that, you have to consider the fact that most HTML formatting tags are being phased out in lieu of style sheets. So, you should definitely start getting comfortable using style sheets or inline styles to format your Web pages, as opposed to the old HTML formatting tags.

> To give the pages at the *24-Hour HTML Café* a consistent look and feel, I created a style sheet that is linked to every page in the site. For your edification and convenience, I copied that style sheet text into an HTML page, which you can access from http://www.24hourHTMLcafe.com/hour14.
>
> Here's a little trick to notice in the htmlcafe.css style sheet: I gave the <p> tag a style with a left margin of 40 pixels. This means that every <p> tag in the *24-Hour HTML Café* pages doesn't just start a new paragraph, but also indents the text 40 pixels. Whenever I don't want indentation, I can leave out the <p> and </p> tags before and after a paragraph or place <p></p> before the paragraph to skip a line without indenting.

Summary

In this hour you learned that a style sheet can control the appearance of many HTML pages at once. It can also give you extremely precise control over typography, spacing, and the positioning of HTML elements. You also learned that by adding a style attribute to almost any HTML tag, you can control the style of any part of an HTML page without referring to a separate style sheet document.

Table 14.1 summarizes the tags discussed in this hour. Refer to the CSS1 and CSS2 style sheet standards at www.w3c.org for details on what options can be included after the <style> tag or the style attribute.

TABLE 14.1 HTML Tags and Attributes Covered in Hour 14

Tag	Attribute	Function
<style>...</style>		Allows an internal style sheet to be included within a document. Used between <head> and </head>.
<link />		Links to an external style sheet (or other document type). Used in the <head> section of the document.
	href="..."	The address of the style sheet.
	type="..."	The Internet content type. (Always "text/css" for a style sheet.)
	rel="..."	The link type. (Always "stylesheet" for style sheets.)

14

TABLE 14.1   continued

Tag	Attribute	Function
`<span>...</span>`		Does nothing at all, except provide a place to put `style` or other attributes. (Similar to `<div>...</div>`, but does not cause a line break.)
	`style="..."`	Includes inline style specifications. (Can be used in `<span>`, `<div>`, `<body>`, and most other HTML tags.)

Q&A

Q Say I link a style sheet to my page that says all text should be blue, but there's a `<span style="font-color: red">` tag in the page somewhere. Will that text come out blue or red?

A Red. Local inline styles always take precedence over external style sheets. Any style specifications you put between `<style>` and `</style>` tags at the top of a page will also take precedence over external style sheets (but not over inline styles later in the same page). This is the cascading effect of style sheets that I mentioned earlier in the hour.

Q Can I link more than one style sheet to a single page?

A Sure. For example, you might have a sheet for font stuff and another one for margins and spacing—just include a `<link />` for both.

Workshop

The workshop contains quiz questions and activities to help you solidify your understanding of the material covered. Try to answer all questions before looking at the "Answers" section that follows.

Quiz

1. Create a style sheet to specify 30-point blue Arial headings, and all other text in double-spaced 10-point blue Times Roman (or the default browser font).

2. If you saved the style sheet you made for question 1 as `corporat.css`, how would you apply it to a Web page named `intro.htm`?

Answers

1. ```
   h1 {font: 30pt blue Arial}
   body {font: 10pt blue}
   ```

2. Put the following tag between the `<head>` and `</head>` tags of the `intro.htm` document:

   ```
   <link rel="stylesheet" type="text/css" href="corporat.css" />
   ```

Exercises

- Develop a standard style sheet for your Web site and link it into all your pages. (Use inline styles for pages that need to deviate from it.) If you work for a corporation, chances are it has already developed font and style specifications for printed materials. Get a copy of those specifications and follow them for company Web pages, too.

- Be sure to explore the official style sheet specs at `www.w3c.org` and try some of the more esoteric style controls I didn't mention in this hour.

14
   ```

HOUR 15

Making the Most of Style Sheets

In the previous lesson you learned a little bit about how to position HTML content using the default approach to CSS positioning, which is known as *relative positioning*. In relative positioning, elements on a page are displayed according to the flow of the page, where each element physically appears after the element preceding it on the page. This is the way elements have been positioned in every HTML document you've seen throughout the book thus far. While relative positioning has its merits, style sheets offer another approach that gives you much more control over how to position elements on a page.

This hour explores HTML positioning as controlled by style sheets. You find out how to carry out relatively and absolute positioning, as well as how to deliberately overlap elements and control how they stack on top of each other. You also find out how to tweak the margins and spacing between elements on a page. By the end of this hour, you'll no longer rely on tables to lay out your pages—you'll realize that style sheets are just too powerful to overlook.

The Whole Scoop on Positioning

I already mentioned that relative positioning is the default type of positioning used by HTML. You can think of relative positioning as being akin to laying out checkers on a checkerboard: The checkers are arranged from left to right, and when you get to the edge of the board you move on to the next row. Elements that are styled with the `block` value for the `display` style property are automatically placed on a new row, while `inline` elements are placed on the same row immediately next to the element preceding them.

> Relative positioning is the default positioning approach used by CSS, so if you don't specify the positioning of a style rule it will default to relative positioning.

The other type of positioning supported by CSS is known as *absolute positioning* because it allows you to set the exact position of HTML content on a page. Although absolute positioning gives you the freedom to spell out exactly where an element is to appear, this position is still relative to any parent elements that appear on the page. In other words, absolute positioning allows you to specify the exact location of an element's rectangular area with respect to its parent's area, which is very different from relative positioning.

As you probably know, with freedom comes responsibility. And with the freedom of placing elements anywhere you want on a page, you can run into the problem of overlap, which is when an element takes up space used by another element. There is nothing stopping you from specifying the absolute locations of elements so that they overlap. In this case, CSS relies on the z-index of each element to determine which element is on the top and which is on the bottom. You learn more about the z-index of elements later in the lesson. For now, let's take a look at exactly how you control whether or not a style rule uses relative or absolute positioning.

The type of positioning (relative or absolute) used by a particular style rule is determined by the `position` property, which is capable of having one of the following two values: `relative` or `absolute`. After specifying the type of positioning, you then specify the specific position using the following properties:

- `left`—The left position offset
- `right`—The right position offset
- `top`—The top position offset
- `bottom`—The bottom position offset

You might think that these position properties only make sense for absolute positioning, but they actually apply to both types of positioning. Under relative positioning, the position of an element is specified as an offset relative to the original position of the element. So, if you set the left property of an element to 25px, the left side of the element will be shifted over 25 pixels from its original (relative) position. An absolute position, on the other hand, is specified relative to the parent of the element to which the style is applied. So, if you set the left property of an element to 25px under absolute positioning, the left side of the element will appear 25 pixels to the right of the parent element's left edge.

You might understand this positioning stuff better by looking at an example. Check out the following HTML code for a very simple Web page:

```
<html>
<head>
<title>Color Blocks</title>
<link rel="stylesheet" type="text/css" href="colors_rel.css" />
</head>

<body>
<div class="one">One</div>
<div class="two">Two</div>
<div class="three">Three</div>
<div class="four">Four</div>
</body>
</html>
```

Admittedly, this page isn't all that interesting, but it's a good way to demonstrate the difference between relative and absolute positioning. Notice in the code that there are several div elements, each with a different class, and therefore a different style rule. Before applying a style sheet to this page, take a look at it in Figure 15.1.

FIGURE 15.1

The Color Blocks sample document is far beyond boring without the help of any style sheets.

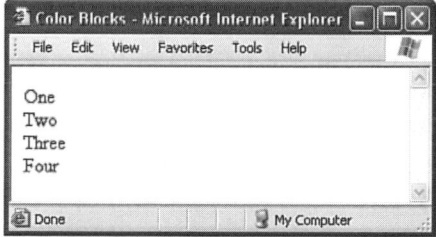

I know, this is an extremely unimpressive page. In fact, it demonstrates perfectly how much style sheets impact otherwise boring content, as you're about to see. Listing 15.1 contains a style sheet for this page that uses relative positioning to arrange the colored squares.

LISTING 15.1   Using Relative Positioning in the `colors_rel.css` Style Sheet

```
div {
  display:block;
  position:relative;
  width:100px;
  height:75px;
  border:10px single black;
  color:black;
  text-align:center;
}

div.one {
  background-color:red;
}

div.two {
  background-color:green;
}

div.three {
  background-color:blue;
}

div.four {
  background-color:yellow;
}
```

This code first sets the `position` style property for the `div` element to `relative`. Since the remaining style rules are inherited from the `div` style rule, they inherit its relative positioning. In fact, the only difference between the other style rules is that they have different background colors. Figure 15.2 shows the Color Blocks page as it is displayed in Internet Explorer using this relative positioning style sheet.

Notice in the figure that the `div` elements are displayed one after the next, which is what you would expect out of relative positioning. To make things more interesting, you can change the positioning to absolute and explicitly specify the placement of the colors. Listing 15.2 contains a modified style sheet for the Color Blocks page that uses absolute positioning to arrange the colors.

LISTING 15.2   Using Absolute Positioning in the `colors_abs.css` Style Sheet

```
div {
  display:block;
  position:absolute;
  width:100px;
  height:75px;
```

LISTING 15.2   continued

```css
    border:10px single black;
    color:black;
    text-align:center;
  }

  div.one {
    background-color:red;
    left:0px;
    top:0px;
  }

  div.two {
    background-color:green;
    left:75px;
    top:25px;
  }

  div.three {
    background-color:blue;
    left:150px;
    top:50px;
  }

  div.four {
    background-color:yellow;
    left:225px;
    top:75px;
  }
```

15

FIGURE 15.2

The Color Blocks sample document is displayed in Internet Explorer using a style sheet with relative positioning.

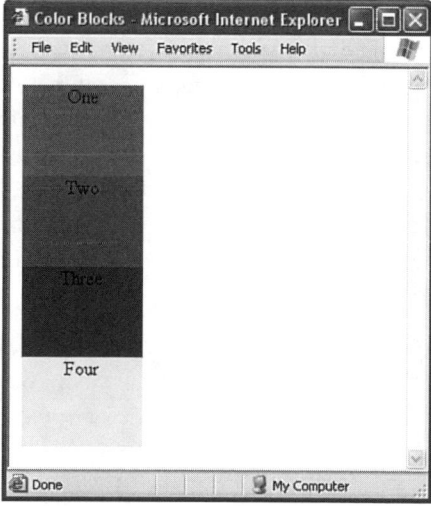

This style sheet sets the `position` property to `absolute`, which is necessary in order for the style sheet to use absolute positioning. Additionally, the `left` and `top` properties are set for each of the inherited `div` style rules. However, the position of each of these rules is set so that the elements will be displayed overlapping each other, as shown in Figure 15.3.

FIGURE 15.3
The Color Blocks sample document is displayed in Internet Explorer using a style sheet with absolute positioning.

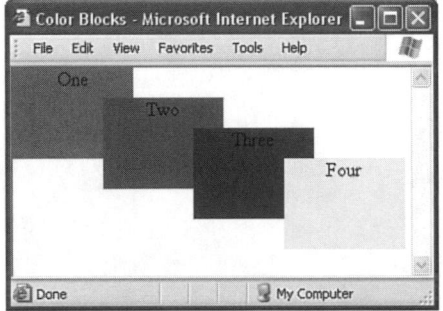

This figure shows how absolute positioning allows you to place elements exactly where you want them. It also reveals how easy it is to arrange elements so that they overlap each other. You might be curious as to how a Web browser knows which elements to draw on top when they overlap. Read on to find out!

Controlling the Way Things Stack Up

There are no doubt situations where you'd like to be able to carefully control the manner in which elements overlap each other on a Web page. The `z-index` style property allows you to set the order of elements with respect to how they stack on top of each other. While the name z-index might sound a little strange, it refers to the notion of a third dimension (Z) that points into the computer screen, in addition to the two dimensions (X and Y) that go across and down the screen. Another way to think of the z-index is the relative position of a single magazine within a stack of magazines. A magazine nearer the top of the stack has a higher z-index than a magazine lower in the stack. Similarly, an overlapped element with a higher z-index is displayed on top of an element with a lower z-index.

The `z-index` property is used to set a numeric value that indicates the relative z-index of a style rule. The number assigned to `z-index` only has meaning with respect to other style rules in a style sheet, which means that setting the `z-index` property for a single rule doesn't really mean much. On the other hand, if you set `z-index` for several style rules

15

that apply to overlapped elements, the elements with the higher z-index values will appear on top of elements with lower z-index values.

> Regardless of the z-index value you set for a style rule, an element displayed with the rule will always appear on top of its parent.

Listing 15.3 contains another version of a style sheet for the Color Blocks sample page that has z-index settings to alter the natural overlap of elements.

LISTING 15.3   The colors_z.css Style Sheet Alters the Z-index of Elements in the Color Blocks Sample Page

```
div {
  display:block;
  position:absolute;
  width:100px;
  height:75px;
  border:10px single black;
  color:black;
  text-align:center;
}

div.one {
  background-color:red;
  z-index:0;
  left:0px;
  top:0px;
}

div.two {
  background-color:green;
  z-index:3;
  left:75px;
  top:25px;
}

div.three {
  background-color:blue;
  z-index:2;
  left:150px;
  top:50px;
}

div.four {
  background-color:yellow;
```

LISTING 15.3   continued

```
        z-index:1;
        left:225px;
        top:75px;
   }
```

The only change in this code from what you saw in Listing 15.2 is the addition of the z-index property in each of the derived div style rules. Notice that the first div has a setting of 0, which should make it the lowest element in terms of the z-index, while the second div has the highest z-index. Figure 15.4 shows the Color Blocks page as displayed with this style sheet, which clearly shows how the z-index affects the displayed content.

FIGURE 15.4
The Color Blocks sample page is displayed using a style sheet that alters the z-index of the colors.

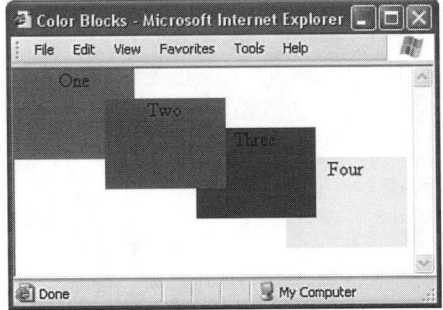

The figure reveals how the z-index style property makes it possible to carefully control the overlap of elements.

Working with Margins

If you look to the left and right of the pages in this book, you'll notice that there is white space that appears between the paragraphs of text and the edge of the pages; this space is known as the margin of the book. Style sheet margins allow you to add empty space around the outside of the rectangular area for an element on a Web page. Following are the style properties that you use to set margins:

- margin-top—Sets the top margin
- margin-right—Sets the right margin
- margin-bottom—Sets the bottom margin
- margin-left—Sets the left margin
- margin—Sets the top, right, bottom, and left margins as a single property

You can specify margins using any of the individual margin properties, or with the single margin property. If you decide to set a margin as a percentage, keep in mind that the percentage is calculated based upon the size of the entire page, not the size of the element. So, if you set the margin-left property to 25%, the left margin of the element will end up being 25% of the width of the entire page. The following code shows how to set the top and bottom margins for one of the colors in the Color Blocks sample page that you've been working with throughout this lesson:

```
div.two {
  background-color:green;
  margin-top:5px;
  margin-bottom:20px;
}
```

In this example, the top margin is set to 5 pixels, while the bottom margin is set to 20 pixels. The results of this code are shown in Figure 15.5.

FIGURE 15.5

The Colo Blocks sample page is displayed using a style sheet that sets top and bottom margins for one of the colors.

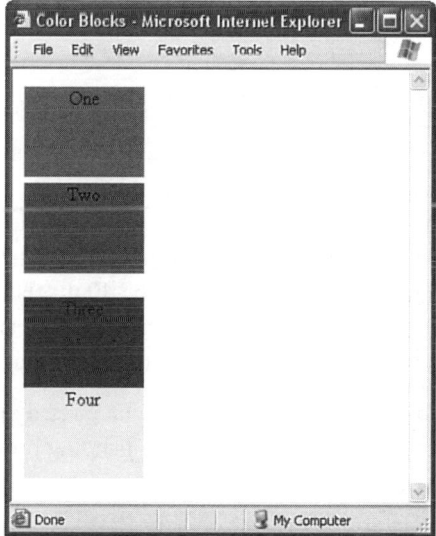

This figure shows how the top and bottom margins appear above and below the second div element. Keep in mind that these margins don't encroach on the content area of any of the colors—they all maintain their original size. In other words, the margins appear around the elements.

If you want to set all of the margins for a style rule, you'll probably want to simplify the code and use the margin property. This property is somewhat flexible in that it offers three different approaches to specifying the margins for a style rule. These different approaches vary based upon how many values you use when setting the property:

- One value—The size of all the margins
- Two values—The size of the top/bottom margins and the left/right margins (in that order)
- Four values—The size of the top, right, bottom, and left margins (in that order)

Following is an example of how you would set the vertical margins (top/bottom) to 5 pixels and the horizontal margins (left/right) to 10% for a style rule:

```
margin:5px 10%;
```

In this code, the top and bottom margins are both set to 5 pixels, while the left and right margins are both set to 10%. Of course, if you wanted to be a little clearer, you could achieve the same effect with the following setting:

```
margin:5px 10% 5px 10%;
```

A Little Padding for Safety

Similar to margins, padding is used to add extra space to elements. However, padding differs from margins in that padding adds space inside the rectangular area of an element, as opposed to around it. As an example, if you create a style rule for an element that establishes a width of 50 pixels and a height of 30 pixels, and then sets the padding of the rule to 5 pixels, the remaining content area will be 40 pixels by 20 pixels. Also, since the padding of an element appears within the element's content area, it will assume the same style as the content of the element, including the background color.

You specify the padding of a style rule using one of the padding properties, which work very much like the margin properties. The following padding properties are available for use in setting the padding of style rules:

- `padding-top`—Sets the top padding
- `padding-right`—Sets the right padding
- `padding-bottom`—Sets the bottom padding
- `padding-left`—Sets the left padding
- `padding`—Sets the top, right, bottom, and left padding as a single property

Similar to margins, you can set the padding of style rules using individual padding properties or the single `padding` property. Padding can also be expressed using either a unit of measurement or a percentage. Following is an example of how you might set the left and right padding for a style rule so that there are 10 pixels of padding on each side of an element's content:

```
padding-left:10px;
padding-right:10px;
```

Also similar to margins, you can set all of the padding for a style rule with a single property, the `padding` property. You can use the same three approaches available for the `margin` property to set the padding property. Following is an example of how you would set the vertical padding (top/bottom) to 12 pixels and the horizontal padding (left/right) to 8 pixels for a style rule:

```
padding:12px 8px;
```

Following is more explicit code that performs the same task by specifying all of the padding values:

```
padding:12px 8px 12px 8px;
```

Keeping Everything Aligned

Knowing that content on a Web page doesn't always fill the entire width of the rectangular area in which it is displayed, it is often helpful to control the alignment of the content. Even if text within a rectangular area extends to multiple lines, alignment still enters the picture because you may want the text justified left or right, or centered. There are a couple of style properties that allow you to control the alignment of Web page content: `text-align` and `vertical-align`.

The `text-align` property aligns an element horizontally within its bounding area, and can be set to `left`, `right`, `center`, or `justify`. The `justify` value performs a full justification on an element. Following is an example of using the `text-align` property to center a hypothetical Web page advertisement:

```
div.ad {
  display:block;
  width:275px;
  margin-bottom:10px;
  border:5px double black;
  color:black;
  background-color:yellow;
  text-align:center
}
```

The last style property defined in this style rule involves setting the `text-align` style to center, which results in the `div.ad` element being centered within its parent. If the parent of this element is the Web page itself, then the element will be centered on the page.

The `vertical-align` property is similar to `text-align` except that it is used to align elements vertically. The `vertical-align` property specifies how an element is aligned with its parent, or in some cases the current line of elements on the page. When I say "current line," I'm really referring to the vertical placement of elements that appear within the same parent element. In other words, I'm talking about inline elements. If several inline elements appear on the same line, you can set their vertical alignments the same to align them vertically. A good example would be a row of images that appear one after the next—the `vertical-align` property allows you to align them vertically.

Following are the acceptable values for use with the `vertical-align` property:

- `top`—Aligns the top of an element with the current line
- `middle`—Aligns the middle of an element with the middle of its parent
- `bottom`—Aligns the bottom of an element with the current line
- `text-top`—Aligns the top of an element with the top of its parent
- `baseline`—Aligns the baseline of an element with the baseline of its parent
- `text-bottom`—Aligns the bottom of an element with the bottom of its parent
- `sub`—Aligns an element as a subscript of its parent
- `super`—Aligns an element as a superscript of its parent

Following is an example of how the `vertical-align` property is used to center text vertically:

```
div.ad {
  display:block;
  width:275px;
  margin-bottom:10px;
  border:5px double black;
  color:black;
  background-color:yellow;
  text-align:center;
  vertical-align:middle
}
```

This code shows how simple it is to modify a style rule so that the element is aligned vertically. In this case, the `div.ad` element is vertically aligned with the middle of its parent.

Managing the Flow of Text

A moment ago I discussed the concept of the "current line," which is an invisible line used to place elements on a page. This line has to do with the flow of elements on a page and comes into play as elements are arranged next to each other across and down the page. Part of the flow of elements is the flow of text on a page. When you mix text with other elements such as images, it's important to control how the text flows around the other elements.

Following are some style properties that provide you with control over text flow:

- `float`—Determines how text flows around an element
- `clear`—Stops the flow of text around an element
- `overflow`—Controls the overflow of text when an element is too small to contain all of the text

The `float` property is used to control how text flows around an element. It can be set to either of the following values: `left` or `right`. These values determine where to position an element with respect to flowing text. So, setting the `float` property to `left` for an image would result in the image being positioned to the left of flowing text.

You can prevent text from flowing next to an element by using the `clear` property, which can be set to `none`, `left`, `right`, or `both`. The default value for the clear property is `none`, indicating that text is to flow with no special considerations for the element. The `left` value causes text to stop flowing around an element until the left side of the page is free of the element. Likewise, the `right` value means that text is not to flow around the right side of the element. The `both` value indicates that text isn't to flow around either side of the element.

The `overflow` property handles overflow text, which is text that doesn't fit within its rectangular area; this can happen if you set the `width` and `height` of an element too small. The `overflow` property can be set to `visible`, `hidden`, or `scroll`. The `visible` setting automatically enlarges the element so that the overflow text will fit within it; this is the default setting for the property. The `hidden` value leaves the element the same size, allowing the overflow text to remain hidden from view. Perhaps the most interesting value is `scroll`, which adds scrollbars to the element so that you can move around and see the text.

Summary

This lesson picked up where the previous lesson left off by continuing to explore the power of style sheets. The focus in this hour had more to do with the positioning of elements on a Web page, and how it can be controlled via CSS style sheets. You started the lesson by learning the difference between relative and absolute positioning, and how each is used to position elements. You then learned about other CSS positioning features such as z-index, margins, padding, and content alignment. You then wrapped up the hour by finding out about a few nifty little style properties that allow you to control the flow of text on a page.

Q&A

Q How do I use positioning and layers to make text and graphics fly around the page? Isn't that what they call dynamic HTML?

A *Dynamic HTML*, or *DHTML*, is a general term that refers to the combination of HTML, style sheets, and scripting to create interactive Web pages. You learn all about scripting in Hour 17, "Web Page Scripting for Non-Programmers," and DHTML in Hour 18, "Setting Pages in Motion with Dynamic HTML."

In a nutshell, scripting lets you use a programming language called JavaScript to modify any HTML content or style sheet information (including positioning) on-the-fly in response to the mouse movements and clicks of people who visit your pages. As you might imagine, this opens up lots of interesting possibilities for making Web pages that are more exciting.

Q How do you know when to use relative versus absolute positioning?

A While there are no set guidelines regarding the usage of relative versus absolute positioning, the general idea is that absolute positioning is only required when you want to exert a fine degree of control over how content is positioned. This has to do with the fact that absolute positioning allows you to position content down to the exact pixel, while relative positioning is much less predictable in terms of how it positions content. This isn't to say that relative positioning can't do a good job of positioning elements on a page, it just means that absolute positioning is more exacting. Of course, this also makes absolute positioning potentially more suscepti-ble to changes in screen size, which you can't really control.

Q If you don't specify the z-index of two elements that overlap each other, how do you know which element will appear on top?

A If the z-index property isn't set for overlapping elements, the element appearing later in the Web page will appear on top. The easy way to remember this is to think of a Web browser drawing each element on a page as it reads it from the HTML document; elements read later in the document are drawn on top of those read earlier.

15

Workshop

The workshop contains quiz questions and activities to help you solidify your understanding of the material covered. Try to answer all questions before looking at the "Answers" section that follows.

Quiz

1. What's the difference between relative and absolute positioning?

2. What CSS style property do you use to control the manner in which elements overlap each other?

3. Write the HTML code to display the words What would you like to, starting exactly at the top-left corner of the browser window, and THROW TODAY? in large type exactly 80 pixels down and 20 pixels to the left of the corner.

Answers

1. In relative positioning, content is displayed according to the flow of a page, where each element physically appears after the element preceding it in the HTML code. Absolute positioning, on the other hand, allows you to set the exact position of content on a page.

2. The z-index style property is used to control the manner in which elements overlap each other.

3.
```
<span style="position: absolute; left: 0px; top: 0px">
What would you like to</span>
<h1 style="position: absolute; left: 80px; top: 20px">
THROW TODAY?</H1>
```

Exercises

- Modify your style sheet from the previous hour's exercises to support absolute positioning. Try placing each element in an exact location on the page.

- Further enhance your style sheet by adding some margins, as well as tweaking the padding of a few elements for a different look.

HOUR 16

Multi-Page Layout with Frames

You've probably come into contact with Web sites where the browser window seemingly allowed you to move around between several different pages. The truth is that the browser really was allowing you to view several pages at once. An HTML feature known as *frames* allows you to divide the browser window into regions that contain separate Web pages; each of these regions is known as a frame. Of course, from the user's perspective, everything comes together to form a single window of Web content, but there are separate pages at work.

Frames are like tables (covered in Hour 13, "Advanced Layout with Tables") in that they allow you to arrange text and graphics into rows and columns. Unlike a table cell, however, any frame can contain links that change the contents of other frames (or itself). For example, one frame could display an index page that changes the page displayed in another frame based upon which links the reader clicks.

To Do

Frames are basically a way of arranging and presenting several Web pages at once. You'll be able to work through this hour faster and get more out of it if you have a few related Web pages ready before you continue.

- If you have an index page or table of contents for your Web site, copy it to a separate directory folder so you can experiment with it without changing the original. Copy a few of the pages that the index links to as well.

- As you read this hour, try modifying the sample frames I present to incorporate your own Web pages.

What Are Frames?

At first glance, Figure 16.1 may look like an ordinary Web page, but it is actually two separate HTML pages, both displayed in the same Web browser window. Each of these pages is displayed in its own *frame*, separated by the horizontal bar.

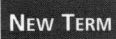 A *frame* is a rectangular region within the browser window that displays a Web page, alongside other pages in other frames.

FIGURE 16.1

Frames allow more than one Web page to be displayed at once.

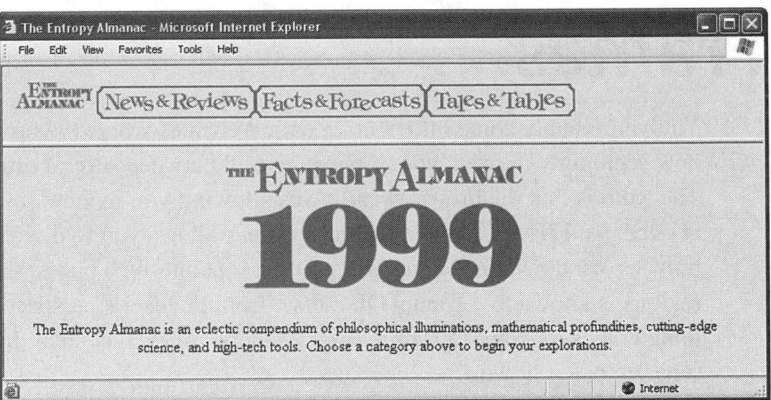

The main advantage of using frames becomes apparent when you click one of the navigational links in the top frame of Figure 16.1. The top frame will not change at all in this example, but a new page will be loaded and displayed in the bottom frame, as in Figure 16.2.

Although frames can certainly be useful, I must admit that I'm not a huge fan of them. The reason is simply because they can sometimes be confusing for users if you overdo it and create too many frames with too many cross links. When implemented properly with only two or three frames, the effect can be helpful, but more than that and you'll likely just cause confusion and frustration among your visitors.

FIGURE 16.2

Clicking Facts & Forecasts in Figure 16.1 brings up a new bottom page, but leaves the top frame the same.

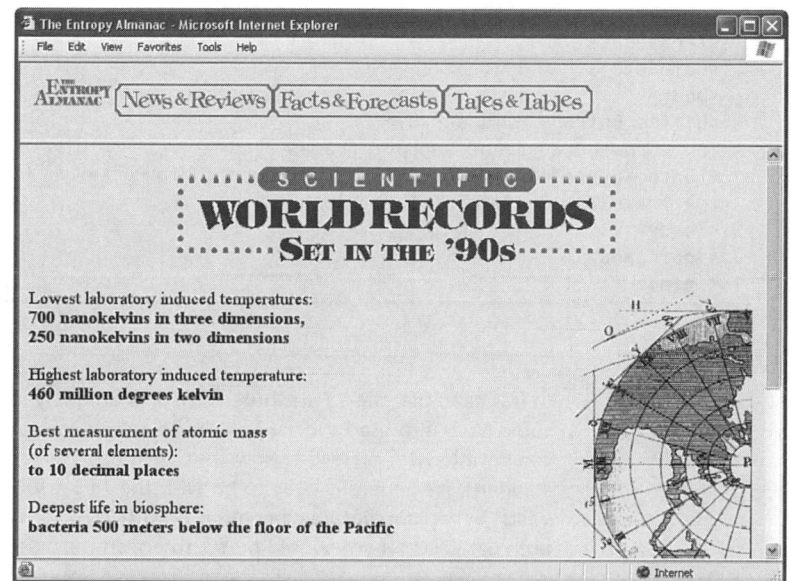

16

Building a Frameset

You might be surprised to find out that frames aren't too difficult to work with in HTML code. So, how did I make the pages in Figures 16.1 and 16.2? First, I created the contents of each frame as an ordinary HTML page. These pages don't contain any tags you haven't already seen in other hours. To put them all together, I used a special kind of page called a *frameset document*.

Creating a Frameset Document

A frameset document actually has no content. It only tells the browser which other pages to load and how to arrange them in the browser window. Listing 16.1 shows the frameset document for the Entropy Almanac site shown in Figures 16.1 and 16.2.

NEW TERM A *frameset document* is an HTML page that instructs the Web browser to split its window into multiple frames, and specifies which Web page should be displayed in each frame.

LISTING 16.1   Frameset Document for the Site in Figure 16.1

```
<html><head><title>The Entropy Almanac</title></head>
<frameset rows="80,*">
  <frame src="banner.htm" id="top" />
  <frame src="greeting.htm" id="main" />
</frameset>
<noframes>
<body>
<h1>The Entropy Almanac</h1>
Your browser does not support frames.
Please <a href="noframes.htm">click here</a> for
the frameless version of this Web site.
</body>
</noframes>
</html>
```

In this example, the id attribute is used to uniquely identify the frames. You could have also used the name attribute, which is popular in HTML 4 but isn't compatible with XHTML 1. Now that most browsers support the XHTML standard, it's generally okay to go with the id attribute instead of name, which helps to maintain compatibility with XHTML. You could also provide both attributes if you would prefer to err on the side of caution.

In the listing there is a <frameset> tag instead of a <body> tag. No tags that would normally be contained in a <body> tag can be within the <frameset> tag. The <frameset> tag in this example includes a rows attribute, meaning that the frames should be arranged on top of each other like the horizontal rows of a table. If you want your frames to be side-by-side, use a cols attribute instead of rows.

You must specify the sizes of the rows or cols, either as precise pixel values or as percentages of the total size of the browser window. You can also use an asterisk (*) to indicate that a frame should fill whatever space is available in the window. If more than one frame has an * value, the remaining space will be divided equally between them.

In Listing 16.1, <frameset rows="80,*"> means to split the window vertically into two frames. The top frame will be exactly 80 pixels tall, and the bottom frame will take up all the remaining space in the window. The top frame contains the document banner.htm (see Listing 16.2), and the bottom frame contains greeting.htm (see Listing 16.3) .

After the framesets in Listing 16.1, I included a complete Web page between the <body> and </body> tags. Notice that this doesn't appear at all in Figures 16.1 or 16.2. All Web browsers that support frames will ignore anything between the <noframes> and </noframes> tags.

The vast majority of browsers in use these days support frames, so the issue of frames compatibility is much less significant than in years past. However, it's still something to consider since it will impact a few users; just include alternative content within the <noframe> tag.

Some Web page publishers actually produce two versions of their site—one with frames and one without. While that's not a terrible option, you can save yourself that hassle by simply including links between all the pages that will appear in your primary frame.

16

LISTING 16.2 The banner.htm Document Serves As a Navigation Bar for the Entropy Almanac Web page

```
<html><head><title>The Entropy Almanac</title></head>
<body background="back.gif"
><a href="greeting.htm" target="main"
><img src="eatiny.gif" border= "0" align="left" /></a
><a href="news.htm" target="main"
><img src="news.gif" border="0" /></a
><a href="facts.htm" target="main"
><img src="facts.gif" border="0" /></a
><a href="tales.htm" target="main"
><img src="tales.gif" border="0" /></a>
</body></html>
```

LISTING 16.3 The greeting.htm Document Acts As a Single Content Frame Within the Entropy Almanac Web page

```
<html><head><title>The Entropy Almanac</title></head><body
background="back.gif"><div align="center"><img src="easmall.gif" /><br />
<img src="1999.gif" /><p>The Entropy Almanac is an eclectic compendium of
philosophical illuminations, mathematical profundities,
cutting-edge science, and high-tech tools. Choose a
category above to begin your explorations.</p>
</div>
</body></html>
```

Because you can't predict the size of the window in which someone will view your Web page, it is often convenient to use percentages rather than exact pixel values to dictate the size of the rows and columns. For example, to make a left frame 20% of the width of the browser window with a right frame taking up the remaining 80%, you would type the following:

```
<frameset cols="20%,80%">
```

An exception to this rule is when you want a frame to contain graphics of a certain size; then you would specify that size in pixels and add a few pixels for the margins and frame borders. This is the case in Listing 16.1, where the images in the top frame are each 42 pixels tall. I allowed 38 extra pixels for margins and borders, making the entire frame 80 pixels tall.

Whenever you specify any frame size in pixels, it's a good idea to include at least one frame in the same frameset with a variable (*) width so that the document can be displayed in a window of any size.

Adding the Frames

Within the `<frameset>` and `</frameset>` tags, you should have a `<frame />` tag indicating which HTML document to display in each frame. (If you have fewer `<frame />` tags than the number of frames defined in the `<frameset>` tag, any remaining frames will be left blank.)

Include a `src` attribute in each `<frame>` tag with the address of the Web page to load in that frame. (You can put the address of an image file instead of a Web page if you just want a frame with a single image in it.)

You can include any HTML page you want in a frame. For smaller frames, however, it's a good idea to create documents specifically for the frames with the reduced display area for each frame in mind. The top frame in Figure 16.1, for instance, is listed in Listing 16.2, and is much shorter than most Web pages because it was designed specifically to fit in a frame under 80 pixels tall.

You may notice that the `<a>` and `<img />` tags in the banner.htm document in Listing 16.2 are arranged a bit strangely. Since I didn't want any space between the graphics, I had to make sure there were no spaces or line breaks between any of the tags. Therefore, I had to put all the line breaks inside the tags. This makes the HTML a bit harder to read, but keeps the images right next to each other on the page.

Linking Between Frames and Windows

The real power of frames begins to emerge when you give a frame a unique name with the `id` attribute (and/or the `name` attribute) in the `<frame />` tag. You can then make any link on the page change the contents of that frame by using the `target` attribute in an `<a>` tag. For example, Listing 16.1 includes the following tag:

```
<frame src="greeting.htm" id="main" />
```

This code displays the `greeting.htm` page in that frame when the page loads and names the frame `"main"`.

In the code for the top frame, which is shown in Listing 16.2, you will see the following link:

```
<a href="facts.htm" target="main"
><img src="facts.gif" border=0 /></a>
```

When the user clicks this link, `facts.htm` is displayed in the frame named `main` (the lower frame). To accomplish this sort of interactivity before the invention of frames, you would have had to use complex programming or scripting languages. Now you can do it with a simple link!

If the `target="main"` attribute hadn't been included, the `facts.htm` page is displayed in the current (top) frame instead.

To save space, I haven't provided a listing of the `facts.htm` page; it's just a regular Web page with no special frame-related features. You can see what the top of it looks like in Figure 16.2, and you can see this whole frameset online at `http://www.24hourHTMLcafe.com/hour16`.

Want to open a page in a new window without using frames? Just use one of the following special names with the `target` attribute of the `<a>` tag. (Example: `<a href="popup.htm" target="_blank">Click here to open the popup.htm document in a new window.</a>`)

- `_blank` loads the link into a new, unnamed window.
- `_top` loads the link into the entire browser window. Use this when you want to get rid of all frames or replace the entire window with a whole new set of frames.
- `_parent` loads the link over the parent frame if the current frame is nested within other frames. (This name does the same thing as `top` unless the frames are nested more than one level deep.)
- `_self` loads the link into the current frame, replacing the document now being displayed in this frame. (You'll probably never use this because you can achieve the same thing by simply leaving out the `target` attribute altogether.)

All other names beginning with an underscore (_) will be ignored.

Nested Frames

By nesting one frameset within another, you can create rather complex frame layouts. For example, the document shown in Figure 16.3 and listed in Listing 16.4 has a total of nine frames. A `cols` frameset is used to split each row of the `rows` frameset into three pieces. Before you get to thinking that I'm contradicting myself when it comes to the complexities of frames, please understand that the purpose of this example is to demonstrate how nested frames work, not to encourage a particular technique.

FIGURE 16.3

This window contains nine frames, some of which are nothing more than blank pages with custom background tiles.

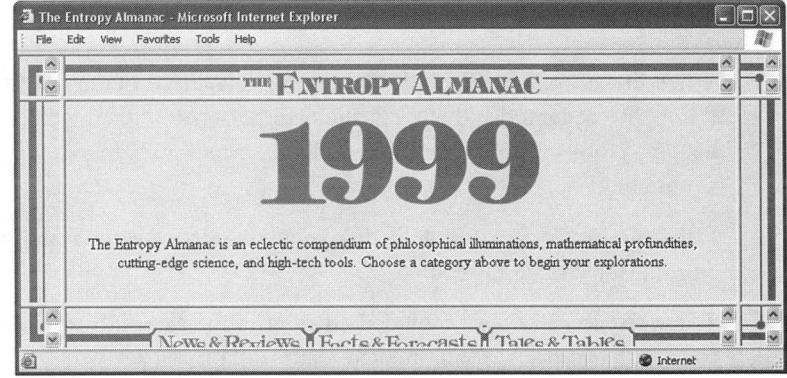

LISTING 16.4 Creating the Page Shown in Figure 16.3 Using Three Horizontal `<frameset>`s Within a Vertical `<frameset>`

```html
<html><head><title>The Entropy Almanac</title></head>
<frameset rows="43,*,43">
  <frameset cols="43,*,43">
    <frame src="ctoplft.htm" id="toplft" />
    <frame src="bordtop.htm" id="top" />
    <frame src="ctoprgt.htm" id="toprgt" />
  </frameset>
  <frameset cols="43,*,43">
    <frame src="bordlft.htm" id="left" />
    <frame src="main.htm" id="main" />
    <frame src="bordrgt.htm" id="right" />
  </frameset>
  <frameset cols="43,*,43">
    <frame src="cbtmlft.htm" id="btmlft" />
    <frame src="bordbtm.htm" id="btm" />
    <frame src="cbtmrgt.htm" id="btmrgt" />
  </frameset>
</frameset>
</html>
```

Figure 16.3 consists of nine separate Web pages laid out in different frames, many of which consist solely of a background image. The corners and side frames contain blank HTML documents, showing nothing more than specially designed background tiles. The top frame is a permanent title graphic, and the bottom frame is a navigation bar similar to the one shown in the previous example. The net effect is to surround the middle frame within a sort of "picture frame" border. Figure 16.4 shows thumbnails of all the background tiles and other graphics incorporated into the pages.

16

FIGURE 16.4

To create the border effect in Figure 16.3, I designed several custom background tiles and matching title graphics.

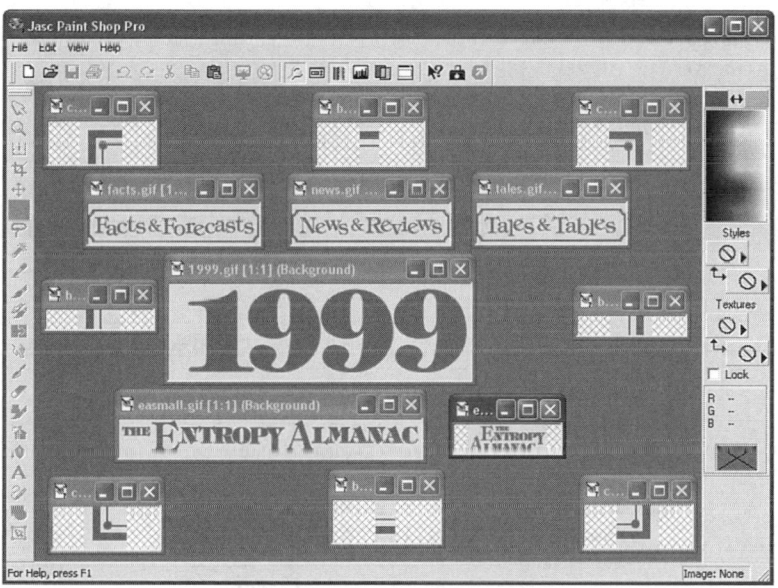

Controlling Frame Margins, Borders, and Scrolling

The problem with the nine-frame arrangement in Figure 16.3 is that it looks ugly and stupid. We can fix that.

The ugly parts are the gray dividers between the frames, which completely ruin the effect of surrounding the center frame with nicely designed graphics. There also isn't enough room in the top and bottom frames to display the graphics without scrollbars. Fortunately, there are HTML commands to get rid of the frame dividers, make more space in small frames by reducing the size of the margins, and force frames not to have scrollbars.

Before you read about these HTML magic tricks, take a look at the dramatic results they can achieve. Figure 16.5 is a nine-frame window displaying the same Web pages shown in Figure 16.3. Obviously, Figure 16.5 looks much nicer! In Listing 16.5, you can see the anti-ugliness medication I gave to the frameset you saw in Figure 16.3.

FIGURE 16.5

This is the page whose code is shown in Listing 16.5. By adding some attributes to the <frame /> *tags, I was able to make the frames look much nicer.*

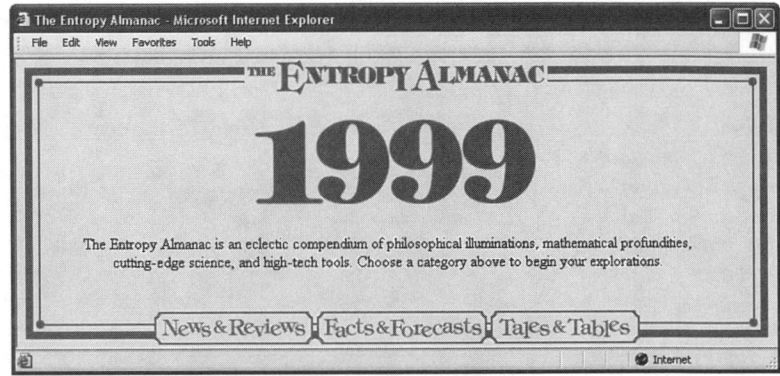

LISTING 16.5   Nine Separate Web Pages Displayed in Nine Frames

```
<html><head><title>The Entropy Almanac</title></head>
<frameset rows="43,*,43" border="0">
  <frameset cols="43,*,43" border="0">
    <frame src="ctoplft.htm" id="toplft"
      scrolling="no" frameborder="0" />
    <frame src="bordtop.htm" id="top"
      scrolling="no" frameborder="0" marginheight="1" />
    <frame src="ctoprgt.htm" id="toprgt"
      scrolling="no" frameborder="0" />
  </frameset>
  <frameset cols="43,*,43" border="0">
    <frame src="bordlft.htm" id="left"
      scrolling="no" frameborder="0" />
    <frame src="main.htm" id="main" frameborder="0" />
    <frame src="bordrgt.htm" id="right"
      scrolling="no" frameborder="0" />
  </frameset>
  <frameset cols="43,*,43" border="0">
    <frame src="cbtmlft.htm" id="btmlft"
      scrolling="no" frameborder="0" />
    <frame src="bordbtm.htm" id="btm"
      scrolling="no" frameborder="0" marginheight="1" />
    <frame src="cbtmrgt.htm" id="btmrgt"
      scrolling="no" frameborder="0" />
  </frameset>
</frameset>
</html>
```

In addition to the `id` and `name` attributes, the `<frame />` tag can take the following special frame-related attributes:

- `marginwidth`—Left and right margins of the frame (in pixels).
- `marginheight`—Top and bottom margins of the frame (in pixels).
- `scrolling`—Display scrollbar for the frame? (`"yes"` or `"no"`)
- `frameborder`—Display dividers between this frame and adjacent frames? (1 means yes, 0 means no)
- `noresize`—Don't allow this frame to be resized by the user.

`marginwidth` and `marginheight` are pretty self-explanatory, but each of the other attributes is discussed in detail in the next few paragraphs.

Normally, any frame that isn't big enough to hold all of its contents will have its own scrollbar(s). The top and bottom frames you saw earlier in Figure 16.3 are examples. If you don't want a particular frame to ever display scrollbars, you can put `scrolling="no"` in the frame tag. Conversely, `scrolling="yes"` forces both horizontal and vertical scrollbars to appear, whether they are needed or not.

> When graphics just fit within a small frame, Netscape Navigator and Microsoft Internet Explorer often display scrollbars that only scroll a few pixels down and have no real purpose. Rather than make the frame bigger (and take up valuable window real estate with empty margin space), you will often want to just turn off the scrollbars with `scrolling="no"`.
>
> The only situation I can think of where you might want to use `scrolling="yes"` is if some graphics won't line up right unless you can count on the scrollbars always being there. Chances are, you'll probably never need `scrolling="yes"`.

People viewing your frames can ordinarily resize them by grabbing the frame border with the mouse and dragging it around. If you don't want anyone messing with the size of a frame, put `noresize="noresize"` in the `<frame />` tag.

Frames are flexible enough to allow you to control the size of frame borders or eliminate borders altogether. This makes a frame document look just like a regular Web page, with no ugly lines breaking it up. Just put a `frameborder="0"` attribute in every single `<frame />` tag—not just in the `<frameset>` tags.

When used together with custom graphics, borderless frames can allow you to create sites that are easier to navigate and more pleasant to visit. For example, when someone visits the site in Figure 16.5 and clicks one of the navigation choices in the bottom frame, the page he chose comes up in the middle frame quickly because the title graphic, navigation buttons, and border graphics all remain in place. The frames also automatically adapt to changes in the size of the browser window, so the nice "picture frame" effect looks just as good at 1,024×768 resolution as it does at 800×600.

Figure 16.6 shows the result of clicking the Facts & Forecasts link in Figure 16.5. Note that the middle frame gets its own scrollbar whenever the contents are too big to fit in the frame.

FIGURE 16.6

Clicking a link at the top of Figure 16.5 brings up a new page in the middle frame, without redrawing any of the other frames.

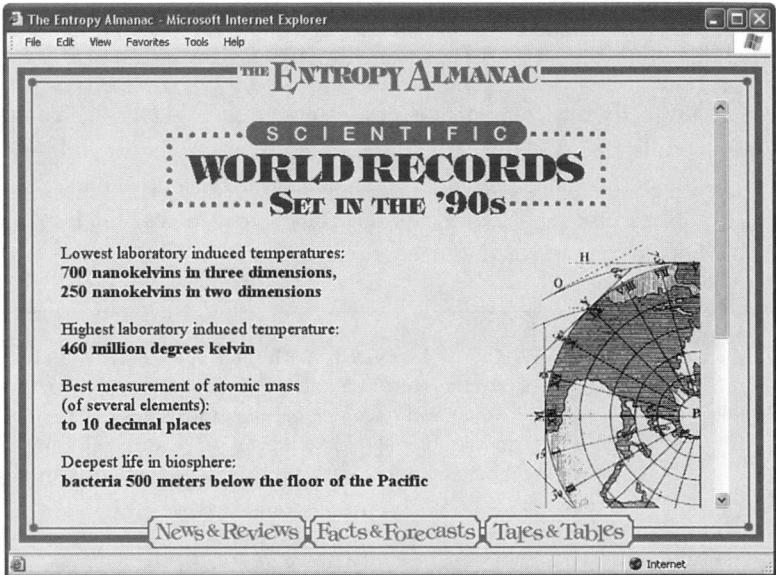

If you'd like to get more advanced with frames, you might want to look into *inline frames*, which are frames that you can place directly within a section of text in a page. Inline frames are created using the <iframe> tag, as the following code demonstrates:

```
<html><head><title>bios</title></head><body>
<h1>Short Bios</h1>
<iframe id="bioframe" src="mybio.htm" width="200" height="200">
</iframe><p>
<a href="yourbio.htm" target="bioframe" >Your Bio</a><p>
<a href="mybio.htm" target="bioframe">My Bio</a>
</body></html>
```

This code displays the page `mybio.htm` in a 200×200-pixel region, underneath the heading Short Bios. If the document `mybio.htm` doesn't fit in that small region, it would have its own little scrollbar(s) next to it. Clicking the Your Bio link would replace the contents of the 200×200-pixel region with `your-bio.htm`. Clicking My Bio would put `mybio.htm` back into that region.

You can view an `<iframe>` example online at `http://www.24hourHTMLcafe.com/hour16`.

16

Summary

In this hour you learned how to display more than one page at a time by splitting the Web browser window into *frames*. You learned to use a *frameset document* to define the size and arrangement of the frames, as well as which Web page or image will be loaded into each frame. You saw how to create links that change the contents of any frame you choose, while leaving the other frames unchanged. You also discovered several optional settings that control the appearance of resizable borders and scrollbars in frames. Finally, you saw how to nest framesets to create complex frame layouts.

Table 16.1 summarizes the tags and attributes covered in this hour.

TABLE 16.1 HTML Tags and Attributes Covered in Hour 16

Tag/Attribute	Function
`<frameset>...</frameset>`	Divides the main window into a set of frames that can each display a separate document.
Attributes	
`rows="..."`	Splits the window or frameset vertically into a number of rows specified by a number (such as 7), a percentage of the total window width (such as 25%), or an asterisk (*) indicating that a frame should take up all the remaining space or divide the space evenly between frames (if multiple * frames are specified).
`cols="..."`	Works similar to `rows`, except that the window or frameset is split horizontally into columns.
`frameborder="..."`	Specifies whether to display a border for a frame. Options are 1 (yes) and 0 (no).
`<frame />`	Defines a single frame within a `<frameset>`.

TABLE 16.1 continued

Tag/Attribute	Function
Attributes	
`src="..."`	The URL of the document to be displayed in this frame.
`id="..."`	A name to be used for targeting this frame with the `target` attribute in `<a href>` links.
`name="..."`	A name to be used for targeting this frame with the `target` attribute in `<a href>` links; not compliant with XHTML, but otherwise equivalent to `id`.
`<marginwidth>`	The amount of space (in pixels) to leave to the left and right side of a document within a frame.
`<marginheight>`	The amount of space (in pixels) to leave above and below a document within a frame.
`scrolling="..."`	Determines whether a frame has scrollbars. Possible values are `yes`, `no`, and `auto`.
`noresize="noresize"`	Prevents the user from resizing this frame (and possibly adjacent frames) with the mouse.
`<noframes>...</noframes>`	Provides an alternative document body in `<frameset>` documents for browsers that do not support frames (usually encloses `<body>...</body>`).
`<iframe>...</iframe>`	Creates an inline frame.
	(`<iframe>` accepts all the same attributes as does `<frame />`.)

Q&A

Q Can I display other people's Web pages from the Internet in one frame, and my own pages in another frame at the same time? What if those sites use frames, too?

A You can load any document from anywhere on the Internet (or an intranet) into a frame. If the document is a frameset, its frames are sized to fit within the existing frame into which you load it.

For example, you could put a hotlist of your favorite links in one frame and have the pages that those links refer to appear in a separate frame. This makes it easy to provide links to other sites without risking that someone will get lost and never come back to your own site. Note, however, that if any link within that site has `target="_top"`, it will replace all your frames.

You should also be aware that framing somebody else's pages so that they appear to be part of your own site may get you in legal trouble. Several major lawsuits are pending on this exact issue, so be sure to get explicit written permission from anyone whose pages you plan to put within one of your frames (just as you would if you were putting images or text from their site on your own pages).

Q Do I need to put a `<title>` in all my frames? If I do, which title will be displayed at the top of the window?

A The title of the frameset document is the only one that will be displayed. `<head>` and `<title>` tags are not required in framed documents, but it's a good idea to give all your pages titles just in case somebody opens one by itself outside any frame.

16

Workshop

The workshop contains quiz questions and activities to help you solidify your understanding of the material covered. Try to answer all questions before looking at the "Answers" section that follows.

Quiz

1. Write the HTML to list the names Mickey, Minnie, and Donald in a frame taking up the left 25% of the browser window. Make it so that clicking each name brings up a corresponding Web page in the right 75% of the browser window.

2. Write a frameset document to make the frame layout pictured here:

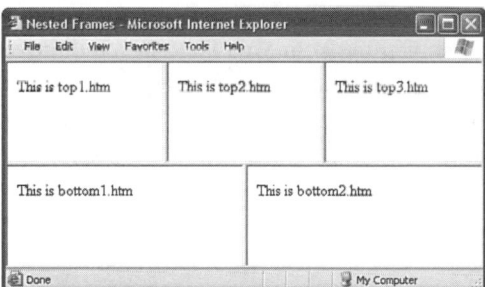

Answers

1. You need five separate HTML documents. The first document is the frameset:

```
<html><head><title>Our Friends</title></head>
<frameset cols="25%,75%">
<frame src="index.htm" />
```

```
<frame src="mickey.htm" id="mainframe" />
</frameset>
</html>
```

Next, you need the index.htm document for the left frame:

```
<html><head><title>Our Friends Index</title></head>
<body>
Pick a friend:<p>
<a href="mickey.htm" target="mainframe">Mickey</a><p>
<a href="minnie.htm" target="mainframe">Minnie</a><p>
<a href="donald.htm" target="mainframe">Donald</a><p>
</body></html>
```

Finally, you need the three HTML pages named mickey.htm, minnie.htm, and don-ald.htm. They contain the information about each friend.

2.
```
<html><head><title>Nested Frames</title></head>
<frameset rows="*,*">
  <frameset cols="*,*,*">
  <frame src="top1.htm" />
  <frame src="top2.htm" />
  <frame src="top3.htm" />
  </frameset>
  <frameset cols="*,*">
  <frame src="bottom1.htm" />
  <frame src="bottom2.htm" />
  </frameset>
</frameset>
</html>
```

Exercises

In Hour 22, "Helping People Find Your Web Pages," you discover out how to make a page that loads another page automatically after a specified time interval. When you combine that trick with frames, you can create all sorts of interesting animated layout effects. Consider what kind of information you might display in this manner.

PART V
Dynamic Web Pages

Hour

HOUR 17

Web Page Scripting for Non-Programmers

Scripting is a polite word for *computer programming*, and that's obviously an enormous topic you're not going to learn much about in a one-hour lesson. Still, there are some awfully handy things you can do in a snap with scripting—and things you can't do any other way. So with a spirit of bold optimism, this hour aims to help you teach yourself just enough Web page scripting to make your pages stand out from the "non-de-script" crowd.

Specifically, you'll learn in this hour how to make the images (or multimedia objects) on your Web pages change in response to mouse movements or mouse clicks, as well as how to jump into the advertising business by adding animated banner ads to your Web pages that cycle between different ad images. Using the JavaScript language, you can do these tasks in a way that is compatible with all major Web browsers.

You'll learn some additional JavaScript tricks in Hour 18, "Setting Pages in Motion with Dynamic HTML." If the ease and power of the few JavaScript commands you learn in these two hours whet your appetite for more (as I think it will), I encourage you to turn to a book such as *Sams Teach Yourself JavaScript in 24 Hours*.

Jazzing Things Up with Interactive Highlighting

If you've used any graphical CD-ROM software application, you have probably seen buttons that light up or change when your mouse passes over them. This looks cool and gives you some visual feedback before you click something, which research shows can reduce confusion and errors—it makes for more intuitive user interfaces.

Although JavaScript can be a tempting option for important Web page elements such as navigation buttons, keep in mind that users have the ability to turn off JavaScript support in their browsers. This is sometimes done as a security measure, and it could seriously hamper the functionality of a Web site that is highly dependent on JavaScript for critical functions. On the other hand, you may decide that the minority of people who disable JavaScript aren't a big enough concern to do away with the cool light-up buttons!

Graphical links that highlight when the mouse is dragged over them are sometimes referred to as *hover buttons*.

You can add the same sort of visual feedback to the links on your Web pages, too. The first step toward achieving that effect is to create the graphics for both the dark and the lit icons. Figure 17.1 shows some pumpkin faces I created in Paint Shop Pro. I made two copies of each pumpkin: one darkened and one illuminated as if it has a candle inside.

FIGURE 17.1

Four graphics images, each with a high-lighted version to replace it when the mouse points to it.

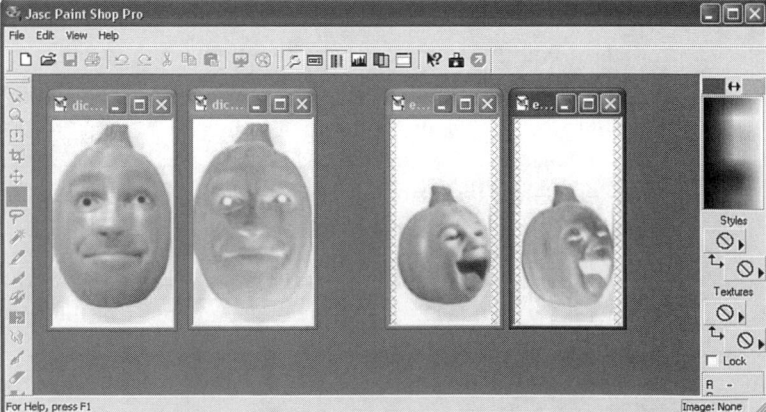

To Do

Do you have any pages that would look flashier or be easier to understand if the navigation icons or other images changed when the mouse passed over them? If so, try creating some highlighted versions of the images, and try modifying your own page as you read the following few paragraphs. Here are a few ideas to get you started:

- Use Paint Shop Pro's text tool to make graphical titles that change color when the mouse points to them.

- Use the Effects, 3D Effects, Buttonize command in Paint Shop Pro with various background colors to make buttons that light up just before they're pressed.

- Use the techniques you learned in Hour 8, "Creating Your Own Web Page Graphics," to make icons that rotate, wiggle, or blink when the mouse passes over them. (You can use a regular, unanimated GIF for the image to present when the mouse isn't pointing to the icon.)

- If you have a list of choices, put a blank (totally transparent) image in front of each choice and make an arrow or bullet icon appear in front of the item to which the mouse is pointing.

Here's how the HTML for a graphical link would look before any scripting is added. This should all look familiar to you. (If it doesn't, review Hour 9, "Putting Graphics on a Web Page," and Hour 12, "Page Design and Layout.")

```
<a href="erica.htm"><img src="ercadark.jpg"
  width="98" height="214" border="0" alt="erica" /></a>
```

The first thing you need to do is give this particular <img> tag its own unique ID within the Web page, which is simply a name you can use to identify the image. You'll use this ID to refer to this specific image on the page when you want to change which image is displayed. We'll name this image erica by putting an id attribute in the <img> tag:

```
<a href="erica.htm"><img id="erica" src="ercadark.jpg"
  width="98" height="214" border="0" alt="erica" /></a>
```

 Don't forget that for maximum backward compatibility, you should use both the id and name attributes in tags such as <img>. I've consistently used only the id attribute throughout the book because name isn't technically supported by XHTML, but if you want to stay compatible with older browsers you might consider using both; just set them both to the same value.

Now for the magic part: You can add JavaScript commands to any link on a Web page by including two special attributes called OnMouseOver and OnMouseOut. With OnMouseOver, you tell the Web browser what to do when the mouse passes over any text or images within that link. With OnMouseOut, you indicate what to do when the mouse moves out of the link area.

In this case, you want the image to change to ercalite.jpg when the mouse passes over the corresponding link and change back to ercadark.jpg when the mouse moves away.

Here's what that looks like in HTML and JavaScript:

```
<a href="erica.htm" OnMouseOver="erica.src='ercalite.jpg'"
OnMouseOut="erica.src='ercadark.jpg'"><img id="erica"
src="ercadark.jpg" width="98" height="214" border="0" alt="erica" /></a>
```

Notice that you need to enclose the name of the image file in single quotation marks (apostrophes), but the whole JavaScript command gets enclosed by double quotation marks (inch marks). This is because the JavaScript code is provided as an attribute, and attributes in HTML must be enclosed within double quotation marks. When you enter JavaScript code like this in your own pages, just follow my example closely, substituting your own image names and graphics files.

Listing 17.1 contains the complete HTML for a Web page using the pumpkin images as links. You can see how the pumpkins light up when the mouse passes over them in Figures 17.2 and 17.3, or online at http://www.24hourHTMLcafe.com/hour17/.

LISTING 17.1　JavaScript-Enhanced HTML for the Page Shown in Figures 17.2 and 17.3

```
<html><head><title>The Olivers</title></head>
<body><div align="center">
<h1>The Oliver Family</h1><a href="erica.htm"
OnMouseOver="erica.src='ercalite.jpg'"
                    OnMouseOut="erica.src='ercadark.jpg'"
><img id="erica" id="erica" src="ercadark.jpg" width="98" height="214"
border="0" alt="Erica" /></a
><a href="dick.htm" OnMouseOver="dick.src='dicklite.jpg'"
                    OnMouseOut="dick.src='dickdark.jpg'"
><img id="dick" src="dickdark.jpg"
width="124" height="214" border="0" alt="Dick" /></a
><a href="jan.htm" OnMouseOver="jan.src='janlite.jpg'"
                    OnMouseOut="jan.src='jandark.jpg'"
><img id="jan" src="jandark.jpg"
width="136" height="214" border="0" alt="Jan" /></a
><a href="ona.htm" OnMouseOver="ona.src='onalite.jpg'"
                    OnMouseOut="ona.src='onadark.jpg'"
><img id="ona" src="onadark.jpg"
width="100" height="214" border="0" alt="Ona" /></a>
<p>Click on a family member to find out all about us.</p>
</div></body></html>
```

FIGURE 17.2

When the mouse passes over the pumpkin with my daughter's face, it lights up and her name (from the alt *attribute) appears.*

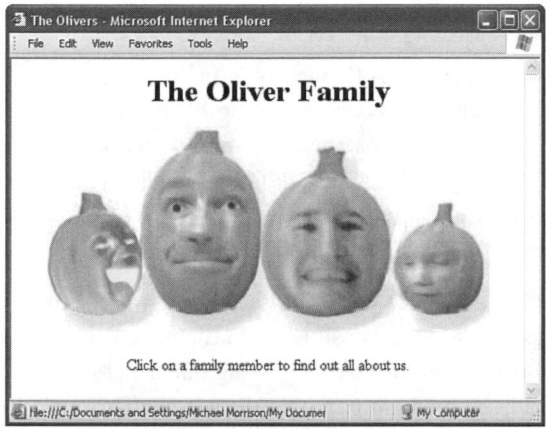

17

FIGURE 17.3

When you move the mouse to my pumpkin, my face lights up instead of Erica's.

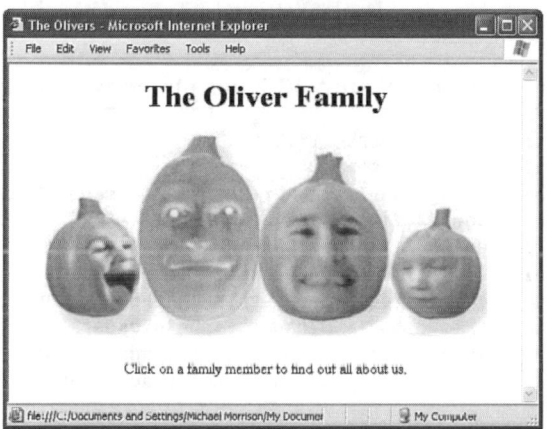

You will usually want the image that the mouse is passing over to light up or change, but you aren't limited to doing it that way. For example, if you wanted all the pumpkins to light up whenever the mouse moved over one of them, you could put the following JavaScript in each <a> tag:

```
<a href="erica.htm" OnMouseOver="erica.src='ercalite.jpg';
dick.src='dicklite.jpg'; jan.src='janlite.jpg'; ona.src='onalite.jpg'"
OnMouseOut="erica.src='ercadark.jpg'";
dick.src='dickdark.jpg'; jan.src='jandark.jpg'; ona.src='onadark.jpg'">
```

As you can see, modifying multiple images is as simple as putting a semicolon (;) after the first JavaScript command and following it with another command. You can put as many commands as you need in the same OnMouseOver (or OnMouseOut) attribute, as long as you separate them with semicolons.

Preloading Images for Speed

The code in Listing 17.1 works flawlessly in both Microsoft Internet Explorer and Netscape Navigator but there is one minor problem: The lit images won't be downloaded from your Web site until someone actually moves the mouse over the image. This can cause a noticeable delay before the highlighted image appears, especially if the person is viewing your page over a slow Internet connection. The end result is a possible lowering of the all-important Gee Whiz Factor (GWF).

You can avoid this annoyance by including some JavaScript code telling the browser to preload the images as soon as possible when the page is displayed. That way, by the time the slow human reader gets around to passing his or her mouse over the link, those images will usually be ready to pop onto the screen. This makes the animations seem to appear without any download delay, giving the page a snappy feel and pumping the GWF back up to truly nerdly levels. Listing 17.2 shows how it's done.

LISTING 17.2   The Page from Figure 17.2 with Images Preloaded

```
<html><head><title>The Olivers</title>
<script language="JavaScript">
<!-- ercalite=new Image(98,214);  ercadark=new Image(98,214);
  dicklite=new Image(124,214); dickdark=new Image(124,214);
  janlite=new Image(136,214);  jandark=new Image(136,214);
  onalite=new Image(100,214);  onadark=new Image(100,214);
  ercalite.src="ercalite.jpg"; ercadark.src="ercadark.jpg";
  dicklite.src="dicklite.jpg"; dickdark.src="dickdark.jpg";
  janlite.src="janlite.jpg";   jandark.src="jandark.jpg";
  onalite.src="onalite.jpg";   onadark.src="onadark.jpg";
//-->
</script></head>
<body><div align="center">
<h1>The Oliver Family</h1>
<a href="erica.htm" OnMouseOver="erica.src='ercalite.jpg'"
                    OnMouseOut="erica.src='ercadark.jpg'"
><img id="erica" id="erica" src="ercadark.jpg"
width="98" height="214" border="0" alt="Erica" /></a>
><a href="dick.htm" OnMouseOver="dick.src='dicklite.jpg'"
                    OnMouseOut="dick.src='dickdark.jpg'"
><img id="dick" src="dickdark.jpg" width="124" height="214" border="0"
alt="Dick" /></a>
><a href="jan.htm" OnMouseOver="jan.src='janlite.jpg'"
                    OnMouseOut="jan.src='jandark.jpg'"
><img id="jan" src="jandark.jpg"
width="136" height="214" border="0" alt="Jan" /></a>
><a href="ona.htm" OnMouseOver="ona.src='onalite.jpg'"
                    OnMouseOut="ona.src='onadark.jpg'"
><img id="ona" src="onadark.jpg"
```

Listing 17.2 continued

```
width="100" height="214" border="0" alt="Ona" /></a>
<p>Click on a family member to find out all about us.</p>
</div></body></html>
```

There are a couple of things worthy of note in this listing. The most important is the `<script>` tag. This is used whenever you need some JavaScript that doesn't go in an attribute of some other tag. You can put `<script>` tags anywhere in the `<head>` or `<body>` section of a document. (The forms example later in this hour talks more about that.)

The `<!--` and `//-->` tags just inside the `<script>` and `</script>` tags are actually comment tags, which have the effect of hiding the script from older browsers that otherwise might become confused and try to display the code as text on the page. You should always put each of these comment tags on a line by itself, as I did in Listing 17.2.

I won't go too deep into an explanation of the JavaScript in the listing because that would get us into a course on computer programming. You don't need to understand exactly how this works in order to copy it into your own pages, using your own image names and graphics files.

You can also use the OnMouseOver and OnMouseOut attributes with imagemaps (which were covered in Hour 11, "Graphical Links and Imagemaps"). For an example of a large interactive imagemap, using no fewer than 24 separate images, move your mouse cursor around the pocket watch at the completed *24-Hour HTML Café* site at http://www.24hourHTMLcafe.com/.

Peeking at the source code shows you exactly how to incorporate JavaScript commands into an imagemap. (It also reveals that the clock is actually five separate images—four imagemaps and the changing image in the center. They don't call me "Tricky Dicky" for nuthin'.)

Also, don't forget that you can use animated GIFs with JavaScripts too! For an example, check out the "Predictions and Fictions" link at http://www.24hourHTMLcafe.com/hour17/.

Creating an Animated Banner Ad

One of the most common uses of scripting is animating images, as you learned earlier in the hour. Although hover buttons and other forms of user interface improvements are certainly helpful, there is a more lucrative approach to animated images that you should consider when it comes to scripting. I'm referring to animated banner ads, which display a succession of advertisements over time. You've no doubt seen these kinds of ads around the Web since ads are now commonplace on virtually all large Web sites.

The first step in putting together an animated banner ad is creating the individual ad images. Banner ads come in all shapes and sizes, but I personally like vertical banner ads that occupy space down the side of a Web page. Figure 17.4 shows a series of three banner ad images that are oriented vertically.

FIGURE 17.4

An animated banner ad consists of several images all created the exact same size.

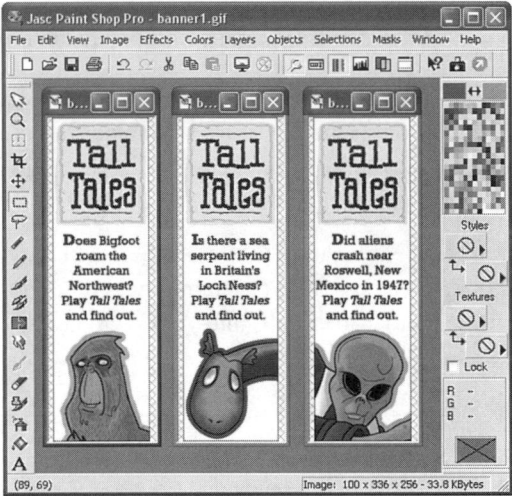

The three images in the figure are displayed one after another to form an animated banner ad. The key to the ad working properly is establishing a timing mechanism so that each ad image is displayed for a few seconds before showing the next one. This can be easily accomplished with JavaScript code, as shown in Listing 17.3.

LISTING 17.3 A Timing Mechanism for Displaying a Series of Ad Banner Images

```
<html><head><title>Tall Tales Banner Ads</title>
<script language="JavaScript">
<!--
var bannerNum = 1;
function rotateBanner() {
  if (++bannerNum > 3)
    bannerNum = 1;
  banner.src = "banner" + bannerNum + ".gif";
  window.setTimeout('rotateBanner();', 3000);
}
//-->
</script></head>
<body onLoad="window.setTimeout('rotateBanner();', 3000);">
<div align="center">
```

LISTING 17.3   continued

```html
<h1>Game Lovers Anonymous</h1>
<table width="500">
<tr>
  <td valign="top">
  <p>Welcome to Game Lovers Anonymous. We love to play
  games, and invite you to support us by visiting our
  sponsors as you enjoy our site.</p>
  </td>
  <td width="100">
  <a href="http://www.talltalesgame.com/">
  <img id="banner" style="border:none" src="banner1.gif">
  </a>
  </td>
<tr>
</table>
</div></body></html>
```

17

This code is another example of JavaScript code that you don't necessarily have to understand inside and out in order to use it effectively in your own Web pages. There are a few things worth pointing out so that you'll understand how to tweak the code to suit your own needs, but beyond that I'm suggesting that you don't worry too much about how it works. The idea is to add some sizzle to your Web pages, not become a programmer overnight.

Figure 17.5 shows the ad banner example page in action. Okay, maybe the printed page is not the best way to show something in action, but you get the picture that you're seeing one of the ad banners as the page is flipping through several of them.

FIGURE 17.5

The JavaScript code in Listing 17.3 produces this vertical banner ad that cycles through three different ad images.

There are several lines of code in Listing 17.3 worth taking a closer look at in order for you to be able to create your own banner ads. Let's start with the JavaScript function that actually changes (rotates) the ad image:

```
function rotateBanner() {
  if (++bannerNum > 3)
    bannerNum = 1;
  banner.src = "banner" + bannerNum + ".gif";
  window.setTimeout('rotateBanner();', 3000);
}
```

The rotateBanner() function is used to change the banner ad image once every 3 seconds. You're probably wondering how the code can possibly know how long to wait before changing an image. This is accomplished in the next to last line of code. See the number 3000? This 3000 is the *wait period* for the banner ad, and is specified in milliseconds— 3000 milliseconds equals 3 seconds. To slow down or speed up how fast the images change, just change this number.

NEW TERM   A *function* is a chunk of JavaScript code grouped together to carry out a specific task such as performing a calculation or in this case, changing an image on the page.

The other important piece of information in the rotateBanner() function is the number of banner ads, which in this code is set to 3 (look at the second line). If you want to provide more banner ad images and have the page cycle through all of them, just change this number to however many images you have. Also, I forgot to mention that this code assumes your banner images are named banner1.gif, banner2.gif, banner3.gif, and so on. If you want to use JPEG images instead of GIFs, just change the fourth line of the code so that the .jpg file extension is used instead.

The other critical line of code in the ad banner example that you absolutely must not leave out is this one:

```
<body onLoad="window.setTimeout('rotateBanner();', 3000);">
```

This code is what gets everything started because it tells the rotateBanner() function to get started showing and changing the images. Notice that the onLoad attribute is used, which is another scripting attribute that results in script code being run whenever a page is first loaded. You may also notice that the number 3000 appears again in this code. This is because you must set an initial wait period for the banner ad to make sure the first image is displayed before changing to the second one.

The Wide World of JavaScript

You've learned enough in this hour to have a head start on JavaScript and to add some snazzy interaction to your Web pages. You've probably also gotten the idea that there's a lot more you can do, and it isn't as hard as you may have thought.

You may also find some scripts online that can be incorporated into a Web page of your own with little or no modification. (Check out the JavaScript-related links at http://www.24hourHTMLcafe.com/hotsites.htm#developer for good places to find scripts.)

When you find scripts you'd like to reuse or experiment with, pay attention to the placement of the JavaScript elements; generally, functions go in the <head> area, preceded by <script language="javascript"> and followed by </script>. The parts of the script that actually carry out the actions when the page is loaded go in the <body> part of the page, but still need to be set aside with the <script> tag. Sections of script that respond to specific events such as mouse moves go in the <a> or <input> tags, with special attributes such as OnMouseOver.

You can also put JavaScript code into a separate file by putting the name of the file in a src attribute within the <script> tag, like the following:

```
<script language="JavaScript" src="bingo.htm"></script>
```

This is especially handy when you are using a script that someone else wrote and you don't want it cluttering up your HTML.

Summary

In this hour you've seen how to use scripting to make the images on your Web pages respond to mouse movements. You've also seen how similar JavaScript commands can be used to change multiple images at once and to create practical Web page features such as animated ad banners. None of these tasks require much in the way of programming skills, though they may inspire you to learn the JavaScript language to give your pages more complex interactive features.

Q&A

Q Are there other, "secret" attributes besides OnMouseOver and OnMouseOut that I can use just as easily? And can I put them anyplace other than in an <a> tag?

A Yes and yes. Each HTML tag has an associated set of JavaScript attributes, which are called *events*. For example, OnClick can be used within the <a> tag to specify a command to be followed when someone clicks that link or form element. Refer to

Appendix C, "Complete HTML 4 and XHTML 1 Quick Reference," for a complete listing of the events you can use in each tag.

Q Doesn't Microsoft use a different scripting language for Internet Explorer?

A Yes. Microsoft definitely would prefer you using its own scripting language based upon Visual Basic called VBScript, but Internet Explorer also supports JavaScript. Some commands work slightly differently in the Microsoft implementation of JavaScript than they do in Netscape Navigator, but the commands covered in this hour work exactly the same in both browsers so you can use them with confidence.

Q I want to display ad banner images that each link to different Web pages. How difficult is this?

A It's not terribly difficult, but it does require a level of JavaScript programming knowledge that is outside the realm of this hour. If you'd like to build on the examples in this hour and tweak them to do more interesting things, I highly recommend you spending some time to learn JavaScript. Otherwise, you should probably stick to using them without major modification.

Workshop

The workshop contains quiz questions and activities to help you solidify your understanding of the material covered. Try to answer all questions before looking at the "Answers" section that follows.

Quiz

1. Say you've made a picture of a button and named it `button.gif`. You also made a simple GIF animation of the button flashing green and white and named it `flashing.gif`. Write the HTML and JavaScript to make the button flash whenever someone moves the mouse pointer over it, and link to a page named `gohere.htm` when someone clicks the button.

2. How would you modify what you wrote for question 1 so that the button starts flashing when someone moves the mouse over it, and keeps flashing even if he or she moves the mouse away?

3. Write the HTML for a JavaScript function that displays five banner ads with a four-second delay between each one.

Answers

1.
```
<a href="gohere.htm"
OnMouseOver="flasher.src='flashing.gif';
OnMouseOut="flasher.src='button.gif'">
<img id="flasher" src="button.gif" border=0 /></a>
```

2.
```
<a href="gohere.htm"
OnMouseOver="flasher.src='flashing.gif'">
<img id="flasher" src="button.gif" border=0 /></a>
```

3.
```
function rotateBanner() {

  if (++bannerNum > 5)
    bannerNum - 1;
  banner.src = "banner" + bannerNum + ".gif";
  window.setTimeout('rotateBanner();', 4000);
}
```

Exercises

Hey, what are you waiting for? Now that you're an HTML expert, get yourself a copy of the new *Sams Teach Yourself JavaScript in 24 Hours* and take the next quantum leap in Web publishing!

17

Hour **18**

Setting Pages in Motion with Dynamic HTML

As we all know, a word must be spelled with all capital letters and no vowels in order to qualify as genuine computer jargon. The latest unpronounceable buzzword along this line is *DHTML*, which stands for *Dynamic HTML*. Like all the best tech-talk, this term means quite a few things, depending on whom you ask.

Everyone agrees that Dynamic HTML brings a new level of power and excitement to Web pages. Everyone also agrees that it has something to do with scripting, animation, and interactivity. Unfortunately, there is still a fair amount of confusion over what exactly constitutes DHTML as a technology. The best way to describe is to say that it's a combination of HTML, style sheets, and scripting. Since you've already learned about all three of these things, you already know a fair amount about DHTML. The key to DHTML is putting them all together to do useful things.

In this hour I will bravely lead you into the wilds of Dynamic HTML. Don't expect to become a DHTML guru in the next 60 minutes, but you can count on coming away with some reusable scripts to animate the contents of your Web pages in ways you couldn't before. You will also emerge with the know-how necessary to put these scripts to work and to modify them for your own purposes.

To Do

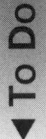

Since the example for this hour involves interactive animation, it's easier to see how everything works if you have the actual page on your computer, instead of just the static pictures in this book. I therefore recommend that you download the example files from the *24-Hour HTML Café* before you continue reading. Here's how:

- Start your Web browser and go to the *24-Hour HTML Café* at
  `http://www.24hourHTMLcafe.com/hour18/`.

- Under The XYZ Files example, you will see a list of seven filenames. Use the right mouse button (or hold down the button if you're using a Macintosh) to click each of these, choosing Save Target As from the pop-up menu each time. Save all seven files in the same folder on your hard drive.

  (The files are `xyzfiles.htm`, `slide.js`, `nodhtml.htm`, `xfolder.gif`, `yfolder.gif`, `zfolder.gif`, and `empty.gif`. The last of these GIF images is invisible, so don't worry if you try to look at it after saving and don't see anything. You also may not see anything if you try to view `slide.js` with a Web browser.)

  Once you have those seven files on your hard drive, you can use your favorite text editor and Web browser to look at them (and, if you're bold, modify them to work with your own graphics and text) as you read the rest of this hour.

▲

Learning How to Fly

For the first part of this hour, your noble quest will be to make some text "fly in" from the edge of a page when that page first comes up in the browser window. Just to make the quest more worthy of pursuit, you'd better make the text slide diagonally, instead of left to right. Naturally, what you really want (and shall no doubt soon gain) is a general-purpose script that you can use to slide any text or graphics any way you want.

While you're at it, why not go wild and ask for a script that can slip things underneath the edge of other things, or slide one layer of text and graphics behind or in front of any number of other layers?

Figures 18.1 and 18.2 are snapshots of a Dynamic HTML Web page with flying text. This is the `xyzfiles.htm` document you were just instructed to download from the *24-Hour HTML Café*, so you may want to look at it on your computer screen now. See how the text glides in from behind the file folders as soon as you pull up the page? Pretty cool, huh?

FIGURE **18.1**
Dynamic HTML lets you animate overlapping layers of text and graphics. This text is emerging from behind some images.

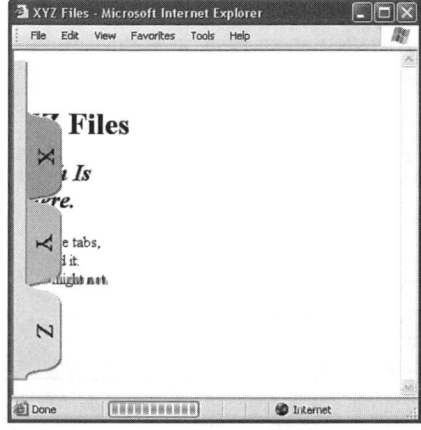

FIGURE **18.2**
The text that was moving in Figure 18.1 has settled into place and stopped.

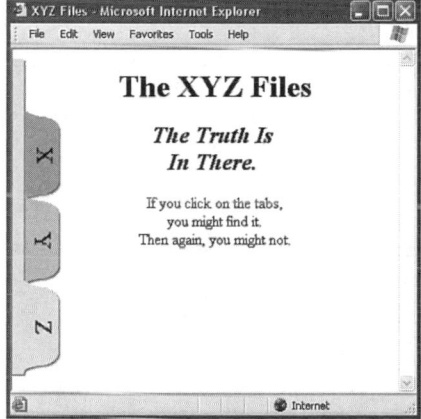

18

To achieve the effect shown in Figures 18.1 and 18.2, your HTML and JavaScript code needs to do all of the following:

1. Check to make sure that the user's Web browser can handle Dynamic HTML and provide some alternative content if it can't.
2. Define and name the layer containing the text; hide it out of sight beyond the edge of the page.
3. Define and name the layers that contain the file tab images. (Each tab is actually assigned its own layer because later in this hour they are all animated separately.)
4. Animate the text layer sliding onto the page.

Listing 18.1 contains the HTML that does all these things, which is part of the XYZ Files Web page. The following sections explain how each of these four tasks is accomplished.

LISTING 18.1   HTML for the Page in Figures 18.1 and 18.2

```
<html><head><title>XYZ Files</title>
<script src="slide.js" language="javascript"></script>
</head>

<!-- Check for DHTML compatibility and if it's okay,
     then fly in the headings and body text -->
<body OnLoad="if (checkDHTML()) {
layername=makeName('intro');
yhop=-2; ygoal=20; xhop=10; xgoal=80; slide() }">

<!-- Tell users of non-JavaScript browsers to go away,
     but hide the message from DHTML-compatible browsers -->
<div style="position: absolute;
            left: -250px; top: 10px; width: 250">
<p>Your browser can't cope with this DHTML page.</p>
<a href="nodhtml.htm">Click here for a regular HTML page.</a>
</div>

<!-- Get the headings and body text ready to fly in -->
<div id="intro" style="text-align: center; z-index: 0;
 position: absolute; left: -260px; top: 88px; width: 260px">
<h1>The XYZ Files</h1>
<h2><i>The Truth Is<br />In There.</i></h2>
If you click on the tabs,<br />you might find it.<br />
Then again, you might not.</div>

<!-- Give each file folder image its own layer -->
<div id="layer1" style="position: absolute;
 left: -250px; top: 10px; width: 300; z-index: 1">
<img src="xfolder.gif" width="300" height="330" /></div>
<div id="layer2" style="position: absolute;
 left: -250px; top: 10px; width: 300; z-index: 2">
<img src="yfolder.gif" width="300" height="330" /></div>
<div id="layer3" style="position: absolute;
 left: -250px; top: 10px; width: 300; z-index: 3">
<img src="zfolder.gif" width="300" height="330" /></div>
```

 All text between <!-- and --> tags in Listing 18.1 (or any other HTML page) is completely ignored by the Web browser. These comments are just reminders the Web page author has written to himself (that's me) and anyone else who might need some hints to understand how the page works (that's you) .

Dividing a Web Page into Layers

Shortly, you'll learn how to detect whether a page is being viewed with a DHTML-compatible Web browser. Granted, the vast majority of users these days have browsers that support DHTML, but it's probably worth checking just so you don't alienate the minority of people using computers built during the stone age (mid 1990s).

Before getting into the browser stuff, let's first take a look at an essential secret of all Dynamic HTML: how to define layers of text and graphics so you can move them around.

Wait—you already know how to do that! Remember that you can use `<div align="center">` to center a bunch of text and graphics on the page. The whole purpose of the `<div>` and `</div>` tags is to define a region of the page (also called a *division* or *layer*) so you can then do something with that whole region at once.

As you found out in Hours 14 and 15 when working with style sheets, centering the contents of a `<div>` region is only one of many possibilities for playing with it. You could also turn all the text in the region red with `<div style="color: red">`, or put a red background behind the region with `<div style="background-color: red">`, or even pick up the whole region and move it to the top-left corner of the browser window with `<div style="position: absolute; left: 0px; top: 0px">`.

Now you're about to learn how to do all these things dynamically, in response to user-initiated events such as mouse movements or link clicks. Of course, you'll need a name for each `<div>` region you want to order around. This name is assigned to a region using the familiar `id` attribute that you've seen several places throughout the book thus far.

For example, the following code from Listing 18.1 defines a layer named `"intro"`:

```
<div id="intro" style="text-align: center; z-index: 0;
 position: absolute; left: -260px; top: 88px; width: 260px">
<h1>The XYZ Files</h1>
<h2><i>The Truth Is<br />In There.</i></h2>
If you click on the tabs,<br />you might find it.<br />
Then again, you might not.</div>
```

18

The `style` attribute positions this layer 88 pixels down from the top edge of the browser window, and negative 260 pixels from the left edge. *Negative* means to the left, so in other words you won't actually be able to see this layer (until you move it) because it's completely outside the viewing window, off to the left side. The `style` attribute also specifies the width of the layer as 260 pixels and indicates that the text should be centered in that 260-pixel–wide region.

Each of the last three `<div>` tags in Listing 18.1 contains a single `<img />` tag, placing a 300×330-pixel image of a file folder on the page. If you look carefully at the `style` attributes for these `<div>` tags, you'll notice that each layer is positioned 250 pixels outside the left edge of the browser window, so that only the rightmost 50 pixels of the image are visible in Figures 18.1 and 18.2. The rest is hidden beyond the edge of the viewing window and will not be revealed until later this hour when I show you how to interactively animate the file folder images.

You'll also notice that all three of these `<div>` layers are placed in exactly the same spot, right on top of one another. The only reason you can see the bottom two folder tabs is that the images covering them are partially transparent GIFs, allowing parts of the image and background beneath to show through.

With all these semi-transparent layers piled on top of one another, you need some way to determine which layer appears in front, which one is in the back, and the stacking order of those layers in between. You can do this by including `z-index:` followed by a number in the `style` attribute of each layer. Higher numbered layers appear in front of lower numbered layers. In Listing 18.1, the `"intro"` layer gets a `z-index` of `0` (the very bottom layer), and the X, Y, and Z file tabs get `z-index`es of `1`, `2`, and `3`, respectively. Figure 18.1 clearly shows the result of this stacking order. (If you gave the `"intro"` layer a `z-index` of `4` or higher, the text would appear in front of the file tabs instead of behind them.)

I apologize for this discussion reading like a flashback to the example from earlier in the lesson, but I wanted to point out that more was going in the example than I originally shared with you. And there's more!

Offering Alternate Content in Plain HTML

There's one more `<div>` layer in Listing 18.1 that I haven't mentioned yet. The code for it looks like the following:

```
<div style="position: absolute;
 left: -250px; top: 10px; width: 250">
Your browser can't cope with this DHTML page.<p>
<a href="nodhtml.htm">Click here for a regular HTML page.</a>
<p></div>
```

Like the `"intro"` layer mentioned earlier, this layer is nothing more than a little text positioned completely out of view beyond the edge of the browser window. The point here is that older browsers that don't support style sheet positioning won't know enough to hide this layer; those browsers' users will see the text telling them how lame their browser is and offering a link to an alternative page—presumably one that doesn't use any Dynamic HTML jugglery.

Figure 18.3 shows what the page from Figures 18.1 and 18.2 looks like when viewed in a Web browser that doesn't support DHTML. Actually, I had a hard time finding a browser these days that doesn't support it, so you're actually seeing a simulation in Internet Explorer of what the page would look like if DHTML wasn't supported. In this example, the `style` and `id` attributes of the `<div>` tags have been disabled, so the contents of all the layers are displayed one after the other down the page.

FIGURE 18.3

When the page in Figures 18.1 and 18.2 is viewed in a browser that doesn't support DHTML, a link to an alternate page appears.

When a user follows the "Click here for a regular HTML page." link in Figure 18.3, she gets the `nodhtml.htm` document shown in Figure 18.4. You can make any page you want and name it `nodhtml.htm` (or change the `"nodhtml.htm"` reference to the page of your choice). Instead of telling the user that her browser isn't advanced enough for your state-of-the-art pages, you might choose instead to simply present equivalent content without the fancy DHTML animation.

FIGURE 18.4

Clicking the link in Figure 18.3 takes the user to a plain-vanilla HTML page, with no DHTML enhancements.

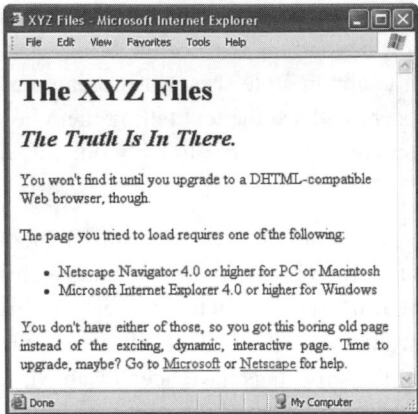

Being Compatible with Incompatible Browsers

With all the layers in place, and users of under-powered browsers properly warned, the only thing left to do is write a little JavaScript to slide the `"intro"` layer onto the page.

Unfortunately, it's not quite that easy. There are still some ugly browser-compatibility issues to resolve first. You've seen how to offer some level of compatibility with browsers that support neither style sheet positioning nor JavaScript. If you want a page that works out in the real world, you also need to be ready for Web browsers that understand older versions of JavaScript but still can't handle advanced stuff like layer animation. If you don't detect and divert those browsers, anyone using those browsers to view your DHTML pages may see all sorts of strange behavior and error messages.

To make matters worse, the two most popular Web browsers use incompatible scripting languages. For some simple applications, like those presented in Hour 17, "Web Page Scripting for Non-Programmers," Netscape Navigator and Microsoft Internet Explorer are compatible enough to write simple scripts that work in both browsers; when you try to do more interesting things, such as moving overlapping layers of text and graphics around, Netscape's JavaScript and Microsoft's JScript are just not talking the same language.

None of this would be a big deal if you were creating Web pages for a corporate intranet where all employees always used exactly the same software. (Such corporations do exist, I'm told, though I'm not sure I believe it.) Most of us, however, want our pages to look good to anyone who pulls them off the Internet, no matter what Web browser the viewer is using. At the very least, we'd like our fancy interactive bells and whistles to work with the latest browsers from Netscape and Microsoft, and perhaps gracefully offer a less exciting page to users of any other Web browser.

Time for the bad news: Achieving this level of compatibility is a huge headache. The good news is that I already got the headache for you, had a beer, got over it, and wrote the necessary scripts so you don't have to. I won't even try to teach you enough to understand how I did it, but if you take a look at Listing 18.2, I will tell you what the JavaScript does and why.

As mentioned in Hour 17, you can either type a script directly into a Web page, between the <script> and </script> tags, or you can put the script in a separate file and indicate the filename with a src attribute in the <script> tag. The Web page in Listing 18.1 uses the latter approach to include the slide.js script listed in Listing 18.2. This allows you to use the same script in as many Web pages as you want without having to maintain multiple copies of the script itself.

LISTING 18.2   slide.js JavaScript File

18

```
// Define all variables and set the default delay to 5ms
var layername, xgoal, ygoal, xhop, yhop, delay=5;

// Check to see if the browser is DHTML-compatible
function checkDHTML() {
  if ((parseInt(navigator.appVersion)>=4) &&
     ((navigator.appName!="Netscape" &&
       navigator.appVersion.indexOf("X11") == -1) ||
      (navigator.appName!="Microsoft Internet Explorer" &&
       navigator.appVersion.indexOf("Macintosh") == -1)))
    { return 1 }
  else
    { document.location="nodhtml.htm"; return 0 }
}

// Construct a valid reference to a layer
// in either Netscape JavaScript or Microsoft JScript
function makeName(layerID) {
  if (navigator.appName=="Netscape")
    { refname = eval("document." + layerID) }
  else
    { refname = eval("document.all." + layerID + ".style") }
  return refname
}
```

LISTING 18.2 continued

```
// Slide over xhop,yhop pixels every delay milliseconds
// until the layer reaches xgoal and ygoal
function slide() {
  if ((parseInt(layername.left) != xgoal) ||
      (parseInt(layername.top) != ygoal))
    { layername.left = parseInt(layername.left) + xhop;
      layername.top = parseInt(layername.top) + yhop;
      window.setTimeout("slide()", delay) }
}
```

 Any line starting with // is ignored by the JavaScript interpreter, the same way anything between <!-- and --> tags is ignored by HTML browsers. The lines starting with // in Listing 18.2 are just comments by the Web page author, reminding anyone who reads the code what each function does.

As you may remember from Hour 17, a *function* is a piece of JavaScript code that can be called on to do a specific task. The first function in Listing 18.2 checks to see if a Web page is being viewed with a DHTML-compatible Web browser. In order to qualify as DHTML-compatible (according to me on this particular Thursday, anyway), a browser must understand some version of JavaScript advanced enough to group text and graphics into layers and dynamically position those layers anywhere on a Web page. The following are the browsers that meet these criteria, which you'll notice encompasses the vast majority of current computer users:

- Netscape Navigator 4 or later for Windows or Macintosh (but not UNIX)
- Microsoft Internet Explorer 4 or later for Windows (but not Macintosh or UNIX)

 Opera is a Web browser that I personally recommend because of its compact nature and ruthless adherence to Web standards. Unfortunately, it's still a minority player in the browser war and therefore probably isn't worth including as a special case in your browser detection code. Fortunately, Opera does such a good job of supporting technologies such as style sheets that you really don't need to do anything special for your pages to work well with it. To learn more about Opera, visit the Opera Web site at http://www.opera.com/.

You'll see how to use the checkDHTML() function on your Web pages momentarily, but first you should know what it does when it detects an incompatible browser. The following line of JavaScript deals with this eventuality:

```
{ document.location="nodhtml.htm"; return 0 }
```

This takes the user to the nodhtml.htm page in Figure 18.4, while sending a signal to the original page to let it know that it shouldn't try to perform any DHTML tricks.

The next function in Listing 18.2, makeName(), is pure black magic. To understand the need for it, you have to realize exactly how Microsoft and Netscape's implementations of JavaScript differ when it comes to handling layers.

To change the position of a layer (for example, the layer named "intro"), you need some way to say "the top of the layer named intro" and "the left side of the layer named intro" in JavaScript—and that's where the trouble starts. To move the layer down so its top edge is 200 pixels from the top edge of the browser window, you need a different command in Netscape Navigator than in Microsoft Internet Explorer. The Netscape way follows:

```
document.intro.top = 200
```

This is the Microsoft way to say the same thing:

```
document.all.intro.style = 200
```

This clearly makes it a pain in the proverbial Back button to write a script that works with both browsers.

Now for the black magic. If you give the makeName() function in Figure 18.1 the name "intro", it gives you either "document.intro" or "document.all.intro.style", depending upon which browser you are using. If you use this result to refer to a layer, it works nicely for Netscapians and Microsofters alike. You will soon see exactly how this works in practice because you're finally ready to see how Dynamic HTML layer animation is accomplished.

Moving a Layer Around with JavaScript

The only two sections of code in Listings 18.1 and 18.2 I haven't explained yet in this hour are the <body> tag in Listing 18.1 and the slide() function in Listing 18.2. Together, they create the effect seen in Figures 18.1 and 18.2: the text layer flying onto the page. The <body> tag looks like this:

18

```
<body OnLoad="if (checkDHTML()) {
 layername=makeName('intro');
 yhop=-2; ygoal=20; xhop=10; xgoal=80; slide() }">
```

Any JavaScript commands you put after OnLoad= in the <body> tag are carried out as soon as the Web page is displayed. (OnLoad is also triggered every time the user clicks the Reload button in Netscape Navigator or the Refresh button in Microsoft Internet Explorer.)

What does the JavaScript in this OnLoad attribute do? First, it starts the checkDHTML() function. If this function detects a DHTML-compatible browser, the following steps are carried out:

1. The makeName() function is given the layer ID "intro" so that it can construct the appropriate Netscape or Microsoft version of the layer name. The result is saved as layername.

2. The numbers -2, 20, 10, and 80 are put into storage boxes (or, if you speak math, *variables*) named yhop, ygoal, xhop, and xgoal. The point is to tell the slide() function where you want the layer moved to and how fast to move it (more on that shortly).

3. The slide() function is called on to "fly in" the layer.

Here's the slide() function from Listing 18.2:

```
function slide() {
  if ((parseInt(layername.left) != xgoal) ||
     (parseInt(layername.top) != ygoal))
   { layername.left = parseInt(layername.left) + xhop;
     layername.top = parseInt(layername.top) + yhop;
     window.setTimeout("slide()", delay) }
}
```

I can't teach enough JavaScript in this hour for you to be able to write your own functions like this, but you can probably get the general gist of how this function works. First, it determines whether the layer referred to by layername is already at the location specified by xgoal and ygoal. If the layer isn't there yet, it moves the layer xhop pixels horizontally and yhop pixels vertically. It then waits for a short time and goes back to the beginning of the function. It keeps on hopping until it reaches the goal.

If xhop is a negative number, the layer will hop to the left instead of to the right. Likewise, the layer will move up instead of down if yhop is negative. The bigger the values of xhop and yhop, the faster the layer will get where it's going. You can also control the length of the pause between hops by changing the value of delay. For example, adding delay=100; to the OnLoad commands just before the slide() would cause a 100-millisecond (1/10th of a second) delay between each step in the layer movement.

In the sample page from Listing 18.1, the `<div style>` attribute initially places the `"intro"` layer at the x,y pixel location (`-260,88`). In the `<body OnLoad>` attribute, `xgoal` and `ygoal` are set to (`80,20`), while `xhop` and `yhop` are set to (`10,-2`). The slide moves the layer from (`-260,88`) to each of the following positions, one after the other, until it finally reaches (`80,20`):

```
(-250,86)    (-240,84) (-230,82) (-220,80) ... etc.
```

I had to be very careful when I chose the values for `xhop` and `yhop` because they must reach the `xgoal` and `ygoal` in exactly the same number of steps. If I had used (`9,-3`) instead of (`10,-2`), the layer would never land on the spot (`80,20`) and would therefore never stop moving! When you use the `slide()` function for your own animations, be sure to grab a calculator and make sure the two sides of the following equation come out to the same number (using the initial x,y position of the layer for `xstart` and `ystart`):

$$(xgoal - xstart) / xhop = (ygoal - ystart) / yhop$$

I could have added some JavaScript to the `slide()` function to check this automatically, but the whole point is that Dynamic HTML functions can be pretty simple and still get the job done.

> If you've programmed in other languages, it may seem strange that there aren't any explicit commands in Listing 18.2 to draw anything on the screen. JavaScript takes care of updating the display automatically as soon as you change the position settings for anything on the Web page.

Interactive Layer Animation

The rest of this hour demonstrates another application of the `slide()` function and shows you how Dynamic HTML can respond to user-initiated events. The goal this time is to modify the XYZ Files example page so that the user can click any of the three file tabs to "pull out" the hidden part of that graphic.

Figures 18.5 and 18.6 show an example: The user clicks the file tab marked X, and that image slides to the right. If the user clicked the tab again, it would slide back into its original location. You could achieve this interactive animation by adding the Dynamic HTML code in Listing 18.3 to the end of the page presented earlier (in Listing 18.1).

FIGURE 18.5

You can make layers respond to the user's actions. Here, the image of the X file slides out in response to a mouse click.

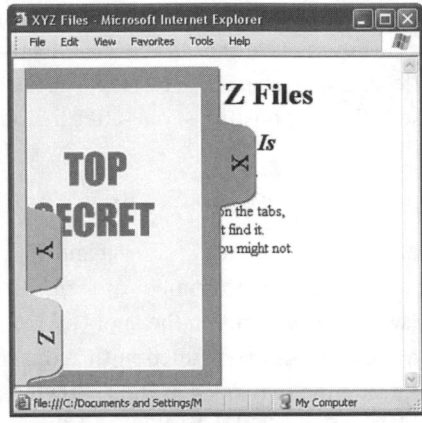

FIGURE 18.6

Notice here and in Figure 18.5 that the moving image stays in front of the text but behind the other two images as it slides.

LISTING 18.3   Enabling the Interactive Behavior Shown in Figures 18.5 and 18.6

```
<!-- Use invisible image links to nowhere as triggers
     to pull out and put away the file folders -->
<div style="position: absolute;
 left: 10px; top: 65px; z-index: 4">
<a href="#" OnClick="layername=makeName('layer1');
 yhop=0; ygoal=10; xhop=40; xgoal=70; slide()">
<img src="empty.gif" width= "35" height="85" border="0" /></a>
</div>
<div style="position: absolute;
 left: 330px; top: 65px; z-index: 5">
<a href="#" OnClick="layername=makeName('layer1');
 yhop=0; ygoal=10; xhop=-40; xgoal=-250; slide()">
<img src= "empty.gif" width="35" height="85" border="0" /></a>
```

LISTING 18.3 continued

```
</div>
<div style="position: absolute;
 left: 10px; top: 155px; z-index: 6">
<a href="#" OnClick="layername=makeName('layer2');
 yhop=0; ygoal=10; xhop=40; xgoal=70; slide()">
<img src="empty.gif" width="35" height="85" border="0" /></a>
</div>
<div style="position: absolute;
 left: 330px; top: 155px; z-index: 7">
<a href="#" OnClick="layername=makeName('layer2');
 yhop=0; ygoal=10; xhop=-40; xgoal=-250; slide()">
<img src="empty.gif" width="35" height="85" border="0" /></a>
</div>
<div style="position: absolute;
 left: 10px; top: 245px; z-index: 8">
<a href="#" OnClick="layername=makeName('layer3');
 yhop=0; ygoal=10; xhop=40; xgoal=70; slide()">
<img src="empty.gif" width="35" height="85" border="0" /></a>
</div>
<div style="position: absolute;
 left: 330px; top: 245px; z-index: 9">
<a href="#" OnClick="layername=makeName('layer3');
 yhop=0; ygoal=10; xhop=-40; xgoal=-250; slide()">
<img src= "empty.gif" width="35" height="85" border="0" /></a>
</div>
</body></html>
```

The first `<div>` layer defined in Listing 18.3 enables the file tab marked X to display the behavior you see in Figures 18.5 and 18.6 (and which you can see on your computer screen by clicking the X tab) .

```
<div style="position: absolute;
 left: 10px; top: 65px; z-index: 4">
<a href="#" OnClick="layername=makeName('layer1');
 yhop=0; ygoal=10; xhop=40; xgoal=70; slide()">
<img src="empty.gif" width="35" height="85" border="0" /></a></div>
```

This layer doesn't change the appearance of the page at all because it contains only a single image (`empty.gif`), which I made completely transparent before saving it in Paint Shop Pro. The `<div style>` tag positions this invisible image directly over the tab of the X file image, in order to give the user something to click. It took some trial and error to find exactly the right spot, as well as the best `width` and `height` for the image. To make it easier, I left out the `border="0"` attribute of the `<img />` tag, making a visible border around the image, until I had found the correct pixel coordinates for it.

The OnClick attribute lets you specify some JavaScript to respond when the mouse clicks something. In future versions of JavaScript, you'll be able to put an OnClick, OnMouseOver, or OnMouseOut attribute in an <img /> tag, but for now that doesn't work, so you have to make the image a link and put the attribute in the <a> tag. In this case, I didn't want the link to actually go anywhere, so I just used href="#" to make a link to the top of the current page (a bit silly, but it works).

> You can also use OnClick and other events in the <area> tag of an imagemap (see Hour 11, "Graphical Links and Imagemaps"), which might have been a more elegant way of achieving the result I was after in this example.

The JavaScript commands in the <a OnClick> attribute are very similar to those you saw earlier in the <body OnLoad> attribute. The makeName() function is used to make a valid layer name; xgoal and ygoal are then set to the destination of the layer, while xhop and yhop are set to the size of each hop on the way there. (Notice that yhop is 0 and ygoal is the same as the initial top: setting, since the image moves only horizontally.) Finally, slide() is called on to do the actual animation.

The second <div> layer in Listing 18.3 is almost the same, but is located 320 pixels further to the right. The xgoal is also 320 pixels further to the left, and xhop is -40 instead of 40. This gives the user a place to click to put away the file folder image after it has been pulled out.

The remaining four <div> layers provide exactly the same interactive behavior for the file tabs marked Y and Z.

Summary

This was undoubtedly the most challenging hour in the book. Don't be surprised or discouraged if you need to read through it more than once and experiment with the sample page to begin successfully adapting the Dynamic HTML code to your own purposes.

If you have any experience with computer programming, you probably gleaned enough from this hour and the previous one to start writing your own JavaScript enhancements to your pages. Even if you have never written a line of computer-language code before in your life, you can still copy the code in the book and use it on your own pages.

In this hour, you've seen how to combine HTML, style sheets, and JavaScript to animate independent layers of text and graphics. You learned how to initiate an animation when a page first loads, or in response to a mouse click on any region of the page.

Of course, all this is only the tip of the Dynamic HTML iceberg. Current scripting languages allow you to modify any of the content or formatting of your pages on-the-fly, in response to a wide variety of events. The latest versions of major Web browsers are finally starting to make it easier to use scripting code in such a way that it is fully compatible with different browsers. The promising future of Dynamic HTML is discussed in Hour 24, "Planning for the Future of HTML."

Q&A

Q Isn't there some way to make layers without using the `style` attribute?

A Yes, but only in older versions of Netscape Navigator that are now obsolete. Netscape invented its own `<layer>` tag, which is unlikely to ever become part of the HTML standard or to be supported by other browsers. If you must know more about this tag, visit `http://devedge.netscape.com/`.

Q In Hours 14 and 15 you stressed the concept of keeping style specifications in a separate document, but in this hour you put all the style stuff right in with the HTML. Aren't you being hypocritical?

A Sort of. It is often a good idea to keep styles in a separate document, and you can combine true style sheets and Dynamic HTML. For example, I could have made a style sheet that included a style like the following:

```
div.peekaboo {position: absolute; left: -250px; top: 10px; width: 300;}
```

I could then have applied that style to each of the three file tab layers with `<div class="peekaboo">`. Doing so, however, would probably have just made the page harder to understand and maintain. When you are working with JavaScript and style-based positioning, I usually find it easier and more efficient to use inline styles than to use separate style sheets.

Q I'm a professional programmer, and I think it was inelegant of you to employ global variables instead of parameter passing in your implementation of the recursive function `slide()`. Furthermore...

A Was that a question? I didn't think so. Get over it, okay?

18

Workshop

The workshop contains quiz questions and activities to help you solidify your understanding of the material covered. Try to answer all questions before looking at the "Answers" section that follows.

Quiz

1. Modify the following Web page so that the Balzout Skydiving heading and fall.gif image drop into place together from above the top edge of the browser window. (Use the slide.js script presented in this hour.)

```
<html><head><title>Take a Dive</title>
</head><body>
<img src="diver.gif" align="left" width="100" height="200" />
<h1>Balzout Skydiving</h1>
Join Richard Balzout for a free chute-packing lesson
on June 15th at the Sewerside Memorial Airfield.
</body></html>
```

2. Now modify the page from Question 1 so that clicking the fall.gif image makes it leap back out of sight.

Answers

1. The following is one possibility. You could change the speed of the fall by adjusting the value of yhop. (This quiz answer is included in the online examples at http://24hourHTMLcafe.com/hour18, by the way.)

```
<html><head><title>Take a Dive</title>
<script src="slide.js" language="javascript">
</script></head><body>
<body OnLoad="if (checkDHTML()) {
 layername=makeName('ComeOnDown');
 yhop=5; ygoal=10; xhop=0; xgoal=10; slide() }">
<div id="ComeOnDown"
 style="position: absolute; left: 10px; top: -210px;">
<img src="diver.gif" align="left" width="100" height="200" />
<h1>Balzout Skydiving</h1></div>
<div style="position: absolute; left: 10px; top: 220px;">
Join Richard Balzout for a free chute-packing lesson
on June 15th at the Sewerside Memorial Airfield.</div>
</body></html>
```

2. Replace the <img /> tag with the following:

```
<a href="#" OnClick="layername=makeName('ComeOnDown');
 yhop=-10; ygoal=-210; xhop=0; xgoal=10; slide()">
<img src="diver.gif" align="left"
 width="100" height="200" border="0" /></a>
```

Exercises

Try combining the techniques you learned in this hour with the JavaScript examples in Hour 17. For example, you might create an animated banner ad that slides across the screen before settling into place, thereby achieving maximum annoyance of Web users! The possibilities are endless, so grab your imagination and get creative!

18

HOUR 19

Gathering Information with HTML Forms

Up to this point, pretty much everything in this book has focused on getting information out to others. (Email links, introduced in Hour 7, "Creating Text Links," are a notable exception.) But HTML is a two-way street; you can use your Web pages to gather information from the people who read them as well.

Web forms allow you to receive feedback, orders, or other information from your Web pages readers. If you've ever used a Web search engine such as Google, HotBot, or Yahoo!, you're familiar with HTML forms. Product order forms are also an extremely popular use of forms.

This lesson shows you how to create your own forms and the basics of how to handle form submissions.

NEW TERM   An HTML *form* is part of a Web page that includes areas where readers can enter information to be sent back to you, the publisher of the Web page.

How HTML Forms Work

Before you learn the HTML tags to make your own forms, you should understand how the information that someone fills out on a form makes its way back to you. You also probably need to have the person who runs your Web server computer set it up to process your forms.

Every form must include a button for the user to submit the form. When someone clicks that button, all the information he filled in is sent (in a standard format) to an Internet address that you specify in the form itself. You have to put a special forms-processing program at that address in order for that information to get to you, or you can choose to receive the formatted information via email.

Almost all ISP companies that offer Web page hosting also provide preprogrammed scripts to their customers for processing forms. You don't need to use a script if you only want to have form information sent to your email address. Scripts allow you to take things a step further by somehow processing form information and possibly saving it to a database or routing it to a Web service such as a secure payment service. A form-processing script usually generates some sort of reply page and sends it back to be displayed for the user.

It's possible to set things up so that much of the information from a form is interpreted and processed automatically. For example, server software exists to authorize a credit card transaction automatically over the Internet, confirm an order to the customer's email address, and enter the order directly into your company's in-house database for shipment. Obviously, setting up that sort of thing can get quite complex, and it's beyond the scope of this book to explain all the things you can do with form data once it has been submitted.

Most ISPs that host Web pages already have a "generic" form-processing script set up and will happily tell you the exact HTML required to use it. If your ISP can't do this, or charges you an extra fee for it, you are frankly probably not using a very good ISP! In that case, you have the following choices:

- Switch to a more helpful Web hosting service.
- Learn advanced server programming.
- Use a form-creation service such as freedback.com to create and process your forms. (Although such services are free and work great, they will display other companies' advertising to everyone who uses your forms.)

▼ To Do

To Do

Before you put a form online, you should do the following:

- Ask your ISP what it offers for form-processing scripts and the exact address to which your forms should send their information. Later in this hour, you'll see where and how to put that address into your forms.

- If you run your own Web server computer, the server software probably came with some basic form-processing scripts. Consult your documentation to set them up properly and find the address on your server where each is located.

- If you're not sure what scripts are available and you want to start with the simplest form-processing approach, configure your forms to simply send the raw form data to your email address. The examples in this hour use such a technique. You can experiment with fancy scripts later.

▲

Creating a Form

Every form must begin with a `<form>` tag, which can be located anywhere in the body of the HTML document. The `form` tag normally has two attributes, `method` and `action`:

```
<form method="post" action="mailto:me@mysite.com">
```

Nowadays, the `method` is almost always `"post"`, which means to send the form entry results as a document. (In some special situations, you may need to use `method="get"`, which submits the results as part of the URL header instead. For example, `"get"` is sometimes used when submitting queries to search engines from a Web form. Since you're not yet an expert on forms, just use `"post"` unless someone tells you to do otherwise.)

The `action` attribute specifies the address to which to send the form data. You have two options here:

- You can type the location of a form-processing program or script on a Web server computer, and the form data will then be sent to that program.

- You can type `mailto:` followed by your email address, and the form data will be sent directly to you whenever someone fills out the form. However, this approach is completely dependent on the user's computer being properly configured with an email client. People accessing your site from a public computer without an email client will be left out in the cold.

The form in Listing 19.1 and Figure 19.1 includes every type of input you can currently use on HTML forms (with one exception: the `button` tag was discussed in Hour 17, "Web Page Scripting for Non-Programmers"). Figure 19.2 shows how the form in Figure 19.1

19

might look after someone fills it out. Refer to these figures as you read the following explanations of each type of input element.

LISTING 19.1 All Parts of a Form Must Fall Between the `<form>` and `</form>` Tags

```
<html><head><title>Guest Book</title></head>
<body>
<h1>My Guest Book</h1>
<p>Please let me know what you think of my Web pages. Thanks!
<form method="post" action="/htbin/generic">
<input id="success" type="hidden" value="me@mysite.com" />
<pre>
What is your name? <input type="text"
                               id="fullname" size="25" />
Your e-mail address: <input type="text"
                          id="e-address" size="25" />
</pre></p>
<p>Check all that apply:<br />
<input type="checkbox" id="likeit" checked="checked" />
I really like your Web site.<br />
<input type="checkbox" id="best" />
One of the best sites I've seen.<br />
<input type="checkbox" id="envy" />
I sure wish my pages looked as good as yours.<br />
<input type="checkbox" id="love" />
I think I'm in love with you.<br />
<input type="checkbox" id="idiot" />
I have no taste and I'm pretty dense,
so your site didn't do much for me.</p>

<p>Choose the one thing you love best about my pages:<br />
<input type="radio" id="lovebest" value="me" checked />
That gorgeous picture of you and your cats.<br />
<input type="radio" id="lovebest" value="cats" />
All those moving poems about your cats.<br />
<input type="radio" id="lovebest" value="burbs" />
The inspiring recap of your suburban childhood.<br />
<input type="radio" id="lovebest" value="treasures" />
The detailed list of all your Elvis memorabilia.</p>

<p>Imagine my site as a book, video, or album.<br />
Select the number of copies you think it would sell:<br />
<select size="3" id="potential">
<option selected>Million copy bestseller for sure!</option>
<option>100,000+ (would be Oprah's favorite)</option>
<option>Thousands (an under-appreciated classic)</option>
<option>Very few: not banal enough for today's public</option>
</select></p>
```

LISTING 19.1   continued

```
<p>How do you think I could improve my site?
<select id="suggestion">
<option selected>Couldn't be better</option>
<option>More about the cats</option>
<option>More Elvis stuff</option>
<option>More family pictures</option>
</select></p>

<p>Feel free to type more praise, marriage proposals,
gift offers, etc. below:<br />
<textarea id="comments" rows="4" cols="55">
I just want to thank you so much for touching my life.
</textarea>
<input type="submit" value="Click Here to Submit" />
<input type="reset" value="Erase and Start Over" /></p>
</form>
</body></html>
```

FIGURE 19.1

The form code shown in Listing 19.1 uses nearly every type of HTML form input element.

19

FIGURE 19.2
*Visitors to your Web
site fill out the form
and then click the
Click Here to Submit
button.*

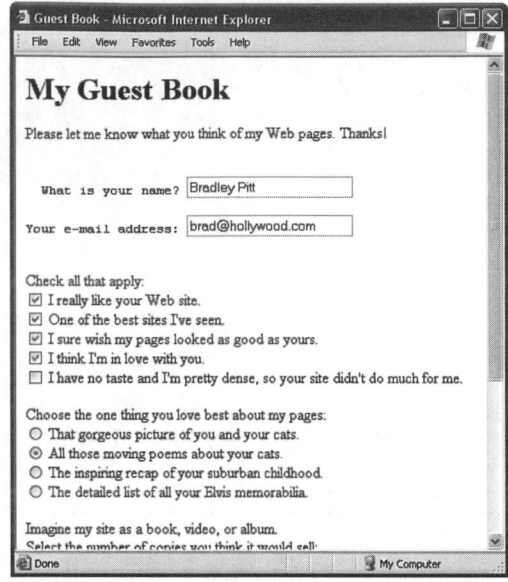

Notice that some of the text in Figures 19.1 and 19.2 is monospaced, meaning that every letter is the same width. Monospaced text makes it easy to
line up a form input box with the box above or below it and can make your
forms look neater. To use monospaced text in all or part of a form, enclose
the text between <pre> and </pre> tags. Using these tags also relieves you
from having to put <br /> at the end of every line because the <pre> tag
puts a line break on the page at every line break in the HTML document.
Another alignment solution for forms involves placing form labels and fields
in two different columns of a table.

Accepting Text Input

To ask the user for a specific piece of information within a form, use the <input /> tag.
This tag must fall between the <form> and </form> tags, but it can be anywhere on the
page in relation to text, images, and other HTML tags. For example, to ask for some-
one's name you could type the following:

```
What's your first name? <input type="text" size="20" maxlength="30"
id="firstname" />
What's your last name? <input type="text" size="20" maxlength="30"
id="lastname" />
```

The type attribute indicates what type of form element to display—a simple one-line text entry box in this case. (Each element type is discussed individually in the following sections.)

The size attribute indicates approximately how many characters wide the text input box should be. If you are using a proportionally spaced font, the width of the input will vary depending on what the user enters. If the input is too long to fit in the box, most Web browsers will automatically scroll the text to the left.

maxlength determines the number of characters the user is allowed to type into the text box. If someone tries to type beyond the specified length, the extra characters won't appear. You can specify a length that is longer, shorter, or the same as the physical size of the text box. size and maxlength are used only for type="text" because other input types (check boxes, radio buttons, and so on) have a fixed size.

If you want the user to enter text without it being displayed on the screen, you can use <input type="password" /> instead of <input type="text" />. Asterisks (***) are then displayed in place of the text the user types. The size, maxlength, and name attributes work exactly the same for type="password" as for type="text". Keep in mind that this technique of hiding a password only provides visual protection—there is no encryption or other protection associated with the password being transmitted.

Identifying Each Piece of Form Data

19

No matter what type an input element is, you must give a name to the data it gathers. You can use any name you like for each input item, as long as each one on the form is different. When the form is sent to you (or to your form-processing script), each data item is identified by name.

For example, if someone entered Jane and Doe in the text box defined previously, you would see something like the following two lines in the email message you get when she submits the form:

```
firstname=Jane
lastname=Doe
```

The following code is a sample email message generated by the form-processing script specified in the form in Listing 19.1. Notice that each data element is identified by the name given to it in Listing 19.1:

```
fullname=Bradley Pitte-
address=brad@hollywood.comlikeit=onbest=onenvy=onlove=onpayment=catspotential=Ve
ry few: not banal enough for today's publicsuggestion=More about the cats
comments=Absolutely stunning. Really. Wow.
```

> Depending upon the specific manner in which your Web server processes email forms, you might see the data in a different format than that shown here.

Including Hidden Data in Forms

Want to send certain data items to the server script that processes a form but don't want the user to see them? Use the `input type="hidden"` attribute. This attribute has no effect on the display at all; it just adds any name and value you specify to the form results when they are submitted.

You might use this attribute to tell a script where to email the form results. For example, the following might indicate that the results should be mailed to me@mysite.com:

```
<input type="hidden" id="mail_to" value="me@mysite.com" />
```

For this attribute to have any effect, someone must create a script or program to read this line and do something about it. My ISP's form script uses this hidden value to determine where to email the form data.

Most scripts require at least one or two hidden input elements. Consult the person who wrote or provided you with the script for details.

Exploring Form Input Controls

There are a variety of different input controls available for retrieving information from the user. You've already learned about some text entry options for forms. The next few sections introduce you to most of the remaining form input options you can use to design forms.

Check Boxes

NEW TERM The simplest input type is a *check box*, which appears as a small square the user can select or deselect by clicking. You must give each check box a name via the `id` attribute. If you want a check box to be checked by default when the form comes up, include the `checked` attribute. For example, the following would make two check boxes:

```
<input type="checkbox" id="baby" checked="checked" /> Baby Grand Piano
<input type="checkbox" id="mini" /> Mini Piano Stool
```

The check box labeled Baby Grand Piano would be checked in this example. (The user would have to click it to turn it off if he didn't want a piano.) The one marked Mini Piano Stool would be unchecked to begin with, so the user would have to click it to turn it on.

When the form is submitted, selected check boxes appear in the form result:

```
baby=on
```

Blank (*deselected*) check boxes do not appear in the form output at all.

The new XHTML and XML standards require all attributes to have an equal sign followed by a value. This explains why I've used checked="checked" to indicate that a check box is checked, as opposed to just checked. This rule applies to all Boolean (true/false, on/off, yes/no, and so on) attributes that you may come across in HTML.

You can use more than one check box with the same name, but different values, as in the following code:

```
<input type="checkbox" id="pet" value="dog"> dog
<input type="checkbox" id="pet" value="cat"> cat
<input type="checkbox" id="pet" value="iguana"> iguana
```

If the user checks both cat and iguana, the submission result includes the following:

```
pet=cat
pet=iguana
```

Radio Buttons

NEW TERM *Radio buttons*, where only one choice can be selected at a time, are almost as simple to implement as check boxes. Just use type="radio" and give each of the options its own input tag, but use the same id for all of the radio buttons in a group:

```
<input type="radio" id="card" value="v" checked="checked" /> Visa
<input type="radio" id="card" value="m" /> MasterCard
```

The value can be any name or code you choose. If you include the checked attribute, that button is selected by default. (No more than one radio button with the same id can be checked.)

19

If the user selects MasterCard from the preceding radio button set, the following is included in the form submission to the server script:

```
card=m
```

If the user doesn't change the default `checked` selection, `card=v` is sent instead.

Selection Lists

 Both *scrolling lists* and *pull-down pick lists* are created with the `<select>` tag. You use this tag together with the `<option>` tag:

```
<select id="extras" size="3" multiple="multiple">
<option selected="selected"> Electric windows</option>
<option> AM/FM Radio</option>
<option> Turbocharger</option>
</select>
```

No HTML tags other than `<option>` and `</option>` should appear between the `<select>` and `</select>` tags.

Unlike the text input type, the `size` attribute here determines how many items show at once on the selection list. If `size="2"` were used in the preceding code, only the first two options would be visible, and a scrollbar would appear next to the list so the user could scroll down to see the third option.

Including the `multiple` attribute allows users to select more than one option at a time, and the `selected` attribute makes an option selected by default. The actual text that accompanies selected options is returned when the form is submitted. If the user selected Electric windows and Turbocharger, for instance, the form results would include the following lines:

```
extras=Electric windows
extras=Turbocharger
```

(As I cautioned you earlier with regard to the `checked` attribute, the new XHTML standard requires you to use `multiple="multiple"` and `selected="selected"`.)

 If you leave out the `size` attribute or specify `size="1"`, the list will create a pull-down pick list. Pick lists cannot allow multiple choices; they are logically equivalent to a group of radio buttons. For example, another way to choose between credit card types follows:

```
<select id="card">
<option> Visa</option>
<option> MasterCard</option>
</select>
```

Text Areas

The `<input type="text">` attribute mentioned earlier allows the user to enter only a single line of text. When you want to allow multiple lines of text in a single input item, use the `<textarea>` and `</textarea>` tags instead. Any text you include between these two tags is displayed as the default entry. Here's an example:

```
<textarea id="comments" rows="4" cols="20">
Please send more information.
</textarea>
```

As you probably guessed, the rows and cols attributes control the number of rows and columns of text that fit in the input box. The `cols` attribute is a little less exact than `rows`, and approximates the number of characters that fit in a row of text. Text area boxes do have a scrollbar, however, so the user can enter more text than fits in the display area.

Submit!

Every form must include a button that submits the form data to the server. You can put any label you like on this button with the `value` attribute:

```
<input type="submit" value="Place My Order Now!" />
```

A gray button will be sized to fit the label you put in the `value` attribute. When the user clicks it, all data items on the form are sent to the email address or program script specified in the `form action` attribute.

You can also include a button that clears all entries on the form so users can start over if they change their minds or make mistakes. Use the following:

```
<input type="reset" value="Clear This Form and Start Over" />
```

If the standard Submit and Reset buttons look a little bland to you, you'll be glad to know that there is an easy way to substitute your own graphics for these buttons. Type the following to use an image of your choice for a Submit button:

```
<input type="image" src="button.gif" />
```

The image named `button.gif` will appear on the page, and the form will be submitted whenever someone clicks that image. You can also include any attributes normally used with the `<img />` tag, such as `border` or `align`. (Hour 9, "Putting Graphics on a Web Page," introduces the `<img />` tag.)

19

The exact pixel coordinates where the mouse clicked an image button are sent along with the form data. For example, if someone entered bigjoe@chicago.net in the form in Figure 19.3, the resulting form data might look like the following:

Anotherone=bigjoe@chicago.net
&x=75
&y=36

Normally you should ignore the x and y coordinates, but some server scripts use them to turn the button into an imagemap.

Listing 19.2 and Figure 19.3 show a very simple form that uses a customized Submit button. (You saw how to make graphics like the signup.gif button in Hour 9, "Creating Your Own Web Page Graphics.")

LISTING 19.2   The <input /> Tag on This page Uses a Custom Graphical Submit Button

```html
<html><head><title>FREE!</title></head>
<body>
<h1>Free Electronic Junk Mail!</h1>
To start receiving junk e-mail from us daily*, enter your
e-mail address below and click on the <i>SignUP!</i> button.
<form method="post" action="/htbin/generic">
<input id="success" type="hidden"
 value="http://24hourHTMLcafe.com/hour8/thanks.htm" />
<input type="text" id="anotherone" size="25" />
<input type="image" src="signup.gif" border="0" align="top" />
</form>
*<small>By clicking the above button, you also agree to the
terms of our Marketing Agreement, which is available upon
request at our offices in Bangkok, Thailand. A fee may be
charged for removal from our list if you elect at a later
date not to receive additional sales literature.</small>
</body></html>
```

FIGURE **19.3**

Forms don't need to be complex to be effective. (They might need to be a little less blunt, though.)

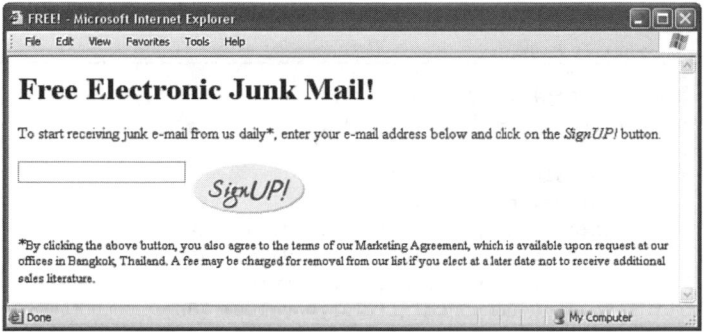

You can make a button that cancels the form and proceeds to another page (ignoring all information the user has entered so far) simply by linking to that other page. Here is an example:

```
<a href="nodice.htm">Click here to cancel.</a>
```

There is no specific form type for a graphical reset button, but you can achieve the same effect by putting an image link to the current page, like this:

```
<a href="thispage.htm"><img src="cancel.gif" /></a>
```

Creating an Online Order Form

One of the most common uses of scripting is making an order form that adds its own totals based upon what items the customer selects. Listing 19.3 contains the code for a sample order form that you can copy to create self-totaling forms yourself.

Though the code for this example is unrealistically simple for any real company's order form (most companies would like at least the address and phone number of the person placing the order), it is a completely functional order form that uses JavaScript to calculate a total for the order. Of course, relying entirely on JavaScript for order taking is a little risky given that some users will undoubtedly disable JavaScript in their browsers. You learned about JavaScript in Hour 17, and also in the previous hour.

Figure 19.4 demonstrates what the order form would look like after a user entered values into the form. The numbers in the Totals column are computed automatically.

19

LISTING 19.3   Simple Order Form Using JavaScript to Automatically Compute
Totals

```
<html><head><title>Parts</title>
<script language="JavaScript">
<!--
 function CalculateTotals(){
   f=document.orderform;
   f.total1.value=parseInt(f.qty1.value)*50;
   f.total2.value=parseInt(f.qty2.value)*295;
   f.total3.value=parseInt(f.qty3.value)*395;
   f.total4.value=parseInt(f.qty4.value)*750;
   f.grandtotal.value=parseInt(f.total1.value)
                     +parseInt(f.total2.value)
                     +parseInt(f.total3.value)
                     +parseInt(f.total4.value);}
//-->
</script></head>
<body>
<h1>Parts Order Form</h1>
<p>Indicate how many of each part you wish to order in the "Qty"
column. The total amount of your order will be calculated
automatically. When you are ready to submit your order, click on
the <b>Make Purchase</b> button.</p>
<form id="orderform" method="post" action="/htbin/generic">
<table border="3"><tr>
<th>Qty</th><th>Part #</th><th>Description</th>
<th>Price</th><th>Total</th></tr>
<tr><td>
<input id="qty1" size="3" OnBlur="CalculateTotals()" /></td>
<td>25791</td><td>Chromated Flywheel Knob</td>
<td align="right">$50</td>
<td><input id="total1" size="7"
     OnFocus="document.orderform.qty2.select();
             document.orderform.qty2.focus();" /></td></tr>
<tr><td>
<input id="qty2" size="3" OnBlur="CalculateTotals()" /></td>
<td>17557</td><td>Perambulatory Dramograph</td>
<td align="right">$295</td>
<td><input id="total2" size="7"
     OnFocus="document.orderform.qty3.select();
             document.orderform.qty3.focus();" /></td></tr>
<tr><td>
<input id="qty3" size="3" OnBlur="CalculateTotals()" /></td>
<td>98754</td><td>Triple-Extruded Colorizer</td>
<td align="right">$395</td>
<td><input id="total3" size="7"
     OnFocus="document.orderform.qty4.select();
             document.orderform.qty4.focus();" /></td></tr>
<tr><td>
```

LISTING 19.3 continued

```
<input id="qty4" size="3" OnBlur="CalculateTotals()" /></td>
<td>47594</td><td>Rediculation Kit (Complete)</td>
<td align="right">$750</td>
<td><input id="total4" size="7"
     OnFocus="document.orderform.qty1.select();
              document.orderform.qty1.focus();" /></td></tr>
<tr><td></td><td></td><td></td>
<td align="right"><b>GRAND TOTAL:</b></td>
<td><input id="grandtotal" size="7"
     OnFocus="document.orderform.qty1.select();
              document.orderform.qty1.focus();" /></td></tr>
</table>
<br /><input type="submit" value="Make Purchase" />
</form>
<script language="JavaScript">
<!--
  f=document.orderform;
  f.qty1.value=0; f.qty2.value=0;
  f.qty3.value=0; f.qty4.value=0;
  f.total1.value=0; f.total2.value=0;
  f.total3.value=0; f.total4.value=0;
  f.grandtotal.value=0;
// -->
</script>
</body></html>
```

FIGURE 19.4

The JavaScript in Listing 19.3 produces this form. Here, the customer has entered some desired quantities and the form has figured out the total cost.

19

Most programmers could probably customize and expand this example quite a bit without knowing anything whatsoever about JavaScript. What's more, this page works on any server and any JavaScript-enabled browser on any operating system.

Even if you don't do programming at all, you can easily adapt the code in Listing 19.3 to your own uses. The following list highlights the key elements of the JavaScript code that you need to understand in order to modify the page for your own purposes.

- I started by giving a name to all the parts of the page I would need to modify. Using the id attribute, I named the `<form>` itself `"orderform"`. I also gave each input element in the form a name, such as `"qty1"`, `"qty2"`, `"total1"`, `"total2"`, and so on.

- The HTML page itself is always named `"document"`, so I refer to the form as `"document.orderform"`. The first input item on that form is `"document.orderform.qty1"`, the `"grandtotal"` input item is `"document.orderform.grandtotal"`, and so forth. You'll notice that I put f=document.orderform at the beginning of each `<script>`. This just saved me some typing, since I could then use the letter f from then on instead of typing out document.orderform as part of every name.

- The function near the top of the page, which I chose to name CalculateTotals(), is the part of the script that actually carries out the computations. This function is pretty straightforward: It multiplies the quantities the user entered by the prices to get the totals, then adds the totals to make a grand total. The only tricky thing here is all that parseInt() business. You have to use parseInt() to indicate that something is a number whenever you want to do computations. (This isn't necessary in most other programming languages. JavaScript is a little weird that way.) If you want to allow numbers that aren't integers, such as 12.5 or 13.333, use parseFloat() instead of parseInt().

- The `<script>` at the bottom of the page just sets all the input elements to 0 when the page first appears. This has to be done after the form itself is defined on the page with the `<form>` and `</form>` tags.

- The real action happens in the `<input>` tags, which respond to the OnFocus and OnBlur events. The OnFocus stuff happens when the user first clicks in (or tabs to) an input box to enter data. The OnBlur commands are triggered when the user is done entering data in a box and moves on to the next one.

- Take a look at the `<input>` tags named qty1, qty2, qty3, and qty4. In each of these, you'll see OnBlur="CalculateTotals()", which simply does all the math in the CalculateTotals function in the top `<script>` every time the user enters a number in the Qty column. (JavaScript takes care of displaying the totals and grand total automatically, so you don't see any explicit command to "print" these numbers.)

- Now look at all the other `<input>` tags. Each contains two commands, similar to the following:

```
OnFocus="document.orderform.qty2.focus();
         document.orderform.qty2.select()"
```

This causes the cursor to skip to the next input box so that the user doesn't get a chance to modify the totals. It also causes whatever data is in that next input box to be selected, so whatever the user types will replace the old data instead of being tacked onto the end of it.

Whew! That may seem like a lot to figure out, especially if you've never done any programming before! With a little experimentation and a few careful readings of this explanation, you should be able to put together a simple automatic order form of your own without any further knowledge of JavaScript.

Summary

This hour demonstrated how to create HTML forms, which allow your Web pages readers to enter specific information and send it back to you via email. You also found that you can set up a script or program to process form data. Your ISP or server software vendor can help you do this. You even learned how to make an order form add its own totals automatically, which could be especially useful in a Web site that accepts online orders for products.

Table 19.1 summarizes the HTML tags and attributes covered in this hour.

TABLE 19.1 HTML Tags and Attributes Covered in Hour 19

Tag/Attribute	Function
`<form>...</form>`	Indicates an input form.
Attributes	
`action="..."`	The address of the script to process this form input.
`method="..."`	How the form input will be sent to the server. Normally set to `post`, rather than `get`.
`<input />`	An input element for a form.
Attributes	
`type="..."`	The type for this input widget. Possible values are `checkbox`, `hidden`, `radio`, `reset`, `submit`, `text`, and `image`.

19

TABLE 19.1   continued

Tag/Attribute	Function
id="..."	The unique name of this item, as passed to the script.
value="..."	The default value for a text or hidden item; for a check box or radio button, the value to be submitted with the form; for reset or submit buttons, the label for the button itself.
src="..."	The source file for an image.
checked="checked"	For check boxes and radio buttons, indicates that this item is checked.
size="..."	The width, in characters, of a text input region.
maxlength="..."	The maximum number of characters that can be entered into a text region.
align="..."	For images in forms, determines how the text and image will align (same as with the `<img />` tag; see Hour 9).
`<textarea>...</textarea>`	Indicates a multiline text entry form element. Default text can be included.

Attributes

id="..."	The name to be passed to the script.
rows="..."	The number of rows this text area displays.
cols="..."	The number of columns (characters) this text area displays.
`<select>...</select>`	Creates a menu or scrolling list of possible items.

Attributes

id="..."	The name that is passed to the script.
size="..."	The number of elements to display. If size is indicated, the selection becomes a scrolling list. If no size is given, the selection is a pop-up menu.
multiple="multiple"	Allows multiple selections from the list.
`<option>...</option>`	Indicates a possible item within a `<select>` element.

Attributes

selected="selected"	With this attribute included, the option will be selected by default in the list.
value="..."	The value to submit if this option is selected when the form is submitted.

Q&A

Q **I've heard that it's dangerous to send credit card numbers over the Internet. Can't thieves intercept form data on its way to me?**

A It is possible to intercept form data (and any Web pages or email) as it travels through the Internet. If you ask for credit card numbers or other sensitive information on your forms, you should ask the company who runs your Web server about secure forms processing. There are several reliable technologies for eliminating the risk of high-tech eavesdroppers, but they typically must pay for them—you will usually need to obtain a security certificate from a secure services provider such as Thawte (`http://www.thawte.com/`).

To put the amount of risk in perspective, remember that it is much more difficult to intercept information traveling through the Internet than it is to look over someone's shoulder in a restaurant or retail store. Even so, you should always utilize secure pages any time you're handling sensitive financial information such as credit card numbers.

Q **I'm not set up to take credit cards or electronic payments. How do I make an order form for people to print out on paper and mail to me with a check?**

A Any form can be printed out. Just leave off the Submit button if you don't want any email submissions; instead, instruct people to fill out the form and select File, Print. Remember to include a link to some other page so they can return to the rest of your Web site after printing the form—and don't forget to tell them where they should send the check! Also, don't forget to include the form elements within the `<form>` tag—some browsers won't display the elements without a `<form>` tag.

Q **Can I put forms on a CD-ROM, or do they have to be on the Internet?**

A You can put a form anywhere you can put a Web page. If it's on a disk or CD-ROM instead of a Web server, it can be filled out by people whether they are connected to the Internet or not. Of course, they must be connected to the Internet (or your local intranet) when they click the Submit button, or the information won't get to you.

19

Workshop

The workshop contains quiz questions and activities to help you solidify your understanding of the material covered. Try to answer all questions before looking at the "Answers" section that follows.

Quiz

1. Write the HTML to create a guestbook form that asks someone for his or her name, sex, age, and email address. Assume that you have a form-processing script set up at /cgi/generic and that you need to include the following hidden input element to tell the script where to send the form results:

   ```
   <input type="hidden" id="mailto" value="you@yoursite.com" />
   ```

2. If you created an image named sign-in.gif, how would you use it as the Submit button for the guestbook in question 2?

Answers

1. ```
   <html><head><title>My Guestbook</title></head>
   <body>
   <h1>My Guestbook: Please Sign In</h1>
   <form method="post" action="/cgi/generic">
   <input type="hidden" id="mailto" value="you@yoursite.com" />
   Your name: <input type="text" id="name" size="20" /><p>
   Your sex:
   <input type="radio" id="sex" value="male" /> male
   <input type="radio" id="sex" value="female" /> female<p>
   Your age: <input type="text" id="age" size="4" /><p>
   Your e-mail address:
   <input type="text" id="email" size="30" /><p>
   <input type="submit" value="sign in" />
   <input type="reset" value="erase" />
   </form>
   </body></html>
   ```

2. Replace

   ```
   <input type="submit" value="Sign In" />
   ```

   with

   ```
   <input type="image" src="sign-in.gif" />
   ```

Exercises

Try creating a form using all of the different types of input elements and selection lists to make sure you understand how each of them works.
   ```

Hour **20**

Embedding Multimedia in Web Pages

Multimedia is a popular buzzword for sound, motion video, and interactive animation. This hour shows you how to include multimedia in your Web pages.

The first thing you should be aware of is that Internet multimedia is still in its youth. Computer multimedia in general is actually relatively new, but Internet multimedia is even newer, and is therefore in a more noticeable state of change. The rapid pace of growth for Internet multimedia creates three obstacles for anyone who wants to include audiovisual material in a Web page:

- There are many incompatible multimedia file formats from which to choose, and none has yet emerged as a clear industry standard.

- Many people do not have Internet connections fast enough to receive high-quality audiovisual data without a long wait.

- HTML tags for including multimedia in Web pages are somewhat inconsistent, although HTML 4 does offer a standard approach that will likely set everything straight in the future.

The moral of the story: Whatever you do today to implement a multimedia Web site, plan on changing it before too long as technologies evolve.

The good news is that you can sidestep all three of these obstacles to some extent today, and they are all likely to become even easier to overcome in the near future. This hour shows you how to put multimedia on your Web pages for maximum compatibility with the Web browser versions that most people are now using. It also introduces you to the new standard way that Web page multimedia is handled by newer Web browsers, which will help to clear up problems in the future.

To Do

Before you see how to place multimedia on your Web pages in any way, you need to have some multimedia content to start with.

Creating multimedia of any kind is a challenging and complicated task. If you're planning to create your own content from scratch, you'll need far more than this book to become the next crackerjack multimedia developer. Once you have some content, however, this hour will show you how to place your new creations into your Web pages.

For those of us who are artistically challenged, a number of alternative ways to obtain useful multimedia assets are available. Aside from the obvious (such as hiring an artist), here are a few suggestions:

1. The Web itself is chock-full of useful content of all media types, and stock media clearinghouses of all shapes and sizes now exist online. See the hotlist at the *24-Hour HTML Café*—`http://www.24hourhtmlcafe.com/hotsites.htm#multimedia`—for links to some of the best stock media sources on the Web.

2. Don't feel like spending any money? Much of the material on the Internet is free. Of course, it's still a good idea to double-check with the author or current owner of the content; you don't want to be sued for copyright infringement. In addition, various offices of the U.S. government generate content which, by law, belongs to all Americans. (Any NASA footage found online, for instance, is free for your use.)

3. Many search engines (google.com, altavista.com, hotbot.com, and so on) have specific search capabilities for finding multimedia files. As long as you are careful about copyright issues, this can be an easy way to find multimedia related to a specific topic.

4. Check out the online forums and Usenet newsgroups that cater to the interests of videographers. As clearly as possible, describe your site and what you want to do with it. Chances are you'll find a few up-and-coming artists who'd be more than happy to let thousands of people peruse their work online.

Placing Multimedia on a Web Page

The following sections show you how to add some audio and video to a Web page in three ways:

1. The "old way" for maximum compatibility with all Web browsers

2. The "today way" that's best for more recent versions of Netscape Navigator and Microsoft Internet Explorer

3. The "new way" that only works with the latest versions of Netscape Navigator and Microsoft Internet Explorer, but will be the official standard technique for the future

> I use Windows AVI video and MIDI sound files in this hour's sample pages. For better compatibility with non-Windows computers, you could use Apple's QuickTime audio/video, the RealAudio/RealVideo, the popular MP3 sound format, or any other media format supported by today's Web browsers. The procedures shown in this hour for incorporating the files into your Web pages are the same, no matter which file format you choose.

Multimedia the Old-Fashioned Way

The simplest and most reliable option for incorporating a video or audio file into your Web site is to simply link it in with `<a href>`, exactly as you would link to another HTML file. (See Hour 3, "Linking to Other Web Pages," for coverage of the `<a>` tag.)

For example, the following line could be used to offer an AVI video of a Maine lobster:

```
<a href="lobstah.avi">Play the lobster video.</a>
```

When the user clicks the words `Play the lobster video`, the `lobstah.avi` video file is transferred to her computer. Whichever helper application or plug-in she has installed automatically starts as soon as the file has finished downloading. If no AVI-compatible helper or plug-in can be found, the Web browser offers her a chance to download the appropriate plug-in or save the video on the hard drive for later viewing.

20

In case you're unfamiliar with *helper applications* (*helper apps* for short), they are the external programs that a Web browser calls on to display any type of file it can't handle on its own. Generally, the helper application associated with a file type is called upon whenever a Web browser can't display that type of file on its own.

Plug-ins are a special sort of helper application that are installed directly into a Web browser, and allow you to view multimedia content directly within the browser window.

Embedding Sound in a Web Page

Over the past few years, Microsoft and Netscape have offered various conflicting solutions to the problem of how to put multimedia on a Web page. Some of these, such as Microsoft's proprietary extensions to the <img> tag, are now completely obsolete.

One non-standard tag has endured, however: Netscape's <embed /> tag is still more compatible with both Netscape and Microsoft browsers than the official HTML 4 <object> tag, which was supposed to replace it. The <object> tag will still likely replace the <embed /> tag in the long run, but the <embed /> tag is still the way to go for now to ensure that the most people will be able to successfully view your multimedia content. An even better approach is to place the <embed> tag inside of an <object> tag, which allows the code to work with virtually all browsers, old and new. You find out more about this approach later in the lesson.

The <embed /> tag enables you to place any type of file directly into your Web page. For the media to appear on the Web page, however, every user must have a plug-in or helper application that recognizes the incoming data type and knows what to do with it.

The media players that come bundled with Internet Explorer and Netscape Navigator can handle most common media types, including WAV, AU, MPEG, MID, EPS, VRML, and many more. Many other plug-ins are also available from other companies to handle almost any type of media file such as the popular PDF Acrobat file format by Adobe.

Netscape maintains a Web page that lists all registered plug-ins and plug-in developers. To check out the current assortment, head to http://home.netscape.com/plugins/. You can see which plug-ins are installed in your Netscape browser by entering about:plugins in the Location bar (where you would normally type an Internet address).

The Plug-ins Development Kit, available for free from Netscape, allows developers to create new plug-ins for their own products and data types. For more information, see Netscape's Web site at http://home.netscape.com/. Of course, most popular plug-ins are available for both Netscape Navigator and Microsoft Internet Explorer.

The following line of HTML would embed a sound clip named `hello.wav` and display the playback controls at the current position on the page, as long as visitors to the page have a WAV compatible plug-in or helper app.

```
<embed src="hello.wav">
```

Notice that, like the `<img>` tag, `<embed />` requires a `src` attribute to indicate the address of the embedded media file. Also like `<img>`, the `<embed />` tag can take `align`, `width`, and `height` attributes. The `src`, `width`, `height`, and `align` attributes are interpreted by the browser just as they would be for a still image. However, the actual display of the data is handled by whichever plug-in or helper application each user may have installed. In the case of sound files, the sound is played and some controls are usually displayed. Which controls actually appear depend on which plug-in or helper application each individual user has installed, so you, as a Web page author, can't know ahead of time exactly what someone will see.

The `<embed />` tag also enables you to set any number of optional parameters, which are specific to the plug-in or player program. For instance, the HTML code in Listing 20.1 includes the following:

```
<embed src="atune.mid" width="1" height="1"
 autostart="true" loop="true" hidden="true" />
```

This causes the music file `atune.mid` to play whenever the page is displayed. As you can see in Figure 20.1, this has no visual effect on the page whatsoever. (Since this book doesn't have any speakers, you can't hear the auditory effect unless you pull the page up online at http://www.24hourHTMLcafe.com/hour20/.)

20

LISTING 20.1   The `<embed />` Tag Embeds Multimedia Files Directly into a Web Page in Netscape Navigator and Microsoft Internet Explorer

```
<html><head><title>Music</title></head>
<body background="wiggles.jpg">
<a href="nosound.htm">
<img src="shutup.gif" border="0" align="right" alt="Stop music">
</a>
<table width="500">
```

LISTING 20.1   continued

```
<tr><td><img src="piano.gif" width="200" height="172"></td></tr>
<tr><td><b>Roaming through the jungle of 'oohs' and 'ahs,'
searching for a more agreeable noise, I live a life of
primitivity with the mind of a child and an unquenchable
thirst for sharps and flats.</b>
&#151;Duke Ellington, <i>Music Is My Mistress</i>
</td></tr></table>
<embed src="atune.mid" width="1" height="1"
 autostart="true" loop="true" hidden="true" />
</body></html>
```

FIGURE 20.1

If you were looking at this page (from Listing 20.1) on a computer with a sound card and speakers, you would hear the atune.mid *file playing.*

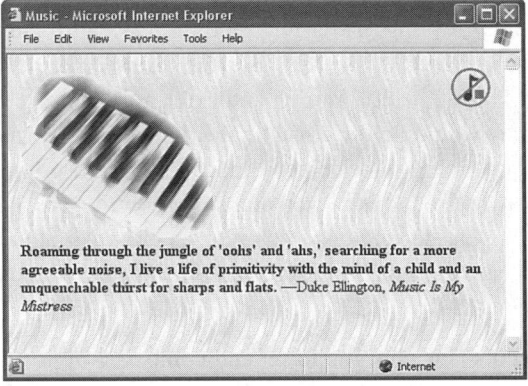

autostart, loop, and hidden are not standard attributes of the <embed /> tag, so the browser simply hands them over to the plug-in program to interpret. Some plug-ins support these attributes—they tell the plug-in to automatically play the video as soon as it loads, to play it over again each time it finishes, and not to display any controls on the Web page. If a user has a different AVI plug-in, or no plug-in at all for handling MIDI (Musical Instrument Digital Interface) files, these attributes will do nothing at all. Refer to the Web pages of each plug-in developer for information on the commands that its plug-in will accept as attributes in the <embed /> tag.

If a suitable plug-in can't be found for an <embed /> tag, both Netscape Navigator and Microsoft Internet Explorer may embed some other helper application (such as Windows Media Player) to play the media file. Therefore, the sound will play successfully in both Netscape Navigator and Microsoft Internet Explorer.

Whenever you set up a Web page to play a sound automatically, it's a good idea to give people some way to turn the sound off. (There's nothing more annoying than surfing the Web with your favorite CD on and hitting a musical Web page that can't be turned off!) The easiest way to turn off a sound is to simply link to a page with no sounds embedded in it. For example, clicking the shutup.gif icon in the upper-right corner of Figure 20.1 loads a silent but otherwise identical page.

Embedding Video in a Web Page

The HTML page in Listing 20.2 demonstrates the use of <embed /> with a video clip in the Windows AVI (Audio-Video Interleave) format. The <embed /> tag in Listing 20.2 also includes the autostart and loop attributes, which tell the plug-in to start playing the video when the page loads and to repeat it as long as the page is being displayed. Figure 20.2 shows the resulting page as viewed in Internet Explorer.

LISTING 20.2   Embedding a Video into a Web Page with the <embed /> Tag

```
<html><head><title>Fractal Video Clip</title></head>
<body>
  <embed src="3dtetra2.avi" autostart="true" loop="true"
  width="160" height="120" vspace="10" hspace="20" align="left" />
<h2>A Spinning 3-D Fractal</h2>
If the video clip to the left doesn't start on its own,
click on it to make it play. Once it starts, you can
right-click on it and choose Pause to make it stop.
</body></html>
```

FIGURE 20.2

This is the page in Listing 20.2 as seen in Internet Explorer. If this page were a computer screen, the fractal would be spinning and a soundtrack would be playing.

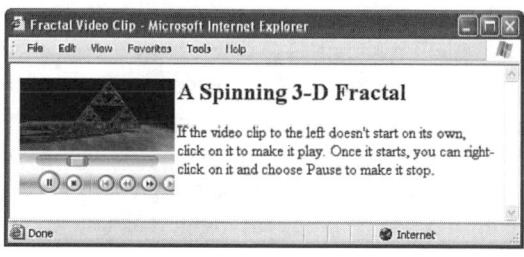

20

Notice that the size of the video is reduced to make room for the Media Player controls. This isn't ideal, since it makes the video appear smaller in Internet Explorer than it does in Netscape Navigator. In the next section of this hour, you learn how to remedy this problem.

When Navigator and Internet Explorer encounter an `<embed />` tag, they basically try their hardest to find some way to embed the media file directly in the Web page. As a Web page author, you can't predict what plug-in or helper application will be selected, but you can at least try to put some instructions on the Web page telling your audience from where to download a suitable player.

> Embedded helper apps currently only work on the Windows platform—they will not function for Macintosh or UNIX users.

You can use `<embed />` with any type of audio, video, or interactive multimedia files as long as your audience has the correct player software installed.

Unfortunately, you as a Web page author have no control over or knowledge of which file types and applications people who visit your pages will have configured on their computers, or even how many visitors will be using a Microsoft Windows operating system. So the exotic uses of `<embed />` are probably best left to corporate intranets or other situations where you have some control over the intended audience's computer setup.

Multimedia the New Way

Netscape's `<embed />` tag has come under fire for a number of reasons, both technical and political. Officially, it has already been made obsolete by a new tag called `<object>`, which has the blessing of Netscape, Microsoft, and the official World Wide Web Consortium (W3C) standards-setting committee. The `<object>` tag will do everything Netscape wants the `<embed />` tag to do, plus a lot more. Or so the story goes.

The problem with the `<object>` tag is that it still isn't supported consistently across different browsers. The problem mainly has to do with the fact that Internet Explorer supported the `<object>` tag for quite some time before it was standardized, and included several proprietary attributes that aren't supported in Netscape Navigator. These inconsistencies have already begun ironing themselves out to some degree, but they are still an issue for the immediate future. Even so, I want to go ahead and show you how to use the `<object>` tag so you'll have some familiarity with it as it continues to catch on.

Following is code to display the fractal video from the previous example using the `<object>` tag instead of the `<embed />` tag:

```
<object data="3dtetra2.avi" type="video/x-msvideo"\
 width="160" height="120" align="left" />
```

As you can see, there isn't really anything tricky in this code other than maybe the `type` attribute, which identifies the type of media being displayed. This media type must be specified as one of the standard Internet MIME types, which you might have heard of. Following are the MIME types for several popular sound and video formats you might want to use in your Web pages:

- WAV Audio—`audio/x-wav`
- AU Audio—`audio/basic`
- MP3 Audio—`audio/mpeg`
- MIDI Audio—`audio/midi`
- AVI—`video/x-msvideo`
- MPEG Video—`video/mpeg`
- QuickTime—`video/quicktime`

NEW TERM   A *MIME type* is an identifier for uniquely identifying different types of media objects on the Internet. MIME stands for Multi-purpose Internet Mail Extensions, and this name comes from the fact that MIME types were originally used to identify email attachments.

These MIME types should be used in the `type` attribute of the `<object>` tag to identify what kind of multimedia object is being referenced in the `data` attribute. That's all it takes to use the new `<object>` tag!

In this hour, you have struggled with a turgid tangle of incompatible HTML extensions and media formats. And if you, the Web page author, find it a bit confusing (as I assure you that I sometimes do), just think how confusing it might be to your audience when your Web page video encounters an uncooperative browser.

My bottom-line advice is this: For now, avoid embedded multimedia if you possibly can. Most people would rather have a good old-fashioned clickable link to the multimedia file. `<a href="hotvideo.avi">hot video (avi for- mat, 240k)</a>` allows people to play the video if and when they want to, or download it and play it from their hard drive. If you have software that can convert between AVI and QuickTime, offer links to the same video in both formats to accommodate both Windows and Macintosh users. (Offer both WAV and AU formats if it's a sound clip.)

To experience both the new and old-fashioned approaches to Web page multimedia yourself, kick back, grab an appropriate beverage, and tune your browser to `http://www.24hourHTMLcafe.com/hour20/`.

20

Earlier in the lesson I mentioned that it's possible to achieve the best of both worlds in terms of embedded multimedia by using both the <object> tag and the <embed> tag. This approach involves wrapping an <object> tag around an <embed> tag, and allows browsers that support either tag to successfully recognize and display multimedia objects. Following is code snippet that demonstrates how this is accomplished:

```
<object classid="clsid:D27CDB6E-AE6D-11cf-96B8-444553540000"
  codebase="http://download.macromedia.com/pub/shockwave/cabs/flash/swflash.cab
  #version=5,0,0,0"
  width="400" height="250" id="myFlash">
  <param name="movie" value="MyFlashMovie.swf">
  <param name="quality" value="high">
  <param name="swliveconnect" value="true">
  <embed src="MyFlashMovie.swf" quality="high" width="400" height="250"
    type="application/x-shockwave-flash"
    pluginspage="http://www.macromedia.com/downloads/"
    name="myFlash" swliveconnect="true">
  </embed>
</object>
```

I realize this code probably is a little more complex than you expected, and this is because of the fact that it specifies an ActiveX plug-in for the <object> tag. The big serial number style code you see in the first line is a unique *class ID* for the Macromedia Shockwave ActiveX control. Every ActiveX control has a unique class ID that is used to identify it from other controls. Several <param> tags are used within the <object> tag to further describe the Shockwave (Flash) multimedia object, including the filename and quality. Each <param> tag includes name and value attributes, which are used to set properties of the multimedia object. If you left out the <embed> tag, the <object> tag that you see here would work perfectly well for displaying the Flash movie MyFlashMovie.swf in browsers that fully support the <object> tag and the Shockwave ActiveX plug-in.

To make the code backward compatible with older browsers, you simply place an <embed> tag inside of the <object> tag. In this case, the <embed> tag specifies the type of the multimedia object as a MIME type using the type attribute. The filename of the object is then specified using the src attribute. Similarly, other parameters of the multimedia object are detailed in the attributes of the <embed> tag.

I realize I haven't gone into an enormous degree of detail when it comes to explaining the inner workings of the <object> tag as it applies to ActiveX controls, but the truth is the code varies a great deal depending on the specific control. So, I encourage you to investigate the specific control you want to use, and assess what parameters it requires.

Summary

In this hour, you've seen how to embed video and sound into a Web page. But remember that the <embed /> tag (and its successor, the <object> tag) can be used to include a vast array of media types besides just AVI and MIDI files. Some of these media types are alternative audio and video formats that aim to achieve greater compression, quality, or compatibility than the Windows standard formats. Others, such as Shockwave and QuickTime VR, add a variety of interactive features that old-fashioned audiovisual media types lack. Table 20.1 summarizes the tags discussed in this hour.

TABLE 20.1 HTML Tags and Attributes Covered in Hour 20

Tag	Attribute	Function
<embed />		Embeds a file to be read or displayed by a Netscape plug-in application.
	src="..."	The URL of the file to embed.
	width="..."	The width of the embedded object in pixels.
	height="..."	The height of the embedded object in pixels.
	align="..."	Determines the alignment of the media window. Values are the same as for the <img> tag.
	vspace="..."	The space between the media and the text above or below it.
	hspace="..."	The space between the media and the text to its left or right.
	border="..."	Draws a border of the specified size in pixels around the media.
<object>...</object>		Inserts images, videos, Java applets, ActiveX controls, or other objects into a document. (See Hour 18 for attributes of the <object> tag.)
<param>...</param>		Runtime settings for an object, such as the width and height of the window it occupies on a page.
	name="..."	A named parameter property.
	value="..."	The value associated with a named parameter property.

20

Q&A

Q I hear a lot about streaming video and audio. What does that mean?

A In the past, video and audio files took minutes and sometimes hours to retrieve through most modems, which severely limited the inclusion of video and audio on Web pages. The goal that everyone is moving toward is streaming video or audio, which will play while the data is being received. This is to say that you will not have to completely download the clip before you can start to watch it.

Streaming playback is now widely supported through Microsoft Internet Explorer's built-in features and Netscape Navigator plug-ins, as well as the popular RealPlayer (http://www.real.com/). The examples in this hour use Windows AVI and WAV audio files to demonstrate both streaming and the old-fashioned download-and-play methods of delivering audiovisual media.

Q How do I choose among audiovisual file formats such as QuickTime, Windows AVI/WAV, RealVideo/RealAudio, and MPEG? Is there any significant difference among them?

A QuickTime is the most popular video format among Macintosh users, though QuickTime players are available for Windows as well. Similarly, AVI and WAV are the video and audio formats of choice for Windows users, but you can get AVI and WAV players for the Macintosh. However, all these are likely to be eclipsed by MPEG as the online audio and video standard of choice within the next few years. MPEG-3, or MP3 for short, is already extremely popular as the high-fidelity audio standard of choice.

How do you choose? If most of your audience uses Windows, pick AVI or WAV. If your audience includes a significant number of Macintosh users, pick QuickTime or at least offer it as an alternative. If cross-platform compatibility is essential, consider the RealVideo or RealAudio format—although only those who download special software from http://www.real.com/ will be able to see that format. And if you're working with recorded audio or music, you should probably consider MP3 or Microsoft's new WMA format.

Workshop

The workshop contains quiz questions and activities to help you solidify your understanding of the material covered. Try to answer all questions before looking at the "Answers" section that follows.

Quiz

1. What's the simplest way to let the widest possible audience see a video on your Web site?

2. Write the HTML to embed a video file named `myvideo.avi` into a Web page so that both Netscape Navigator and Microsoft Internet Explorer users will be able to see it.

3. What tag is replacing `<embed />` and will work with recent versions of major Web browsers?

Answers

1. Just link to it:

```
<a href="myvideo.avi">my video</a>
```

2. Use the following HTML:

```
<embed src="myvideo.avi" />
```

3. `<object>`

Exercises

- If you include multimedia elements that require special players, you might need a special page to help people understand and set up what they need to make the most of your site. A link to that page should be prominently located near the top of your home page, steering newcomers aside just long enough to give them a clue.

- The techniques and tags covered in this hour for embedding media also work with Macromedia Flash files. To find out how you can use Flash to put interactive animations in your Web pages, check out the Flash home page at `http://www. macromedia.com/software/flash/`.

20

PART VI
Building a Web Site

Hour

HOUR 21

Organizing and Managing a Web Site

The first 20 hours of this book led you through the design and creation of your own Web pages and the graphics to put on those pages. Now it's time to stop thinking about individual Web pages and start thinking about your Web site as a whole.

This hour shows you how to organize and present multiple Web pages, so that people will be able to navigate among them without confusion. You also read about ways to make your Web site memorable enough to visit again and again.

Because Web sites can be (and usually should be) updated frequently, creating pages that can be easily maintained is essential. This hour shows you how to add comments and other documentation to your pages so that you—or anyone else on your staff—can understand and modify your pages.

To Do

By this point in the book, you should have enough HTML knowledge to produce most of your Web site. You have probably made a number of pages already, and perhaps even published them online.

As you read this hour, think about how your pages are organized now and how you can improve that organization. Don't be surprised if you decide to do a redesign that involves changing almost all of your pages—the results are likely to be well worth the effort!

> If you have been using a simple text editor such as Windows Notepad or Macintosh SimpleText to create your HTML pages, this is an excellent time to consider trying out an interactive Web site management software package such as Microsoft FrontPage or Macromedia Dreamweaver. Aside from helping you write HTML quickly, these programs offer time-saving ways to modify and keep track of many pages at once.
>
> On the other side of the coin, these programs cost a fair amount of money and are not at all necessary for managing a small- to medium-sized Web site. Unless you plan to have at least 50 Web pages on your site, or unless you were planning to buy a version of Microsoft Office that includes FrontPage anyway, you may save the most time and money by using the simple text editor and file transfer software you already know how to use.

When One Page Is Enough

Building and organizing an attractive and effective Web site doesn't always need to be a complex task. In some cases, you can effectively present a great deal of useful information on a single page, without a lot of flashy graphics. In fact, there are several advantages to a single-page site:

- All the information on the site downloads as quickly as possible.
- The whole site can be printed out on paper with a single print command, even if it is several paper pages long.
- Visitors can easily save the site on their hard drive for future reference, especially if it uses a minimum of graphics.
- Links between different parts of the same page usually respond more quickly than links to other pages.

Figure 21.1 shows the first part of a Web page that serves its intended audience better as a single lengthy page than it would as a multi-page site. It contains about eight paper pages worth of text explaining how to participate in a popular email discussion list.

FIGURE 21.1

A good table of contents can make a lengthy page easy to navigate.

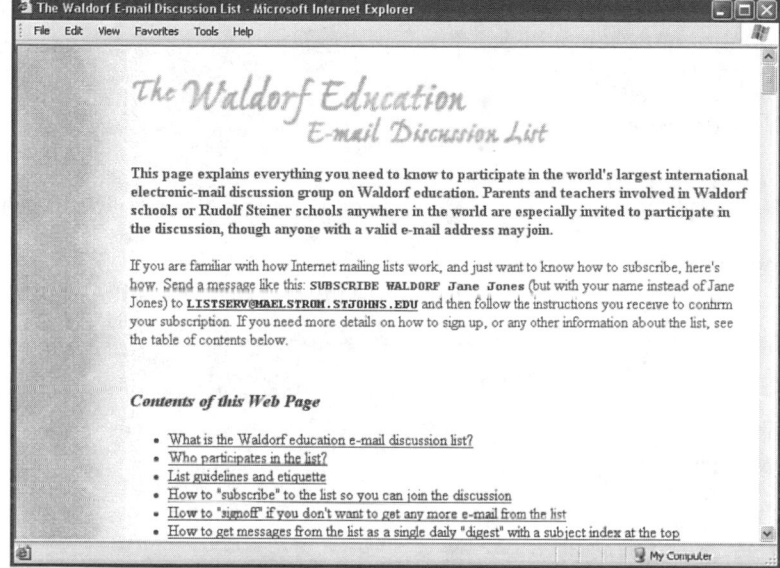

The page begins, as most introductory pages should, with a succinct explanation of what the page is about and who would want to read it. A detailed table of contents allows readers to skip directly to the reference material in which they are most interested. (Refer to Hour 7, "Creating Text Links," for a refresher on how to build a table of contents.)

As Figure 21.2 shows, each short section of the page is followed by a link back up to the table of contents, so navigating around the page feels much the same as navigating around a multi-page site. Since the contents of the page are intended as a handy reference, its readers will definitely prefer the convenience of being able to bookmark or save a single page instead of 8 or 10 separate pages.

Having seen all the fancy graphics and layout tricks in the book, you may be tempted to forget that a good old-fashioned outline is often the clearest and most efficient way to organize a Web site. Even if your site does require multiple pages, a list like the table of contents in Figure 21.1 may be the best way to guide people through a relatively small Web site—or subsections of a larger one.

21

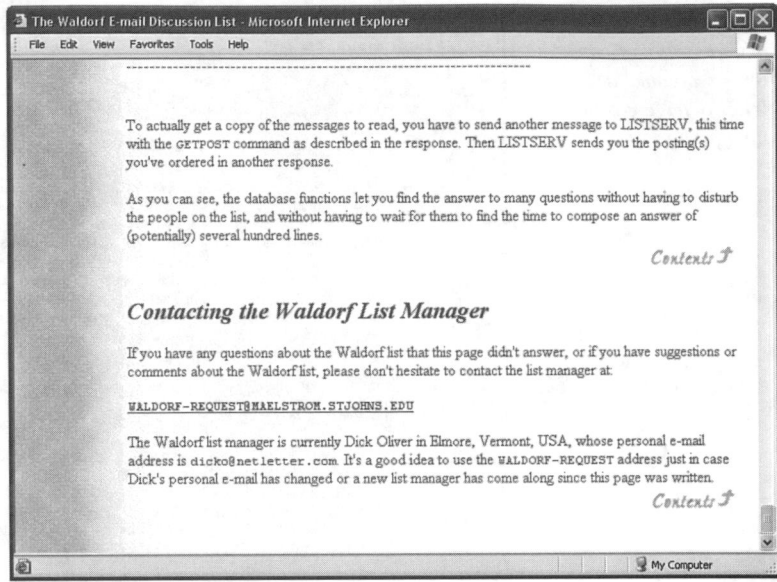

FIGURE 21.2
*Always provide a link
to the table of contents
after each section of a
long Web page.*

Organizing a Simple Site

Though single-page sites have their place, most companies and individuals serve their readers better by dividing their site into short, quick-read pages with graphical navigation icons to move between the pages. That way, the entire site doesn't have to be downloaded by someone seeking specific information.

The goal of the home page in Figure 21.3, like the goal of many Web sites today, is simply to make the organization "visible" on the Internet. Many people today immediately turn to the World Wide Web when they want to find out about an organization, or find out whether a particular type of organization exists at all. A simple home page should state enough information so that someone can tell whether she wants to find out more. It should then provide both traditional address and telephone contact information and an electronic mail address, either directly on the home page or via a prominent link (like the About Us button in Figure 21.3).

One of the most common mistakes beginning Web site producers make is having each page on the site look different than the one before. Another equally serious mistake is using the same, publicly available clip art that thousands of other Web authors are also using. Remember that on the Internet, one click can take you around the world. The only way to make your pages memorable and recognizable as a cohesive site is to make all your pages adhere to a unique, unmistakable visual theme.

FIGURE 21.3

This small-business home page uses distinctive graphics and no-nonsense text to quickly convey the intended mood and purpose.

Regardless of how large your site is, it's a good idea to organize your resources. For example, I always place the images for my Web pages in a separate folder named `images`. Similarly, if you have files that are available for download, you could place them in a folder called `downloads`. In the image example, you would refer to images in the `images` folder like this:

```
<img src="images\myimage.gif" alt="" />
```

For example, when someone clicks the Products link in Figure 21.3, he is taken to the page in Figure 21.4. The visual reiteration of the link as a title and the repetition of the background, logo, and link graphics all make it immediately obvious that this page is part of the same site as the previous page. (Reusing as many graphics from the home page as possible also speeds display since these images are already cached on the reader's computer.) Another helpful little detail on this page is the highlighting of the navigation graphic near the top of the page—the spaceship graphic is colored in to indicate that this is the Products page. (If you would like to view this site online, go to `http://www.stalefishlabs.com/`.)

21

Clicking Products in Figure 21.3 takes you here. The graphical theme makes it instantly clear that this is part of the same site.

The page in Figure 21.4 avoids another common disease that beginning Web authors too often catch; I call it the "construction site" syndrome. If you've looked around the Internet very much, I'm sure you're as sick as I am of cute little road worker icons and dead-end pages that say nothing but Under Construction. Please remember that when you put your pages on the Internet, you are publishing them just as surely as if a print shop were running off 10,000 copies. No publisher would ever annoy readers by printing a brochure, book, or newspaper with useless pages saying only Under Construction. Don't annoy your readers, either: If a page isn't ready to go online, *don't put it online* until it is ready, and don't put any links to it on your other pages yet.

Organizing a Larger Site

For complex sites, sophisticated layout and graphics can help organize and improve the looks of your site when used consistently throughout all of your pages. To see how you can make aesthetics and organization work hand-in-hand, look at a site that needs to present a large volume of information to several different audiences.

Figure 21.5 shows the top part of the Center for Journal Therapy home page. This site currently provides access to the equivalent of about 75 paper pages of text, in the form of

25 electronic documents. As the Center for Journal Therapy continues to publish newsletters, directories, and instructional materials, the site is likely to expand to hundreds of paper pages' worth of information. (If you would like to view this site online, go to http://www.journaltherapy.com/.)

FIGURE 21.5

The links on the left side of this page lead to a surprising wealth of information.

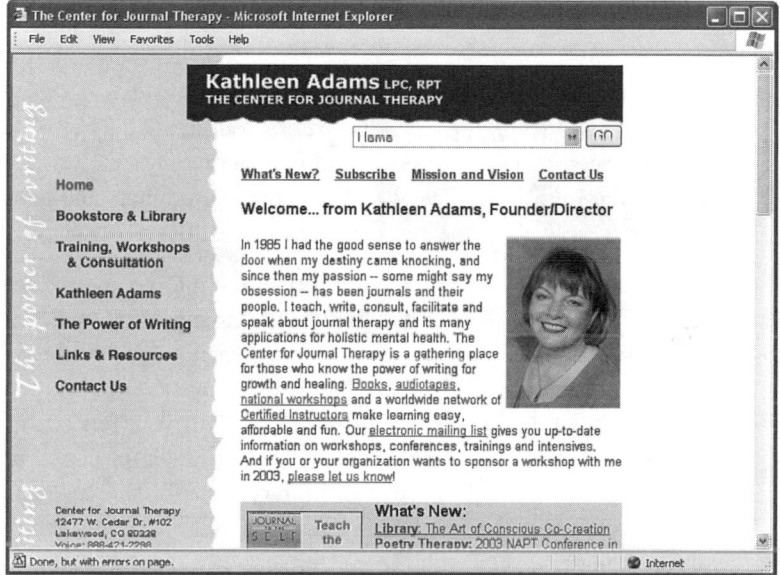

The first page a visitor sees should always begin by explaining what the site is about and provide enough introductory information to "hook" the intended audience while getting rid of anyone who really has no interest. The Center for Journal Therapy site does this with a photo and note from Kay Adams, whose face and name are well known by much of the target audience. After the welcome note, the home page offers brief sections with the headings, "What is Journal Therapy?," "About the Center for Journal Therapy," and "About Kathleen Adams," followed by the address, telephone numbers, and email address of the organization. This is a worthy model for any organization's home page to imitate, though in cases where a prominent personality is not a main feature of the site it's usually best to skip the "Welcome" and go straight into the "What is..." introduction.

If there's one thing I would change about the page in Figure 21.5, it would be the lack of emphasis on benefits to the reader. It is absolutely essential—especially for commercial sites or any site intending to serve the needs of some audience—to make the very first words on the page explain *why* it

21

> would benefit a reader to look further. Research shows that you have 3 to 5
> seconds to convince visitors that your site is worth their attention before
> they head elsewhere, possibly never to return. Use those seconds wisely!
> (Hint: Is the phrase "Welcome to the Home Page of..." worth wasting two of
> those precious seconds on?)

The Center for Journal Therapy site is intended to serve at least three distinct groups:
therapists and laypersons just discovering journal therapy, professionals who already use
journal therapy in their practice, and journal therapy instructors. Many other Web sites
are similar in that they need to address both newcomers and people who are already
knowledgeable about the site's subject.

The site in Figures 21.5 and 21.6 is organized into six main categories (not counting
Home), accessible through the link icons that appear on the left side of each page. It's
important to notice that these icons were chosen to give each of the three different audiences a choice that would clearly meet their needs. Always organize the main links on
your site according to the questions or desires of your readers, not the structure of the
information itself. For example, some of the same information is available in the Links &
Resources and in the Bookstore & Library on this site. This redundancy serves both audiences well because it gives them a place to find everything they need without wading
through material they aren't interested in.

FIGURE 21.6

*You get this page when
you click Bookstore &
Library in Figure 21.5.*

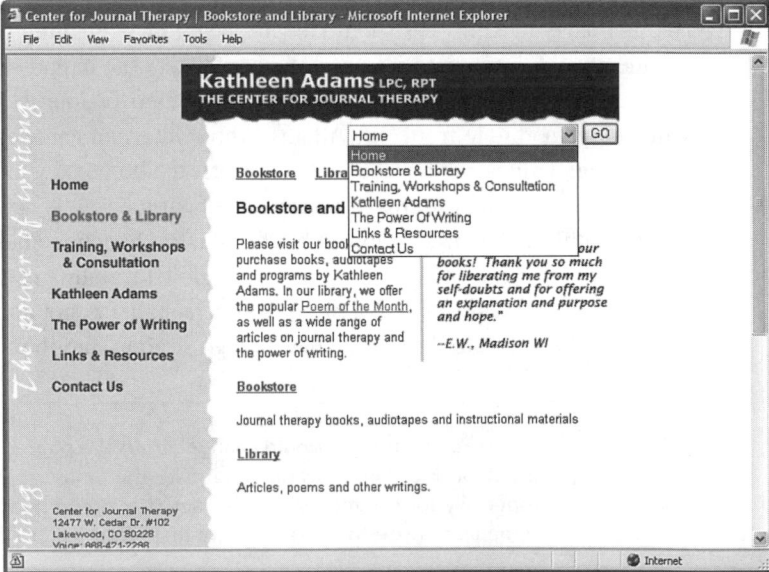

Figure 21.6 is the page you would get if you clicked Bookstore & Library in Figure 21.5. The graphics at the top provide a strong visual relationship to the original page, and the drop-down navigation menu provides quick access to the rest of the site, including the home page. All the contact information is also repeated at the bottom of the page; it's almost never a bad idea to put your name, address, and phone number on all the major pages of your site if you want to encourage readers to contact you.

Providing topic-specific link pages like this one is a much less confusing way of organizing large quantities of information than some of the alternatives that beginning Web publishers often choose instead. It's all too common to see home pages with a dozen or more links arranged in a long list or string of buttons. That many links all in one group will inevitably confuse readers and make your site hard to use.

In all aspects of your site design, keep in mind the following fact: Studies have repeatedly shown that people become confused and annoyed when presented with more than seven choices at a time, and people feel most comfortable with five or fewer choices. Therefore, you should avoid presenting more than five links (either in a list or as graphical icons) next to one another and never present more than seven at once. When you need to present more than seven text links, break them into multiple lists with a separate heading for each five to seven items.

It will also help your readers navigate your site without confusion if you avoid putting any page more than two (or at most three) links away from the home page and always send readers back to a main category page (or the home page) after reading a subsidiary page.

Clicking "The Center for Journal Therapy" at the very top of Figure 21.6 will take the reader back to the home page. The link uses an absolute address (http://www.journaltherapy.com/) instead of a relative address (welcome.htm), so that anyone who saves the page on his hard drive can still go to the online site by clicking this link. See Hour 3, "Linking to Other Web Pages," for a review of absolute and relative addresses.

Including Comments in a Page

Whenever you type an HTML page, keep in mind that you or someone else will almost certainly need to make changes to it someday. Simple text pages are easy to read and revise, but complex Web pages with graphics, tables, and other layout tricks can be quite difficult to decipher.

21

As you saw in Hour 18, "Setting Pages in Motion with Dynamic HTML," you can enclose comments to yourself or your co-authors between `<!--` and `-->` tags. These comments will not appear on the Web page when viewed with a browser, but can be read by anyone who examines the HTML code with a text editor, a word processor, or the Web browser's View, Source command.

To include comments in a JavaScript script, put `//` at the beginning of each comment line. (No closing tag is needed for JavaScript comments.) In style sheets, start comments with `/*` and end them with `*/`.

The HTML `<!--` and `-->` tags will not work properly in scripts or style sheets!

You can and should, however, include one `<!--` tag just after a `<script>` or `<style>` tag, with a `-->` tag just before the matching `</script>` or `</style>`. This hides the script or style commands from older browsers that would otherwise treat them as regular text and display them on the page.

One handy usage of comments is to hide parts of a Web page that are currently under construction. Rather than make the text and graphics visible and explain that they're under construction, you can hide them from view entirely with some carefully placed comments.

To Do

It will be well worth your time now to go through all the Web pages, scripts, and style sheets you've created so far and add any comments that you or others might find helpful when revising them in the future.

1. Put a comment explaining any fancy formatting or layout techniques before the tags that make it happen.

2. Use a comment just before an `<img />` tag to briefly describe any important graphic whose function isn't obvious from the `alt` message.

3. Always use a comment (or several comments) to summarize how the cells of a `<table>` are supposed to fit together visually.

4. If you use hexadecimal color codes (such as `<font color="#8040b0">` or `<div style="color: #8040b0">`), insert a comment indicating what the color actually is (bluish-purple).

5. Indenting your comments helps them stand out and makes both the comments and the HTML easier to read. Don't forget to use indentation in the HTML itself to make it more readable, too.

Summary

This hour has given you examples and explanations to help you organize your Web pages into a coherent site that is informative, attractive, and easy to navigate.

This hour also discussed the importance of making your HTML easy to maintain by adding comments and indentation to your HTML code.

Q&A

Q I've seen pages that ask viewers to change the width of their browser window or adjust other settings before proceeding beyond the home page. Why?

A The idea is that the Web page author can offer a better presentation if she has some control over the size of reader's windows or fonts. Of course, few people ever bother to change their settings, so these sites often look weird or unreadable. You'll be much better off using the tips you learn in this book to make your site readable and attractive at any window size and a wide variety of browser settings. The better organized your site is, the more usable it will be for visitors.

Q Won't lots of comments and spaces make my pages load slower when someone views them?

A All modems compress text when transmitting it, so adding spaces to format your HTML doesn't usually change the transfer time at all. You'd have to type hundreds of comment words to cause even one extra second of delay when loading a page. It's the graphics that slow pages down, so squeeze your images as tightly as you can (refer to Hour 12, "Page Design and Layout"), but use text comments freely.

Q Will you look at my site and give me some suggestions on how to improve it?

A I'd like to, really. Truly I would. If I looked at all my readers' sites and offered even a tiny bit of wisdom for each, however, I would be at it for hours every day. I have looked at hundreds of reader sites, and my advice usually amounts to this: Your site looks pretty or ugly and you have the basic idea of HTML, but you need to make it clearer, first, who your site is intended for—in the first sentence or heading; second, what earthly good your site is going to do them; and third, what you want them to do as a result of visiting your site. All the great graphics and HTML-manship in the world can't substitute for clearly and consistently answering those three questions for yourself and for your site's visitors.

21

Workshop

The workshop contains quiz questions and activities to help you solidify your understanding of the material covered. Try to answer all questions before looking at the "Answers" section that follows.

Quiz

1. What are three ways to help people stay aware that all your pages form a single site?

2. What two types of information should always be included in the home page that people encounter at your site?

3. If you want to say, "Don't change this image of me. It's my only chance at immortality," to future editors of a Web page, but you don't want people who view the page to see that message, how would you do it?

Answers

1. (a) Use consistent background, colors, fonts, and styles.

   (b) Repeat the same link words or graphics on the top of the page the link leads to.

   (c) Repeat the same small header, buttons, or other element on every page of the site.

2. (a) Enough identifying information so that she can immediately see the name of the site and what it is about.

   (b) Whatever the most important message you want to convey to your intended audience is, stated directly and concisely.

3. Put the following immediately before the `<img />` tag:

   ```
   <!-- Don't change this image of me.
        It's my only chance at immortality. -->
   ```

Exercises

Grab a pencil (the oldfangled kind) and sketch out your Web site as a bunch of little rectangles with arrows between them. Sketch a rough overview of what each page will look like by putting squiggles where the text goes and doodles where the images go. Each arrow should start at a doodle icon that corresponds to the navigation button for the page the arrow leads to. Even if you have the latest whiz-bang Web site management tools, sketching your site by hand can give you a much more intuitive grasp of which pages on your site will be easy to get to and how the layout of adjacent pages will work together—all before you invest time in writing the actual HTML to connect the pages together.

21

Hour **22**

Helping People Find Your Web Pages

The HTML tags and techniques you discover in this hour won't make any visible difference in your Web pages, which may come as a surprise. However, they are extremely important in that they will help make your Web pages much more visible to your intended audience. For most Web authors, this may be the easiest—but most important—hour in the book. You learn how to make links to your pages appear at all the major Internet search sites whenever someone searches for words related to your topic or company. There are no magic secrets that guarantee you'll be at the top of every search list, but there are many reliable and effective techniques you can employ to make sure your site is as easy to find as possible.

This hour also shows you how to make one page automatically load another, how to forward visitors to pages that have moved, and how to document a page's full Internet address.

Publicizing Your Web Site

Presumably, you want your Web pages to attract someone's attention or you wouldn't bother to create them. If you are placing your pages only on a local network or corporate intranet or are distributing your pages exclusively on disk or by email, helping people find your pages may not be much of a problem. If you are adding your pages to the millions upon millions of others on the Internet, however, bringing your intended audience to your site is a very big challenge indeed.

To tackle this problem, you need a basic understanding of how most people decide which pages they will look at. There are basically three ways that people can become aware of your Web site:

- Somebody tells them about it and gives them the address; they enter that address directly into their Web browser.
- They follow a link to your site from someone else's site.
- They find your site listed in a search site such as Google, Yahoo!, or HotBot.

You can make all three of them happen more often if you invest some time and effort. To increase the number of people who hear about you through word-of-mouth, well, use your mouth—and every other channel of communication available to you. If you have an existing contact database or mailing list, announce your Web site to those people. Add the site address to your business cards or company literature. Heck, go buy TV ads broadcasting your Internet address if you have the money. In short, do the marketing thing. Good old-fashioned word-of-mouth marketing is still the best thing going, even on the Internet.

Getting links to your site from other sites is also pretty straightforward—though that doesn't mean it isn't a lot of work. Find every other Web site related to your topic and offer to add a link to those sites if they add one to yours. If there are specialized directories on your topic, either online or in print, be sure you are listed. There's not much I can say in this book to help you with that, except to go out and do it.

What I can help you with is the third item: being visible at the major Internet search sites. I'm sure you've used at least one or two of the big search sites: Google, Yahoo!, MSN Search, AllTheWeb, Alta Vista, Excite, and Lycos. (The addresses of these sites are as follows: `google.com`, `yahoo.com`, `search.msn.com`, `alltheweb.com`, `altavista.com`, and so on.)

The popularity and usefulness of search engines are not etched in stone. In other words, you'll find that search engines come in and out of vogue according to the whims of the Web community, as well as the technical details of how they perform searches. For this reason, you might want to visit http://www.searchengine.watch/ for a recent assessment of the most popular search engines.

22

These sites are basically huge databases that attempt to catalog as many pages on the Internet as possible. They all use automated processing to build the databases, though some (such as Yahoo!) emphasize quality by having each listing checked by a human. Others (such as HotBot) prefer to go for quantity and rely almost entirely on programs called robots or spiders to crawl around the Internet hunting for new pages to index. Still others (such as Google) use highly sophisticated techniques of ranking pages based upon how they are linked to from other pages.

NEW TERM A *robot* (also called a *spider*) is an automated computer program that spends all day looking at Web pages all over the Internet and building a database of the contents of all the pages it visits.

As the spiders and humans constantly add to the database, another program, called a *search engine*, processes requests from people who are looking for Web pages on specific topics. The search engine looks in the database for pages that contain the key words or phrases that someone is looking for and sends that person a list of all the pages that contain those terms.

NEW TERM A *search engine* is an automated computer program that looks in a database index for pages containing specific words or phrases. Some people use the term *Internet directory* to indicate a search engine whose database was built mostly by people instead of robots. (Lately, it's become vogue in some circles to call search engines *portals.*)

Listing Your Pages with the Major Search Sites

If you want people to find your pages, you absolutely must submit a request to each of the six major search sites to index your pages. Each of these sites has a form for you to fill out with the address, a brief description of the site, and in some cases a category or list of keywords with which your listing should be associated. These forms are easy to fill out; you can easily do all six of them in an hour with time left over to list yourself at one or two specialized directories you might have found as well. (How did you find the specialized directories? Through the major search sites, of course!)

Even though listing with the major search engines is easy and quick, it can be a bit confusing: Each of them uses different terminology to identify where you should click to register your pages. Table 22.1 may save you some frustration; it includes the address of each major search engine, along with the exact wording of the link you should click to register.

TABLE 22.1   Registering Your Site with a Search Engine

Search Engine Address	How to Register Your Page
google.com	Click Jobs, Press, and Help in the lower-right corner of the Google home page, and then click Submitting Your Site on the right side of the page.
yahoo.com	Go to the category you want to be listed under and click Suggest a Site at the bottom of the page.
search.msn.com	Click Submit a Web site... near the lower-right corner of the page.
alltheweb.com	Click Submit Site at the bottom of the page.
altavista.com	Click Submit a Site at the bottom of the Alta Vista home page.
excite.com	Click Submit Your Site near the top of the Excite home page, just above and to the right of the main search box.
lycos.com	Click Site Submit near the top of the Lycos home page, just below the main search box.

NEW TERM   *URL* stands for Uniform Resource Locator, which is just a fancy name for the address of a Web page.

There are sites that provide one form that automatically submits itself to all the major search engines, plus several minor ones. (`http://www.submit-it.com` and `http://www.hypersubmit.com/` are popular examples.) Many of these sites attempt to sell you a premium service that lists you in many other directories and indexes as well. Depending upon your target audience, these services may or may not be of value, but I strongly recommend that you go directly to each of the six most popular search sites and use their own forms to submit your requests to be listed. That way you can be sure to answer the questions (which are slightly different at every site) accurately, and you will know exactly how your site listing will appear at each of them.

Wait! Before you rush off this minute to submit your listing requests, read the rest of this hour. Otherwise, you'll have a very serious problem, and you will have already lost your best opportunity to solve it.

To see what I mean, imagine this scenario: You publish a page selling automatic cockroach flatteners. I have a roach problem, and I'm allergic to bug spray. I open my laptop, brush the roaches off the keyboard, log on to my favorite search site, and enter *cockroach* as a search term. The search engine promptly presents me with a list of the first 10 out of 10,254 Internet pages containing the word *cockroach*. You have submitted your listing request, so you know your page is somewhere on that list.

Did I mention that I'm rich? And did I mention that two roaches are mating on my foot? You even offer same-day delivery in my area. Do you want your page to be number 3 on the list, or number 8,542? Okay, now you understand the problem.

Providing Hints for Search Engines

Fact: There is absolutely nothing you can do to guarantee that your site will appear in the top 10 search results for a particular word or phrase in any major search engine (short of buying ad space from the search site, that is). After all, if there were, why couldn't everyone else who wants to be number 1 on the list do it, too? What you can do is avoid being last on the list and give yourself as good a chance as anyone else of being first.

Each search engine uses a slightly different method for determining which pages are likely to be most relevant and should therefore be sorted to the top of a search result list. You don't need to get too hung up about the differences, though, because they all use some combination of the same basic criteria. The following list includes almost everything any search engine considers when trying to evaluate which pages best match one or more keywords. The first three of these criteria are used by almost every major search engine, and most of them also use at least one or two of the other criteria.

- Do the keywords appear in the <title> tag of the page?
- Do the keywords appear in the first few lines of the page?
- How many times do the keywords appear in the entire page?
- Do the keywords appear in a <meta /> tag in the page?
- How many other pages in my database link to the page?
- How many times have people chosen this page from a previous search list result?
- Is the page rated highly in a human-generated directory?

> Yahoo! is unique among search engines in that real people analyze and categorize Web sites that are added to its directory.

Clearly, the most important thing you can do to improve your position is to consider what word combinations your intended audience is most likely to enter. I'd recommend that you not concern yourself with common single-word searches; the lists they generate are usually so long that trying to make it to the top is like playing the lottery. Focus instead on uncommon words and two- or three-word combinations that are most likely to indicate relevance to your topic. Make sure those terms and phrases occur several times on your page, and be certain to put the most important ones in the <title> tag and the first heading or introductory paragraph.

> Some over-eager Web page authors put dozens or even hundreds of repetitions of the same word on their pages, sometimes in small print or a hard-to-see color, just to get the search engines to sort that page to the top of the list whenever someone searches for that word. This practice is called *search engine spamming*.
>
> Don't be tempted to try this sort of thing—all the major search engines immediately delete any page from their database that sets off a "spam detector" by repeating the same word or group of words in a suspicious pattern. It's still fine (and quite beneficial) to have several occurrences of important search words on a page. Make sure, however, that you use the words in normal sentences or phrases, and the spam police will leave you alone.

Of all the search engine evaluation criteria just listed, the use of <meta /> tags is probably the most poorly understood. Some people rave about <meta /> tags as if using them could instantly move you to the top of every search list. Other people dismiss <meta /> tags as ineffective and useless. Neither of these extremes is true.

A <meta /> tag is a general-purpose tag you can put in the <head> portion of any document to specify some information about the page that doesn't belong in the <body> text. Most major search engines allow you to use <meta /> tags to give them a short description of your page and some keywords to identify what your page is about. For example, your automatic cockroach flattener order form might include the following two tags:

```
<meta name="description"
 content="Order form for the SuperSquish cockroach flattener." />
<meta name="keywords"
 content="cockroach, roaches, kill, squish, supersquish" />
```

> Always place <meta /> tags *after* the <head>, <title>, and </title> tags but *before* the closing </head> tag.
>
> According to the new XHTML standards, <title> must be the very first tag in the <head> section of every document.

The first of these tags ensures that the search engine has an accurate description of your page to present on its search results list. The second slightly increases your page's ranking on the list whenever any of your specified keywords are included in a search query.

You should always include <meta /> tags with name="description" and name="keywords" attributes in any page that you request a search engine to index. Doing so may not have a dramatic effect on your position in search lists, and not all search engines look for <meta /> tags, but it can only help.

> In the unlikely event that you don't want a page to be included in search engine databases at all, you can put the following <meta /> tag in the <head> portion of that page.
>
> <meta name="robots" content="noindex">
>
> This causes some search robots to ignore the page. For more robust protection from prying robot eyes, ask the person who manages your Web server computer to include your page address in his or her robots.txt file. (She will know what that means and how to do it.) All major search spiders will then be sure to ignore your pages.

To give you a concrete example of how to improve search engine results, consider the page in Listing 22.1 and Figure 22.1. This page should be fairly easy to find since it deals with a specific topic and includes several occurrences of some uncommon technical terms for which people interested in this subject would be likely to search. However, there are several things you could do to improve the chances of this page appearing high on a search engine results list.

LISTING 22.1   A Page That Will Present Some Problems During an Internet Site
Search

```html
<html><head><title>Fractal Central</title></head>
<body background="bacfrac.jpg" text="#003399">
<div align="center">
<img src="fraccent.gif" height="149" width="320" /></div>
<table cellspacing="10">
<tr>
  <td valign="top">
  <table border="2" cellpadding="10" width="133">
  <tr><td align="center">Discover the latest software, books
  and more at our online store.<br /><a href="ordform.htm">
  <img src="ordform.gif" border="0" height="55" width="111" />
  </a></td>
</tr>
</table>
</td><td valign="top"><h2>A Comprehensive Guide to the<br />
Art and Science of Chaos and Complexity</h2>
<p>What's that? You say you're hearing about "fractals" and
"chaos" all over the place, but still aren't too sure what they
are? How about a quick summary of some key concepts:</p>
<ol><li><p>Even the simplest systems become deeply complex and
richly beautiful when a process is "iterated" over and over,
using the results of each step as the starting point of the next.
This is how Nature creates a magnificently detailed 300-foot
redwood tree from a seed the size of your fingernail.</p></li>
<li><p>Most "iterated systems" are easily simulated on computers,
but only a few are predictable and controllable. Why? Because a
tiny influence, like a "butterfly flapping it's wings," can be
strangely amplified to have major consequences such as completely
changing tomorrow's weather in a distant part of the world.</p></li>
<li><p>Fractals can be magnified forever without loss of detail,
so mathematics that relies on straight lines is useless with them.
However, they give us a new concept called "fractal dimension" which
can measure the texture and complexity of anything from coastlines
to storm clouds.</p></li>
<li><p>While fractals win prizes at graphics shows, their chaotic
patterns pop up in every branch of science. Physicists find
beautiful artwork coming out of their plotters. "Strange attractors"
with fractal turbulence appear in celestial mechanics. Biologists
diagnose "dynamical diseases" when fractal rhythms fall out of sync.
Even pure mathematicians go on tour with dazzling videos of their
research.</p></li>
</ol>
<p>Think all these folks may be on to something?</p>
<div align="center"><ahref="http://netletter.com/nonsense/">
<img src="findout.gif" height="20" width="150" border="0" />
</a></div>
</td></tr></table>
</body></html>
```

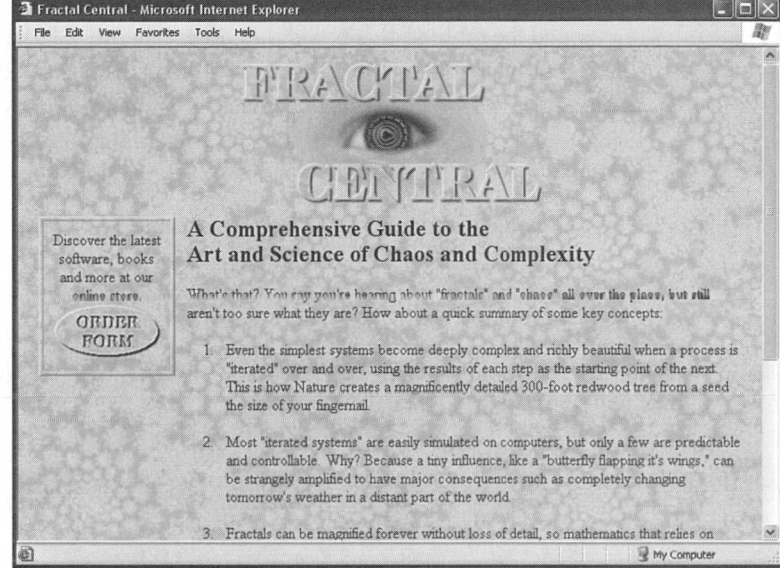

FIGURE 22.1

The first part of the page in Listing 22.1, as it appears in a Web browser.

22

The contents of the page in Listing 22.2 and Figure 22.2 look to a human being almost the same as the page in Listing 22.1 and Figure 22.1. To search robots and search engines, however, these two pages appear quite different. The following list summarizes the changes and explains why I made each modification:

1. I added some important search terms to the `<title>` tag and the first heading on the page. The original page didn't even include the word *fractal* in either of these two key positions.

2. I added `<meta />` tags to assist some search engines with a description and keywords.

3. I added an `alt` attribute to the first `<img />` tag. Not all search engines read and index `alt` text, but some do.

4. I took out the quotation marks around technical terms (such as `"fractal"` and `"iterated"`) because some search engines consider *"fractal"* to be a different word than *fractal*. I could have used the HTML character entity `&quot;` to make the quotation marks, in which case the search robot would have disregarded them, but I chose instead to simply italicize the words. If you really need to use quotation marks around content in a page, make sure to use `&quot;` instead of `"` so that your pages will adhere to XHTML standards.

5. I added the keyword *fractal* twice to the text in the order form box. I also
    rearranged the table so this box didn't appear in the HTML code before the <h1>
    heading or the main body text. Since search sites give special importance to words
    occurring early in the HTML document, it's important not to put table columns (or
    <script> or <style> tags) before the text containing your most important search
    words.

It is impossible to quantify how much more frequently people searching for information
on fractals and chaos were able to find the page in Listing 22.2 versus the page in Listing
22.1, but it's a sure bet that none of the changes could do anything but improve the
page's visibility to search engines. As is often the case, the improvements made for the
benefit of the search spiders probably made the page's subject easier for humans to recognize and understand as well.

LISTING 22.2   An Improvement on the Page in Listing 22.1

```
<html><head><title>Fractal Central:
A Guide to Fractals, Chaos, and Complexity</title>
<meta name="description"
 content="A comprehensive guide to fractal geometry,
          chaos science and complexity theory." />
<meta name="keywords"
 content="fractal, fractals, chaos science, chaos theory,
          fractal geometry, complexity, complexity theory" />
</head>
<body background="bacfrac.jpg" text="#003399">
<div align="center">
<img src="fraccent.gif" height="149" width="320"
 alt="Fractal Central" />
<h2>A Comprehensive Guide to Fractal Geometry, Chaos Science and Complexity
Theory</h2>
</div>
<table cellspacing="10"><tr><td valign="top">
<p>What's that? You say you're hearing about <i>fractals</i> and
<i>chaos</i> all over the place, but still aren't too sure what they
are? How about a quick summary of some key concepts:</p>
<ol><li><p>Even the simplest systems become deeply complex and
richly beautiful when a process is <i>iterated</i> over and over,
using the results of each step as the starting point of the next.
This is how Nature creates a magnificently detailed 300-foot
redwood tree from a seed the size of your fingernail.</p></li>
<li><p>Most <i>iterated systems</i> are easily simulated on computers,
but only a few are predictable and controllable. Why? Because a
tiny influence, like a "butterfly flapping it's wings," can be
strangely amplified to have major consequences such as completely
changing tomorrow's weather in a distant part of the world.</p></li>
<li><p>Fractals can be magnified forever without loss of detail,
```

LISTING 22.2   continued

```
so mathematics that relies on straight lines is useless with them.
However, they give us a new concept called <i>fractal dimension</i>
which can measure the texture and complexity of anything from
coastlines to storm clouds.</p></li>
<li><p>While fractals win prizes at graphics shows, their chaotic
patterns pop up in every branch of science. Physicists find
beautiful artwork coming out of their plotters. <i>Strange
attractors</i> with fractal turbulence appear in celestial
mechanics. Biologists diagnose <i>dynamical diseases</i> when
fractal rhythms fall out of sync. Even pure mathematicians go on
tour with dazzling videos of their research.</p></li>
</ol><p>Think all these folks may be on to something?</p>
<div align="center">
<a href="http://netletter.com/nonsense/">
<img src="findout.gif" height="20" width="150" border="0" />
</a></div></td>
<td valign="top">
  <table border="2" cellpadding="10" width="133">
  <tr><td align="center">Discover the latest fractal software,
  books and more at the <b>Fractal Central</b> online store.
  <br /><a href="ordform.htm">
  <img src="ordform.gif" border="0" height= "55" width="111" />
  </a>
</td></tr></table>
</td></tr></table>
</body></html>
```

FIGURE 22.2

The first part of the page in Listing 22.2, as it appears in a Web browser.

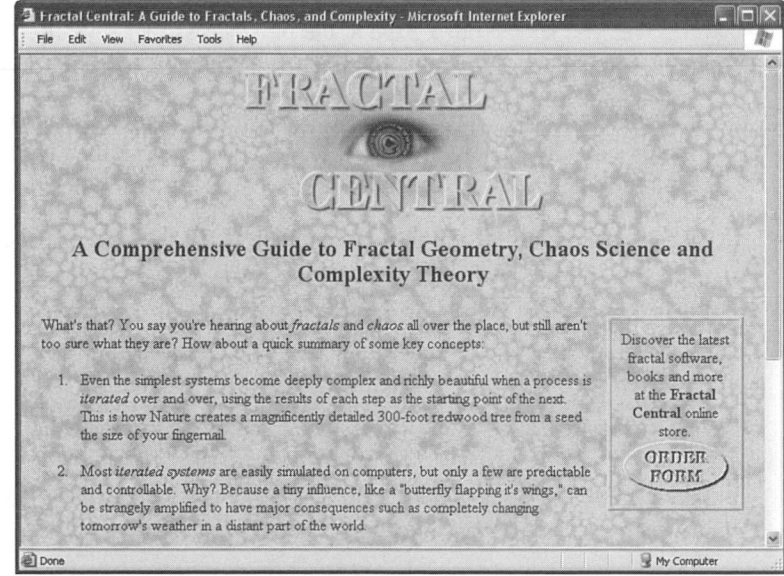

If you read the popular science and computer magazines, you have probably found claims that XML, the "HTML of the future," will make it much easier to find what you're looking for on the Internet. You might be wondering how to get the Web pages you create hooked up to this magical new searching miracle.

The good news is that XML will indeed eventually make online searching easier and more efficient. You'll read more about how XML works and how it achieves this and other goals in the next hour, "Using XML to Describe Data." The bad news is that neither XML nor its young offspring, XHTML, can make it any easier for people to find your pages today or even this year.

While you're waiting for The Next Big Thing to hit, you might want to keep an eye on future developments in Web searching by stopping by the Search Engine Watch site at http://www.searchenginewatch.com/ every month or so.

Loading Another Page Automatically

When you are managing a Web site, it may become necessary to move some pages from one address to another. You might decide, for example, to change the service provider or your whole site's domain name. You might just reorganize things and move some pages into a different directory folder.

What happens, then, when someone visits his or her favorite Web page on your site after you've moved it? If you don't want your visitor to be stranded with a Not Found error message, you should put a page at the old address that says This page has moved to... with the new address (and a link to it).

Chances are you've encountered similar messages on the Internet yourself. Some of them probably employed the neat trick you're about to learn; they automatically transferred you to the new address after a few seconds, even if you didn't click a link.

In fact, you can make any page automatically load any other page after an amount of time you choose. The secret to this trick is the <meta /> tag, which goes in the <head> section of a page and looks like the following:

```
<meta http-equiv="refresh" content="5; url=nextpage.htm" />
```

Replace 5 with the number of seconds to wait before loading the next page and replace nextpage.htm with the address of the next page to load.

For example, the page in Listing 22.3 looks like Figure 22.3 when viewed in a Web browser. After 5 seconds (during which a GIF animation counts down from 5 to 0), the

<meta /> tag causes the page at http://www.24hourHTMLcafe.com/hour22/there.htm (Listing 22.4 and Figure 22.4) to appear.

> For the impatient, I also included a link to the there.htm page, which some-one could click before the 5 seconds is up. Also, some very old Web browsers don't recognize <meta />, so you should always put a normal link on the page leading to the same address as the <meta /> refresh tag.

LISTING 22.3 The <meta /> Tag Causes the Web Browser to Automatically Load the Page Shown in Figure 22.4 After 5 Seconds

```
<html><head><title>New Address Notice</title>
<meta http-equiv="refresh"
content="6; URL=http://www.24hourHTMLcafe.com/hour22/there.htm" />
</head>
<body bgcolor="black" text="silver" link="red" vlink="white">
<div align="center">Nicholas' home page is now located at
<a href="http://www.24hourHTMLcafe.com/hour22/there.htm">
www.24hourHTMLcafe.com/hour22/there.htm</a>.
<h2 style="color: red">You will arrive in</h2>
<p><font color="red"><img src="countdn.gif" /></p>
<h2 style="color: red">seconds.</h2>
</div>
</body></html>
```

FIGURE 22.3

This is the page con-tained in Listing 22.3. I used a GIF anima-tion (countdn.gif) to entertain readers while they're waiting for the next page.

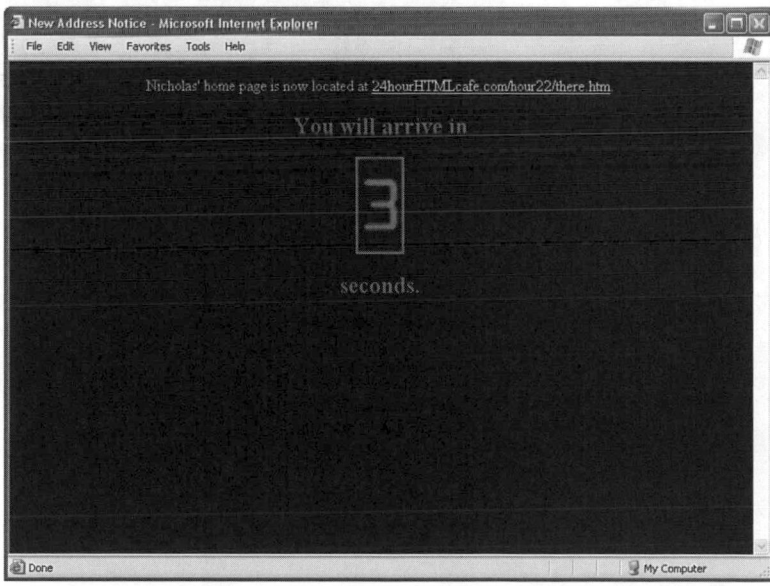

LISTING 22.4   The \<base /\> Tag in This PageHhas Nothing to Do with Page Forwarding; \<base /\> Is Discussed in the Next Section of This Hour

```
<html><head><title>New Arrival Notice</title>
<base href="http://www.24hourHTMLcafe.com/hour22/there.htm">
</head>
<body bgcolor="black" text="silver" link="red" vlink="white">
<div align="center">
<h2><font color="red">You have arrived.<p><img src="nicholas.jpg"></p>
<p>So has Nicholas.<br />(Age zero and counting.)</p></font></h2>
</div>
</body></html>
```

FIGURE 22.4

This is the page shown in Listing 22.4. The page in Listing 22.3 and Figure 22.3 forward to this page automatically after the 5-second delay.

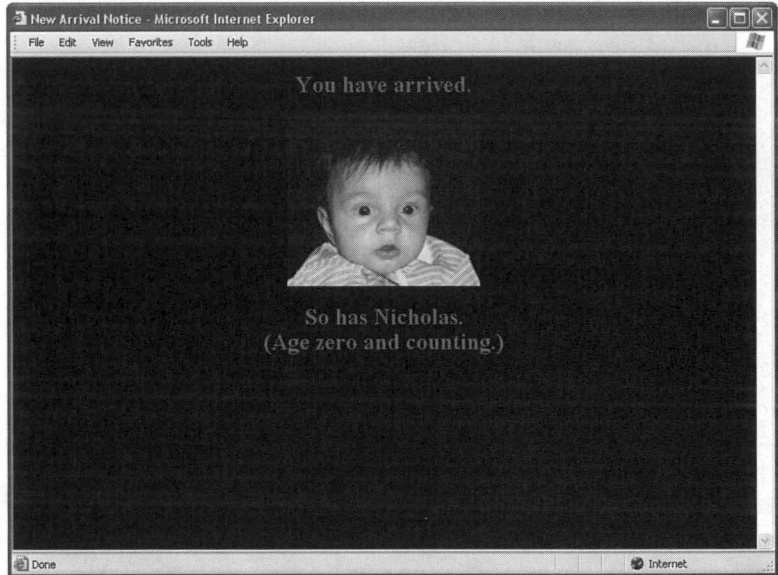

Documenting the Full Address of a Page

Suppose you create a Web page advertising your business, and a customer likes your page so much that she saves it on her hard drive. A couple of days later, she wants to show a friend your cool site, but guess what? She forgot to bookmark it, and of course the page doesn't contain a link to itself. She clicks the links to your order form, but they are only filename links (such as `<a href="orderform.htm">`); they don't work from her hard drive unless the order form is on her hard drive, too. You have lost two eager customers.

22

One way to avoid this heartbreaking scenario is to always use complete addresses starting with http:// in all links. However, this makes your pages difficult to test and maintain.

You could also include a link to your home page's full address on every page, including the home page itself. Yet there's a more elegant way to make a page remember where it came from.

The <base /> tag lets you include the address of a page within the <head> section of that page, like this:

```
<html><head>
 <title>My Page</title>
 <base href="http://www.myplace.com/mypage.htm" />
</head>
<body> ...The actual page goes here... </body>
</html>
```

For the HTML authors whose job is to maintain this page, the <base /> tag provides convenient documentation of where this page should be put.

Even more importantly, all links within the page behave as if the page were at the <base /> address—even if it isn't. For example, if you had the page in Listing 22.4 on your hard drive and you opened it with a Web browser, all images on the page would be loaded from the online site at http://24hourHTMLcafe.com/hour22/ rather than from the hard drive. The links would also lead to pages in the hour22 directory at http://24hourHTMLcafe.com/, instead of pages on the hard drive.

Few Web page authors use (or even know about) the <base /> tag. Many who do know about it don't like the hassle of changing it when they want to test a page (including images and links) on their hard drive. I've tried to give you enough information in this hour to choose for yourself whether the <base /> tag is worthwhile for you—though I will mention that I never use it myself, nor do any of the professional Web page designers I have worked with.

If you do choose to use the <base /> tag, don't put it in your pages until you're ready to upload them to the Web server. That way you can test them with all the images and link pages on your hard drive and then add the <base /> tag at the last minute, to enjoy the benefits it offers once your pages are online.

Summary

This hour showed you how to make a page remember its own address and how to make a page load another page automatically. It also taught you how to provide hints to search engines (such as Google, Yahoo!, HotBot, Alta Vista, Excite, and Lycos) so that people can find your pages more easily on the Internet. Table 22.2 lists the tags and attributes covered in this hour.

TABLE 22.2 HTML Tags and Attributes Covered in Hour 22

Tag/Attribute	Function
`<meta />`	Indicates meta-information about this document (information about the document itself). Most commonly used to make a page automatically load another page or reload itself. Used in the document `<head>`.
	Attributes
`http-equiv="..."`	Gives a command to the Web browser or server. For example, `http-equiv="refresh"` will cause a new page to load automatically.
`name="..."`	Can be used to specify which type of information about the document is in the `content` attribute. For example, `name="author"` means the author's name or ID is in `content`.
`content="..."`	The actual message or value for the information specified in `http-equiv` or `name`. For example, if `http-equiv="refresh"`, `content` should be the number of seconds to wait, followed by a semicolon and the address of the page to load.
`<base />`	Indicates the full URL of current document. This optional tag is used within `<head>`.
	Attributes
`href="..."`	The full URL of this document.
`<link />`	Indicates a link from this entire document to another (as opposed to `<a>`, which can create multiple links in the document); see Hour 16.

Q&A

Q I have lots of pages in my site. Do I need to fill out a separate form for each at each search site?

A No. If you submit just your home page (which is presumably linked to all the other pages), the search spiders will crawl through all the links on the page (and all the links on the linked pages, and so on) until it has indexed all the pages on your site.

22

Q I submitted a request to be listed with a search engine, but my page never comes up, even when I enter my company's unique name. What can I do?

A All the big search engines offer a form you can fill out to instantly check whether a specific address is included in their database. If you find that it isn't, you can submit another request form. Sometimes it takes days or even weeks for the spiders to get around to indexing your pages after you submit a request. Yahoo! is particularly infamous for being way behind on index requests because they employ human beings to check every page they list.

Q When I put keywords in a `<meta />` tag, do I need to include every possible variation of spelling and capitalization?

A Don't worry about capitalization; almost all searches are entered in all lowercase letters. Do include any obvious variations or common errors in spelling as separate keywords.

Q Can I use the `<meta />` tag to make a page automatically reload itself every few seconds or minutes?

A Yes, but there's no point in doing that unless you have some sort of program or script set up on your Web server computer to provide new information on the page. This technique can be useful in special scenarios, however. As an example, sites that display live information such as sports scores would benefit greatly from being automatically reloaded every few seconds.

Workshop

The workshop contains quiz questions and activities to help you solidify your understanding of the material covered. Try to answer all questions before looking at the "Answers" section that follows.

Quiz

1. If you publish a page about puppy adoption, how could you help make sure the page can be found by people who enter *puppy*, *dog*, and/or *adoption* at all the major Internet search sites?

2. Suppose you recently moved a page from `http://mysite.com/oldplace/thepage.htm` to `http://mysite.com/newplace/thepage.htm`, but you're not quite sure if you're going to keep it there yet. How would you automatically send people who try the old address to the new address, without any message telling them there was a change?

3. What are three ways to make sure that people who save one of your pages on their hard drive can find your site online from it, even if they forget to add it to their Bookmarks or Favorites list?

Answers

1. First, make sure *puppy*, *dog*, and *adoption* all occur frequently on your main page (as they probably already do), and title your page something like Puppy Dog Adoption. While you're at it, put the following `<meta />` tags in the `<head>` portion of the page:

```
<meta name="description"
content="dog adoption information and services" />
<meta name="keywords" content="puppy, dog, adoption" />
```

Finally, put your page online and go to `google.com`, `yahoo.com`, `hotbot.com`, `altavista.com`, `lycos.com`, and `excite.com` to fill out each of their page submission forms.

2. Put the following page at `http://mysite.com/oldplace/thepage.htm`:

```
<html><head><meta http-equiv="refresh" content="0;
http://mysite.com/newplace/thepage.htm></head>
</html>
```

3. (a) Include a link to the site, using the full Internet address, on every page. Here is an example:

```
The address of this page is:
<a href="http://mysite.com/home.htm">
http://mysite.com/home.htm</a>
```

(b) Use full Internet addresses in all links between your pages. Here is an example:

```
This is my home page. From here you can
<a href="http://mysite.com/personal.htm">
find out about my exciting personal life</a>, or
<a href="http://mysite.com/work.htm">
find out about my boring work life</a>.
```

(c) Use the `<base />` tag to specify the full Internet address of a page. Here is an example:

```
<head><base href="http://mysite.com/home.htm" />
<title>My Home Page</title></head>
```

Exercises

Can you think of some fun and useful ways to employ automatically changing pages (with the `<meta http-equiv="refresh">` tag)? I bet you can.

Hour **23**

Using XML to Describe Data

You've probably heard the buzzword and just thought it was another fly-by-night geek term with no real meaning or significance. I'm talking about XML, and while it certainly qualifies as a geek term, it is by no means insignificant. Next to HTML itself, XML is positioned to have the most widespread ramifications of any Web technology to date. The interesting thing about XML is that its impact will go largely unnoticed by most Web users. Unlike HTML, which reveals itself in flashy text and graphics, XML is more of an under-the-hood kind of technology. So prepare to get a little bit dirty as this hour introduces you to XML and its relevance to the Web.

Introducing XML

Before you can understand what XML is and why it may be a key to the future of computer communication, you first have to meet its mother. Her name is *SGML*, or *Standard General Markup Language*. She is a venerable, time-worn standard for describing other mark-up languages. HTML is just one of many languages that can be defined in SGML. Others include specialized languages for library indexing, print publications management, mathematical formulas, molecular chemistry, and so on. Though no one SGML browser can render all these specialized document types, any SGML browser can read the *document type definition* (*DTD*) and figure out how to render those elements of the document type that it understands while ignoring the rest.

It would be ideal if Web browsers could read any SGML document type instead of being limited to HTML documents. The problem with this idea is that SGML is so complex and powerful that it can be very difficult to learn and implement. If this book were about SGML, the title would be something like *Sams Teach Yourself SGML in a Year and a Half*.

XML was created to bridge the gap between HTML, which is easy to learn but kinda wimpy, and SGML, which gives you God-like powers, but may require several reincarnations to master. Like SGML, XML allows you to define your own special-purpose tags and implement complex link relationships between documents. Like HTML, XML is simple enough to learn fairly quickly because it avoids all the more esoteric (and least commonly used) aspects of SGML.

XML is a general-purpose language, which includes all the HTML tags but also allows specialized extensions of the language to be easily defined without losing compatibility with the core language. XML standardizes the format of the most common types of information while freely allowing unlimited special cases for proprietary formats and new technology. This means that you can both ensure complete compatibility between the widest variety of software and easily develop unique information formats to meet your individual needs.

Using XML, you can create a unique markup language to model just about any kind of information, including Web page content. Knowing that XML is a language for creating other markup languages, you could create your own version of HTML using XML. You could also create a markup language called CFLML (Chinese Food Lovers Markup Language), for example, which you could use to keep track of your favorite Chinese cooking recipes. The point is that XML lays the ground rules for organizing information in a consistent manner, and that information can be anything from Web pages to recipes.

One of the really nifty things about XML is that it looks very familiar to anyone who has used HTML to create Web pages. Going back to our Chinese recipe example, check out the following XML code, which reveals what a hypothetical CFLML document might look like:

```
<food>
  <item name="Crab Wontons" type="appetizer" rating="good">
```

```
    <ingredient name="Crab Meat" amount="2 cans" />
    <ingredient name="Wonton Wrap" amount="12 oz package" />
    ...
  </item>
  <item name="Beef and Broccoli" type="entree" rating="yummy">
    <ingredient name="Steak" amount="1 lb" />
    <ingredient name="Broccoli" amount="2 stalks" />
    ...
  </item>
</food>
```

23

This XML (CFLML) code includes two recipes: Crab Wontons and Beef and Broccoli. If you study the code, you'll notice that tags are used to describe the recipes much as tags are used in HTML code to describe Web pages. However, in this example the tags are unique to the CFLML language. It's not too hard to understand the meaning of the code thanks to the descriptive tags. For example, by looking at the <ingredient> tags for each recipe you can ascertain what goes into each. Keep in mind that you could create an application that used CFLML to share information with other lovers of Chinese cooking.

> Unlike HTML, which consists of a predefined set of tags such as <head>, <body>, and <img>, XML allows you to create custom markup languages with tags that are unique to a certain type of data, such as recipes.

The recipe example demonstrates how flexible XML is in solving data structuring problems. For example, you can open up any XML document in a text editor such as Windows Notepad and view or edit the code. The fact that XML is pure text also makes it very easy for applications to shuttle data between one another across networks, and also across different computing platforms such as Windows, Macintosh, and Linux. XML essentially establishes a platform-neutral means of structuring data, which is ideal for networked applications, including Web-based applications.

XML Meets HTML

One of the main goals of XML is to separate the content of information from the presentation of it. There are a variety of reasons why this is a good idea, and they all have to do with improving the organization and structure of information. Although presentation plays an important role in any Web site, modern Web applications are evolving to become driven by data of very specific types such as financial transactions. It turns out that HTML is a very poor markup language for representing such data. With its support for custom markup languages, XML opens the door for carefully describing data and the relationships between pieces of data. Imagine much more intelligent search engines that are capable of searching based upon the meaning of words, not just matching the text in them.

 You might have noticed that I've used the word document instead of page when referring to XML data. You can no longer think of the Web as a bunch of linked pages. Instead, you should think of it as linked documents. A page is an inherently visual thing, while a document can be anything ranging from a resume to stock quotes to recipes.

To understand how XML impacts HTML, consider that HTML is a relatively unstructured markup language that could benefit from the rules of XML. The natural merger of the two technologies is to make HTML adhere to the rules and structure of XML. To accomplish this merger, a new version of HTML was formulated that adheres to the stricter rules of XML. The XML-compliant version of HTML is known as XHTML. I've mentioned XHTML several times throughout the book, and you learn even more about it in the next lesson. You might also want to take a look at Appendix D, "Migrating from HTML to XHTML," to learn more about the coding differences between HTML and XHTML.

XML and Web Browsers

One of the stumbling blocks to learning XML is figuring out exactly how to use it. You now understand how XML complements HTML, but you still probably don't have a good grasp on how XML data is used in a practical scenario. More specifically, you're probably curious about how to view XML data. There is no such thing as a generic XML viewer or browser, at least not in a sense that a Web browser is an HTML viewer. An "XML viewer" is simply an application that lets you view XML code, which is normally just a text editor. To view XML code according to its meaning, you must use an application that is designed to work with a specific XML language. If you think of HTML as an XML language, a Web browser is an application designed specifically to interpret the HTML language and display the results. Another way to view XML documents is with style sheets, which offer a better approach to formatting Web pages. You learned in Hours 14 and 15 that style sheets work in conjunction with HTML code to describe in more detail how HTML data is to be displayed in a Web browser. Style sheets play a similar role when used with XML.

One last point to make in regard to viewing XML with Web browsers is that Internet Explorer allows you to view XML code directly. This is a neat feature of Internet Explorer because it automatically highlights the code so that the tags and other content are easy to see and understand. Additionally, Internet Explorer allows you to expand and collapse sections of the data just as you can expand and collapse folders in Windows Explorer. Figure 23.1 shows an XML document as viewed in Internet Explorer.

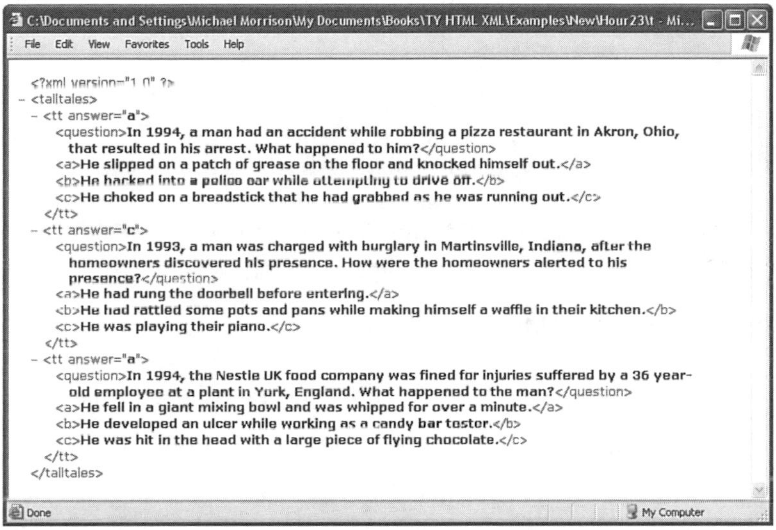

FIGURE 23.1

Opening an XML document in Internet Explorer allows you to view the code with color highlighting.

Although Internet Explorer provides a neat approach to viewing XML code, you'll probably rely on a simple text editor to view any XML code that you develop.

Inside the XML Language

The XML language relies heavily on three fundamental building blocks: elements, attributes, and values. An element is used to describe or contain a piece of information; elements form the basis of all XML documents. Elements consist of two tags: an opening tag and a closing tag. Opening tags appear as words contained within angle brackets (<food>), while closing tags appear within angle brackets that have a forward-slash (/) before the tag name (</food>). Following is an example of a pair of tags you might use to keep up with information about a pet:

```
<pet>
</pet>
```

Keep in mind that the purpose of tags is to denote pieces of information in an XML document, so it is rare to see a pair of tags with nothing between them. Instead, tags typically contain text content and/or additional tags. Following is an example of how the `pet` element can contain additional content, which in this case is a couple of empty `friend` elements:

```
<pet>
  <friend />
  <friend />
</pet>
```

> It's important to note that an *element* is a logical unit of information in an XML document, while a *tag* is a specific piece of XML code. That's why I always refer to an element by its name, such as `pet`, while tags are always referenced just as they appear in code, such as `<pet>`.

Similar to HTML, XML also supports attributes, which consist of an attribute name and a corresponding attribute value separated by an equal symbol (=). The value of an attribute appears to the right of the equal symbol, and must appear within quotes:

```
<friend name="Augustus"/>
```

Attributes aren't limited to empty elements—they are just as useful with non-empty elements. Additionally, you can use several different attributes with a single element. Following is an example of how several attributes are used to describe a pet in detail:

```
<pet name="Maximillian" type="pot bellied pig" age="3">
```

As you can see, attributes are a great way to tie small pieces of information to an element. Of course, you already knew this from your experience with HTML.

Dissecting an Element

A *non-empty element* is an element that contains text or additional elements within its opening and closing tags. When elements are contained within other elements, they are known as *nested elements*.

To understand how nested elements work, consider an apartment building. Individual apartments are contained within the building, while individual rooms are contained within each apartment. Within each room there may be pieces of furniture that in turn are used to store belongings. In XML terms, the belongings are nested in the furniture, which are nested in the rooms, which are nested in the apartments, which are nested in the apartment building. Following is how the apartment building might be coded in XML:

```
<apartmentbldg>
  <apartment>
    <room type="bedroom">
      <furniture type="armoire">
        <belonging type="t-shirt" color="navy" size="xl" />
        <belonging type="sock" color="white" />
        <belonging type="watch" />
      </furniture>
    </room>
  </apartment>
</apartmentbldg>
```

It's important to realize that non-empty elements aren't just used for nesting purposes. Non-empty elements often contain text content, which appears between the opening and closing tags. Following is an example of how you might decide to change the belonging element so that it isn't empty:

```
<furniture type="desk">
  <belonging type="letter">
    Dear Sir,
    I am pleased to announce that you may have won our sweepstakes. You
    are one of the lucky finalists in your area, and if you would just
    purchase five or more magazine subscriptions then you may eventually
    win some money. Or not.
  </belonging>
</furniture>
```

In this example, my ticket to an early retirement appears as text within the belonging element. You can include just about any text you want in an element, with the exception of a few special symbols, which you learn about a little later in the lesson.

Five Rules of XML

I've mentioned already that XML is a more rigid language than HTML, which means that you have to pay attention when coding XML or XHTML documents. The key to XML's accuracy lies in a few simple rules:

1. Tag names are case sensitive
2. Every opening tag must have a corresponding closing tag (unless it is abbreviated as an empty tag)
3. A nested tag pair cannot overlap another tag
4. Attribute values must appear within quotes
5. Every document must have a root element

23

Admittedly, the last rule is one that I haven't prepared you for, but the others should make sense to you. First off, rule number 1 states that XML is a case-sensitive language, which means that `<pet>`, `<Pet>`, and `<PET>` are all different tags. Generally speaking, XML standards encourage developers to use either lowercase tags or mixed case tags, as opposed to the uppercase tags found in some HTML Web pages.

The second rule reinforces what you've already learned by stating that every opening tag (`<furniture>`) must have a corresponding closing tag (`</furniture>`). Of course, the exception to this rule is the empty tag (`<belonging />`). Rule 3 continues to nail down the relationship between tags by stating that tag pairs cannot overlap each other. This really means that a tag pair must be completely nested within another tag pair. Perhaps an example will better clarify this point:

```
<pets>
  <pet name="Maximillian" type="pot bellied pig" age="3">
  </pet>
  <pet name="Augustus" type="goat" age="2">
</pets>
  </pet>
```

The problem with this code is that the second `pet` element isn't properly nested within the `pets` element. To fix the problem, you must either move the closing `</pet>` tag so that it is enclosed within the `pets` element, or move the opening `<pet>` tag so that it is outside of the `pets` element.

Getting back to the XML commandments, rule 4 reiterates the earlier point regarding quoted attribute values. It simply means that all attribute values must appear in quotes. So, the following code breaks this rule because the `name` attribute value `Maximillian` doesn't appear in quotes:

```
<friend name=Maximillian/>
```

The last XML commandment is the only one that I haven't really prepared you for because it deals with an entirely new concept: the root element. The *root element* is the single element in an XML document that contains all other elements in the document, and every XML document must have one. In the apartment example, the `apartmentbldg` element is the root element because it contains all of the other elements in the document (the `apartment` elements). To make a quick comparison to HTML, the `html` element in a Web page is the root element.

Creating an XML Document

As with HTML, the best way to get a handle on XML is to take a look at a complete document. Although you can store just about any kind of information in an XML document, I want to use as an example the data for a trivia game called Tall Tales. This XML document allows you to store trivia questions and answers in a structured format. One of the main question types is called a "tall tale" in the game. It's a multiple-choice question consisting of three possible answers. Knowing this, it stands to reason that the XML document will need a means of coding each question plus three different answers. In order for the answers to have any meaning, you must also provide the correct answer, which can be placed in the main element for each question/answer group.

Earlier in this lesson, you learned that every XML document must have a root element. In this case, the root element is named `talltales` to match the name of the game. Within the `talltales` element there will be several questions, each of which has three possible answers. Each question is coded with an element named `question`, and each of the three answers with the three letters `a`, `b`, and `c`. It's important to group each question with its respective answers, so you'll need an additional element for this. This element is called `tt` to indicate that the question type is a tall tale. The only remaining piece of information is the correct answer, which can be identified as an attribute of the `tt` element named `answer`.

Just in case I went a little too fast with this description of the Tall Tales document, let's recap the explanation with the following list of elements that are used within the document:

- `talltales`—The root element of the document
- `tt`—A tall tale question and its associated answers
- `question`—A question
- `a`—The first possible answer to a question
- `b`—The second possible answer to a question
- `c`—The third possible answer to a question

> In practice, you'll likely create an XML document so that it adheres to a set of tags and attributes as outlined in a DTD (Document Type Definition). A DTD acts as a template for an XML language, and makes it possible to validate an XML document for technical accuracy. DTDs are a little beyond the scope of this lesson, but I wanted you to understand that they are often used in XML.

In addition to these elements, an attribute named answer is used in the `tt` element to indicate which of the three answers (`a`, `b`, or `c`) is correct. With this information in mind, take a look at the following code for a complete `tt` element:

```
<tt answer="a">
  <question>
    In 1994, a man had an accident while robbing a pizza restaurant in Akron,
Ohio, that resulted in his
    arrest. What happened to him?
  </question>
  <a>He slipped on a patch of grease on the floor and knocked himself out.</a>
  <b>He backed into a police car while attempting to drive off.</b>
  <c>He choked on a breadstick that he had grabbed as he was running out.</c>
</tt>
```

This code reveals how a question and its related answers are grouped within a `tt` element. Now that you've seen the code for a single question, check out the following complete XML document that includes three trivia questions:

```
<?xml version="1.0"?>

<talltales>
  <tt answer="a">
    <question>
      In 1994, a man had an accident while robbing a pizza restaurant in Akron,
      Ohio, that resulted in his arrest. What happened to him?
    </question>
    <a>He slipped on a patch of grease on the floor and knocked himself out.</a>
    <b>He backed into a police car while attempting to drive off.</b>
    <c>He choked on a breadstick that he had grabbed as he was running out.</c>
  </tt>

  <tt answer="c">
    <question>
      In 1993, a man was charged with burglary in Martinsville, Indiana, after
      the homeowners discovered his presence. How were the homeowners alerted to
      his presence?
    </question>
    <a>He had rung the doorbell before entering.</a>
    <b>He had rattled some pots and pans while making himself a waffle in their
kitchen.</b>
    <c>He was playing their piano.</c>
  </tt>

  <tt answer="a">
    <question>
      In 1994, the Nestle UK food company was fined for injuries suffered by a
      36 year-old employee at a plant in York, England. What happened to the
      man?
    </question>
    <a>He fell in a giant mixing bowl and was whipped for over a minute.</a>
    <b>He developed an ulcer while working as a candy bar tester.</b>
    <c>He was hit in the head with a large piece of flying chocolate.</c>
  </tt>
</talltales>
```

Except for the first line, this code should all make sense to you given the earlier explanation of the Tall Tales trivia data. The first line of code is the XML declaration, which notifies a Web browser of the XML version that an XML document is using. Following is the standard XML declaration for XML 1.0:

```
<?xml version="1.0"?>
```

This code looks somewhat similar to an opening tag for an element named xml with an attribute named version. However, the code isn't actually a tag at all. Instead, this code is known as a *processing instruction*, which is a special line of XML code that passes information to the application that is processing the document. In this case, the processing instruction is notifying the application that the document uses XML 1.0. Processing instructions are easily identified by the <? and ?> symbols that are used to contain each instruction.

You now have your first complete XML document that has some pretty interesting content ready to be processed and served up for viewing.

Styling an XML Document

Short of developing a custom application from scratch, the best way to view XML documents is to use a style sheet. Style sheets allow you to determine exactly how to display data in an XML document. While style sheets can improve the appearance of HTML Web pages, as you saw in Hours 14 and 15, they are especially important for XML because Web browsers typically don't understand what the custom tags mean in an XML document.

Keep in mind that the purpose of a style sheet is to determine the appearance of XML content. This means that you can use styles in a style sheet to control the font and color of text, for example. You can also control the positioning of content, such as where an image or paragraph of text appears on the page. Styles are always applied to specific elements. So, in the case of the trivia document, the style sheet should include styles for each of the important elements that you want displayed: tt, question, a, b, and c.

The idea with the Tall Tales style sheet is to format the data so that each question is displayed followed by each of the answers in a smaller font and different color. Following is the code for the TallTales.css style sheet:

```
tt {
  display: block;
  width: 750px;
  padding: 10px;
  margin-bottom: 10px;
  border: 4px double black;
  background-color: silver;
}
```

```
question {
  display: block;
  color: black;
  font-family: Times, serif;
  font-size: 16pt;
  text-align: left;
}

a, b, c {
  display: block;
  color: brown;
  font-family: Times, serif;
  font-size: 12pt;
  text-indent: 15px;
  text-align: left;
}
```

Although you now have an XML document and a style sheet for it, you haven't associated the two. To attach the style sheet to the trivia document, add the following line of code just after the XML declaration in the document:

```
<?xml-stylesheet type="text/css" href="TallTales.css"?>
```

You'll recognize this line of code as a processor instruction, which is evident by the `<?` and symbol>?> symbols. This processor instruction notifies the application processing the document (the Web browser) that the document is to be displayed using the style sheet `TallTales.css`. After adding this line of code to the document, it is displayed in Internet Explorer in a format that is much easier to read (Figure 23.2).

FIGURE 23.2

A simple style sheet provides a means of formatting the data in an XML document for convenient viewing.

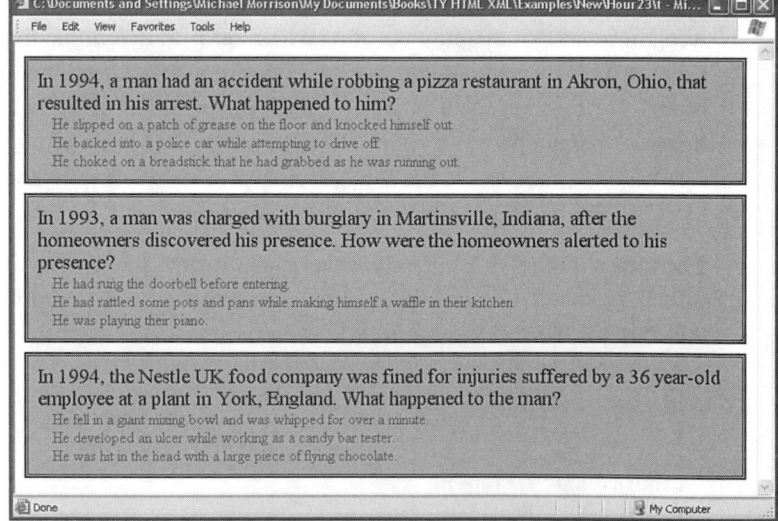

As you can see, the style sheet does wonders for making the XML document viewable in a Web browser. You've now successfully created your first XML document, along with a style sheet to view it in a Web browser.

Summary

XML is one of those industry buzzwords that everyone has heard of and not all that many people truly understand. Fortunately, you're now in the know when it comes to XML and its role in the present and future of the Web. Perhaps more importantly, you found out how to use XML to structure data in such a way that it is more understandable and can be processed easier than straight HTML. XML is obviously a much larger topic than this lesson, or even this book, could hope to fully explore, but you now have the groundwork in place should you choose to learn more.

This lesson started off by introducing you to the basics of XML and how it relates to other technologies such as HTML. You then took a peek inside the XML language to see how XML documents are structured. And finally, you wrapped up the hour by creating a complete XML document, along with a style sheet for it that allows you to view the document in a Web browser.

Q&A

Q Is it possible to create custom tags in HTML, as I can in XML?

A No. HTML is a markup language that consists of a predefined set of tags that each has a special meaning to Web browsers. If you were able to create custom tags in HTML, Web browsers wouldn't know what to do with them. XML, on the other hand, isn't necessarily tied to Web browsers, and therefore has no notion of a predefined set of tags.

Q How do I keep up with what the latest version of XML is?

A The latest (and only) version of XML to date is version 1.0. To find out about new versions as they are released, please visit the World Wide Web Consortium (W3C) Web site at http://www.w3c.org/. Keep in mind, however, that XML is a relatively stable technology, and isn't likely to undergo version changes nearly as rapidly as more dynamic technologies such as XHTML or even HTML. You can also find out about the latest versions of XHTML and HTML at the W3C Web site.

Q What happens if an XML document breaks one or more of the five rules covered in this hour?

23

A Obviously, your computer will crash immediately and quite likely catch on fire. No, actually nothing tragic will happen unless you attempt to process the document using an XML application or tool. Even then, you will likely get an error message instead of any kind of fatal result. XML applications expect documents to follow the rules, so they will likely notify you of the errors whenever they are encountered. Even Web browsers are pretty good at reporting errors in XML documents, which is in sharp contrast to how loosely they interpret HTML Web pages.

Workshop

The workshop contains quiz questions and activities to help you solidify your understanding of the material covered. Try to answer all questions before looking at the "Answers" section that follows.

Quiz

1. What is the significance of the root element of an XML document?
2. How would you code an empty element named `movie` with an attribute named `format` that is set to `dvd`?

Answers

1. The root element of an XML document contains all of the other elements in the document; every document must have a root element.
2. `<movie format="dvd />`

Exercises

- Add another trivia question to the `TallTales.xml` document, complete with three possible answers. Then view the document in a Web browser using the `TallTales.css` style sheet to see the new question.
- Modify the `TallTales.css` style sheet so that the questions and answers are displayed in different colors.

Hour **24**

Planning for the Future of HTML

Almost everything you have learned in this book is likely to work flawlessly with HTML-compatible software for many years to come. There are tens of millions of pages of information written in standard HTML, and even as that standard evolves, tomorrow's Web browsers and business software will retain the capability to view today's Web pages.

Some of the most exciting applications of HTML, however, are still rapidly developing. This hour introduces the latest HTML extensions and helps you understand what these new capabilities will enable you to do.

To Do

When this hour was written, "now" meant mid-2003. Because you are living in "the future," you can check to make sure my crystal ball wasn't too cloudy, with the help of the following Web sites:

- Your best two sources for the latest HTML standards (and proposed future standards) are the World Wide Web Consortium site (http://www.w3.org/) and the HTML Compendium (http://www.html-compendium.org/).

- To see how the standards are actually implemented in the latest Web browsers, and to see what nonstandard HTML extensions might be available, visit the Microsoft (`http://www.microsoft.com/`) and Netscape Web sites (`http://home.netscape.com/`).

You can also get copies of the latest Web browser updates from these two Web sites.

HTML Beyond the Web

The intimate familiarity with HTML you gained from reading this book will be one of the most important (and profitable) skills that anyone can have both in the present and coming years. However, most of the HTML pages you create in your lifetime will probably not be Web pages.

To understand why, and to see the big picture of where HTML is headed, consider the following features of the latest HTML standard:

- Through style sheets and scripting, HTML gives you precise control over the appearance and functionality of virtually any textual and graphical information.
- All major programming languages, interactive media, and database formats can also be seamlessly integrated with HTML.
- HTML's extended character sets and fonts can now be used to communicate in the native script of almost any human language in the world.
- Data security standards have finally made it practical to carry out financial and other sensitive transactions with HTML, and to manage confidential or restricted-access information.
- All future versions of the Microsoft Windows operating system will use HTML as a fundamental part of the user interface. Nearly all current versions of office productivity software also support HTML, with some of them highly reliant on HTML (and XML) as a standard data format.

All this adds up to a very near future where HTML will, without a doubt, play a central role—it might even be accurate to say **the** central role—in the display and exchange of almost all information across all computers and computer networks on earth. This sounds important because it is important. However, this hour will make a case that HTML will have an even more important role than that to play. To understand how that can be so, we'll need to take another step back to see an even bigger picture: the changing role of the computer itself in our society.

From Calculators to Wireless Communicators

The computer was once considered a device for accounting and number crunching. Then it evolved into a device for crunching all types of information, from words and numbers to graphics and sounds. Today and tomorrow, the computer is above all a communications device; its primary use is the transmission of information between people.

In many workplaces today, you can use a computer to access business information every day without knowing much more than how to click links and scroll through long pages—and you can do so without knowing which information is coming from your computer, which is coming from the server down the hall, and which is coming from other servers perhaps thousands of miles away.

Users who become accustomed to seeing highly readable and attractive pages of information on their computer screens are losing the tiny bit of tolerance they have left for cryptic icons, unadorned text messages, and idiosyncratic menu mazes. They will soon expect their computer screens to always be as easy to read and interact with as is the Web.

24

Those who make their millions supplying computer software are well aware of that expectation, and are expending an unprecedented amount of research and development effort toward fulfilling it. Along the way, the central metaphor for interacting with computers changed from the "window" of the 1980s "desktop" to the "page" of the 1990s "World Wide Web." This metaphor is already changing to accommodate the needs and capabilities of users in this first decade of the new millennium, where wireless handheld devices and networks are rapidly becoming a standard part of daily life.

HTML as the New User Interface

As the role of the computer evolves, HTML is becoming more and more central to nearly everything we do with computers. HTML is the de facto global standard for connecting all types of information in a predictable and presentable way.

HTML gives you a painless and reliable way to combine and arrange text, graphics, sound, video, and interactive programs. Unlike older proprietary page layout standards, HTML was originally designed for efficient communication among all kinds of computers worldwide.

The prominence of HTML, however, does not mean that Web browsers will be a major category of software application in the coming years. In fact, the Web browser as a distinct program has already nearly disappeared. Microsoft Internet Explorer, for instance, does much more than retrieve pages from the World Wide Web. It lets you use HTML pages as the interface for organizing and navigating through the information on your own computer, including directory folders and the Windows Desktop itself. In conjunction with HTML-enabled software such as Microsoft Office, HTML becomes the common standard interface for word processing, spreadsheets, and databases. Netscape Navigator is also much more than a Web browser. It uses HTML to integrate all types of media into email, discussion groups, schedule management, business documents, and collaborative project management.

Meanwhile, HTML support is being included in virtually every major software release so that every program on your computer will soon be able to import and export information in the form of HTML pages. In a nutshell, HTML is the glue that holds together all the diverse types of information on our computers and ensures that it can be presented in a standard way that will look the same to anyone in the world.

In situations where HTML doesn't provide the structure necessary to accurately describe information, XML is filling in as a universal data format. So, while HTML may suffice to serve as the glue for different kinds of visual information, XML serves as the glue for information that isn't so easily seen: electronic orders, automatic funds transfers, mobile phone settings, and so forth. XML provides a highly structured alternative to HTML for representing information on the Web.

In a business world that now sees fast, effective communication as the most common and most important task of its workers, the "information glue" of HTML and XML has the power to connect more than different types of media. They are the hidden adhesive that connects a business to its customers and connects individual employees to form an efficient team. Knowing how to apply that glue—the skills you gained from this book—puts you in one of the most valuable roles in any modern organization.

The Digital Media Revolution

The most important changes in the next few years might not be in HTML itself, but in the audience you can reach with your HTML pages. Many Web site developers hope that Internet-based content will have enough appeal to become the mass-market successor to television and radio. Less optimistic observers note that the global communications network has a long way to go before it can even deliver television-quality video to most users, or reach a majority of the world's populace at all.

I won't pretend to have a magic mirror that lets me see how and when HTML becomes a mass-market phenomenon, but one thing is certain: All communication industries, from television to telephony, are moving rapidly toward exclusively digital technology. As they do so, the lines between communication networks are blurring. New Internet protocols promise to optimize multimedia transmissions at the same time new protocols allow wireless broadcasters to support two-way interactive transmissions. The same small satellite dish can give you both Internet access and high-definition TV.

Add to this the fact that HTML is the only widely supported worldwide standard for combining text with virtually any other form of digital medium. Whatever surprising twists and turns digital communication takes in the future, it's difficult to imagine that HTML won't be sitting in the driver's seat, with XML in the passenger's seat I might add!

Over a million people can already access the Internet without a "real computer"—via TV set-top boxes and from WebTV, Inc., cable TV companies, digital satellite services, and even telephones and pagers. These devices are only the first wave of much more ubiquitous appliances that provide HTML content to people who wouldn't otherwise use computers. Full-blown handheld computers such as those powered by Microsoft's Pocket PC operating system allow you to surf the Web from anywhere wirelessly. And for those less gadget-savvy, all of the popular home video game systems are on the verge of providing Web access in addition to their online gaming services.

24

The prospect of mass-market HTML access is obviously a great opportunity for HTML page authors. However, it can also present a number of challenges when designing HTML pages because many people might see your pages on low-resolution TV screens or on small handheld devices. See this hour's "Preparing Yourself for Tomorrow" section for some pointers on making sure your HTML pages can be enjoyed and understood by the widest possible audience.

XHTML, the New HTML

So far in this hour I've noted how HTML is in the right place at the right time to enable several key changes in business and interpersonal communication. As the people and companies of the world become more connected and dependent upon one another, HTML's capability to make all information technology easier to use and less constrained by geography seems almost magical.

Even more magically, HTML has enabled an explosion of new media formats and incompatible file types, while at the same time providing the first truly universal format for exchanging all types of information. The limitations of the HTML language itself have stood in the way of it truly fulfilling this important role, however. To address these limitations, the World Wide Web Consortium created XML, which you learned about in the previous hour.

Although XML has a lot to offer, it does pose a few problems, not the least of which is that the HTML and XML standards are almost—but not quite—compatible with one another. To smooth out these technical bumps, the W3C created a 100% XML-compliant version of HTML 4, called (you guessed, didn't you?) XHTML 1.

Does that mean there will never be an HTML 5 standard? Sort of. There will undoubtedly be more tags and attributes added to HTML in the future, but the result will probably be called XHTML 2 instead of HTML 5. Actually, XHTML 2 is already in the works, while HTML is only enjoying minor tweaks here and there.

The most important thing for you to know about XHTML? How to write your Web pages for compatibility with it, while still remaining compatible with HTML-based Web browsers. If you learned HTML from this book, you have nothing to worry about because every example in the book and on the accompanying Web site (`http://www.24hourHTMLcafe.com`) is compatible with both HTML 4 and XHTML 1 in terms of the HTML code itself. XHTML does require a few technical details that I didn't include in the examples throughout the book to keep things simple. Please refer to Appendix D, "Migrating from HTML to XHTML," to find out more about making your pages absolutely 100% XHTML compatible.

If you have some older HTML pages that you need to convert for XHTML and XML compatibility, the following checklist will get you there (refer to Appendix D for more information):

1. In HTML, it doesn't matter whether tags are uppercase, lowercase, or a mixture of both. In XHTML, all tags must be lowercase. For example, use `<body>` instead of `<BODY>`.

2. Closing tags are often optional in HTML, but are always required in XHTML for any tag that *encloses* (refers to) some content. For example, every paragraph must begin with a `<p>` tag and end with a `</p>` tag. Likewise, every `<li>` list item must have a closing `</li>`, every `<td>` table data cell must have a closing `</td>`, and so forth.

3. HTML tags that don't enclose any content (such as `<br>`, `<hr>`, and `<img>`) must now contain a slash (examples: `<br />` `<hr />` `<img src="pic.gif" />`). This tells XHTML interpreters not to expect a closing tag.

4. In XHTML, all attribute values must be enclosed in quotation marks. For example, `<img src=pic.gif border=1>` was valid HTML, but it must be written as `<img src="pic.gif" border="1" />` to be valid XHTML.

5. All attributes must have values in XHTML. For example, `<input type="checkbox" checked>` should technically now be written as `<input type="checkbox" checked="checked">`.

6. Certain special characters are not allowed in HTML because in contexts it might be hard to tell if they were meant as part of a markup tag. XHTML forbids the same characters, but is much stricter about not allowing them to appear in embedded style sheets and scripts. The forbidden characters and the codes you must replace them with are shown in Table 24.1.

This is another case where I deserve a little slap on the wrist for not following my own advice religiously; for clarity, I have used the single quotation mark character instead of `&#39;` in some of the JavaScript examples in this book.

TABLE 24.1 Characters You Should Avoid Using in XHTML Pages

Replace This...	With This...
& (ampersand)	`&amp;` or `&#38;`
" (quotation/inch mark)	`&quot;` or `&#34;`
< (open angle-bracket)	`&lt;` or `&#60;`
> (close angle-bracket)	`&gt;` or `&#62;`
[(open square bracket)	`&#91;`
] (closed square bracket)	`&#93;`
' (apostrophe/single-quote)	`&#39;`

If you have a number of HTML pages that you'd like to convert to XHTML-compatible format, I strongly recommend that you download the free HTML-Kit software from `http://www.chami.com/html-kit/`. This free program includes a module called HTML-Tidy, which automatically changes HTML to conform to the rules mentioned here and also reports any other problems or incompatibilities it finds.

HTML-Kit is also a friendly and well-designed text editor with many handy features for writing new HTML and XHTML pages. I used HTML-Kit 1 to convert and edit every sample file in this book, and didn't encounter any bugs or errors; you shouldn't hesitate to trust your precious pages to it. (One caveat: HTML-Tidy changes the line breaks and spacing of your code, so you may have to do some reformatting by hand if you like to neatly indent your code.)

24

Once you've converted your pages over to XHTML, you will want to *validate* them to make sure the conversion was a complete success. The W3C provides a free online validation service that you can use to see if your pages adhere completely to the official XHTML standard. The validation service is located at http://validator.w3.org/, and allows you to browse HTML files on your own computer for validation or files that are already published on the Web. I strongly encourage you to try out the validation service, because it represents the final word on the accuracy of XHTML code.

HTML Applications of the Future

The near-universal compatibility of HTML and XML provides a big incentive to format any important document as a Web page—even if you have no immediate plans for putting it on the World Wide Web. You can create a single page that can be printed on paper, sent as an email message, displayed during a board meeting presentation, and posted for reference on the company intranet. You can also take the traditional route and format the page separately for each of these applications—and edit each file with a different software program when the information needs to be updated. Now that most business software supports the HTML standards, many organizations are trying to get employees to consistently use it for all important documents.

Yet the great migration to HTML goes beyond what you might have thought of as "documents" in the old days. Combined with XML, style sheets, JavaScript, and other technologies, HTML-based presentations can in many cases replace what was once done with proprietary data formats, specialized software, or more traditional programming languages. Here are a few of the other areas where HTML is finding application beyond the Web:

- *Kiosks* with HTML-based interactive content are popping up everywhere. They look like ATMs on steroids, and they're helping sell records and movie tickets, expand department store displays, and even automate the paying of parking tickets.

- Information-rich CD-ROM titles are fast migrating to HTML. *Encyclopaedia Britannica* is entirely HTML-based, which enables them to offer the content on CD-ROM, the Web, or a combination of both for maximum speed and up-to-the-minute currency. Because CD-ROM drives display multimedia so much faster than most Internet connections, dynamic HTML presentations that are too media intensive to be done on today's World Wide Web become possible. DVD-ROM drives are even faster and hold much more information, making them ideally suited to large multimedia "sites."

- Corporate HTML-based newsletters are now often created in HTML for the company intranet, and printed on paper for delivery to employees or customers who won't see them on the Web. The traditional difference between online and paper presentations was that graphics needed to be high-resolution black-and-white for printing and low-resolution color for computer screens. Today's inexpensive color printers, however, do a great job making low-res color images look great in an HTML-based newsletter.

- Teachers are finding that tests and educational worksheets are easier to administer as HTML pages and can include many types of interactive content that isn't possible on paper. Simple HTML documents can be passed out on floppy disks, writeable CDs, or memory cards for students who lack access to the Internet.

- Vertical market users often buy a computer specifically to run a certain custom-designed application or set of applications. The value-added resellers and systems integrators that provide these systems are delivering machines configured to start displaying HTML pages. This can help step users through the use of the machine or replace old-fashioned *idiot menus* with a more attractive and sophisticated interface without sacrificing ease of use.

I could list many more creative and beneficial uses of HTML beyond run-of-the-mill Web pages, but the point is clear: If you need to present any type of information, seriously consider HTML as an alternative to the specialized software or programming tools that you would have used for the job a couple of years ago.

Preparing Yourself for Tomorrow

If you've your way through most of this book's hours, you already have one of the most important ingredients for future success in the new digital world: a solid working knowledge of HTML and XHTML.

Chances are that your primary reason for learning HTML at this time was to create some Web pages, but I hope this hour has convinced you that you'll be using XHTML for far more than that in the future. Here are some of the factors you should consider when planning and building your Web site today so that it will also serve you well tomorrow:

- Whenever you run into something that you'd like to do on a Web page, but can't with HTML as it stands today, include a comment in the page so you can add that feature when it becomes possible in the future. The multimedia and interactive portions of your site are likely to need more revisions to keep up with current technology than will the text and graphics portions. When possible, keep the more

24

cutting-edge elements of your site separate and take especially good care to document them well with the `<!--` and `-- >` comment tags.

- Though high-bandwidth interactive media may high hig hbe the wave of the future, avoid it today except when developing for disk-based media or a fast local intranet. Even when everyone is using 56Kbps or faster modems, many people will move on to a different site before they'll wait for a large interactive movie or presentation to download, initialize, and start working.

- Because style sheets give you complete control over the choice and measurements of type on your Web pages, it is a good idea to study basic typography now if you aren't familiar with it. Understanding and working with things such as *leading*, *kerning*, *em spaces*, and *drop caps* have long been essential for producing truly professional-quality paper pages. It will soon be essential for producing outstanding Web pages, too.

- When you design your pages, don't assume that everyone who sees them will be using a computer. Televisions, video telephones, game consoles, and many other devices might have access to them as well. Some of these devices have very low-resolution screens (with as few as 320×200 pixels). Though it's difficult to design a Web page to look good at that resolution, you'll reach the widest possible audience if you do.

- Several new standards have been issued by the World Wide Web Consortium that will increasingly impact the Web as time goes by. These include

  Portable Network Graphics (*PNG*)

  Synchronized Multimedia Interface Language (*SMIL*)

  Scalable Vector Graphics (*SVG*)

  Mathematics Markup Language (*MathML*)

  eXtensible Style Sheet Language (*XSL*)

  On the privacy and security front, new standards include:

  Platform for Internet Content Selection (*PICS*)

  Platform for Privacy Preferences (*P3P*)

  Digital Signature standard (*Dsig*)

  Since these advances are likely to both expand the potential capabilities of your Web site and change some of the methods you currently use to build Web pages, you should visit the w3c.org site and take the time to learn a little about each of them.

You'll find links to several online reference and learning resources at the *24-Hour HTML Café* at `http://www.24hourHTMLcafe.com/`.

In addition to providing an easy way to review all the sample pages and HTML techniques covered in this book, this site offers many example pages this book didn't have room for.

You'll also find links to hundreds of Web sites created by this book's readers. You're sure to pick up some great ideas for your own pages!

Summary

This hour has provided a bird's-eye view of the future of HTML. It discussed the new roles that HTML will play in global communications and briefly introduced how HTML relates to the new XML standard. Finally, it offered some advice for planning and constructing Web pages today that will continue to serve you well into the future.

Q&A

Q **What is the difference between *digital communication* and other communication, anyway? Does *digital* mean it uses HTML?**

A When information is transferred as distinct bits of information, which are essentially numbers, it's called *digital*. It's much easier to store, retrieve, and process information without losing or changing it when it is transferred digitally. Any information from a computer (including HTML) is by its nature digital, and in the not-too-distant future, all telephone, television, radio, and even motion picture production will be digital.

Q **How soon can I start designing Internet Web pages that aren't limited by what I can transfer over a 56Kbps modem?**

A That depends on who you want to read your pages. There will be millions of 56Kbps modems in use for many years to come. A growing number of people will have 1Mbps (1,000Kbps) or faster cable, copper-optic, and wireless connections, so things are looking up. Before long, the number of 1Mbps users will surpass the number of 56Kbps users. That difference of 18× in speed will lead more and more Web page publishers to offer separate high-speed and low-speed sites; many are already offering media content in varying sizes for each connection speed.

Q **I keep hearing people talk about a language called WML that has something to do with the wireless Internet. What is it?**

A WML stands for Wireless Markup Language, and indeed, it allows you to create Web pages specially suited for devices that connect to the Internet wirelessly. Since most wireless devices are limited in terms of processing power, memory, and most importantly, screen size, WML is considerably slimmer than HTML/XHTML. Pages created in WML are designed for display by *microbrowsers*, which are scaled down browsers that run on wireless devices. The good news is that WML is very easy to use, especially given your knowledge of HTML. To find out more about WML, visit the Wireless Developer Network at `http://www.wirelessdevnet.com/`.

Workshop

The workshop contains quiz questions and activities to help you solidify your understanding of the material covered. Try to answer all questions before looking at the "Answers" section that follows.

Quiz

You've taken 23 quizzes in 24 hours! Instead of taking another, may I suggest that you congratulate yourself for a job well done, take a break, and treat yourself to something special? You deserve it.

Exercises

Back from your break yet? Now that you've learned HTML and have your Web site online, this book can still help you make it better and better. You may want to review the Q&A sections throughout the book and Appendix A, "Readers' Most Frequently Asked Questions." Be sure to also stick a bookmark at the beginning of Appendix C, the "Complete HTML 4 and XHTML 1 Quick Reference." Exploring the "Exercises" sections that you might have skipped the first time around will help build your HTML skills as well.

I'm sure you haven't yet explored all the oodles and oodles of entertaining examples and tutorial tips at the *24-Hour HTML Café*. That's `www.24hourHTMLcafe.com`, where the JavaScript is hot and the HTML never stops flowing. See you there!

Part VII
Appendixes

Appendix **A**

Readers' Most Frequently Asked Questions

I have read and carefully collated more than 1,000 questions and suggestions sent to me by readers of this book's previous editions. This feedback has influenced everything in this edition, from the overall outline to the specific notes, tips, and quiz questions. I've tried to incorporate the answers to readers' questions into the text at just the point in each hour when you would have found yourself asking those questions.

This appendix is for those times when you may have overlooked or forgotten a key point in the book. It's also a chance for me to answer those questions that just didn't fit under any particular topic. These questions are presented in order of frequency: Number 1 is the most commonly asked question, number 2 is the next, and so on down to number 24. (A good number. I had to stop somewhere!)

In cases where the answer is clearly explained in the book, I just refer you to the relevant part of that hour. In cases where you might need a little more from me, I provide a succinct answer here and may also refer to an online resource that can help.

The 24 Top Questions from Readers of *Sams Teach Yourself HTML in 24 Hours*

1. **What should I read next?**

   Try *Sams Teach Yourself JavaScript in 24 Hours* or *Sams Teach Yourself Paint Shop Pro 7 in 24 Hours*, which are available at most bookstores, including online at www.amazon.com.

2. **I'm stuck on my first page. It didn't work. What did I do wrong?**

   The first is always the hardest. If you see all the HTML when you try to view the file (by selecting File, Open in your Web browser), or if you see some weird characters at the top of the page, you haven't saved the file in plain text or ASCII text format. If you can't figure out how to do that in your word processor, use the Notepad or TextEdit editor that came with your computer instead. (WordPad is especially problematic in this regard.)

   For more guidance on making your first page, carefully go over the first To Do section and "A Simple Sample Page" in Hour 2, "Create a Web Page Right Now."

   Also, remember that you don't have to be connected to the Internet to edit and view Web pages on your hard drive. (If your Web browser tries to connect to the Internet every time you start it, change the home page in your browser settings to a page on your hard drive.)

3. **Graphics or media files don't work/don't show online.**

   There are several common pitfalls you may encounter when putting graphics on a Web page:

   - Make sure the graphics file is in the same folder as the HTML document that refers to it. (If you're trying to refer to it in a different folder, review the "Relative Addresses" section of Hour 3, "Linking to Other Web Pages.")
   - Make sure the graphics file is saved in GIF or JPEG format. Open the file with Paint Shop Pro (or another graphics program) and use File, Save As to save it again just to be sure.
   - Make sure the capitalization of the filename and the `src=` attribute in the `<img />` tag match. `MyImage.gif` and `myimage.GIF` are not the same to most Web servers!

- To get rid of the blue line around a graphic, put border="0" in the <img /> tag.
- This one's unlikely, but possible: Do you have Automatically Load Images turned off under Edit, Preferences, Privacy & Security in Netscape Navigator, or Show Pictures turned off under Tools, Internet Options, Advanced in Microsoft Internet Explorer?
- True story: One reader spent four days trying to figure out why none of his images worked. He was typing <img scr= instead of <img src= every single time. Don't laugh—just check *your* page for typos.

Refer to Hour 9, "Putting Graphics on a Web Page." If you're having trouble arranging graphics on the page, you'll find many helpful hints in all four chapters of Part IV, "Web Page Design."

Audio and video files are trickier and more prone to problems. There's no practical way to make them work in every version of every popular browser, but refer to Hour 20, "Embedding Multimedia in Web Pages," for as much help as I can give.

4. **How do I get forms to work on my server?**

Ask your ISP to help you set up a forms-processing script. If your ISP can't do it, you either need to find one that is willing to actually provide some service or use a third-party form-processing service, such as www.freedback.com. You can also simply have form information sent to your email address, but this approach is a little unreliable because it is dependent on every user having their email properly configured through their Web browser.

5. **How do I put a counter on my page?**

You probably don't need one, since most ISPs send you a detailed report each week, summarizing exactly how many times each of your pages was accessed. You should expect (read: demand) this, but some Web hosting services (especially free ones, or those outside North America) just won't provide it. In that case, you need to set up a CGI script on your server. That isn't terribly difficult, and you'll find the code and some advice on how to do it at www.developer.com and other Web development sites.

6. **I'm confused about frames. Mine don't work, and I don't understand why. Do you?**

Frames are tricky. It may take a couple readings of Hour 16, "Multi-Page Layout with Frames" and some experimentation before everything clicks and you see how the whole thing works. Here are some tips that may help:

- Remember that you can right-click in any frame and pick This Frame, View Frame Source in Netscape Navigator or View Source in Microsoft Internet

A

Explorer to see the HTML for that frame. Selecting View, Source from the main menu shows you the HTML for the frameset document.

- The only way to make a link change the contents of two or more frames at once is to link to a new frameset and include `target="_top"` in the `<a>` link tag.

- You also use `target="_top"` when you want to break out of all the frames and go back to a regular single-page document.

7. **How do I pursue a career in Web page design, and how much should I charge to make someone a Web page?**

As in any competitive business (and Web page design is a very competitive business), you need a solid marketing plan to be successful. If you've already found some clients, the amount you charge them is obviously up for negotiation. As a general rule, the going rate for experienced Web developers is between $25 and $50 per hour. If you are still learning, expect to charge less than that, unless you are already a professional graphics or publications designer with a loyal client base.

8. **How do I make password-protected pages?**

Consult your ISP to see what kinds of security options it has available. For true password protection, you will need to utilize secure pages, or at least a script of some sort that limits access to users who can enter a verified password.

9. **Where can I find Java applets/prewritten JavaScript?**

Try `www.developer.com`, `www.javascript.com`, and `javascript.internet.com`, or look in any of the major Internet search sites under *Java* or *JavaScript*.

10. **I can't get a link to work. What could be wrong?**

Check the spelling and capitalization of the `href` link and the file to which you're trying to link. Some links will work on your hard drive, but fail on the Web server if the capitalization doesn't match. (This is because Windows doesn't care about capitalization of filenames, but UNIX does.) Also, review Hour 3 to make sure you understand the finer points of relative and absolute addressing.

11. **I am having trouble getting JavaScript code to work, even though I'm pretty sure I got the syntax right.**

Please don't imagine for a moment that Microsoft and Netscape could possibly have bugs in their Web browsers, especially in the sacred JavaScript module. You are the problem. To redeem yourself, you must build a shrine next to your computer, paste gilt-edged pictures of Bill Gates and Marc Andreessen to it, and humbly offer it cold pizza thrice daily. If you do this with a clean heart and pure mind, all problems with code implementation will still be your own darn fault, but at least Microsoft may decide not to take legal action against you for it.

12. **Where can I get more help creating graphics and multimedia?**

   If you use Paint Shop Pro for graphics, try the tutorials at www.jasc.com or read *Creating Paint Shop Pro Web Graphics*, which is available through the Jasc online store. Learning to work with audio and video is a more ambitious endeavor, but my *Web Page Wizardry: Wiring Your Site for Sound and Action* gives you a good head start. I also contributed chapters on working online audio and video to *Web Publishing Unleashed: Professional Reference Edition*. Both books can be purchased at any major bookseller. Another option is to use an online media gallery, or clip art site, such as Microsoft's Design Gallery Live (dgl.microsoft.com).

13. **How do I put more "bells and whistles" (a chat room, a hit counter, password protection, interactive sound, a pull-down list of links, and things of that nature) on my site?**

   Most of those involve JavaScript or CGI scripting (advanced stuff) to make them work. To help you go beyond what this book teaches, I've assembled a list of advanced developer resources at

   http://www.24hourHTMLcafe.com/hotsites.htm#developer.

14. **How do I get a message to scroll along the bottom?**

   You'll find JavaScript for that at both www.developer.com and www.javascript.com.

15. **How do I put files on a Web site for download?**

   Just upload the file in the same place you put your Web pages and use a regular HTML link, like the following:

   ```
   <a href="bigfile.zip">Click here to download bigfile.zip.</a>
   ```

   Keep in mind that an image linked in this manner will likely open up within the browser window, which may not be the desired effect if you're placing the image online for download. The solution is for the user to save the image to their local computer once it is opened in the browser.

16. **How do I put a browser on a disk? Do I need to if I publish Web pages on a disk?**

   Most people have a Web browser on their computer these days, but if you want to provide one just in case, you need permission from the browser company. I recommend Opera (www.opera.com), which is small enough to fit on a single 1.4MB floppy disk and allows distribution of free time-limited evaluation copies.

17. **When I try to download Paint Shop Pro or the FTP software you recommended, the download is deathly slow or stops altogether. Can you help?**

A

I'm afraid there's not much I (or you) can do, except recommend that you try again later. And you thought you needed a car to get in a traffic jam?

18. **Should I use Java applets and other advanced stuff?**

    Not unless you need to do something you can't do any other way. Basic HTML is faster, more widely compatible, and easier to maintain.

19. **How do I make a form for people to fill out and print?**

    They can fill out and print any HTML form. Just tell them to do it. See the Q&A section at the end of Hour 19, "Gathering Information with HTML Forms." Make sure the form elements are still placed within a `<form>` tag, even if you don't plan on having the form submitted electronically.

20. **How do I justify text so it lines up with both margins?**

    If you have a flat-panel screen, you could try scissors and glue. Or just use the `text-align` CSS style like this: `style="text-align: justify"`.

21. **How do I publicize my site, and how do I find advertisers for my site?**

    The first section of Hour 22, "Helping People Find Your Web Pages," will help some, but mostly you'll need to come up with your own marketing/PR plan tailored to your specific situation.

    There are a number of Web advertising services and companies that will pay independent Web publishers like you to run ads or affiliate with them in other potentially profitable ways. Most pay you a small amount each time a visitor clicks one of their ads. (See `http://www.sitecash.com/guide.htm` for some possibilities.)

22. **How do I create HTML pages or links within email messages?**

    Just type regular HTML like you would to make a Web page. Most advanced email programs nowadays (especially those bundled with Microsoft Internet Explorer and Netscape Navigator) allow you to create and view mail in HTML. You format it just as you would a document—no HTML experience required. Generally speaking, if a Web address is preceded by `http://` in an email, most email programs will automatically convert it into a link.

23. **How do I open a link in a new window?**

    Use `target="_blank"` in your `a href` link tag.

24. **How do I link to a database and let people search my site?**

    You'll probably need to give a software company some money for a good answer to that one. More than likely your Web hosting service already supports a particular kind of database, and might be able to provide you with guidance for building pages that are capable of accessing a database.

APPENDIX B

HTML Learning Resources on the Internet

General HTML and XHTML Information

The *24-Hour HTML Café*—the companion site to *Sams Teach Yourself HTML 4 in 24 Hours*, 6th Edition, including an online version of this appendix:

```
http://www.24hourHTMLcafe.com/
```

The World Wide Web Consortium (W3C):

```
http://www.w3.org/
```

The Compendium of HTML Elements:

```
http://www.htmlcompendium.org/
```

Microsoft Internet Explorer Web browser:

http://www.microsoft.com/windows/ie/

Netscape DevEdge Online:

http://devedge.netscape.com/

The HTML Writer's Guild:

http://www.hwg.org/

The Web Developer's Virtual Library:

http://www.wdvl.com/

XHTML.org:

http://www.xhtml.org/

Wireless Developer Network—Wireless Web pages:

http://www.wirelessdevnet.com/

Web Page Design

Creating Graphics for the Web:

http://www.widearea.co.uk/designer/

The WDVL Style Guide:

http://www.wdvl.com/Authoring/Style/Guides/WDVL.html

Web Pages That Suck:

http://www.webpagesthatsuck.com/

HTML Help (Web Design Group):

http://www.htmlhelp.com/

Software

Paint Shop Pro—A highly recommended Windows graphics and animation editor:

http://www.jasc.com/

GIF Construction Set—Another alternative for creating animated graphics:

http://www.mindworkshop.com/alchemy/gcsdemo.html

Adobe Photoshop Elements:

http://www.adobe.com/products/photoshopel/main.html

Mapedit— A Tool for Windows and X11 for Creating Imagemap Map Files:

http://www.boutell.com/mapedit/

Shareware.com—Best source for almost any type of free or inexpensive software for all types of computers:

http://shareware.cnet.com/

WinSite Windows Software Archive:

http://www.winsite.com/

Graphics

Barry's Clip Art Server:

http://www.barrysclipart.com/

216-color square:

http://www59.metronet.com/colors/

Color Triplet Chart:

http://quasar.unl.edu/tutorials/rgb.html

Microsoft Design Gallery Live:

http://dgl.microsoft.com/

B

Multimedia and Virtual Reality

Sound Central—Free sound files in a variety of formats:

http://www.soundcentral.com/

MIDIworld—Music files:

http://www.midiworld.com/

Stock Video/Film Footage:

http://www.cinema-sites.com/Cinema_Sites_PROD4.html

RealAudio and RealVideo:

http://www.real.com/

Windows Media:

http://www.windowsmedia.com/

Apple QuickTime:

http://www.apple.com/quicktime/

Macromedia's Shockwave Player:

http://www.macromedia.com/

Macromedia's Flash Player:

http://www.macromedia.com/

Multimedia Authoring:

http://www.mcli.dist.maricopa.edu/authoring/

The VRML Repository:

http://www.web3d.org/vrml/vrml.htm

Advanced Developer Resources

Webreference—Tutorials and references to HTML and related technologies:

http://www.webreference.com/

Netscape's JavaScript Guide:

http://developer.netscape.com/docs/manuals/communicator/jsguide4/index.htm

JavaScript.com—The Definitive JavaScript Resource:

http://www.javascript.com/

Developer.com Resource Directories:

http://www.developer.com/directories/

Microsoft Developer Network (MSDN) Developer Network

http://msdn.microsoft.com/

Search Engine Submission Tips:

http://searchenginewatch.com/webmasters/index.html

The TrueDoc Web Typography Center:

`http://www.truedoc.com/webpages/intro/`

Microsoft's TrueType Typography Pages:

`http://www.microsoft.com/truetype/`

HTML Validators

HTML-Kit and HTML Tidy—Web page editor that also converts to XHTML 1:

`http://www.chami.com/html-kit/`

Htmlchek—Checks compatibility with older HTML 2 and 3 standards:

`http://uts.cc.utexas.edu/~churchh/htmlchek.html`

Weblint—Paid-subscription HTML validation service:

`http://www.unipress.com/cgi-bin/WWWeblint`

Directories with HTML Information

HotWired's WebMonkey:

`http://hotwired.lycos.com/webmonkey/`

HTML Goodies:

`http://www.htmlgoodies.com/`

Yahoo! World Wide Web:

`http://www.yahoo.com/Computers/Internet/World_Wide_Web/`

Cool Site of the Day:

`http://cool.infi.net/`

B

Web Site Services

The List—Internet Service Providers Buyer's Guide:

`http://thelist.internet.com/`

freedback.com—Free form processing service:

`http://www.freedback.com/`

GuestPage—free guestbook service:

`http://www.guestpage.com/`

The Counter—Free Web counter/tracker:

`http://www.thecounter.com/`

Affiliate Guide—Info on companies that pay you to promote them on your site:

`http://www.sitecash.com/guide.htm`

TrainXchange—Advertise your site/exchange ads with other sites:

`http://www.ntwp.net/trainxchange/`

Microsoft bCentral Submit It!—Register Your pages with hundreds of search sites, paid service:

`http://www.submit-it.com/`

Open Directory Project—The largest, most comprehensive human-edited directory of the Web:

`http://dmoz.org/about.html`

Free Web Site Hosting

Yahoo! Geocities:

`http://geocities.yahoo.com/`

Angelfire:

`http://www.angelfire.lycos.com/`

Cybercities:

`http://www.cybercities.com/`

Tripod:

`http://www.tripod.lycos.com/`

Appendix C

Complete HTML 4 and XHTML 1 Quick Reference

HTML 4 is an ambitious attempt to meet the needs of Web developers worldwide, both casual and professional. XHTML 1 is a reformulation of HTML 4 as an XML application, allowing extensions to the language to be more easily defined and implemented. This appendix provides a quick reference to all the elements and attributes of HTML 4 and XHTML 1.

This appendix is based upon the information provided in the *HTML 4.0 W3C Recommendation*, revised in December, 1999, and the *XHTML 1.0 W3C Recommendation*, revised in January, 2000. The latest versions of these standards can be found at the World Wide Web Consortium (W3C) Web site at `http://www.w3.org/`.

Your obvious concern might be why this book is focused on such out-of-date technologies. The answer is that the technologies supported by the latest Web browsers are always a few years behind the work of the W3C. Think of the W3C as the long-range architects of the Web, while the Web designers (you) and browser vendors are the builders in the field who use only tried and true technologies.

The W3C is already busy working on XHTML 2, as well as a newer version of HTML. However, both of these technologies are still at least a year or more away from being supported in popular Web browsers. Just as you wouldn't want to take a pill that the FDC hadn't put through rigorous testing, neither would you want to adopt a Web technology that wasn't carefully designed.

To make the information readily accessible, this appendix organizes HTML elements by their function in the following order:

- Structure
- Text phrases and paragraphs
- Text font elements
- Lists
- Links
- Tables
- Frames
- Embedded content
- Style
- Forms
- Scripts

The elements are listed alphabetically within each section, and the following information is presented:

- Usage—A general description of the element
- Start/End Tag—Indicates whether these tags are required, optional, or illegal

- Attributes—Lists the attributes of the element with a short description of their effect
- Empty—Indicates whether the element can be empty
- Notes—Relates any special considerations when using the element and indicates whether the element is new, deprecated, or obsolete

NEW TERM   Several elements and attributes have been *deprecated*, which means they have been outdated by the current HTML version, and you should avoid using them. The same or similar functionality is provided by using new features.

Following this, the common attributes and intrinsic events are summarized.

> HTML 4 reorganized several fundamental attributes that apply to a significant number of elements. These are referred to within each element listing as core, i18n, and events. Flip ahead to the end of this appendix to see the specific attributes associated with each of these attribute groups.

Structure

HTML relies on several elements to provide structure to a document (as opposed to structuring the text within) as well as provide information that is used by the browser or search engines.

<bdo>...</bdo>

Usage	The bidirectional algorithm element used to selectively turn off the default text direction.
Start/End Tag	Required/Required.
Attributes	core.
	lang="..." The language of the document.
	dir="..." The text direction (ltr, rtl). Mandatory attribute.
Empty	No.
Notes	Strict DTD.

C

 Hour 23 briefly covered DTDs (Document Type Definitions), which are used to describe what kind of XML language a particular XML document is based upon, such as XHTML.

There are three versions of HTML 4/XHTML 1: Strict (pure HTML 4), Transitional (elements within the Strict DTD plus additional elements held over from HTML 3.2), and Frameset (Transitional plus frames). Each one relies upon a DTD to specify which elements and attributes are to be used, and the DTD is noted in this reference for each HTML element.

`<body>...</body>`

Usage	Contains the document's content.
Start/End Tag	Optional/Optional.
Attributes	`core`, `i18n`, `events`.
	`background="..."` Deprecated. URL for the background image.
	`bgcolor="..."` Deprecated. Sets background color.
	`text="..."` Deprecated. Text color.
	`link="..."` Deprecated. Link color.
	`vlink="..."` Deprecated. Visited link color.
	`alink="..."` Deprecated. Active link color.
	`onload="..."` Intrinsic event triggered when the document loads.
	`onunload="..."` Intrinsic event triggered when document unloads.
Empty	No.
Notes	Strict DTD. There can be only one `<body>`, and it must follow the `<head>`. The `<body>` element can be replaced by a `<frameset>` element. The presentational attributes are deprecated in favor of setting these values with style sheets.

Comments <!-- ... -->

Usage	Used to insert notes or scripts that are not displayed by the browser.
Start/End Tag	Required/Required.
Attributes	None.
Empty	Yes.
Notes	Comments are not restricted to one line and can be any length. The end tag is not required to be on the same line as the start tag.

<div>...</div>

Usage	The division element is used to add structure to a block of text.
Start/End Tag	Required/Required.
Attributes	core, i18n, events.
	align="..." Deprecated. Controls alignment (left, center, right, justify).

 You will notice that the oft-used align attribute has been deprecated. This affects a large number of elements whose rendered position was controlled by setting the alignment to a suitable value, such as right or center. Also deprecated is the <center> element. The W3C strongly encourages users to begin using style sheets to modify the visual formatting of an HTML document.

C

Empty	No.
Notes	Strict DTD. Cannot be used within a p element. The align attribute is deprecated in favor of controlling alignment through style sheets.

<!doctype...>

Usage	Version information appears on the first line of an HTML document and is an SGML declaration rather than an element.

`<h1>`...`</h1>` Through `<h6>`...`</h6>`

Usage	The six headings (h1 is uppermost, or most important) are used in the body to structure information in a hierarchical fashion.
Start/End Tag	Required/Required.
Attributes	core, i18n, events.
	align="..." Deprecated. Controls alignment (left, center, right, justify).
Empty	No.
Notes	Strict DTD. Visual browsers will display the size of the headings in relation to their importance, `<h1>` being the largest and `<h6>` the smallest. The align attribute is deprecated in favor of controlling alignment through style sheets.

`<head>`...`</head>`

Usage	This is the document header and contains other elements that provide information to users and search engines.
Start/End Tag	Optional/Optional.
Attributes	i18n.
	profile="..." URL specifying the location of meta data.
Empty	No.
Notes	Strict DTD. There can be only one `<head>` per document. It must follow the opening `<html>` tag and precede the `<body>`.

`<hr />`

Usage	Horizontal rules are used to separate sections of a Web page.
Start/End Tag	Required/Illegal.

Attributes	core, events, i18n.
	align="..." Deprecated. Controls alignment (left, center, right, justify).
	noshade="..." Deprecated. Displays the rule as a solid color.
	size="..." Deprecated. The size of the rule.
	width="..." Deprecated. The width of the rule.
Empty	Yes.
Notes	Strict DTD.

`<html>...</html>`

Usage	The html element contains the entire document.
Start/End Tag	Optional/Optional.
Attributes	i18n.
	version="..." Deprecated. URL of the document type definition specifying the HTML version used to create the document.
Empty	No.
Notes	Strict DTD. The version information is duplicated in the `<!doctype...>` declaration and is therefore not essential.

`<meta />`

Usage	Provides information about the document.
Start/End Tag	Required/Illegal.
Attributes	i18n.
	http-equiv="..." HTTP response header name.
	name="..." Name of the meta information.
	content="..." Content of the meta information.
	scheme="..." Assigns a scheme to interpret the meta data.

C

Empty	Yes.
Notes	Strict DTD.

`<span>...</span>`

Usage	Organizes the document by defining a span of text.
Start/End Tag	Required/Required.
Attributes	core, i18n, events.
Empty	No.
Notes	Strict DTD. This element is new to HTML 4.

`<title>...</title>`

Usage	This is the name you give your Web page. The `<title>` element is located in the `<head>` element and is displayed in the browser window title bar.
Start/End Tag	Required/Required.
Attributes	i18n.
Empty	No.
Notes	Strict DTD. Only one title allowed per document.

Text Phrases and Paragraphs

Text phrases (or blocks) can be structured to suit a specific purpose, such as creating a paragraph. This should not be confused with modifying the formatting of the text.

`<abbr>...</abbr>`

Usage	Used to define abbreviations.
Start/End Tag	Required/Required.
Attributes	core, i18n, events.
Empty	No.

| Notes | Strict DTD. This element is new to HTML 4. The material enclosed by the tag is the abbreviated form, whereas the long form is defined by attributes within the tag. |

`<acronym>...</acronym>`

Usage	Used to define acronyms.
Start/End Tag	Required/Required.
Attributes	`core, i18n, events.`
Empty	No.
Notes	Strict DTD. This element is new to HTML 4.

`<address>...</address>`

Usage	Provides a special format for author or contact information.
Start/End Tag	Required/Required.
Attributes	`core, i18n, events.`
Empty	No.
Notes	Strict DTD. The ` ` element is commonly used inside the `<address>` element to break the lines of an address.

`<blockquote>...</blockquote>`

Usage	Used to display long quotations.
Start/End Tag	Required/Required.
Attributes	`core, i18n, events.`
	`cite="..."` The URL of the quoted text.
Empty	No.
Notes	Strict DTD.

C

`<br />`

Usage	Forces a line break.
Start/End Tag	Required/Illegal.
Attributes	`core`, `i18n`, `events`.
	`clear="..."` Deprecated. Sets the location where next line begins after a floating object (`none`, `left`, `right`, `all`).
Empty	Yes.
Notes	Strict DTD.

`<cite>...</cite>`

Usage	Cites a reference.
Start/End Tag	Required/Required.
Attributes	`core`, `i18n`, `events`.
Empty	No.
Notes	Strict DTD.

`<code>...</code>`

Usage	Identifies a code fragment for display.
Start/End Tag	Required/Required.
Attributes	`core`, `i18n`, `events`.
Empty	No.
Notes	Strict DTD.

`<del>...</del>`

Usage	Shows text as having been deleted from the document since the last change.
Start/End Tag	Required/Required.

Attributes	core, i18n, events.
	cite="..." The URL of a linked document explaining the change.
	datetime="..." Indicates the date and time of the change.
Empty	No.
Notes	Strict DTD. This element is new to HTML 4.

`<dfn>...</dfn>`

Usage	Defines an enclosed term.
Start/End Tag	Required/Required.
Attributes	core, i18n, events.
Empty	No.
Notes	Strict DTD.

`<h1>...</h1>—<h6>...</h6>`

Usage	Text heading.
Start/End Tag	Required/Required.
Attributes	core, i18n, events.
Empty	No.
Notes	Strict DTD.

`<ins>...</ins>`

Usage	Shows text as having been inserted in the document since the last change.
Start/End Tag	Required/Required.
Attributes	core, i18n, events.
	cite="..." The URL of a linked document explaining the change.

C

datetime="..."   Indicates the date and time of the change.

Empty	No.
Notes	Strict DTD. This element is new to HTML 4.

\<kbd\>...\</kbd\>

Usage	Indicates text a user would type.
Start/End Tag	Required/Required.
Attributes	core, i18n, events.
Empty	No.
Notes	Strict DTD.

\<p\>...\</p\>

Usage	Defines a paragraph.
Start/End Tag	Required/Optional.
Attributes	core, i18n, events.
	align="..." Deprecated. Controls alignment (left, center, right, justify).
Empty	No.
Notes	Strict DTD.

\<pre\>...\</pre\>

Usage	Displays preformatted text.
Start/End Tag	Required/Required.
Attributes	core, i18n, events.
	width="..." Deprecated. The width of the formatted text.
Empty	No.
Notes	Strict DTD.

`<q>...</q>`

Usage	Used to display short quotations that do not require paragraph breaks.
Start/End Tag	Required/Required.
Attributes	core, i18n, events.
	cite="..." The URL of the quoted text.
Empty	No.
Notes	Strict DTD. This element is new to HTML 4.

`<samp>...</samp>`

Usage	Identifies sample output.
Start/End Tag	Required/Required.
Attributes	core, i18n, events.
Empty	No.
Notes	Strict DTD.

`<strong>...</strong>`

Usage	Stronger emphasis.
Start/End Tag	Required/Required.
Attributes	core, i18n, events.
Empty	No.
Notes	Strict DTD.

C

`<sub>...</sub>`

Usage	Creates subscript.
Start/End Tag	Required/Required.
Attributes	core, i18n, events.
Empty	No.
Notes	Strict DTD.

`<sup>...</sup>`

Usage	Creates superscript.
Start/End Tag	Required/Required.
Attributes	`core, i18n, events`.
Empty	No.
Notes	Strict DTD.

`<var>...</var>`

Usage	A variable.
Start/End Tag	Required/Required.
Attributes	`core, i18n, events`.
Empty	No.
Notes	Strict DTD.

Text Formatting Elements

Text characteristics such as the size, weight, and style can be modified using these elements, but the HTML 4 specification encourages you to use style sheets instead (see Hours 14 and 15).

`<b>...</b>`

Usage	Bold text.
Start/End Tag	Required/Required.
Attributes	`core, i18n, events`.
Empty	No.
Notes	Strict DTD.

`<basefont />`

Usage	Sets the base font size.
Start/End Tag	Required/Illegal.

Attributes	`size="..."` Deprecated. The font size (1 through 7 or relative, which is +3).
	`color="..."` Deprecated. The font color.
	`face="..."` Deprecated. The font type.
Empty	Yes.
Notes	Transitional DTD. Deprecated in favor of style sheets.

`<big>...</big>`

Usage	Large text.
Start/End Tag	Required/Required.
Attributes	`core, i18n, events.`
Empty	No.
Notes	Strict DTD.

`<center>...</center>`

Usage	Centered text.
Start/End Tag	Required/Required.
Attributes	`core, i18n, events.`
Empty	No.
Notes	Transitional DTD. Deprecated.

`<font>...</font>`

Usage	Changes the font size and color.
Start/End Tag	Required/Required.
Attributes	`size="..."` Deprecated. The font size (1 through 7 or relative, which is +3).
	`color="..."` Deprecated. The font color.
	`face="..."` Deprecated. The font type.
Empty	No.
Notes	Transitional DTD. Deprecated in favor of style sheets.

C

`<i>...</i>`

Usage	Italicized text.
Start/End Tag	Required/Required.
Attributes	core, i18n, events.
Empty	No.
Notes	Strict DTD.

`<s>...</s>`

Usage	Strikethrough text.
Start/End Tag	Required/Required.
Attributes	core, i18n, events.
Empty	No.
Notes	Transitional DTD. Deprecated.

`<small>...</small>`

Usage	Small text.
Start/End Tag	Required/Required.
Attributes	core, i18n, events.
Empty	No.
Notes	Strict DTD.

`<strike>...</strike>`

Usage	Strikethrough text.
Start/End Tag	Required/Required.
Attributes	core, i18n, events.
Empty	No.
Notes	Transitional DTD. Deprecated.

<tt>...</tt>

Usage	Teletype (or monospaced) text.
Start/End Tag	Required/Required.
Attributes	core, i18n, events.
Empty	No.
Notes	Strict DTD.

<u>...</u>

Usage	Underlined text.
Start/End Tag	Required/Required.
Attributes	core, i18n, events.
Empty	No.
Notes	Transitional DTD. Deprecated.

Lists

You can organize text into a more structured outline by creating lists. Lists can be nested.

<dd>...</dd>

Usage	The definition description used in a <dl> (definition list) element.
Start/End Tag	Required/Optional.
Attributes	core, i18n, events.
Empty	No.
Notes	Strict DTD. Can contain block-level content, such as the <p> element.

C

<dir>...</dir>

Usage	Creates a multi-column directory list.
Start/End Tag	Required/Required.

Attributes	core, i18n, events.
	compact="compact" Deprecated. Compacts the displayed list.
Empty	No.
Notes	Transitional DTD. Must contain at least one list item. This element is deprecated in favor of the <ul> (unordered list) element.

<dl>...</dl>

Usage	Creates a definition list.
Start/End Tag	Required/Required.
Attributes	core, i18n, events.
	compact="compact" Deprecated. Compacts the displayed list.
Empty	No.
Notes	Strict DTD. Must contain at least one <dt> or <dd> element in any order.

<dt>...</dt>

Usage	The definition term (or label) used within a <dl> (definition list) element.
Start/End Tag	Required/Optional.
Attributes	core, i18n, events.
Empty	No.
Notes	Strict DTD. Must contain text (which can be modified by text markup elements) .

<li>...</li>

Usage	Defines a list item within a list.
Start/End Tag	Required/Optional.

Attributes	core, i10n, events.
	type="..." Deprecated. Changes the numbering style (1, a, A, i, I), ordered lists, or bullet style (disc, square, circle) in unordered lists.
	value="..." Deprecated. Sets the numbering to the given integer beginning with the current list item.
Empty	No.
Notes	Strict DTD.

`<menu>...</menu>`

Usage	Creates a single-column menu list.
Start/End Tag	Required/Required.
Attributes	core, i18n, events.
	compact="compact" Deprecated. Compacts the displayed list.
Empty	No.
Notes	Transitional DTD. Must contain at least one list item. This element is deprecated in favor of the `<ul>` (unordered list) element.

`<ol>...</ol>`

Usage	Creates an ordered list.
Start/End Tag	Required/Required.
Attributes	core, i18n, events.
	type="..." Deprecated. Sets the numbering style (1, a, A, i, I).
	compact Deprecated. Compacts the displayed list.
	start="..." Deprecated. Sets the starting number to the chosen integer.
Empty	No.
Notes	Strict DTD. Must contain at least one list item.

C

`<ul>...</ul>`

Usage	Creates an unordered list.
Start/End Tag	Required/Required.
Attributes	`core`, `i18n`, `events`.
	`type="..."` Deprecated. Sets the bullet style (`disc`, `square`, `circle`).
	`compact="compact"` Deprecated. Compacts the displayed list.
Empty	No.
Notes	Strict DTD. Must contain at least one list item.

Links

Hyperlinking is fundamental to HTML. These elements enable you to link to other documents, other locations within a document, or external files.

`<a>...</a>`

Usage	Used to define links and anchors.
Start/End Tag	Required/Required.
Attributes	`core`, `i18n`, `events`.
	`charset="..."` Character encoding of the resource.
	`name="..."` Defines an anchor.
	`href="..."` The URL of the linked resource.
	`target="..."` Determines where the resource will be displayed (user-defined name, `_blank`, `_parent`, `_self`, `_top`).
	`rel="..."` Forward link types.
	`rev="..."` Reverse link types.
	`shape="..."` Enables you to define client-side imagemaps using defined shapes (`default`, `rect`, `circle`, `poly`).

coords-"..." Sets the size of the shape using pixel or percentage lengths.

Empty	No.
Notes	Strict DTD.

`<base />`

Usage	All other URLs in the document are resolved against this location.
Start/End Tag	Required/Illegal.
Attributes	href="..." The URL of the linked resource.
	target="..." Determines where the resource will be displayed (user-defined name, _blank, _parent, _self, _top).
Empty	Yes.
Notes	Strict DTD. Located in the document `<head>`.

`<link />`

Usage	Defines the relationship between a link and a resource.
Start/End Tag	Required/Illegal.
Attributes	core, i18n, events.
	charset="..." The character encoding of the resource.
	href="..." The URL of the resource.
	rel="..." The forward link types.
	rev="..." The reverse link types.
	type="..." The Internet content type.
	media="..." Defines the destination medium (screen, print, projection, braille, speech, all).
	target="..." Determines where the resource will be displayed (user-defined name, _blank, _parent, _self, _top).

C

Empty	Yes.
Notes	Strict DTD. Located in the document `<head>`.

Tables

Tables are meant to display data in a tabular format. Before the introduction of HTML 4, tables were widely used for page layout purposes, but with the advent of style sheets, this is being discouraged by the W3C.

`<caption>...</caption>`

Usage	Displays a table caption.
Start/End Tag	Required/Required.
Attributes	`core, i18n, events.`
	`align="..."` Deprecated. Controls alignment (`left, center, right, justify`).
Empty	No.
Notes	Strict DTD. Optional.

`<col />`

Usage	Groups individual columns within column groups in order to share attribute values.
Start/End Tag	Required/Illegal.
Attributes	`core, i18n, events.`
	`span="..."` The number of columns the group contains.
	`width="..."` The column width as a percentage, pixel value, or minimum value.
	`align="..."` Horizontally aligns the contents of cells (`left, center, right, justify, char`).
	`char="..."` Sets a character on which the column aligns.

	`charoff="..."` Offset to the first alignment character on a line.
	`valign="..."` Vertically aligns the contents of a cell (`top`, `middle`, `bottom`, `baseline`).
Empty	Yes.
Notes	Strict DTD.

`<colgroup>...</colgroup>`

Usage	Defines a column group.
Start/End Tag	Required/Optional.
Attributes	`core, i18n, events.`
	`span="..."` The number of columns in a group.
	`width="..."` The width of the columns.
	`align="..."` Horizontally aligns the contents of cells (`left`, `center`, `right`, `justify`, `char`).
	`char="..."` Sets a character on which the column aligns.
	`charoff="..."` Offset to the first alignment character on a line.
	`valign="..."` Vertically aligns the contents of a cell (`top`, `middle`, `bottom`, `baseline`).
Empty	No.
Notes	Strict DTD. This element is new to HTML 4.

`<table>...</table>`

Usage	Creates a table.
Start/End Tag	Required/Required.
Attributes	`core, i18n, events.`
	`align="..."` Deprecated. Controls alignment (`left`, `center`, `right`, `justify`).

C

`bgcolor="..."`   Deprecated. Sets the background color.

`width="..."`   Table width.

`cols="..."`   The number of columns.

`border="..."`   The width in pixels of a border around the table.

`frame="..."`   Sets the visible sides of a table (`void`, `above`, `below`, `hsides`, `lhs`, `rhs`, `vsides`, `box`, `border`).

`rules="..."`   Sets the visible rules within a table (`none`, `groups`, `rows`, `cols`, `all`).

`cellspacing="..."`   Spacing between cells.

`cellpadding="..."`   Spacing in cells.

`summary="..."`   Provides a text description of the table for accessibility purposes.

Empty	No.
Notes	Strict DTD.

<tbody>...</tbody>

Usage	Defines the table body.
Start/End Tag	Optional/Optional.
Attributes	`core`, `i18n`, `events`.

`align="..."`   Horizontally aligns the contents of cells (`left`, `center`, `right`, `justify`, `char`).

`char="..."`   Sets a character on which the column aligns.

`charoff="..."`   Offset to the first alignment character on a line.

`valign="..."`   Vertically aligns the contents of cells (`top`, `middle`, `bottom`, `baseline`).

Empty	No.
Notes	Strict DTD. This element is new to HTML 4.

`<td>...</td>`

Usage	Defines a cell's contents.
Start/End Tag	Required/Optional.
Attributes	`core`, `i18n`, `events`.

`abbr="..."` Abbreviated name.

`axis="..."` `axis` names listing row and column headers pertaining to the cell.

`nowrap="..."` Deprecated. Turns off text wrapping in a cell.

`bgcolor="..."` Deprecated. Sets the background color.

`rowspan="..."` The number of rows spanned by a cell.

`colspan="..."` The number of columns spanned by a cell.

`align="..."` Horizontally aligns the contents of cells (`left`, `center`, `right`, `justify`, `char`).

`char="..."` Sets a character on which the column aligns.

`charoff="..."` Offset to the first alignment character on a line.

`valign="..."` Vertically aligns the contents of cells (`top`, `middle`, `bottom`, `baseline`).

`headers="..."` Header information for a cell.

`scope="..."` Indicates whether a cell provides header information for other cells.

`width="..."` Deprecated. The width of a cell.

`height="..."` Deprecated. The width of a cell.

Empty	No.
Notes	Strict DTD.

C

`<tfoot>...</tfoot>`

Usage	Defines the table footer.
Start/End Tag	Required/Optional.
Attributes	`core, i18n, events`.

`align="..."` Horizontally aligns the contents of cells (`left, center, right, justify, char`).

`char="..."` Sets a character on which the column aligns.

`charoff="..."` Offset to the first alignment character on a line.

`valign="..."` Vertically aligns the contents of cells (`top, middle, bottom, baseline`).

Empty	No.
Notes	Strict DTD. This element is new to HTML 4.

`<th>...</th>`

Usage	Defines the cell contents of the table header.
Start/End Tag	Required/Optional.
Attributes	`core, i18n, events`.

`axis="..."` Abbreviated name.

`axes="..."` `axis` names listing row and column headers pertaining to the cell.

`nowrap="..."` Deprecated. Turns off text wrapping in a cell.

`bgcolor="..."` Deprecated. Sets the background color.

`rowspan="..."` The number of rows spanned by a cell.

`colspan="..."` The number of columns spanned by a cell.

`align="..."` Horizontally aligns the contents of cells (`left, center, right, justify, char`).

`char="..."`   Sets a character on which the column aligns.

`charoff="..."`   Offset to the first alignment character on a line.

`valign="..."`   Vertically aligns the contents of cells (`top`, `middle`, `bottom`, `baseline`).

`headers="..."`   Header information for a cell.

`scope="..."`   Indicates whether a cell provides header information for other cells.

`width="..."`   Deprecated. The width of a cell.

`height="..."`   Deprecated. The width of a cell.

Empty	No.
Notes	Strict DTD.

`<thead>...</thead>`

Usage	Defines the table header.
Start/End Tag	Required/Optional.
Attributes	`core, i18n, events.`

`align="..."`   Horizontally aligns the contents of cells (`left, center, right, justify, char`).

`char="..."`   Sets a character on which the column aligns.

`charoff="..."`   Offset to the first alignment character on a line.

`valign="..."`   Vertically aligns the contents of cells (`top, middle, bottom, baseline`).

Empty	No.
Notes	Strict DTD. This element is new to HTML 4.

C

<tr>...</tr>

Usage	Defines a row of table cells.
Start/End Tag	Required/Optional.
Attributes	`core`, `i18n`, `events`.

`align="..."`　Horizontally aligns the contents of cells (`left`, `center`, `right`, `justify`, `char`).

`char="..."`　Sets a character on which the column aligns.

`charoff="..."`　Offset to the first alignment character on a line.

`valign="..."`　Vertically aligns the contents of cells (`top`, `middle`, `bottom`, `baseline`).

`bgcolor="..."`　Deprecated. Sets the background color.

Empty	No.
Notes	Strict DTD.

Frames

Frames create new "panels" in the Web browser window that are used to display content from different source documents; frames allow you to build a Web page composed of several other Web pages.

<frame />

Usage	Defines a frame.
Start/End Tag	Required/Illegal.
Attributes	`core`.

`name="..."`　The name of a frame.

`src="..."`　The source to be displayed in a frame.

`frameborder="..."`　Toggles the border between frames (`0`, `1`).

marginwidth="..." Sets the space between the frame border and content.

marginheight="..." Sets the space between the frame border and content.

noresize Disables sizing.

scrolling="..." Determines scrollbar presence (auto, yes, no).

longdesc="..." A URL to a long description of the frame; for browsers without frames.

Empty	Yes.
Notes	Frameset DTD. This element is new to HTML 4.

<frameset>...</frameset>

Usage	Defines the layout of frames within a window.
Start/End Tag	Required/Required.
Attributes	core.

rows="..." The number and size/proportion of rows.

cols="..." The number and size/proportion of columns.

onload="..." The intrinsic event triggered when the document loads.

onunload="..." The intrinsic event triggered when the document unloads.

Empty	No.
Notes	Frameset DTD. This element is new to HTML 4. Framesets can be nested.

<iframe>...</iframe>

Usage	Creates an inline frame.
Start/End Tag	Required/Required.

C

Attributes   `core`.

                                    `name="..."` The name of the frame.

                                    `src="..."` The source to be displayed in a frame.

                                    `frameborder="..."` Toggles the border between frames
                                    (`0`, `1`).

                                    `marginwidth="..."` Sets the space between the frame
                                    border and content.

                                    `marginheight="..."` Sets the space between the frame
                                    border and content.

                                    `scrolling="..."` Determines scrollbar presence (`auto`,
                                    `yes`, `no`).

                                    `align="..."` Deprecated. Controls alignment (`left`,
                                    `center`, `right`, `justify`).

                                    `height="..."` Height.

                                    `width="..."` Width.

                                    `longdesc="..."` A URL to a long description of the
                                    frame; for browsers without frames.

Empty   No.

Notes   Transitional DTD. This element is new to HTML 4.

`<noframes>...</noframes>`

Usage   Alternative content when frames are not supported.

Start/End Tag   Required/Required.

Attributes   `core`, `i18n`, `events`.

Empty   No.

Notes   Frameset DTD. This element is new to
                                    HTML 4.

Embedded Content

NEW TERM Also called *inclusions*, embedded content applies to images, imagemaps, Java applets, and other multimedia or programmed content that is placed in a Web page to provide additional functionality.

`<applet>...</applet>`

Usage	Includes a Java applet.
Start/End Tag	Required/Required.
Attributes	`core`.
	`codebase="..."` The URL base for the applet.
	`archive="..."` Identifies the resources to be pre-loaded.
	`code="..."` The applet class file.
	`object="..."` The serialized applet file.
	`alt="..."` Displays text while loading.
	`name="..."` The name of the applet.
	`width="..."` The height of the displayed applet.
	`height="..."` The width of the displayed applet.
	`align="..."` Deprecated. Controls alignment (`left`, `center`, `right`, `justify`).
	`hspace="..."` The horizontal space separating the image from other content.
	`vspace="..."` The vertical space separating the image from other content.
Empty	No.
Notes	Transitional DTD. Applet is deprecated in favor of the `<object>` element.

C

`<area />`

Usage	The `<area>` element is used to define links and anchors.
Start/End Tag	Required/Illegal.
Attributes	core, i18n, events.

`shape="..."` Enables you to define client-side imagemaps using defined shapes (default, rect, circle, poly).

`coords="..."` Sets the size of the shape using pixel or percentage lengths.

`href="..."` The URL of the linked resource.

`target="..."` Determines where the resource will be displayed (user-defined name, _blank, _parent, _self, _top).

`nohref="..."` Indicates that the region has no action.

`alt="..."` Displays alternative text.

`onfocus="..."` The event that occurs when the element receives focus.

`onblur="..."` The event that occurs when the element loses focus.

Empty	Yes.
Notes	Strict DTD.

`<img />`

Usage	Includes an image in the document.
Start/End Tag	Required/Illegal.
Attributes	core, i18n, events.

`src="..."` The URL of the image.

`alt="..."` Alternative text to display.

`align="..."` Deprecated. Controls alignment (left, center, right, justify).

height="..."   The height of the image.

width="..."   The width of the image.

border="..."   Border width.

hspace="..."   The horizontal space separating the image from other content.

vspace="..."   The vertical space separating the image from other content.

usemap="..."   The URL to a client-side imagemap.

ismap="ismap"   Identifies a server-side imagemap.

longdesc="..."   A URL to a long description of the image; for browsers that don't display images.

Empty	Yes.
Notes	Strict DTD.

<map>...</map>

Usage	When used with the <area> element, creates a client-side imagemap.
Start/End Tag	Required/Required.
Attributes	core, i18n, events.

name="..."   The name of the imagemap to be created.

Empty	No.
Notes	Strict DTD.

<object>...</object>

Usage	Includes an object.
Start/End Tag	Required/Required.
Attributes	core, i18n, events.

declare="declare"   A flag that declares but doesn't create an object.

classid="..."   The URL of the object's location.

C

`codebase="..."` The URL for resolving URLs specified by other attributes.

`data="..."` The URL to the object's data.

`type="..."` The Internet content type for data.

`codetype="..."` The Internet content type for the code.

`standby="..."` Show message while loading.

`align="..."` Deprecated. Controls alignment (`left`, `center`, `right`, `justify`).

`height="..."` The height of the object.

`width="..."` The width of the object.

`border="..."` Displays the border around an object.

`hspace="..."` The space between the sides of the object and other page content.

`vspace="..."` The space between the top and bottom of the object and other page content.

`usemap="..."` The URL to an imagemap.

`shapes=` Enables you to define areas to search for hyperlinks if the object is an image.

`name="..."` The URL to submit as part of a form.

Empty	No.
Notes	Strict DTD. This element is new to HTML 4.

`<param />`

Usage	Initializes an object.
Start/End Tag	Required/Illegal.
Attributes	`name="..."` Defines the parameter name.
	`value="..."` The value of the object parameter.
	`valuetype="..."` Defines the value type (`data`, `ref`, `object`).
	`type="..."` The Internet medium type.

Empty	Yes.
Notes	Strict DTD. This element is new to HTML 4.

Style

Style sheets (both inline and external) are incorporated into an HTML document through the use of the `<style>` element.

`<style>...</style>`

Usage	Creates an internal style sheet.
Start/End Tag	Required/Required.
Attributes	`i18n`.
	`type="..."` The Internet content type.
	`media="..."` Defines the destination medium (`screen`, `print`, `projection`, `braille`, `speech`, `all`).
	`title="..."` The title of the style.
Empty	No.
Notes	Strict DTD. Located in the `<head>` element.

Forms

 *Forms* create an interface for the user to select options, enter information, and return data to the Web server for processing.

`<button>...</button>`

Usage	Creates a button.
Start/End Tag	Required/Required.
Attributes	`core`, `i18n`, `events`.
	`name="..."` The button name.
	`value="..."` The value of the button.
	`type="..."` The button type (`button`, `submit`, `reset`).
	`disabled="..."` Sets the button state to disabled.

C

onfocus="..."   The event that occurs when the element receives focus.

onblur="..."   The event that occurs when the element loses focus.

Empty	No.
Notes	Strict DTD. This element is new to HTML 4.

<fieldset>...</fieldset>

Usage	Groups related controls.
Start/End Tag	Required/Required.
Attributes	core, i18n, events.
Empty	No.
Notes	Strict DTD. This element is new to HTML 4.

<form>...</form>

Usage	Creates a form that holds controls for user input.
Start/End Tag	Required/Required.
Attributes	core, i18n, events.

action="..."   The URL for the server action.

method="..."   The HTTP method (get, post). get is deprecated.

enctype="..."   Specifies the MIME (Internet media type).

onsubmit="..."   The intrinsic event that occurs when the form is submitted.

onreset="..."   The intrinsic event that occurs when the form is reset.

target="..."   Determines where the resource will be displayed (user-defined name, _blank, _parent, _self, _top).

accept="..." The list of content types acceptable by the server.

accept-charset="..." The list of character encodings.

| Empty | No. |
| Notes | Strict DTD. |

`<input />`

Usage	Defines controls used in forms.
Start/End Tag	Required/Illegal.
Attributes	core, i18n, events.

type="..." The type of input control (text, password, checkbox, radio, submit, reset, file, hidden, image, button).

name="..." The name of the control (required except for submit and reset).

value="..." The initial value of the control (required for radio and check boxes).

checked="checked" Sets the radio buttons to a checked state.

disabled="..." Disables the control.

readonly="..." For text password types.

size="..." The width of the control in pixels except for text and password controls, which are specified in number of characters.

maxlength="..." The maximum number of characters that can be entered.

src="..." The URL to an image control type.

alt="..." An alternative text description.

usemap="..." The URL to a client-side imagemap.

align="..." Deprecated. Controls alignment (left, center, right, justify).

C

onfocus="..."   The event that occurs when the element receives focus.

onblur="..."   The event that occurs when the element loses focus.

onselect="..."   Intrinsic event that occurs when the control is selected.

onchange="..."   Intrinsic event that occurs when the control is changed.

accept="..."   File types allowed for upload.

Empty	Yes.
Notes	Strict DTD.

`<isindex />`

Usage	Prompts the user for input.
Start/End Tag	Required/Illegal.
Attributes	core, i18n.

prompt="..."   Provides a prompt string for the input field.

Empty	Yes.
Notes	Transitional DTD. Deprecated.

`<label>...</label>`

Usage	Labels a control.
Start/End Tag	Required/Required.
Attributes	core, i18n, events.

for="..."   Associates a label with an identified control.

onfocus="..."   The event that occurs when the element receives focus.

onblur="..."   The event that occurs when the element loses focus.

Empty	No.
Notes	Strict DTD. This element is new to HTML 4.

`<legend>...</legend>`

Usage	Assigns a caption to a `fieldset`.
Start/End Tag	Required/Required.
Attributes	`core, i18n, events`.
	`align="..."` Deprecated. Controls alignment (`left, center, right, justify`).
Empty	No.
Notes	Strict DTD. This element is new to HTML 4.

`<optgroup>...</optgroup>`

Usage	Used to group form elements within a `<select>` element.
Start/End Tag	Required/Required.
Attributes	`core, i18n, events`.
	`disabled="disabled"` Not used.
	`label="..."` Defines a group label.
Empty	No.
Notes	Strict DTD. This element is new to HTML 4.

`<option>...</option>`

Usage	Specifies choices in a `<select>` element.
Start/End Tag	Required/Optional.
Attributes	`core, i18n, events`.
	`selected="selected"` Specifies whether the option is selected.
	`disabled="disabled"` Disables control.
	`label="..."` Defines a label for the group of options.

C

value="..."   The value submitted if a control is submitted.

Empty	No.
Notes	Strict DTD.

`<select>...</select>`

Usage	Creates choices for the user to select.
Start/End Tag	Required/Required.
Attributes	core, i18n, events.

name="..."   The name of the element.

size="..."   The width in number of rows.

multiple="multiple"   Allows multiple selections.

disabled="disabled"   Disables the control.

onfocus="..."   The event that occurs when the element receives focus.

onblur="..."   The event that occurs when the element
loses focus.

onselect="..."   Intrinsic event that occurs when the
control is selected.

onchange="..."   Intrinsic event that occurs when the
control is changed.

Empty	No.
Notes	Strict DTD.

`<textarea>...</textarea>`

Usage	Creates an area for user input with multiple lines.
Start/End Tag	Required/Required.
Attributes	core, i18n, events.

name="..."   The name of the control.

rows="..."   The width in number of rows.

cols-"..." The height in number of columns.

disabled="disabled" Disables the control.

readonly="readonly" Sets the displayed text to read-only status.

onfocus="..." The event that occurs when the element receives focus.

onblur="..." The event that occurs when the element loses focus.

onselect="..." Intrinsic event that occurs when the control is selected.

onchange="..." Intrinsic event that occurs when the control is changed.

Empty   No.

Notes   Strict DTD. Text to be displayed is placed within the start and end tags.

Scripts

Scripts make it possible to process data and perform other dynamic events. Scripts are included in Web pages thanks to the <script> element, which also identifies the specific scripting language being used (JavaScript, VBScript, and so on.).

<script>...</script>

Usage   The <script> element contains client-side scripts that are executed by the browser.

Start/End Tag Required/Required.

Attributes   type="..." Script language Internet content type.

language="..." Deprecated. The scripting language, deprecated in favor of the type attribute.

src="..." The URL for the external script.

defer="defer" Indicates that the script doesn't alter document content.

C

Empty	No.
Notes	Strict DTD. You can set the default scripting language in the `<meta />` element.

`<noscript>...</noscript>`

Usage	Provides alternative content for browsers unable to execute a script.
Start/End Tag	Required/Required.
Attributes	core, i18n, events.
Empty	No.
Notes	Strict DTD. This element is new to HTML 4.

Common Attributes and Events

Four attributes are abbreviated as core in the preceding sections. They are

- id="..."   A global identifier.
- class="..."   A list of classes separated by spaces.
- style="..."   Style information.
- title="..."   Provides more information for a specific element, as opposed to the `<title>` element, which entitles the entire Web page.
- accesskey="..."   Sets the keyboard shortcut used to access an element.
- tabindex="..."   Sets the tab order of an element.

Two attributes for internationalization (i18n) are abbreviated as i18n:

- lang="..."   The language identifier.
- dir="..."   The text direction (ltr, rtl).

The following intrinsic events are abbreviated events:

- onclick="..."   A pointing device (such as a mouse) was single-clicked.
- ondblclick="..."   A pointing device (such as a mouse) was double-clicked.
- onmousedown="..."   A mouse button was clicked and held down.
- onmouseup="..."   A mouse button that was clicked and held down was released.
- onmouseover="..."   A mouse moved the cursor over an object.

- `onmousemove="..."`   The mouse was moved.
- `onmouseout="..."`   A mouse moved the cursor off an object.
- `onkeypress="..."`   A key was pressed and released.
- `onkeydown="..."`   A key was pressed and held down.
- `onkeyup="..."`   A key that was pressed has been released.

C

APPENDIX **D**

Migrating from HTML to XHTML

Although the relationship between HTML and XHTML has been covered in several places throughout the book, I felt it would be beneficial to have all of the information in one place. This appendix serves as a reference for quickly obtaining the information regarding the differences between HTML 4 and XHTML 1, which are the primary two Web standards involved in Web page creation.

Differences Between XHTML 1 and HTML 4

XHTML 1 is a version of HTML 4 that plays by the more rigid rules of XML. Fortunately, most of the differences between XHTML and HTML don't dramatically impact the overall structure of HTML documents. Migrating an HTML document to XHTML is more a matter of cleaning and tightening up the code rather than converting it to a new language.

Following is a list of the primary differences between XHTML and HTML, with a focus on what XHTML requires that HTML doesn't:

- Element and attribute names must be in lowercase (`<a href="index.html">`)
- End tags are required for non-empty elements (`<p>Howdy!</p>`)
- Empty elements must consist of a start-tag/end-tag pair or an empty element (`<br />`)
- Attribute values must always be quoted (`href="index.html"`)
- Attribute names cannot be used without a value (`ismap="ismap"`)
- An XHTML namespace must be declared in the `html` element
- The `head` and `body` elements cannot be omitted
- The `title` element must be the first element in the `head` element
- Documents must use the `id` attribute to uniquely name elements on the page; the `name` attribute is deprecated in XHTML for this particular purpose

Based upon your newfound knowledge of XML, none of these differences should come as too much of a surprise. Fortunately, they are all pretty easy to find and fix in HTML documents, which makes the move from HTML to XHTML relatively straightforward.

XHTML and Document Validity

All XHTML documents must have a document type definition, or DTD, which is used to identify XHTML as the language for the Web page. Instead of developing a single DTD for XHTML, the W3C went a step further and developed three DTDs, which are all included in the XHTML specification. These DTDs provide varying levels of detail for XHTML, which result in three different classifications of XHTML documents. The idea is that you can use a more minimal XHTML DTD if you don't need to use certain XHTML language features, or you can use a more thorough DTD if you need additional features. The three XHTML DTDs are classified as follows, in order of increasing features:

- Strict—No HTML presentation elements are available (`font`, `table`, and so on.); style sheets must be used to format documents for display
- Transitional—HTML presentation elements are available for formatting documents
- Frameset—Frames are available, as well as HTML presentation elements

The Strict DTD is a minimal DTD that is used to create very clean XHTML documents without any presentation tags. Documents created from this DTD require style sheets in order to be formatted for display. The Transitional DTD builds on the Strict DTD by adding support for presentation tags. This DTD is useful in performing a quick conversion of HTML documents when you don't want to take the time to develop style sheets. The Frameset DTD is the broadest of the three DTDs, and includes support for creating Web pages with frames.

You must declare the DTD for all XHTML documents in a document type declaration at the top of the document. A Formal Public Identifier (FPI) is used in the document type declaration to reference one of the standard XHTML DTDs. Following is an example of how to declare the Strict DTD in a document type declaration:

```
<!DOCTYPE html PUBLIC "-//W3C//DTD XHTML 1.0 Strict//EN"
  "http://www.w3.org/TR/xhtml1/DTD/xhtml1-strict.dtd">
```

It isn't terribly important that you understand the details of the FPI in this code. The main point is that it identifies the Strict XHTML DTD. The Transitional DTD is specified using similar code, as the following example reveals:

```
<!DOCTYPE html PUBLIC "-//W3C//DTD XHTML 1.0 Transitional//EN"
  "http://www.w3.org/TR/xhtml1/DTD/xhtml1-transitional.dtd">
```

Finally, the Frameset DTD is specified with the following code, which shouldn't come as much of a surprise based on the two previous document type declarations:

```
<!DOCTYPE html PUBLIC "-//W3C//DTD XHTML 1.0 Frameset//EN"
  "http://www.w3.org/TR/xhtml1/DTD/xhtml1-frameset.dtd">
```

The significance of these three document type declarations is that you must place one of them at the top of every XHTML Web page that you create in order for it to qualify as a valid XHTML document. You will usually want to use the Transitional DTD unless your pages use frames, in which case you'll need the Frameset DTD. The Strict DTD is only for pages where you're completely relying on style sheets for the page formatting, which is fairly rare.

Declaring XHTML Namespaces

In addition to declaring an appropriate DTD in a document type declaration, a valid XHTML document must also declare an XHTML namespace in the html element. Following are the three XHTML namespaces, which are associated with the three DTDs you just learned about:

- Strict—http://www.w3.org/TR/xhtml1/strict
- Transitional—http://www.w3.org/TR/xhtml1/transitional
- Frameset—http://www.w3.org/TR/xhtml1/frameset

D

The xmlns namespace declaration attribute is used to declare an XHTML namespace in the html element. This namespace must match the DTD specified in the document type declaration. Following is an example of how to specify the strict namespace:

```
<html xmlns="http://www.w3.org/TR/xhtml1/strict">
...
</html>
```

Converting HTML Documents to XHTML

Although it's great to dream about the prospect of creating Web pages from scratch using XHTML, the reality is that you are likely to have HTML documents that you will want to convert to XHTML at some point in the future. Fortunately, it isn't too terribly difficult to bring HTML 4 documents up to par with the XHTML 1 specification. You've already learned about the ways in which XHTML documents differ from HTML documents. These differences are your guide to converting HTML to XHTML.

Following is a checklist to use as a guide while performing the conversion from HTML to XHTML:

1. Add a document type declaration that declares an appropriate XHTML DTD, usually the Transitional DTD
2. Declare an XHTML namespace in the html element that matches the DTD
3. Convert all element and attribute names to lowercase
4. Match every start tag with an end tag
5. Replace > with /> at the end of all empty tags
6. Enclose all attribute values in quotes (")
7. Make sure all elements and attributes are defined in the XHTML DTD declared in the document type declaration
8. Convert special characters to entity references; for example, " becomes " (see Table 24.1 in Hour 24 for more details)

The good news is that this book has already taught you good enough coding habits that steps 3 through 6 shouldn't be a problem. The remaining steps are then just a matter of placing the appropriate standard code in your pages. If you carry out each of these steps, you should arrive at a legitimate XHTML document that conforms to all of the rules of the XHTML 1 standard.

INDEX

Symbols

<> (angle brackets), 367
* (asterisk), 246
\ (backslash), 44
© (copyright), 99
{} (curly braces), 213
.. (double dot), 45
"" (double quotation marks), 264
= (equal sign), 303, 368
/ (forward slash), 44, 57, 367
. (period), 221
(pound sign), 109-111
? (question mark), 374
'' (quotation marks), 77
® (registered trademark), 99
; (semicolon), 265
'' (single quotation marks), 264
<? symbol, 374

--> tag, 340, 407
//--> tag, 267
<!--tag, 267, 340, 407
™ (trademark), 99
_ (underscore), 249

Numbers

3D Effects, Buttonize command (Effects menu), 263
3D Effects, Chisel command (Effects menu), 128
24-Hour HTML Café Web site, 19, 397
216-color square Web site, 399

A

<a> tag, 40-41, 106, 111, 249, 422-423
</a> tag, 106, 422-423
<a href> tag, 109-111, 145, 317
<a href> links, drive letters, 67
<a id> tag, 109
A tool, 128
<abbr> tag, 410
</abbr> tag, 410
About Us button, 334
absolute addresses, 44-45
absolute positioning, 217, 228-232
absolute value, 228
accessing files, Web servers, 63
accesskey attribute, 444
account names, 54

lang, 444
link, 111
loop, 320-321
marginheight, 253
marginwidth, 253
maxlength, 301
method, 297
multiple, 304
name, 106, 172, 246, 324
noresize, 253
OnClick, 290
onLoad, 270, 286
OnMouseOut, 263-267,
   290
OnMouseOver, 263-267,
   290
rows, 246, 305
rowspan, 200
scrolling, 253
selected, 304
shape, 173
size, 96, 301, 304
src, 283, 319
start, 83
style, 222, 280
tabindex, 444
target, 249
text alignment, 76
title, 444
type, 83, 301, 323
types, 323
usemap, 173-174
valign, 199
value, 305, 324
vlink, 111
vspace, 186
width, 173, 198, 319
XML, 368-370
xmlns, 450
audio. *See* **sound**
automatically loading, Web
   pages, 356-358
autostart attribute, 320-321

B

<b> tag, 92-94, 416
</b> tag, 92, 416
background attribute, 201
background banners,
   187-190
background color, 127,
   154-155
background property, 220
background tiles, 157-163
background-color property,
   219
backgrounds, HTML tables,
   201
backslash \, 44
backward compatibility,
   code, 324
banner ads, 267-270
banners
   background, 187-190
   creating, 126-129
   repeating, 187
   transparent, 188
bare-bone pages, 30
Barry's Clip Art Server
   Web site, 399
<base> tag, 423
<base /> tag, 359, 423
<basefont /> tag, 416-417
<bdo> tag, 405
</bdo> tag, 405
bgcolor, 155
bgcolor attribute, 201
<big> tag, 93, 417
</big> tag, 417
block value, 217
<blockquote> tag, 81, 411
</blockquote> tag, 411
Blue slider, 125
Blur command (Image
   menu), 162

Blur More filter, 162
Blur, Blur and Colors com-
   mand (Image menu), 162
<body> tag, 111, 154, 285,
   406
</body> tag, 406
boldface, 92-96
bookmarks, Web pages, 30
border attribute, 186, 196
border property, 218-219
border-bottom property,
   218-219
border-color property, 218
border-left property,
   218-219
border-right property,
   218-219
border-style property, 218
border-top property,
   218-219
border-width property, 218
borders
   frames, 251-255
   Web pages, 183-187
bottom property, 228
boxes, check, 302-303. *See*
   also **dialog boxes**
**
 tag, 31, 412**
<br clear="all" /> tag, 186
<br clear="left" /> tag, 186
<br clear="right" /> tag,
   186
**
 tag, 32**
browsers. *See* **Web browsers**
browsing Web, 12
bullets, HTML lists, 81-82
<button> tag, 437-438
</button> tag, 437-438
buttons
   About Us, 334
   Add File, 133
   Choose File, 29

columns, HTML table spans, 200

commands

Animation menu, Insert Frames, From File, 133

coded. *See* HTML tags

Colors menu

Adjust, Brightness/Contrast, 125, 162

Adjust, Gamma Correction, 125

Decrease Color Depth, 129, 132, 160

Set Palette Transparency, 160

View Palette Transparency, 160

Edit menu

Animation Properties, 135

Copy, 41, 55

Frame Properties, 134

Paste, 41, 56

Preferences, 29

Preferences, Appearance, 95

Effects menu

3D Effects, Buttonize, 263

3D Effects, Chisel, 128

Effect Browser, 129

Insert Image Transition, 136

Insert Text Effect, 136

File menu

Jasc Software Products, Launch Animation Shop, 133

New, 127

Open, 29

Open Page, 29

Preferences, General Program Preferences, 160

Publish Web, 58

Save As, 26-28, 109, 125, 130

Format menu, Make Plain Text, 26

HTML, viewing, 15

Image menu

Blur, 162

Blur, Blur and Colors, 162

Canvas Size, 127

Crop, 127

Effects, Buttonize, 128

Effects, Chisel, 128

Effects, Cutout, 128

Effects, drop Shadow, 128

Noise, Add, 162

Resize, 124

JavaScript, Web page links, 263

Selections menu, Convert to Seamless Pattern, 161

style sheets, viewing, 214

Tools menu

Internet Options, 28

Internet Options, Fonts, 95

Transfer menu, Upload, 62

View menu

Animation, 134

Normal Viewing (1:1), 124

Page Source, 35

Source, 35

comments

future preparations, 385

Web pages, 339-340

communication, digital, 380

comparisons, 447-448

compatibility

backward, 324

DHTML, 282-285

frames, 247

XHTML, 382

XML, 364

Compendium of HTML Elements Web site, 397

Composer (Netscape), 57

compression

graphics, 122

JPEGs, 125-126

Compression Factor setting, 126

computer multimedia, 315

computers, history, 379

ComputeTotals() function, 310

connections, Internet, 10

controls, input, 302-305

Convert to Seamless Pattern command (Selections menu), 161

converting

graphics to links, 145

HTML, 382-383

HTML to XHTML, 450

Cool Site of the Day Web site, 401

coordinates, imagemaps, 170-171

coords attribute, 173

Copy command (Edit menu), 41, 55

copyright (©), 99

corporate newsletters, 385

Counter (The) Web site, 402

counters

hit, Web sites, 395

Web pages, 393

Effects, Cutout, 128
Effects, Drop Shadow, 128
Noise, Add, 162
Resize, 124
imagemaps
client-side, 167, 172-174
coordinates, 170-171
creating, 170-172
defined, 167
hotspots, 170
JavaScript, 267
server-side, 167
text links, 174
when to use, 168, 170
images. *See* **graphics;**
imagemaps
<img /> tag, 144-146,
434-435
<img align="absbottom"/>
tag, 147
<img align="absmiddle"/>
tag, 147
<img align="bottom"/> tag,
147
<img align="center"/> tag,
147
<img align="left"/> tag, 146
<img align="middle"/> tag,
147
<img align="right"/> tag,
146
<img align="top"/> tag, 147
<img src> tag, 144
<img> tag, id attribute, 263
indentation, 219
indexes, alphabetical, 109
Initial Local Directory
option, 62
Initial Remote Directory
option, 62
inline frames, 254-255
inline styles, 222-223

inline value, 217
<input /> tag, 300, 439-440
input, text (HTML forms),
300-301
input controls, 302-305
Insert Frames, From File
command (Animation
menu), 133
Insert Image Transition
command (Effects menu),
136
Insert Text Effect command
(Effects menu), 136
inset value, 218
Instant Alphabetical Index
link, 109
interactive highlighting,
262-265
interactive layer animation,
DHTML, 287-290
interactive media, future
preparations, 386
interactive sound, Web sites,
393
interfaces, user, HTML,
379-380
interlaced GIFs, 131-132
<ins> tag, 413
</ins> tag, 413
Internet
connections, 10
directories, 347
graphics, 144
history of, 11
multimedia, 315
Web space, setting up,
52-53
Internet Explorer. *See*
Microsoft Internet
Explorer
Internet Options command
(Tools menu), 28

Internet Options, Fonts
command (Tools menu),
95
Internet service providers
(ISPs), locating, 10
intranets, 12
defined, 51
HTML pages, publishing,
66
invisible HTML tables,
202-203
<isindex /> tag, 440
ISPs (Internet service
providers), locating, 10
italics, 92-96

J

Jasc Software Products,
Launch Animation Shop
command (File menu), 133
Jasc, Inc. Paint Shop Pro,
120-121, 124
Java, applets, 394, 396
JavaScript, 262
commands, Web page
links, 263
functions, 270, 284
GIFs, 267
imagemaps, 267
layers, moving, 285-287
preloading graphics,
266-267
prewritten, 394
saving, 271
slide.js file, 283-284
timing mechanisms, ban-
ner ads, 268-269
troubleshooting, 394

Q-R

S

<s> tag, 418
</s> tag, 418
<samp> tag, 415
</samp> tag, 415
Sams Teach Yourself JavaScript in 24 Hours, 392
Sams Teach Yourself Paint Shop Pro 7, 392
Sams Teach Yourself Paint Shop Pro in 24 Hours, 121
Save As command (File menu), 26-28, 109, 125, 130
Save Options dialog box, 126
Save Password check box, 57
saving
  animations, 135
  files, 26
  graphics, Web pages, 142-144
  JavaScript, 271
  photographs, 122
  progressive JPEGs, 131
Scalable Vector Graphics (SVG), 386
scanners, 122
scripting
  banner ads, creating, 267-270
  graphics, preloading, 266-267
  interactive highlighting, 262-265
  JavaScript, 271
<script> tag, 267, 283, 443-444
</script> tag, 283, 443-444

scripts
  comments, 340
  form-processing, HTML forms, 296-297
  hiding, 267
scrolling frames, 251-255
scrolling attribute, 253
scrolling lists, 304
scrolling messages, Web sites, 395
search engine spamming, 350
Search Engine Submission Tips Web site, 400
Search Engine Watch Web site, 356
search engines. *See* search sites
search sites, 346
  hints, 352-356
    <meta /> tag, 350-351
    keywords, 349-350
  Web page evaluations, 353-354
  Web sites, listing, 347-349
searching Web sites, database links, 396
security, password-protected Web pages, 394
<select> tag, 304, 442
</select> tag, 304, 442
selected attribute, 304
selection lists, 304
Selections menu commands, Convert to Seamless Pattern, 161
self-totaling forms, creating, 307
semi-transparent layers, 280
semicolon (;), 265
server-side imagemaps, 167

servers
  forms, 393
  Web
    defined, 52
    files, accessing, 63
    HTML pages, transferring, 54-63
Set Palette Transparency command (Colors menu), 160
Set the Transparency Value to the Current Background Color option, 160
SGML (Standard General Markup Language), 363
shape attribute, 173
Shareware.com Web site, 399
Shockwave Player (Macromedia) Web site, 400
shortcuts. *See* keyboard shortcuts
single quotation marks (''), 264
single-page Web sites, 332-333
Site Label option, 60
Site Settings Edit button, 61
sites, search, 346-347. *See also* Web sites
  listing Web sites, 347-349
  Web page evaluations, 353-354
size
  banners, 126-127
  buttons, 126-127
  graphics, 122
  HTML tables, 198
  photographs, 123
size attribute, 96, 301, 304

Your Guide to Computer Technology

www.informit.com